WILLIAM CLARK

AND THE SHAPING OF THE WEST

LANDON Y. JONES

University of Nebraska Press
Lincoln

Copyright © 2004 by Landon Y. Jones.
All rights reserved. Published by arrangement with
Farrar, Straus and Giroux, LLC.
Manufactured in the United States of America

∞

First Nebraska paperback printing: 2009

Library of Congress Cataloging-in-Publication Data
Jones, Landon Y., 1943–
William Clark and the shaping of the West /
Landon Y. Jones.
p. cm.
Originally published: New York: Hill and Wang, c2004.
Includes bibliographical references and index.
ISBN 978-0-8032-2697-5 (pbk.: alk. paper)
1. Clark, William, 1770–1838. 2. Explorers—West
(U.S.)—Biography. 3. Governors—Missouri—
Biography. 4. West (U.S.)—Discovery and exploration.
5. Frontier and pioneer life—West (U.S.) 6. Indians
of North America—Wars—1750–1815. 7. Indians
of North America—Wars—1815–1875. 8. Indians of
North America—West (U.S.) 9. Clark, George Rogers,
1752–1818. 10. Clark family. I. Title.
F592.7.C565J66 2009
973.5092—dc22
[B]
2009022744

Frontispiece: William Clark, c. 1810, attributed to
John Wesley Jarvis (1780–1840). Courtesy of Missouri
History Museum, St. Louis.

To my mother,

Ellen Edmondson Jones

CONTENTS

Maps • *ix*

PROLOGUE: *A Dark and Bloody Ground* • 3
ONE: *America's First West: 1722–1772* • 13
TWO: *General George Rogers Clark: 1772–1789* • 24
THREE: *Lieutenant Billy Clark: 1789–1795* • 49
FOUR: *Soldier and Citizen: 1795–1803* • 87
FIVE: *"Ocian in view! O! the joy!": 1803–1806* • 114
SIX: *This Wild Country: 1806–1809* • 147
SEVEN: *Life without Lewis: 1809–1813* • 180
EIGHT: *Territorial Governor: 1813–1820* • 214
NINE: *"The Red-headed Chief": 1820–1829* • 256
TEN: *Resistance and Removal: 1829–1838* • 296

Notes • 335
Bibliography • 365
Acknowledgments • 375
Index • 379

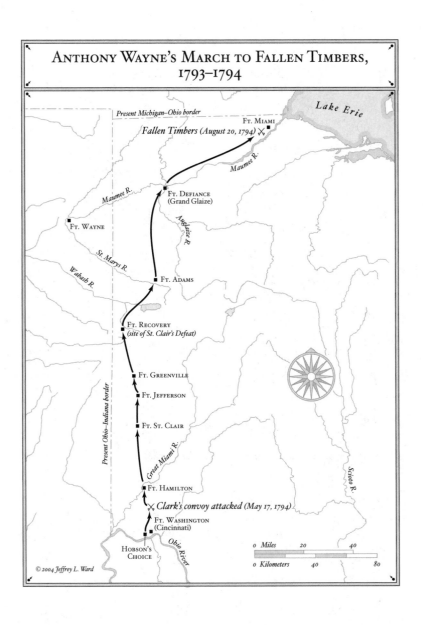

ANTHONY WAYNE'S MARCH TO FALLEN TIMBERS, 1793–1794

Lake Erie

Present Michigan–Ohio border

FT. MIAMI

Fallen Timbers (August 20, 1794) ✕

Maumee R.

Maumee R.

FT. DEFIANCE
(Grand Glaize)

FT. WAYNE

Auglaize R.

St. Marys R.

Wabash R.

FT. ADAMS

FT. RECOVERY
(site of St. Clair's Defeat)

FT. GREENVILLE

FT. JEFFERSON

FT. ST. CLAIR

Present Ohio–Indiana border

Great Miami R.

Scioto R.

FT. HAMILTON

✕ *Clark's convoy attacked (May 17, 1794)*

FT. WASHINGTON
(Cincinnati)

HOBSON'S
CHOICE

Ohio River

0 Miles   20   40

0 Kilometers   40   80

© 2004 Jeffrey L. Ward

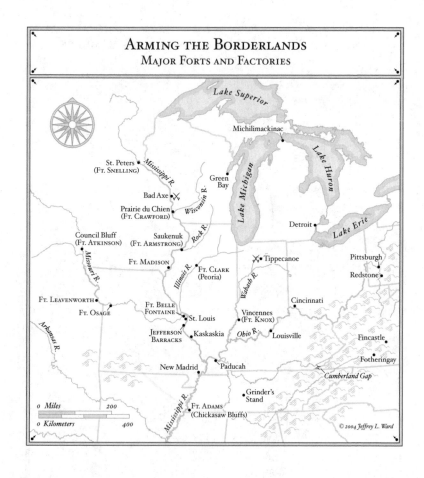

ARMING THE BORDERLANDS
MAJOR FORTS AND FACTORIES

Lake Superior

Michilimackinac

St. Peters
(FT. SNELLING)

Mississippi R.

Green
Bay

Lake Michigan

Lake Huron

Bad Axe

Prairie du Chien
(FT. CRAWFORD)

Wisconsin R.

Detroit

Lake Erie

Council Bluff
(FT. ATKINSON)

Saukenuk
(FT. ARMSTRONG)

Rock R.

Tippecanoe

Pittsburgh

FT. MADISON

Redstone

FT. CLARK
(Peoria)

Illinois R.

Wabash R.

FT. LEAVENWORTH

Missouri R.

FT. OSAGE

FT. BELLE
FONTAINE

Cincinnati

St. Louis

Vincennes
(FT. KNOX)

Ohio R.

Fincastle

JEFFERSON
BARRACKS

Kaskaskia

Louisville

Arkansas R.

Fotheringay

New Madrid

Paducah

Cumberland Gap

Grinder's
Stand

0 Miles   200

0 Kilometers   400

Mississippi R.

FT. ADAMS
(Chickasaw Bluffs)

© 2004 Jeffrey L. Ward

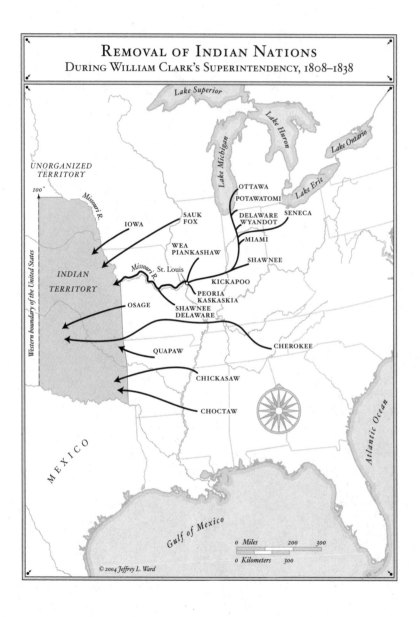

Removal of Indian Nations
During William Clark's Superintendency, 1808–1838

Lake Superior

Lake Huron

Lake Michigan

Lake Ontario

Lake Erie

UNORGANIZED
TERRITORY

100°

Missouri R.

OTTAWA
POTAWATOMI

DELAWARE
WYANDOT

SENECA

IOWA

SAUK
FOX

MIAMI

WEA
PIANKASHAW

SHAWNEE

Missouri R.   St. Louis

INDIAN
TERRITORY

KICKAPOO

PEORIA
KASKASKIA

Western boundary of the United States

OSAGE

SHAWNEE
DELAWARE

QUAPAW

CHEROKEE

CHICKASAW

CHOCTAW

MEXICO

Atlantic Ocean

Gulf of Mexico

0   Miles   200   300

0   Kilometers   300

© 2004 Jeffrey L. Ward

WILLIAM CLARK

AND THE SHAPING OF THE WEST

A DARK AND BLOODY GROUND

In the cold morning air of February 1, 1792, a detachment of 150 soldiers on horseback rode toward the headwaters of the Wabash River in Indian country north of the Ohio. The troops were mounted militiamen led by Lieutenant Colonel James Wilkinson, the newly appointed commander of the western army. Just thirty-four, Wilkinson had won an early reputation for brilliance during the Revolutionary War in Boston and in the New Jersey campaign at Trenton and Princeton. His social connections through his marriage to a prominent Philadelphian, Ann Biddle, had further helped smooth his rise in the army, despite his reputation for intrigue.

The soldiers found it slow going. On either side of them were the blackened branches of the Ohio hardwood forest, dense with trees reaching a circumference and height that were almost unimaginable. There were red and white oaks and maples 100 to 150 feet tall, enormous chestnuts and buckeyes 18 feet in girth. Along the frozen river bottoms stood huge thickets of cane, with stalks 12 to 20 feet high, tall enough to hide a man on horseback. The hollowed-out trunks of the sycamores, called buttonwoods, could shelter a family. Running up the branches and through the treetops was the forest's most distinctive feature: ropy tangles of wild grapevines that in warmer months made a canopy so dark and forbidding that no underbrush could grow beneath it.

For years, Indian hunters had burned scattered clearings into the impenetrable Ohio woodlands to flush out deer and to create meadows to attract herds of elk and eastern bison. Settlers later found another way to clear fields: they notched dozens of closely arrayed trees, each halfway through. They would then topple one of the goliaths, which would in turn bring down an entire stand in a succession of deafening crashes.

Wilkinson and his troops approached the Wabash on a rough road that had been cut into the forest the previous autumn. A fresh snowfall blanketed the ground twenty inches deep. As their horses snorted and pawed through the drifts, the soldiers began to realize that the piles of snow in front of them were covering up a multitude of objects strewn about the road. As they rode on, they discovered increasing numbers of cartridge boxes, pieces of uniforms, carcasses of horses and mules, firelocks, knapsacks, and other debris.

Just before 10:30 a.m., a few miles from a branch of the Wabash, they began to find the bodies. First they stumbled on a few, almost imperceptible beneath mounds of soft snow. But then they found dozens of corpses, many of them dragged into the open by scavenging animals. Almost all had been grotesquely mutilated—stripped naked, scalped, genitals cut off, "stakes as thick as a person's arm drove through their bodies," one officer in the party later reported in a letter.[1]

Buffeted by a strong, cold wind, the soldiers tried to bury the victims, most of them men, but there were also many women and children among them. The icy soil was hard as granite, and, as Winthrop Sargent, an adjutant general and secretary of the Northwest Territory, wrote in his report, the task was difficult, "the bodies being frozen down to the ground, quite covered with snow, and breaking into pieces in tearing them up."[2] A genteel Harvard graduate who was once known as the best-dressed man in the Continental Army (he was said to own a field kit made by Paul Revere), Sargent rode bleakly around the site, noticing that many trees had been stripped of twigs and branches by the ferocity of the gunfire.

The soldiers pulled together several ruined wagons and gun carriages and burned them in order to salvage their ironwork. But they were unable to locate the six cannons that had been carried by the destroyed army. They concluded that the Indians must have thrown them into the river, now covered with a hard shell of ice. In the end, Wilkinson's party buried about one hundred bodies, placing them in several shallow mass graves hacked into the ground. Many of the dead, they observed, bore a disturbing sign: their mouths had been stuffed with handfuls of dirt.

The rich lands north of the Ohio River had been occupied since the late 1730s by the Shawnee and Delaware tribes, which had moved from Pennsylvania and the Susquehanna Valley under pressure from the Iroquois League and European settlers. They were joined by Wyandots and Miamis from the Northwest. Supported by alliances with French and, later, British traders along the Great Lakes, the Indian nations clustered in villages along the latticework of rivers draining the region—the Wabash, Maumee, Scioto, Sandusky, and Great and Little Miami. Their towns were substantial, with log houses filled with European trade goods and surrounded by enormous cultivated fields of corn, beans, and squash.

The tribes thought they had finally found security north of the Ohio River. They had reluctantly given up their hunting grounds in Kentucky after the Revolution and had signed treaties defining the Ohio as both the southern boundary of their territory and the limit of the expanding American republic. But colonial immigrants from Virginia and Pennsylvania continued to swarm into the Indian lands north of the Ohio. Unable to evict the American settlers after a few desultory attempts, the new federal government decided instead to demonstrate its control of the Northwest Territory the only way it knew how: with displays of military force designed to awe the Indians into submission.

The first army raised by the United States was commanded by Brigadier General Josiah Harmar, a Philadelphian and veteran of the Revolution. But in the autumn of 1790, Harmar's force of regulars and militia was humiliatingly defeated in a series of ambushes led by the war chiefs Blue Jacket of the Shawnees and Little Turtle of the Miamis. The following spring and summer, Wilkinson and another Continental Army general, Charles Scott, led successive retaliatory raids by Kentucky militiamen into Shawnee country, burning thousands of acres of crops, looting villages, and digging up corpses from Indian graveyards in order to take their scalps.

In the fall of 1791, the federal government prepared to mount its most ambitious effort to punish the Indians. President Washington, in his third year of office, ordered an army organized at Fort Washington, an outpost on the north bank of the Ohio (now Cincinnati). Its commander would be Major General Arthur St. Clair, another Revolutionary War veteran, an early president of the Continental Congress, and the governor of the newly formed Northwest Territory. Born in Scotland and educated at the University of Edinburgh, St. Clair was a patrician known for his long, flowing hair and pompous manner. At age fifty-five, he had not seen military service in years and suffered from debilitating bouts with gout. St. Clair was ordered by Secretary of War Henry Knox to build "a strong and permanent" fort in the heart of Indian country at Kekionga, or Miamitown, the complex of villages at the headwaters of the Maumee River near present-day Fort Wayne, Indiana. St. Clair was promised 1,200 federal troops supported by 2,000 citizen-soldier "levies" enlisted for six-month tours of duty. But by the time he arrived at Fort Washington in the summer of 1791, St. Clair was already behind schedule and below force. He had suffered an incapacitating attack of gout in his left arm and hand. Worse, he could muster only one-half the troops he had been promised—and many of those were social outcasts literally "collected from the streets and prisons of the cities."[3] The few supplies the army had on hand were inadequate or of inferior quality, thanks to an absentee quartermaster and profiteering contractors. Uniforms and shoes were poorly made, gunpowder of poor quality, axes broken, and muskets in need of repair. Even the blacksmith's traveling forges had no anvils.

Alarmed by the drunkenness and lack of discipline among his troops—Indians had managed to steal one hundred horses hobbled beneath the walls of Fort Washington—St. Clair moved his men six miles away to Ludlow's Station. Ostensibly, he wanted to find fresh forage for the army's horses, but as St. Clair acknowledged, the real reason was "to deprive [the men] of the means of intoxication" available in the village outside the fort.[4]

In the second week of September, St. Clair's army of 625 regulars, 1,675 levies, and 470 militiamen began its ponderous march north into the Ohio country. Leading the columns were 120 axe-wielding "road-cutters" assigned the task of clearing two parallel roads through the thick forest. In front of them were scouts and another party of armed militiamen whose duty was to protect the road-cutters. Then came an advance guard and the infantry in two columns dragging artillery pieces. Behind them were horses with tents and provisions, a small herd of cattle with their own guards, more riflemen and scouts, and a mounted rear guard. Trailing the army were camp followers—several dozen civilian packers, haulers, laundrywomen, cooks, helpers, and family members.

As they proceeded north, St. Clair's troops planned to build a series of log forts to protect their dangerously stretched supply lines. Camped on the Great Miami River, they began chopping trees on September 11, the day of the winter's first frost. When the square fortification, fifty yards to a side, was finished, St. Clair named it Fort Hamilton. Soon the army was on the march again, through the thick Ohio timber. Slowed by desertions and dull axes, it made only twenty-two miles in five grueling days. Frustrated by the slow progress, the deputy commander, Major General Richard Butler, changed the order of march to cut just a single road wide enough for the gun carriages. When St. Clair learned of the change, he angrily reprimanded Butler, who from that point on avoided talking to St. Clair. The commander, said Butler, who like many soldiers had an Indian wife and had fathered half-Shawnee children, "know[s] little about managing Indians."[5]

By the time the army halted on October 12 to build its second outpost on a small creek about seventy miles above Fort Washington, the weather had turned. A hard frost was followed by hail and sheets of freezing rain. An additional three hundred Kentucky militiamen had caught up and joined the force, but they were ill trained and ill equipped and regarded with suspicion by the army regulars. The enlistment of levies was slowing, and desertions were increasing. With supplies limited, St. Clair was forced to put his already hungry troops on half rations. Faced with mass defections, the increasingly anxious officers turned to draconian discipline. Soldiers found sleeping on duty were given fifty lashes. Two artillerymen who attempted to desert and another man who shot a comrade were sentenced to death. They were hanged in front of the assembled army on October 22.

On October 30, having finished a crude log fortification called Fort Jefferson, the army was on the move again—except for its commander. St. Clair had been felled by another attack of gout and "it was supposed he would not be able to proceed," his aide-de-camp, Major Ebenezer Denny, wrote in his journal.[6] But an unorthodox solution was found. When his men were unable to hoist St. Clair into a saddle, they constructed a litter "made to carry him like a corpse between two horses."[7]

That night, the soldiers lay awake amid a terrifying lightning storm, "with trees and limbs falling around and in the midst of us." But for the occasional blinding flashes, the darkness was complete, "[which] in an enemy's country, occasioned some concern," wrote Major Denny. In the morning, camped in the bottom of a frozen creek, the army could not find sufficient forage to strengthen its horses and was forced to leave piles of baggage in the road. With only enough flour left for two days of bread, the militia became openly mutinous; between sixty and seventy men decamped and started back to the Ohio. St. Clair ordered three hundred of his best troops to pursue them in order to prevent the deserters from plundering a column of 212 packhorses bringing up the army's provisions. His civilian adjutant general Winthrop Sargent confided to his diary, "I have to regret that we are hereby deprived for a time of a corps of 300 effective men . . . which must be estimated as the best in the service."[8]

The army's advance guards began seeing increasing evidence of Indians. A scout stumbled into one deserted Indian camp and discovered seven horses with "U.S." brands, apparently among those stolen from Fort Washington weeks earlier. The tracks of fifteen Indians on horseback were found along the banks of a stream, made by a scouting party just hours before the army arrived. Still, St. Clair remained confident that the noise and ostentatious display of his army on the march would discourage any attackers. He wrote Knox, "The few Indians that have been seen were hunters only, who we fell upon by accident."[9]

Watching St. Clair's columns from the day he left Fort Washington were scouts from the largest and best-organized Indian army ever gathered in North America. Among the chiefs were Little Turtle and Blue Jacket, the aging Delaware Buckongahelas, and a young Shawnee scout, Tecumseh. This was the same confederation of Indians that had humiliated Brigadier General Harmar a year earlier; now the entire American army was floundering through the wilderness into its grasp.

Gathering his force on a prairie within the limits of the present-day city of Fort Wayne, Indiana, the forty-five-year-old Little Turtle decided to march. He organized his 1,400 warriors into parties of twenty, with four hunters in each group to procure food. The Indian army moved rapidly up the St. Marys River, covering fifty miles in four days through the sleet and snow. The confederacy included a scattering of white men. They were the British Indian agents Matthew Elliott and Alexander McKee, stationed at Detroit; the notorious American turncoat Simon Girty; and William Wells, a redheaded American. Once an Indian captive,

Wells now lived with the Miamis and had married Little Turtle's daughter, Sweet Breeze. The Indians, Girty claimed later, "were never in greater heart to meet their enemy, nor more sure of success—they [were] determined to drive them to the Ohio."[10]

On the evening of November 3, St. Clair pitched camp on a rise of land on the banks of what he thought was a branch of the St. Marys River, which flowed north to the Great Lakes. In fact, he was on the Wabash, still in the Ohio watershed and just east of the present Indiana border. Since the troops were fatigued from the long day's march, St. Clair did not order any trees felled for a protective log breastwork. Instead, he posted the Kentucky militia as an advance guard on the far side of the creek, three hundred yards away from the regulars. The location ahead of the army had another advantage: it would deter potential deserters among the militia.

St. Clair retired to his tent amid occasional gunshots from the sentinels, who were firing nervously at Indians they believed "to lie skulking about in considerable numbers."[11] Around midnight, a militia captain named Jacob Slough returned from a reconnaissance patrol badly shaken: he had come across several large parties of Indians in the woods. Concluding that "the camp would be attacked in the morning," Slough reported what he had seen to General Richard Butler. "He stood some time," Slough testified later to the congressional inquiry, "and, after a pause, thanked me for my attention and vigilance, and said, as I must be fatigued, I had better go and lie down."[12] Butler, still smarting from perceived slights, never delivered the message to St. Clair.

Before sunrise the next morning, Winthrop Sargent visited the militia encampment and was disturbed to learn that the expected scouting patrols had not yet been sent out. He then returned to the camp's headquarters. There he was stopped by a bizarre sound, one he had never heard before: "not terrible, as has been represented, but more resembling an infinitude of horse-bells suddenly opening to you than any other sound I could compare it to."[13]

The noise was the blended war cries of at least one thousand Indians. Little Turtle and Blue Jacket had begun their attack.

Although the accounts of the ensuing battle taken from surviving eyewitnesses differ in their details, all of them agree on two points: the battle lasted about three hours, and it was a scene of indescribable horror.

The Indians' first rounds of point-blank gunfire felled dozens of the untrained militiamen and threw the rest into pandemonium. Discarding their rifles, the Kentuckians splashed and floundered across the stream and burst into the campfires of the surprised main army. As the militia milled about in confusion—"cowardly in the most shameful degree," Sargent said—the Indians quickly encircled the entire army, firing from behind trees and logs.[14] Soon "the ground was literally covered with dead and dying men," a quartermaster, Benjamin Van Cleve, reported.[15] One group of Indian warriors led by William Wells, whose brother Samuel was fighting on the opposite side with St. Clair's army, concentrated its fire on the artillerymen. "Men and officers were seen falling in every direction," reported Denny. "The distress of the wounded made the scene such as can scarcely be conceived."[16]

St. Clair, still gout-stricken, emerged from his tent and attempted to mount his horse. But, rearing in fright, it could not be controlled by four men before it was shot through the head. Another horse was saddled and led up to the general, but before he could be hoisted into its saddle, it, too, was killed, along with the servant holding it. His pains forgotten, St. Clair finally gave up and directed his forces on foot, leading several bayonet charges that momentarily forced the Indians to give ground. In his report afterward, Sargent acknowledged that the often-criticized general had been "cool and brave" under fire.[17]

The clouds of smoke rising from the guns gave the Indians further cover to sweep a deadly crossfire over the campground. After ninety minutes, all but one of the artillery officers had been killed and the cannons were silenced. As the soldiers fell back, the warriors began tomahawking and scalping the dead and wounded on the battle's outskirts. In the frigid air, it presented a scene that, as recalled by Major Jacob Fowler a half century later, was hard to forget: "The bodies of the dead and dying were around us, and the freshly scalped heads were reeking with smoke, and in the heavy morning frost looked like so many pumpkins through a cornfield in December."[18]

More and more officers were falling. General Richard Butler, who had neglected to pass on the warning of an imminent attack, was shot from his horse and left propped up against a tree, gripping his pistol. Lieutenant Colonel William Oldham, the militia commander who had failed to send out the patrols at dawn, fell mortally wounded. The troops were rendered increasingly useless. Sargent observed dryly later that the female camp followers "exerted themselves upon this day and drove out the skulking militia and fugitives of other corps from under wagons and hiding places by firebrands and the usual weapons of their sex."[19]

At around 9:30, St. Clair concluded that his army's only hope of survival would be to abandon the field of combat. A drummer sounded a retreat that could barely be heard over the din of gunfire and war whoops. St. Clair successfully mounted one of the few remaining horses and led a pell-mell charge for the stump-filled road that his men had so laboriously cut into the wilderness. "The retreat was a precipitate one; it was in fact a flight," he acknowledged later. "But the most disgraceful part of the business is that the men threw away their arms and accoutrements even after the pursuit (which continued for about four miles) had ceased."[20]

One soldier remembered running "for several miles . . . admist [sic] the groans of dying men and the dreadful sight of bloody massacres on every side perpetrated by the Indians on the unfortunate creatures they overtook."[21] The quartermaster, Van Cleve, fell toward the rear of the retreat, "where the Indians were tomahawking the old and wounded men." Discarding his heavy boots to gain speed and running through "ice as thick as a knife blade," he pulled ahead of "half a dozen persons, I thought it would occupy some time [for the enemy] to massacre them before my turn would come."[22]

The fleeing American survivors covered the twenty-nine miles back to Fort Jefferson in eight or ten hours, staggering into the post just after sunset. Stragglers came in hours and days later, including one man who walked in, scalped, with a tomahawk still stuck in his head. Left behind to occupy the Indians were his wounded comrades and an unprecedented trove of plunder: six cannons, two forges, four ox-teams, two baggage wagons, 316 harnessed packhorses, 400 tents, 1,200 muskets and bayonets, 163 axes, 89 spades, and huge quantities of medical and cooking supplies.

The Indians scalped Richard Butler and cut out his heart in order to divide its pieces among the participating tribes. The mouths of the dead were filled with dirt, mocking the Americans' land-hunger. All told, about 630 soldiers out of 1,400 under arms were killed, along with at least half of the two-hundred-odd camp followers. When General Anthony Wayne sent a detachment to the battlefield two years later to finish the burial job Wilkinson's men had begun, they counted six hundred skulls and so many bones that "when we came to lay down in our tents at night, we had to scrape [them] together and carry them out to make our beds."[23]

The Indians gave varying counts of their dead, but the total was not more than forty; they had killed three times as many Americans as the Sioux confederacy would later annihilate at Little Big Horn. St. Clair's Defeat remains the most one-sided loss in the history of the United States military. For three centuries, Indians had been confronting the European empires over these lands, but on the Wabash they had finally dealt the invaders a devastating blow. Without question, the confederated tribes were at that moment the dominant force in the Ohio Valley.

The great tribes of the Ohio Valley would never again realize such power. Almost from the moment of their victory, the tide of violence in the West began to turn against them. Over the ensuing five decades, defeated by treaties and raw force, the Indians would be driven out of the eastern United States. The same brutal process would repeat itself west of the Mississippi.

Both removals would be made possible by a man who joined the territorial militia in 1790 with a commission signed by Arthur St. Clair and Winthrop Sargent. By his good fortune he had not joined the march to the Wabash, though he would live the rest of his life with its bloody legacy. He was William Clark.

CHAPTER ONE

AMERICA'S FIRST WEST

1722–1772

The first people known to live in the Piedmont plateau of Virginia were the Monacans. They were a Siouan-speaking people who, with the Mannahoac tribe, dominated an area that extended north from the Roanoke River valley to the Potomac, and from the fall line, or head of navigation, at Richmond and Fredericksburg to the Blue Ridge Mountains on the west. These agricultural tribes had lived in the Piedmont for three hundred years, but in 1722 their rich lands had been opened to white settlers by the Treaty of Albany.

As the first whites arrived, the Monacans began to leave Virginia to live with the Catawbas in the south. They could anticipate the changes coming to their world by the arrival of honeybees. When the "white man's fly" appeared, Indians knew that settlers were dangerously close. Since there were always more hollow trees in the old-growth forests to the west than in the cleared fields to the east, the bees naturally went west. The honeybees were thought to keep about a hundred miles in advance of white migration all the way across North America.

In 1749, John Clark and his new wife, Ann Rogers, were among the first whites in the area vacated by the Monacans. They packed their belongings and moved from the tidewater county of King and Queen, Virginia, to a home in the hills of the western Piedmont. There the young couple—he was twenty-four, she just fifteen—settled on land John had inherited from his father. It was on the Rivanna River in the newly created Albemarle County, just two miles east of the future location of

Charlottesville, but in the mid-eighteenth century it was America's first West.

Among the Clarks' neighbors was Peter Jefferson, a husky surveyor and land speculator who fourteen years earlier had patented a thousand acres on a nearby plantation he called Shadwell. His son Thomas later would recall that Peter Jefferson was "the third or fourth settler, about the year 1737, of the part of the country in which I live."[1] Along the horizon to the west lay the long, lazy profile of the Blue Ridge Mountains. Beyond them, through Rockfish Gap, was the backcountry, a land still controlled by Indians and rarely visited by whites.

The first John Clark had arrived from Britain early in the seventeenth century, probably under the "headrights" system, a guarantee from Virginia's colonial government that any man who paid his passage to America would receive fifty acres of land when he got there. As a result, he got his start not as a clerk—the origin of his eponymous surname—but as a farmer on the James River. John passed his name down to a succession of eldest sons alternatively called John and Jonathan until it reached John Clark of Drysdale Parish, King and Queen County. At the same time, his heirs inherited from his Scottish-born wife a family attribute known genetically as an amino acid variation in the melanocortin 1 receptor but universally called red hair. John Clark of Drysdale Parish had a full shock of sandy red hair.

Ann Rogers's side of the family arrived literally fresh off the boat. Her father, John Rogers, was born in the Chesapeake Bay aboard the ship carrying his parents to Virginia around 1680. Her mother, Rachel, was a descendant of the Bird family—but not, as sometimes claimed, of Virginia's celebrated Byrd clan. Acquiring land as a surveyor—in those days a surveyor's fee could amount to one-third of the property surveyed—John Rogers settled with Rachel and their nine children in Drysdale Parish, at the base of a finger of land extending into the Chesapeake Bay. There the Rogers and Clark families intermingled closely enough that when Ann married John Clark in 1747, she was marrying her second cousin.

In Albemarle, the newly arrived Clarks were not large landholders. They had inherited just 410 acres, marked off in the county deed book as "beginning at 3 bushes standing on south side of the Rivanna" and continuing "238 poles to 3 red oak saplings standing on the east side of a branch between 2 mountains." Their farm would later be dwarfed by the 11,000 acres Thomas Jefferson accumulated for his plantations. But like virtually all of their countrymen, John and Ann Clark saw the acquisition of land as the best way to build and hold wealth. John Clark's father, Jonathan, may have signed his will with an illiterate's X mark, but he was still able to leave two farms and other property to his two sons.

Like many other emigrants whose families were from the borderlands of northern England and Scotland, John and Ann were comfortable in the colonial backcountry. They built a cabin that was most likely a simple structure of square-hewn logs, in the convention of the times, with sides facing east and west and a fireplace at one end. The floor would have been puncheon—split logs laid with the flat side up—over hard-packed clay. A spring for fresh water flowed nearby.

Two redheaded sons were born there: Jonathan in 1750 and George Rogers in 1752. But then the young couple encountered a problem. Success in the leading cash crop, tobacco, depended on access to tidewater ports and European markets. But they soon realized that they were above the fall line on the Rappahannock and the Rivanna was not deep enough nor the roads sturdy enough to carry heavy wagons from the Piedmont.

Meanwhile, disturbing news was coming from the North. Relative calm had prevailed for decades in the North American backcountry as a result of an uneasy equilibrium between the French and British colonists and the Indians courted by both powers. While the British had a far greater population—the 1.25 million British colonists far outnumbered 60,000 French Canadians—the French enjoyed warmer relations with the Indians thanks to the chain of fur-trading posts they had built stretching from the St. Lawrence River to Detroit and Michilimackinac and down the Ohio and Mississippi rivers to New Orleans.

Conflict erupted, as always, over land. In 1752, a group of Virginia land speculators known as the Ohio Company acquired a huge grant from the English Crown and cut a road from the headwaters of the Potomac across the Allegheny divide to the Youghiogheny and Monongahela rivers. The prospect of English settlers flooding into the Ohio watershed so alarmed the French that they evicted the immigrants and built a new fort at the Forks of the Ohio, now the location of Pittsburgh.

A combined army of French and Indians then forced the surrender of the twenty-two-year-old George Washington and his Virginia militia at Fort Necessity in Pennsylvania in July 1754. That was the opening engagement of the conflict known in North America as the French and Indian War and in Europe as the Seven Years War. A year later, an invading British army led by Major General Edward Braddock stumbled into an Indian ambush near the Forks of the Ohio, suffering casualties of 1,000 of the 1,400 men under arms.

Large tribes like the Delawares and the Shawnees were mounting their own independent resistance to the American invaders. Bands of Indians continued to move up and down the "Warrior's Path" through the Shenandoah Valley, just over the ridge from the Clark family cabin. So when a bachelor uncle died and left John Clark 170 acres of farmland near the Rappahannock in the southwestern corner of Caroline County, twenty-five miles from the coast, John saw his opportunity. He sold his Albemarle farm, and the family returned to the central tidewater, east of the fall line. The American push westward typically produced a counter-migration to the east in its wake, and the Clarks were part of that first backwash. It would be the last time a member of the Clark family would move any direction but west.

The Clarks settled on gently rolling land in Caroline County, located at the first rise of land from the coastal plain. The house began to fill with children. In quick order after Jonathan and George Rogers came Ann (1754), John (1757), Richard (1760), Edmund (1762), Lucy (1765), and Eliza (1768). Then, on August 1, 1770, another redheaded boy arrived. The parents named him William, perhaps after his great-grandfather, William John Clark. William was followed three years later by the last of the ten Clark children, a daughter named Frances but forever called Fanny. The six sons and four daughters were an average complement for rural families, for whom more hands meant more help in the fields. Daniel Boone's wife, Rebecca, bore ten children, and John Clark's brother, Benjamin, is said to have fathered thirty-one children with two wives, including twenty-nine sons—though only six survived to maturity.

The Clarks were landed gentry who did not find working with their hands to be beneath them. Still, they were not the only ones who worked their land. Living with them was the other most important form of property in Virginia: enslaved African-Americans. In the seventeenth century, Africans had begun to replace indentured whites and enslaved Indians as the essential source of labor on the plantations. The new tobacco and cotton economies on the Chesapeake were far more labor-intensive than the mixed-crop farming that had preceded them. By the 1730s, two thousand slaves were arriving in the Chesapeake ports every year. Half of them were Ibos from the most-desired ports of origin in Gambia and the Bight of Biafra. By the time of the American Revolution, there were 200,000 slaves in Virginia, and wealthy planters like Jefferson and Washington had 200 slaves apiece. As relatively modest landholders, the Clarks never owned more than two dozen slaves.

Throughout the Chesapeake, slave families lived in parallel universes with their white owners. Men worked in the fields, and women did household chores—cooking, cleaning, and mending—though some would be sent into the fields at harvest time. Among the possessions Africans lost upon arriving in the colonies were their names. Slaves could be named after the day they arrived, Tuesday or Easter, or receive classical names like Caesar or Scipio that mocked their lack of status.

John Clark had inherited from his father a slave named Old York, presumably because he had disembarked on the York River, then the center of the slave trade in the region. Old York and his wife, Rose, had several children, including a son, also called York, who became William Clark's playmate, and eventually his servant.

When the time came for schooling, the elder boys, Jonathan and George Rogers, were sent back to King and Queen County to live with their maternal grandfather, where they could study under Donald Robertson, the husband of Ann Clark's younger sister Rachel. The Scottish-born Robertson, a graduate of the University of Edinburgh, ran a well-known academy on the Mattaponi River, where another of his students was the young James Madison. Boarders studied history, geography, and arithmetic—and paid tuition of £13 a year, though Robertson willingly accepted in-kind equivalents, including brandy, wheat, cider, and "Half-homony beans."

Formal study for the remaining children began after Jonathan and George Rogers left Robertson's school: copies of their lesson books were handed down through the family. Jonathan's leather-bound "Cyphering Book" was passed from brother to sister and eventually to "Billy," as William was called. The book's topics included "Simple Interest" and "The Rule of Three Direct" and calculation questions reflecting the daily concerns of rural Virginians:

> "When the days are 9 hours long I can travail from here to Williamsburg in 9 days, how many days will I be going the same journey when the days are 14½ [hours] long."
> "If 10 horses in 14 days eat 14 bushels of oats, [how many] will serve 18 horses in 165 days?"
> "How many feet of plank that is 13¼ inches broad will floor a room that is 24 foot long by 24½ broad?"

Schoolboys could still be schoolboys. Scattered among the lesson plans are notations such as "John Clark Loves Nancy Patterson," or "Miss Fanny, fair and witty, Not to wise not to pretty," and

> *William Clark is a spark*
> *And he loves to shoot a gun*
> *He left a fart behind catch*
> *And it sounded like a drum.*

One entry—a ribald story about a farmer's wife who calls a hired man named Jack to catch a mouse she claims has run up her petticoat—was earthy enough to have been partially bowdlerized later by a pen-wielding Clark descendant.

Other notations in the book suggest a darker side of colonial life. There was a premium on good paper, so when children were finished with copying, parents used their books for notepaper. Thus, this draft of a note in John Clark's hand appears in the family copying book under the date of April 7, 1776:

Let the Bearer Cupit [Cupid] pass
to Mr. John Wollers meeting
And he pass home Monday morning.
John Clark.

Plantation owners would write such notes to tear out and hand to a traveling slave to assure other whites that the man was not a runaway. A slave apprehended away from his owner's land without permission could be arrested and whipped. In this case, three months before the signing of the Declaration of Independence, John Clark was giving his slave Cupid safe passage to attend a nearby Sunday church service.

Other participants in the lives of the Clark family included scattered Indian peoples who had lived among the European settlers for more than a century. Once-powerful tribes like the Powhatans had long since been decimated by war and disease. Of the two million native peoples living east of the Mississippi when Columbus arrived, only an estimated 250,000 remained. John Clark's small plantation in Caroline County was close enough to the main road between the colonial capitals at Philadelphia and Williamsburg that Indian travelers would pass by frequently.

While Indians and whites examined one another with suspicion as well as awe, they were not enemies every day. Frequent interaction was important to both groups, and they started to adopt each other's habits as soon as they first came into contact. It began at the table: white and native Virginians both ate Indian corn (maize), beans, squash, hominy, pumpkins, sunflower seeds, and jerked venison. Indians and whites both carried cornmeal in powder horns and made cornbread, which was originally known as "journey cake" but became "Johnny cake" in a tidewater accent.

The Indians' growing reliance on imported trade products resulted in the gradual abandonment of goods they made for themselves. They needed European weapons and ammunition, woolen cloaks, shirts made from the mixture of linen and wool known as "linsey-woolsey," vermilion and verdigris for skin-painting, kettles and spoons, knives and hatchets, needles and scissors, and tools of every kind. Their traditional wampum beads made from whelk and quahog shells were replaced with beads hollowed out by steel tools in Albany, New York. In return, to satisfy the European craving for felt hats made of beaver pelts, the Indians over-hunted their lands and depleted the region's supply of game. "A modern Indian cannot subsist without Europeans," said the British superintendent John Stuart. "What was only conveniency at first is now become necessity."[2]

He could have said the same about the colonists. Indians built better canoes than the Europeans and were far more at home in the wilderness.

Newly arrived whites typically did not know how to hunt, since shooting wild game was a privilege reserved for leisured aristocrats in eighteenth-century Britain and France. The Indians taught them to set fire to a forest to create meadows for game, or hunt by "jacklighting"—using flaming torches to encircle and freeze deer in their tracks at night before shooting them.[3]

Some Europeans became "half-Indian" or "white savages."[4] These frontiersmen dressed in buckskin hunting shirts, leggings, and moccasins, wearing their hair long and greased with bear oil. "Their whole dress," said an English visitor, "is also very singular, and not very materially different from that of the Indians."[5] In turn, Indians adopted some, but hardly all, European fashions. They wore manufactured clothes but continued to slit their ears and tattoo their faces. A traveler observed four Shawnee chiefs "in white men's dress, except breeches, which they refuse to wear, instead of which they have a girdle round them with a piece of cloth drawn through their legs and turned over the girdle, and appears like a short apron before and behind."[6]

The log-cabin style of home construction, first brought to the colonies by Swedes and Finns, was spread throughout America as much by Indians as by white settlers. Travelers frequently remarked on the similarity of Indian villages, their streets likewise lined with log dwellings, to white communities. Labor in both Indian and white villages was also broadly equivalent. Indian men and white men did most of the hunting, while white women and Indian women worked in the fields and cooked.[7]

Women from both groups were often the first to interact with outsiders, and intermarriage between colonial men and native women had been commonplace throughout North America since the time of John Rolfe and Pocahontas. A vocabulary of Shawnee and Delaware words compiled in 1785 is peppered with translations of such phrases as "I love you" and "Will you sleep with me?"[8] The common-law wife of Sir William Johnson, the British superintendent of Indians north of Virginia, was Molly Brant, the sister of the Mohawk chief Joseph Brant. Visitors to Johnson's home unfamiliar with the interlocking worlds of whites and Indians were startled to find Indians seated at the dinner table politely speaking English. Conversely, the Shawnee captive James Kenney was astonished when an Indian woman "boiled some water in a small copper kettle, with which she made some tea in a tea-pot, using cups and saucers of yellow-ware."[9]

From the outset, the Europeans' idea of the Indian had been a blank slate on which they could project their prejudices. Indians were originally seen not as racial inferiors but as white men in a less developed state of culture, not unlike English peasants before the Romans arrived. American natives were thought to be a simple, malleable people who, once they came to understand the benefits of European faith and civilization, would embrace them. If the English colonists described Indians as "savages," "pagans," or "brutes," they were commenting on their unfortunately primitive stage of development, but not on their capacity for improvement.

Early English settlers regarded Indians as not significantly different in skin color from their own. Captain John Smith reported that his Indian neighbors at Jamestown were "a colour browne when they are of any age, but they are borne white."[10] Sir Walter Raleigh likewise observed, "They were never said to be red but 'brown and tawnie.'"[11] Even their darker hue was thought to result from the Indians' ritualistic skin-painting and what William Wood called "the sun's livery."[12] Not until the three-century struggle for power in eastern North America entered its bitterest phase in the mid-eighteenth century would the word "redskins" become the epithet of choice for warriors who painted themselves red for battle.[13]

The conclusion of the Seven Years War with the fall of Quebec and the ensuing Treaty of Paris in 1763 changed everything for the Indian nations. The French abandoned the continent, ceding to Britain all of their lands in Canada and east of the Mississippi and turning over New Orleans and the Louisiana territory west of the Mississippi to Spain (which had yielded Florida to Britain). No longer able to find a strategic middle ground by playing the contending European powers against one another, the tribes were left with few options. Instead of dealing with Frenchmen who wanted their trade but not their land, the native peoples were confronted by a line of settlement advancing from the east. The world of mutual dependence and accommodation, in which Indians and whites could find a place for one another, was disappearing.

In the Ohio Valley, the Delawares and Shawnees lashed out against the enemies—both whites and rival tribes—who had driven them from their original homes in the East. The British official Lord Jeffrey Amherst enforced a repressive Indian policy that went so far as to include distributing blankets infected with smallpox. The result was a bloody rebellion led by the Ottawa chief Pontiac. By the summer of 1763, more than two thousand settlers had been killed in Pontiac's War, and the British had lost nearly every trading fort in the west.

In an attempt to buffer the Indians from the traders, as well as to prevent settlers and land speculators from establishing breakaway colonies, King George III signed the Proclamation of 1763, which drew a line down the crest of the Appalachians and declared that neither colonial governments nor the King's subjects could survey, settle, or purchase land west of it. For the first time, the English backcountry was defined as Indian land, which would be kept "as open and Wild as possible for the purposes of Hunting."[14] As it would turn out, however, defining the land was the necessary first step toward acquiring it.

Few colonists took the proclamation as anything other than a temporary delay in their inevitable march across the mountains. Fur traders continued to cross into the Ohio Valley, and men like George Washington told their friends to begin surveying before it was too late. The competing colonial governments in Virginia and Pennsylvania made no attempt to hold back the settlers. Between 1765 and 1768 alone, an estimated thirty thousand settlers surged across the mountains to settlements like Redstone Creek on the Monongahela River.

Faced with increasing encroachments by whites on recognized tribal lands, the British authorities responded in a manner that set the pattern of Indian relations that would prevail for a century: unable to enforce their laws, they decided to rewrite them. Unable to protect Indian lands, they took them.

In the autumn of 1768 the British superintendent William Johnson convened more than two thousand Iroquois at Fort Stanwix on the Upper Mohawk River for the stated purpose of redrawing the boundary line farther west. But, in an unauthorized and illegal step, Johnson then purchased from the Iroquois a vast tract of land south and east of the Ohio River that included much of the present states of Kentucky, Tennessee, North Carolina, South Carolina, Georgia, and Alabama. The Iroquois did not occupy these lands, but claimed to have taken them from the Shawnees. For £10,000, they thereby ceded to the Crown all the hunting grounds of the Shawnees south of the Ohio and the overlapping claims of the Cherokees.

The land companies that had sprung up around the colonies were quick to seize the rich opportunity. Supported by many of the most prominent men in the colonies, they rushed to lobby in London for land grants in the newly available region. Schemes were hatched to create what amounted to proprietary colonies, fancifully named Transylvania and the State of Franklin. Among the stakeholders in various speculating companies were Thomas Jefferson, Benjamin Franklin, and Sir William Johnson himself. Most of the new investors would remain in the East.

Rejecting any restrictions on their movements, American colonists began to press across the northern end of the Alleghenies into the Upper Ohio Valley. "They do and will remove as their avidity and restlessness incite them," complained Virginia's royal governor, Lord Dunmore. "They acquire no attachment to Place; but wandering about seems engrafted in their nature; they do not conceive that Government has any right to forbid their taking possession of a vast tract of country."[15]

Farther south, Daniel Boone began leading backcountry hunts across the Blue Ridge Mountains into a fertile land that the Iroquois called *Kanta-ke*. Huge herds of buffalo, elk, and deer roamed through the hardwood forests, "rolling fat, and weary for the rifle shot," as one writer put it.[16] The Shawnees had once lived there, but they had been driven north of the Ohio by the Iroquois, who now shared the region with the Cherokees as a common hunting ground.

At some point, the enticing rumors about the earthly paradise across the mountains reached the Clark family of Caroline County. They lived midway between the market centers at Richmond and Fredericksburg—close enough to keep up on news carried by travelers but remote enough to steep them in the ways of provincial Virginia. John Clark knew that to guarantee his children's future, the family would need more land. The course they and thousands of their countrymen took to get it led directly to the snowfields of St. Clair's Defeat.

CHAPTER TWO

GENERAL GEORGE ROGERS CLARK
1772–1789

In the spring of 1772, George Rogers Clark was nineteen years old. He was a strapping redhead who stood about six feet tall, with hooded blue eyes and bristling eyebrows that gave him a commanding presence. Intellectually curious and well read, he included among his friends men like Thomas Jefferson and George Mason, the lawyer-squire of nearby Gunston Hall. From his maternal grandfather, George Rogers Clark had learned the craft of surveying and its argot of roods, poles, perches, meresmen, and chainmen.

In the spring of 1772, George Rogers equipped himself with surveyor's instruments and a copy of *Euclid's Elements* and made his way over the Appalachian Front to the Monongahela River and Fort Pitt. There he and several friends "inclined to make a tour of this new world" pushed their canoes into the Ohio—La Belle Rivière, the French called it—and embarked on the first of the river expeditions into the western country that would define the lives of the Clark brothers for the following four decades.[1]

Floating down the Ohio, the travelers found a land of rugged hills and dense forests filled with red and white oak, honey and black locust, sugar maple, hickory, black walnut, sycamore, hemlock, cedar, beech, and buckeye—all trees that flourished in highly fertile soils. Huge saline springs, called salt licks, drew enormous numbers of white-tailed deer, elk, and eastern bison, as well as predators like black bears, wolves, and mountain lions. The forests teemed with wild turkeys, grouse, quail, Canada geese, passenger pigeons, Carolina parakeets, and ivory-billed woodpeckers. A subsequent English visitor, Francis Baily, proclaimed the Long Reach of the Ohio to be "the most beautiful place I ever saw in my life."[2]

The men ventured as far as the mouth of the Great Kanawha River, in what is now West Virginia, carefully skirting the Indian settlements along the "Indian coast" on the north side of the Ohio. Below the Kanawha, the rugged hills on the south bank, called the "Virginia shore," gave way to the rolling bluegrass country drained by the Kentucky River. Unlike the French who originally descended the river, these men were hunting not for furs but for land. Satisfied with what he had seen, George Rogers made his way back overland to Caroline County, where he enthusiastically told his family about the wonders in Kentucky.

Within a few months, George Rogers returned to the Ohio Valley—this time joined by his father, a neighbor, and several African-American slaves. At Fish Creek, 40 miles below Wheeling, they stopped and made a so-called tomahawk claim by blazing trees at "a bottom of fine land."[3] His father then left for Virginia, but George Rogers and a single companion pressed on another 170 miles before returning to Fish Creek.

The two men spent the winter clearing the dense undergrowth and preparing fields for a spring planting. Fields were never rendered completely clear; backwoodsmen typically girdled large trees, slicing the bark in bands about two feet above the ground to kill them, before burning the surrounding underbrush. A cleared field could take on a bizarre appearance, studded with blackened stumps and gnarled trees rising like specters above the growing corn. Even untended fields in these fertile lands could produce bumper harvests. Travelers reported cornstalks "eight or ten feet and sometimes twelve to fifteen feet [high]."[4] Kentuckians later bragged that if they left a crowbar in a field overnight, it would sprout seedlings of ten-penny nails.

In April 1773, George Rogers joined a band of speculators surveying lands in the interior of Kentucky. He visited Caroline County briefly, but by early fall he was headed back to the Ohio despite his father's "onease apprehensions" that he and his brother Jonathan might not return in time to witness their sister Ann Clark's marriage to Owen Gwathmey on October 25.

John Clark had other reasons to be uneasy. The Shawnees, who had never accepted the Iroquois' right to cede their territory in the Treaty of

Stanwix, began to resist the colonial invasion of their lands. The Americans came by two routes. The first, along the buffalo trace through the Cumberland Gap in the south, was an arduous overland trek that was cheaper and offered better protection from roaming Indian hunters. But it was only slightly better as hostilities increased. In October, a Shawnee war party captured Daniel Boone's teenage son, James; after pulling out the nails on his fingers and toes, they tomahawked him to death.

The northern route to the Ohio Valley and Kentucky was more perilous. Travelers floated down the Monongahela through the Redstone country to Fort Pitt at the Forks of the Ohio. Indians could easily locate them on the river. The region was made even more unstable by clashes between competing land companies from Virginia and Pennsylvania, which were nearly at war over border disputes. During the winter of 1773–'74, Virginia governor Lord Dunmore and his western agent Dr. John Connolly escalated the conflict by seizing and holding hostage several Shawnee chiefs who had gone to Fort Pitt to plead for peace. Dunmore then gave orders to his militia to fire on any Indians traveling with rival Pennsylvania traders.

After his sister Ann's wedding, George Rogers Clark returned to the mouth of the Little Kanawha in the spring of 1774 with a band of ninety Virginians planning to defy the Crown and descend the Ohio in order to settle in Kentucky. Upon learning that unknown Indians had plundered and scalped several white traders, Clark and his friend Michael Cresap led their men on reprisals that left at least two Shawnees dead.

Informed that a hunting party of Mingos, members of a breakaway tribe of the Iroquois confederacy, was camped at Yellow Creek, fifty miles below Fort Pitt, Cresap and Clark made plans to attack them as well. But after learning that the Indian party was peaceful and included women and children, the two men had second thoughts and turned around. "Every person present particularly Cresap (upon Reflection) was opposed to the projected Measure,"[5] Clark later recalled of their change of heart.

Two days later, these same Mingos canoed across the Ohio to visit with a nearby party of whites. Two brothers named Daniel and Joseph Greathouse plied three Indians with rum, rendering them insensate. After the other warriors were tricked into emptying their rifles in a shooting match, the whites killed them all. The victims included the family of a friendly Oneida chief, Tah-gah-ju-te, who had taken the name of Logan from a white official. Logan's sister, who was pregnant, was strung up by her thumbs and grotesquely mutilated.

The Americans' inability to distinguish friend from foe among the Indians, and a willingness to treat either one brutally, once again had disastrous consequences. Logan vowed revenge, promising that ten of the hated "Long Knives," as the natives called Virginians because of the swords they carried, would die for each of his murdered relatives. The wave of Indian assaults created a general panic among whites in the Ohio Valley as thousands of colonists fled back across the Appalachians to safety.

Lord Dunmore now had the excuse he needed to permit his land-hungry Virginians to preempt the rival Pennsylvanians in the struggle for Indian territory. He called up the Virginia militia, using the promise of Indian plunder to recruit volunteers, and sent Daniel Boone to warn Virginia surveyors traveling unaware in Kentucky. Dunmore raised about three thousand troops, including George Rogers Clark, who was sworn in as a militia captain. In July and August 1774, the young captain joined an expedition that burned Shawnee cabins and crops along the Muskingum River, north of the Ohio. It was his first Indian campaign.

The final stage of what would become known as Lord Dunmore's War came in the fall, when Dunmore organized a two-pronged attack on the Shawnees' villages on the Scioto River. Clark joined one force led by Lord Dunmore that moved down the Ohio from Fort Pitt to Wheeling. The other, commanded by Colonel Andrew Lewis, marched overland to Point Pleasant at the mouth of the Kanawha, in present-day West Virginia.

While Lewis and his 1,100 Virginians waited on the banks of the Ohio for Dunmore to arrive, a small army of 300 Shawnee and Delaware warriors led by Cornstalk and Blue Jacket crossed the river and attacked at dawn on October 10. The Battle of Point Pleasant ended in a stalemate, with seventy whites and at least twenty Indians killed and about two hundred men wounded on each side. But when the remaining Indians were first to withdraw from the field, the Virginians claimed victory and then crossed the river, marching north to the largest Shawnee villages at Chillicothe.

In the resulting Treaty of Camp Charlotte—the first such negotiation witnessed by George Rogers Clark—the Shawnees yielded all rights to the lands south of the Ohio and agreed not to cross the river. The Virginians now claimed all of Kentucky as part of Fincastle County, bounded to the

north by the Indian coast of the Ohio. But the treaty council is best remembered for a chief who refused to attend. He was Logan, the grieving
Mingo leader, who instead sent the following speech to Dunmore:

> I appeal to any white man to say, if ever he entered Logan's cabin
> hungry, and he gave him not meat; if ever he came cold and
> naked, and he clothed him not? During the course of the last long
> and bloody war, Logan remained idle in his cabin, an advocate
> for peace. Such was my love for the whites, that my countrymen
> pointed as they passed, and said, "Logan is the friend of the white
> men." I had even thought to have lived with you but for the in-
> juries of one man. Colonel Cresap, the last spring, in cold blood
> and unprovoked, murdered all the relations of Logan, not sparing
> even my women and children. There runs not a drop of my blood
> in the veins of any living creature. This called on me for revenge.
> I have sought it; I have killed many; I have fully glutted my
> vengeance. For my country, I rejoice at the beams of peace. But
> do not harbor a thought that mine is the joy of fear. Logan never
> felt fear. He will not turn on his heel to save his life. Who is there
> to mourn for Logan? Not one.[6]

Thomas Jefferson admiringly reprinted Logan's speech in his 1785
Notes on the State of Virginia, calling it equal to "the whole orations of
Demosthenes and Cicero."[7] Jefferson's goal was less to praise Indians
than to rebut the French Count de Buffon in their debate over the supposed degeneracy of species natural to the Americas. To Jefferson and
many of his fellow citizens, Indians were necessarily both dignified and
dispensable; Logan stood squarely in the moccasins of the Noble Savage,
and in the way of American expansion. Among white colonists the idea
that Indians were a race tragically and inevitably doomed to extinction
had arisen in tandem with the tribes' ongoing destruction. As for the particulars, Jefferson found it expedient to scapegoat men like Cresap rather
than to assign culpability for the vanishing Indians to his countrymen's
wholesale assault on their lands and culture. George Rogers Clark later
cleared Cresap's name; the Greathouse brothers had carried out the
murders.

With the Shawnees confined north of the Ohio, emigrants began to flood from Virginia back into Kentucky. Many were veterans who, during their service with Dunmore's militia, had seen for the first time the fertile lands across the Appalachians.[8] Among them was George Rogers Clark, who went to work surveying plots for the Ohio Company. In May 1775, he descended the Ohio from Wheeling with a group of travelers, including a raffish young Englishman named Nicholas Cresswell.

Floating downstream—his canoes were christened *Charming Sally* and *Charming Polly*—Cresswell found the Virginian to be "an intelligent man" fluent in topics ranging from Indian burial mounds to the uses of bloodroot salve to treat rattlesnake bites. Along the way, Cresswell observed a land he thought was "rich beyond conception"—high praise from a native of Derbyshire.[9] Clark and Cresswell hunted for bison and wild turkey and breakfasted on pancakes made with turtle eggs gathered on the banks of the river. In the habit of men of the Enlightenment, they measured everything from the circumference of a gigantic sycamore (51 feet) to the distance between the eyes of a dead catfish (6 inches).

By late spring Clark had reached Harrodsburg, Kentucky's first permanent settlement. Pioneer stations like Harrodsburg were not picturesque outposts, but rather squalid clusters of cabins surrounded by a crude log palisade and reeking of "putrified flesh, dead dogs, horse, cow, hog excrement and human odour."[10] Here Clark saw his future. He told his family that he planned to settle on property he was surveying near present-day Frankfort. "A richer and more Beautifull Cuntry than this I believe has never been seen in America yet," he exulted. He set about "Ingrosing all the Land I possibly Can, " and predicted that once their father had seen it, "he will never rest until he gets in it to live."[11]

Meanwhile, in March 1775, a land speculator named Richard Henderson had persuaded the Cherokees to sell 20 million acres of Kentucky and Tennessee to his proposed Transylvania Colony. By the terms of Henderson's Treaty of Sycamore Shoals—which was transparently illegal—the Cherokees were to be paid with a pile of trade goods worth £10,000. Even before the treaty was signed, Henderson hired Daniel Boone and a party of thirty settlers to cut a road through the Cumberland Gap and establish a new frontier station in Kentucky called Boonesborough. Back in Williamsburg, Dunmore protested Henderson's violation of the Proclamation of 1763—but largely because he wanted to protect Virginia's (and his own) claims to the same land.

More ominous words came from a Cherokee war chief named Dragging Canoe (Tsiyu-Gûnsíni) who warned his people against the sale of their tribal lands. "New cessions would be applied for," he said, "and finally the country which the Cherokees and their forefathers had so long occupied would be called for; and a small remnant which may then exist of their nation, once so great and formidable, will be compelled to seek a retreat in some far distant wilderness." Kentucky, Dragging Canoe told Henderson in a prescient phrase, would become "a dark and bloody ground."[12]

News of the April 1775 battles of Lexington and Concord opening the Revolution did not get to Kentucky until July. The struggle itself would not reach the Virginia backcountry for another two years. Instead, the settlers were more concerned with the problem at hand: Indian resistance to their continued expansion. Encouraged by the British, mixed war parties of Mingos, Shawnees, Delawares, and Wyandots were banding together to attack settlers west of the Appalachian gateways at Redstone and the Cumberland Gap. Just as Europeans began to describe themselves for the first time as "whites" when facing the Indians—giving up their early self-identification as Swedes, or Irish, or Germans—so too did once-rival Indian tribes begin to find their common identity as "Red Men" confronting a single enemy. The shifting and complex interrelationship between white settlers and native peoples was becoming a deepening racial divide.

Worried about protecting his own surveys in Kentucky from "Carolina Dick" Henderson's immense landgrab, George Rogers Clark returned to Virginia to petition the colonial government to assume jurisdiction over the conflicting land claims. From Caroline County, the rest of the Clark family eagerly eyed his progress in the west. Father John Clark was "determined to go to Kentucky," George Rogers reported to Jonathan, but was concerned about reports of "disturbances [there] with the Indians."[13]

In fact, the Mingos, Shawnees, and Cherokees were successfully mounting their assault on the invading pioneers, who began to pull back to safety across the mountains. By the spring of 1776, fewer than two hundred settlers remained in isolated and thinly defended forts at Harrodsburg, Logan's Station, and Boonesborough.

At this moment, twenty-three-year-old George Rogers Clark made the decision that turned him into the most galvanizing American leader west of the Appalachians. He had always had a reputation for charisma and charm. Cresswell, who never suffered fools lightly, remembered Clark as a sophisticated figure in a rough-hewn world who "always behaved well while he stayed with us."[14] Another contemporary agreed that Clark's "appearance, well calculated to attract attention, was rendered particularly agreeable by the manliness of his deportment and the intelligence of his conversation."[15]

Acting on no authority but his own, Clark called a town meeting in Harrodsburg on June 8, 1776. Short on food, short on gunpowder, and disillusioned with Henderson, the settlers duly elected Clark and John Gabriel Jones as their delegates to petition the Commonwealth of Virginia to assume their colony's governance and protection. Within a few weeks, Clark and Jones were back in Williamsburg after a harrowing overland journey during which they were threatened by both Indian attacks and the dreaded "scald feet," a disabling inflammation caused by wet moccasins. "The Skin seems too hot on every part of our Feet," Clark remembered, resulting "in greater torment than I ever before or since Experienced."[16]

In Virginia, George Rogers traveled to the home of the new governor, Patrick Henry, a friend of the Clark family, to argue for the protection of Kentucky. As a member of Virginia's Revolutionary convention of 1775, eldest brother Jonathan Clark had been sitting in the pews when Henry gave his ringing "Give Me Liberty or Give Me Death!" oration in a Richmond church. (Jonathan, typically, mentioned not the speech but the weather in his diary.) Now the younger George Rogers was poised to rally Henry by his own oratory.

George Rogers made his case forcefully. "By God, if the country is not worth protecting, it is not worth having!" he is said to have bellowed at the governor. If only to counter Henderson's land ambitions, the Virginia executive council approved the delivery of twenty-five kegs of powder to Clark and carved the new Kentucky County out of Fincastle County. In March 1777, the first Kentucky County militia was organized. Its commander: the newly commissioned Major George Rogers Clark, age twenty-four.

By this time, the Revolution had come to Indian country. The Mingos, still bitter over the murder of Logan's family and their loss of land after Lord Dunmore's War, mounted more attacks on Americans in the Upper Ohio Valley. The British enlisted Indian allies all along the frontier, supplying them with weapons, including scalping knives. Thomas Jefferson's single description of native peoples in the Declaration of Independence—that the King had "endeavored to bring on the inhabitants of our frontiers, the merciless Indian Savages"—had become a self-fulfilling prophecy.

The Iroquois and the Shawnees took up arms with the Mingos, though some Shawnee bands began to migrate west to the Mississippi Valley. Those who remained found themselves in a brutal conflict increasingly characterized by atrocities on both sides. When the stepson of Daniel Boone's friend Hugh McGary was killed, the enraged McGary "killed an Indian that he found had his [dead] stepson's shirt on, and cut him up and fed him to the dogs."[17]

Ever since the Battle of Point Pleasant, Cornstalk, the principal chief of the Mequachake division of Shawnees, had pursued a policy of peace with the Americans. In doing so, he aligned himself against war chiefs like Blackfish, the leader of a roaming guerrilla force of two hundred Chillicothe Shawnees that later captured and adopted Daniel Boone. But Cornstalk's attempts to broker peace or at least neutrality were frustrated by the continuing incursions of settlers and land speculators. He told the American Indian agent George Morgan:

> [A]ll our Lands are covered by the white people, & we are jealous that you still intend to make larger strides—We never sold you our Lands which you now possess on the Ohio between the Great Kanawha & the Cherokee, & which you are settling without ever asking our leave, or obtaining our consent.

The peace-seeking Cornstalk ended with a plea rather than a threat:

> I open my hand & pour into your heart the cause of our discontent in hopes that you take pity on us your younger Brethren, and send us a favorable Answer, that we may be convinced of the sincerity of your profession.[18]

Cornstalk, however, soon found it difficult to keep in check the tribe's militant young men, who wished to "run off to where the evil Spirit leads them."[19] In the fall of 1777, Cornstalk crossed the Ohio to warn the Americans at Fort Randolph that factions of his tribe were joining the British. The commander, Captain Matthew Arbuckle, promptly took Cornstalk as a hostage against future tribal violence, along with Cornstalk's son Elinipsico and two other men named Red Hawk and Petalla.

A few days later, a hunter from a group of visiting Virginia militiamen was killed and scalped near Fort Randolph. Outraged, the avenging militiamen stormed the cabin where Arbuckle held Cornstalk and the other hostages. After threatening to shoot the guards, the militiamen killed all four Indian prisoners, including those attempting to flee up a chimney, and mutilated their bodies. Cornstalk was said to have accepted his fate with equanimity, reportedly saying, "I can die but once and it is all one to me now or at another time."[20] But that version may have been popularized because it seemed to absolve the soldiers of responsibility for his death.

The murder of the accommodating Cornstalk joined the slaughter of Logan's family as a flashpoint in the bloody history of the Ohio Valley. From then on, the Shawnees believed that no peace with the Long Knives was possible. Instead, they chose to unite with the British as implacable foes of the American invaders. If there ever had been a hope of accommodation, the American General Edward Hand wrote resignedly, "it is now vanished."[21]

At the end of 1777, George Rogers Clark traveled to his parents' home in Caroline County and on to Williamsburg. There he again met with Patrick Henry. If the Indians continued to attack unopposed, Clark said, they would push the settlers out of Kentucky. They could then attack across the Appalachians and open a new front of the war along the western borders of the colonies. The only way to stop them was to cut off their supplies from the British. Clark then made a bold proposal: he would take the war directly into Indian territory by capturing the major British outposts—at Detroit, along the Wabash, and in the Illinois country along the east bank of the Mississippi above the Kaskaskia River.

Clark said he would need a regiment of five hundred militiamen, more than Virginia could readily afford. But his friends Thomas Jefferson, George Mason, and George Wythe supported the plan and promised that Virginia would award land grants in the West as incentives to the men under his command. Jefferson, who changed his view of the Indians as circumstances demanded, said the goal was to punish those Indians who have "massacred many of the Inhabitants upon the Frontiers of this Commonwealth, in the most cruel and barbarous Manner, and it is intended to revenge the Injury and punish the Aggressors by carrying the War into their own Country."[22]

By the following spring, George Rogers Clark, now promoted to lieutenant colonel, was at Redstone Creek with 150 men—well short of the strength he requested but enough to begin the campaign. He enlisted a few dozen more soldiers and perhaps eighty emigrants and adventurers. Clark told them that their objective was to protect the Kentucky settlements. None of those assembled knew the real scope and difficulty of the enterprise he had actually planned.

Clark and his group waited until the ice floes on the Ohio broke up, hurtling downstream in the engorged and roiling river. On May 27, 1778, the men reached the Falls of the Ohio, the only navigational obstacle between Fort Pitt and the Mississippi. Here the river dropped twenty-six feet in two miles as it tumbled in a series of rapids over an exposed Devonian coral reef.

Clark's men camped on an island opposite present-day Louisville, posting guards on their boats to deter deserters. When Clark finally revealed that they would be marching deeper into Indian country, some militiamen did attempt to flee. But after spending a month to settle and train his makeshift army, Clark recalled, "We left our little island and running about a mile up the river in order to gain the main channel, we shot the Falls at the very moment the sun was under a great eclipse, which caused various conjectures on the part of the superstitious among us."[23]

The party proceeded to Fort Massac, an abandoned French outpost opposite the mouth of the Tennessee River, near present-day Paducah, Kentucky. Hiding their boats nearby, they struck out overland across Illinois in order to avoid discovery by British agents or Indians possibly waiting at the junction of the Ohio and the Mississippi. The goal: Kaskaskia, a bustling town of about a thousand whites and blacks that was the first and largest French settlement on the Mississippi above New Orleans. In a typical shift of allegiance, Kaskaskia's French-born governor, Phillippe François de Rastel, the Chevalier de Rocheblave, now reported to the British in Detroit.

The 175 men of Clark's Illinois Regiment were typical backwoodsmen, which is to say they looked like Indians. They wore hunting shirts, sometimes made of deerskin but more often linsey-woolsey. On the chest was a pouch in which a hunter could carry provisions such as parched corn or jerked venison. Dangling from ornamented belts worn around the waist and over the shoulder would be a knife, tomahawk, shot pouch, and "patchen pouch" for the pieces of oiled cloth that greased the barrels of the Kentucky rifles before a shot was rammed home. Slung over the hunter's shoulders was his powder horn, an item of particular pride. A good horn was scraped so thin that it became translucent and allowed the level of remaining powder to be seen at a glance. Below the waist, the men wore leather breeches or cloth trousers, with leggings and boots that rose to mid-thigh to protect them from thorns, insects, and snakes. When they slept, they tied their moccasins to their rifles in order to find them quickly in the dark.[24]

The troops covered 120 miles in six days, approaching Kaskaskia undetected on the evening of July 4. They then swept clamorously through the town in the middle of the night, rousing Rocheblave and his wife, still in their nightclothes, and announcing that any citizens found on the streets would be shot on sight. "Greater silence, I suppose, never reigned among the inhabitants of a town," Clark wrote afterward.[25]

Quickly determining that the French inhabitants were frightened of the Long Knives' reputation for ferocity, Clark moderated his initial show of force with conspicuous displays of mercy and fairness—a psychological tactic that became his signature. "I considered that the greater the shock I could give them in the beginning, the more appreciative they would be later of my lenity and the more valuable as friends," he reasoned. "This I conceived to accord with human nature as I observed it in many instances."[26]

The next evening he sent Major Joseph Bowman and thirty men north to secure Cahokia and the other undefended settlements scattered along the bottomlands under the bluffs across the Mississippi from St. Louis, which was in Spanish territory.

Clark then turned to his most critical task: to persuade the powerful tribes of the Illinois and Wabash rivers country either to abandon their British allies and side with the Americans or to at least remain neutral. "The treaties we made during the three or four weeks beginning about the last of August were negotiated in a different fashion, probably, than any others in America prior to that time," he recalled. "I had always been convinced that our general conduct of Indian affairs was wrong. Inviting them to treaties was considered by them in a different manner than we realized; they imputed it to fear on our part, and the giving of valuable presents confirmed them in this opinion."[27]

At the end of the first day of the treaty-making at Cahokia, Clark refused to shake hands with the chiefs "until the heart could be given also"—a statement that immediately impressed them that he "did not speak with a double tongue." The next morning, after pretending to sleep unguarded as a sign of his courage, Clark delivered a lengthy speech equal to any Indian's in its oratorical power.

"I am a man and a warrior, not a councilor," he told them.

> I carry War in my right hand and in my left Peace . . . I was sent to bloody the paths of those who continue the effort to stop the course of the rivers, but to clear the roads that lead from us to those who wish to be in friendship with us . . . I know that a mist is yet before your eyes; I will dispel the clouds in order that you may see clearly the cause of the war between the Big Knives and the English . . . Here is a bloody belt and a white one. Take whichever you please.[28]

Few white men had ever talked to the tribes like that before, in their own idiom and with absolute confidence. The next morning they told Clark they would take the belt of peace and would "cast the tomahawk into the river where it could never be found again." Clark's tactic of not courting the Indians had worked. "They parted from us with every appearance of perfect satisfaction." So completely had George Rogers won the Indians' confidence that, years later, if he were present at a council, he was the only white man with whom they would speak.

The final and most dramatic act of the Illinois campaign began in December. Clark learned that the English commander at Detroit, Lieutenant Governor Henry Hamilton, had led a motley army of British regulars, Indians, and French Canadian conscripts through the Maumee and Wabash watersheds and had captured the American-held Fort Patrick Henry, named for the Virginia governor, at Vincennes, near the present Indiana-Illinois border. The Scots-Irish Hamilton was detested by the Virginians, who called him the "Hair-buyer" because he had accepted scalps brought in by Indian raiding parties. Anticipating that

Hamilton could use the renamed Fort Sackville as a staging-point to re-capture both the Illinois country and Kentucky, Clark "saw but one al-ternative which was to attack the enemy in his stronghold."[29]

On February 5, Clark and his 170 men left Kaskaskia and began one of the most remarkable marches in military history. They would "Risque the whole on a Single Battle," he wrote to Patrick Henry.[30] In the dead of winter, they intended to cross 180 miles of Illinois prairies and streams, inundated at the time by freezing rains. The men struggled through the mud and ice, making 25 or 30 miles a day. Clark had learned something about motivating groups of men on the move. "I permitted them to shoot game . . . and to feast on it like Indians at a war dance—each company taking turns to invite the other to its feast . . . I myself and my principal officers conducted ourselves like woodsmen, shouting now and then and running through the mud and water the same as the men themselves. Thus, insensible of their hardships and without complaining, our men were conducted through difficulties far surpassing anything we had ever experienced before."[31]

They reached the twin branches of the Wabash on February 13. There they found that the five-mile-wide swamp between the rivers was flooded to depths of three feet and more. With no option other than to push on, the troops ferried and portaged across the chest-high sheets of frigid wa-ter, holding their rifles and ammunition above their heads as a drummer boy diverted them "by floating on his drum and other tricks."[32]

Once his force was within the sound of the fort's morning cannon, Clark decided to sever the British from the support of the French resi-dents of Vincennes. He sent a message into the town announcing his presence and paraded his flag-bearing troops around the nearby hillsides, like spear-carriers in *Aïda*, "in a fashion calculated to magnify our num-bers."[33] The ruse worked; the town was soon under his control.

Hamilton's French militiamen then deserted, leaving his 70 defend-ers hopelessly outnumbered and under siege by Clark's regiment of 170. A formal exchange of notes followed.

Clark to Hamilton:

Sir In order to save yourself from the Impending Storm that now Threatens you I order you to Immediately surrender yourself up with all your Garrison Stores &c. for If I am obliged to storm, you may depend upon such Treatment justly due to a Murderer beware of destroying Stores of any kind or any papers or letters that is in your possession or hurting one house in the Town for by heavens if you do there shall be no Mercy shewn you.

G. R. Clark[34]

Hamilton's reply:

Govr. Hamilton begs leave to acquaint Col. Clark that he and his Garrison are not disposed to be awed into any action Unworthy of British subjects.

H. Hamilton[35]

The standoff ended when an Indian raiding party, previously sent out by Hamilton, rode up to the fort, unaware that the Americans had surrounded it. Before the warriors could escape, Clark's men captured several of the band. One of them, in a coincidence not unusual in the backcountry, turned out to be the abducted son of one of Clark's lieutenants. Four captive Indians were then dragged into the field in front of the fort. "I now had a fair opportunity of making an impression,"[36] George Rogers wrote. In full view of the appalled British soldiers and their allies, Clark ordered the four captives tomahawked to death and their bodies thrown into the river.

Clark had made his point. Hamilton quickly agreed to meet with him outside the fort. In his later report, the British commander accused Clark of personally participating in the slayings: "Colonel Clarke yet reeking with the blood of these unhappy Victims . . . spoke with rapture of his late achievement, while he washed off the blood from his hands stained in this inhuman sacrifice."[37]

When Clark refused to accept any terms other than unconditional surrender, Hamilton asked him why. Clark replied that he intended to put to death those British soldiers who had incited Indians against the Americans. Whom do you mean? Hamilton asked. Clark promptly named Major Jehu Hay, causing that officer, who was standing at his commander's side, to so visibly blanch that Hamilton was embarrassed.

On the next morning, February 25, 1779, Hamilton surrendered his entire garrison to Clark's Long Knives. Sparing Hay, Clark appointed his own first cousin, Captain John Rogers, to take Hamilton and his officers in irons back to prison at Williamsburg. On the way, the group passed through Caroline County, where young Billy Clark was still living with his family.

Back east, the Revolution had led to American defeats and draws. British-led Indians had killed Americans in Pennsylvania, and the British had captured Savannah, Georgia. But at the age of twenty-six, George Rogers Clark had become the first early hero of the Revolution, the "Hannibal of the West" who had driven the British out of the Illinois country. No American of the period could equal him in military enterprise and experience in dealing with Indians. He had forestalled a planned assault by the British and their combined Shawnee and Cherokee allies against Kentucky and possibly Virginia. He was commended by the Continental Congress, and his childhood neighbor Thomas Jefferson would come to regard Clark as the most able frontiersman of his generation.

But in the coming months, Clark was unable either to consolidate his gains by establishing trade with the Indians or to muster adequate forces to march on the British stronghold at Detroit, despite his typically audacious conviction that a small army "conducted with spirit" could easily rout the British "and put an end to the Indian war."[38] By the following year, the British would be back in the Old Northwest, again inciting the Indians in raids against the Long Knives.

Clark remained in Kentucky, organizing the militia's defenses during the "Hard Winter" of 1779–'80, when temperatures fell so abruptly that maple trees splintered with gunshot-like cracks from the pressure of freezing sap. Clark's regiment now included his younger brother Richard. "I have given Dicky a Lieutenants Commission," he wrote their father. "If I can get him to Imbrace the Air of an officer I don't doubt but that he may make a good appearance in a short time."[39]

In the spring of 1780, the Revolution in the East was going poorly: the British regulars had landed in South Carolina; Charleston had fallen. Thomas Jefferson, who had succeeded Patrick Henry as governor of Virginia, assigned Clark to build a fort at the junction of the Ohio and Mississippi rivers to protect the western front. Clark and his men floated down from Louisville and chose a site on a quarter acre of high ground at Iron Banks, on the eastern side of the Mississippi five miles below the mouth of the Ohio. In May they built Fort Jefferson, the westernmost outpost of the American republic.

Just a few days after completing the fort, George Rogers was summoned by the Spanish governor of St. Louis, Fernando de Leyba. Spain had declared war against England the previous year, and now a British-led force of nearly a thousand Sioux, Sauks, Foxes, Ojibwas, and Winnebagos was rumored to be descending from the Great Lakes to seize St. Louis and New Orleans and take control of all Louisiana.

Poling and rowing one hundred miles upstream against the Mississippi current, Clark and his party arrived at Cahokia and St. Louis just one day before the attack began on May 26, 1780. St. Louis was then a village of about eight hundred mostly French Creole inhabitants, so remote that Virginia officials literally had no idea where it was located.[40] The villagers called it "Pancore"—from the French *pain court* (bread shortage)—because they were chronically in need of foodstuffs.

Clark was the first representative of the new American government to visit this strange place. The unexpected arrival of the feared Long Knife surprised the attackers, who believed his regiment was still at the Falls of the Ohio. After a vigorous resistance was mounted by the local militia, the British and Indians halted their advance on the outskirts of St. Louis and withdrew after only minor skirmishes. St. Louis was appropriately grateful, and the American troops warmly celebrated—though there is no evidence to support a persistent Clark family legend that at the time George Rogers had a thwarted romance with de Leyba's sister Teresa.

By now George Rogers's attitude toward the Indians had hardened. Their continued support of the British and opposition to settlements on their lands led him to agree with Jefferson that the only way to influence the tribes was "to excel them in barbarity."[41] After his captivity, Henry Hamilton wrote that Clark had told him "that he had made a vow never to spare woman or child of the Indians."[42] Jefferson's words were just as chilling. "We must leave it to yourself to decide on the object of the campaign," he wrote Clark on New Year's Day of 1780. "If against these Indians, the end proposed should be their extermination, or their removal . . . The same world would scarcely do for them and us."[43]

Returning to Kentucky in the summer of 1780, George Rogers organized the first of the punitive raids into Indian country that would occupy him for several years. On August 2, he led one thousand militiamen—the largest American force yet assembled beyond the Appalachians—across the Ohio at the mouth of the Licking River. They marched up the Little Miami River toward the main Shawnee villages at Chillicothe and Piqua. These were multiethnic, European-style communities, where residents spoke several languages and were fully dependent on small manufacturing and trade for their survival.

The army made such a clamor during its march that it frightened off available game and the natives. The Shawnees abandoned the first village so precipitously that the militia found kettles of roasted corn and green beans still boiling over their fires.[44] "We Burnt the Town & Cut down their Corn," Clark reported. Moving on to Piqua, they found "well built cabins located along the river each surrounded by a strip of corn."[45] Here the Indians made a stand in a ferocious rifle battle, giving way only as the Americans' cannons routed them and darkness fell. The fighting was vicious and hand-to-hand; an Indian woman was killed by a soldier's "ripping up her Belly & otherwise mangling her."[46] Clark's force lost about fourteen men, and the Indians three times as many. Among the casualties was "a white man dressed fine in Indian dress," killed trying to flee to the Americans' lines.[47] He turned out to be Clark's first cousin Joseph Rogers, who had been captured four years earlier and adopted by the tribe.

The troops then spent two days at the Shawnee villages burning eight hundred acres of cornfields and digging up graves to take scalps from corpses. The American strategy was to lay waste the Indian food supplies late in the season, when it would be too late to replant. If the Indians could not be defeated militarily, they would be starved into submission. "Having done the Shawanese all the mischief in our power; after destroying the Picawey settlmnts, I returned to this post," George Rogers reported to Jefferson.[48]

In the fall, Clark returned to Virginia for the first time in three years. His father, John, had been commissioned earlier as a lieutenant in the Caroline County militia at the age of thirty-nine. But he would be outdone by his sons. Five of the six Clark boys were serving in Revolutionary armies. The only brother not under arms was the youngest, Billy. To the redheaded ten-year-old, his brother George Rogers must have seemed a dashing and romantic figure, a war hero brimming with tales of his military expeditions down the Ohio River, of negotiations with Indians and

British enemies, and, most compellingly, of the rich lands that could be theirs once the Indians were cleared. Just a year earlier a family friend had written Jonathan that "People are Runing Mad for Kentucky hereabouts," and now the entire Clark family was burning to do the same.[49]

But there would be no Kentucky land for any Virginians if the Indians and their British allies continued to control it. On Christmas Day of 1780, Jefferson wrote a long letter to George Rogers Clark authorizing a new expedition "into the hostile country beyond the Ohio, the principal object of which is to be the reduction of the British post at Detroit." The result would be to add to "the Empire of liberty"—Jefferson's first use of his famous phrase—"an extensive and fertile Country thereby converting dangerous Enemies into valuable friends."

There were now two wars of independence taking place. One was the struggle of the American colonies to achieve independence from the British empire. The other was the struggle of the Indian tribes of North America to preserve their independence in the face of the steady march of the Europeans into their homelands. The old balance of power in the backcountry, in which Indians had successfully coexisted with foreign trading partners for generations, had collapsed. In its place was a killing field.

In the coming months, George Rogers Clark fought in both wars. Before he returned west, he was assigned by Jefferson to a unit of 240 Virginians under the command of Baron Friedrich von Steuben. In early January 1781, Clark saw his only fighting on the eastern front when he and his men faced a British force under the traitorous Benedict Arnold at Hood's Ferry on the James River. They inflicted thirty casualties without losing a single soldier.[50]

Back on the Ohio and promoted to brigadier general, Clark found that the Indians had renewed their attacks on the frontier stations. One hundred thirty-one Kentuckians had been killed or captured in the first nine months of the year. "Whole families are destroyed without regard to Age or Sex," a desperate John Floyd told Jefferson. "Infants are torn from their Mothers Arms and their Brains dashed out against Trees . . . Not a week Passes some weeks scarcely a day with out some of our distressed Inhabitants feeling the fatal effects of the infernal rage and fury of those Execreable Hellhounds."[51]

Clark's own reputation began to suffer. In the spring, the detachment he had left at Fort Jefferson had been forced to abandon the post after repeated raids from the neighboring Chickasaws. A group of Pennsylvania militia moving down the Ohio was attacked by an Indian force led by the Mohawk chief Joseph Brant; more than one hundred Pennsylvanians were killed or captured. Some settlers blamed George Rogers for the disaster.[52] Clark's own expedition into Indian country collapsed in the face of a shortage of supplies and troops. Rumors of his drinking bouts, which first surfaced during the construction of Fort Jefferson, became more frequent. An officer wrote that Clark "has lost the confidence of the people and it is said become a sot; perhaps something worse."[53]

The surrender of Lord Cornwallis at Yorktown in October 1781 ended the major fighting with the British on the eastern seaboard, but nothing changed on the western front. Dragging Canoe's prediction of a "dark and bloody" future proved increasingly accurate. In March 1782, a band of militiamen from the Monongahela region descended on the Moravian mission town of Gnudenhutten (Glad Huts), where a group of Christian Delawares had gathered to harvest winter corn left standing in the fields. The militia commander, David Williamson, rounded up the converts and told them they would be escorted to Fort Pitt for their protection. But when his men discovered that these devout Indians used teakettles, cups and saucers, and other appointments of Europeans, they concluded that the Indians could have acquired them only by murdering whites. After a vote, the Virginians decided what to do. The next morning they marched the forty-two men, twenty women, and thirty-four children into two houses and systematically slaughtered them with clubs and hatchets. One militiaman, Charles Builderback, reputedly killed fourteen Indians with a cooper's mallet before announcing, "My arms faile me. Go on with the work. I have done pretty well."[54]

The reprisals were no less ghastly. In May, Colonel William Crawford, a personal friend of George Washington's, led an army of Pennsylvanians that was routed by the Wyandots north of the Ohio. Crawford lost fifty men and was captured. Clark's future brother-in-law William Croghan talked to an escaped prisoner who had witnessed Crawford's fate: "Col. Crawford was led by a long rope to a high stake, to the top of which the rope about the colonel was tied; all around the stake a great quantity of red hot coals were laid, on which the poor colonel was obliged to walk barefoot, and at the same time the Indians firing squibs of powder at him, while others poked burning sticks on every part of his body; thus they continued torturing him for about two hours." Seeing Simon Girty, a white who had joined the Indians, standing nearby, Crawford pleaded for Girty to shoot him. "Don't you see I have no gun?" Girty replied. The Indians then scalped Crawford and struck his bare skull with sticks. "Being now nearly exhausted, he lay down on the burning embers, when the squaws put shovels full of coals on his body, which dying as he was, made him move and creep a little . . ."[55]

In the crazy quilt of the borderlands, where the ultimate winners and losers were impossible to predict, the most successful strategy was often the most opportunistic one. Girty and his three brothers were odd mirror images of the Clark brothers. A Pennsylvanian, Simon Girty had been captured as an adolescent and raised by the Senecas. After he was released, he became an interpreter for the Continental Congress in 1776—only to desert and join the British as an Indian agent north of the Ohio. In August 1782, he and the British agent Alexander McKee led a Shawnee army that ambushed 160 frontiersmen from central Kentucky at the battle of Blue Licks. Among the sixty American officers and men killed were Daniel Boone's son Israel and Clark's friend Colonel John Todd, a founder of Lexington, Kentucky, who had served in the Illinois campaign.

By now the entire Ohio Valley was aflame with hatred, brutality, and fear. One military commander estimated that Indians had killed 860 Kentuckians since Daniel Boone had led the first settlers to the territory—a casualty rate higher than that of the Continental Army itself. George Rogers was instructed by the Virginia government to build a series of defensive forts along the Ohio. They would be supported by a fleet of "row galleys," eighty-foot oared keelboats equipped with artillery and hinged bulwarks that could be hoisted to defend the crew against attack. In the end, only Fort Nelson was completed at the Falls of the Ohio, patrolled by a single galley, the *Miami*.

The atmosphere of dread was felt by families throughout the region. The onetime Noble Savages were now seen as little more than demonic fiends. Settlers tried to poison Indians by leaving crops impregnated with arsenic and warned their children to be good "or the Shawnees will catch you."[56] Indian mothers had equal reason to give their own children nightmares about the Long Knives. "The white Americans," said a British traveler, "have the most rancorous antipathy for the whole race of Indians; and nothing is more common than to hear them talk of extirpating them totally, from the face of the earth, men, women, and children."[57]

A pioneer woman remarked that after two sanguinary years in Kentucky, she was so astonished to see a young man dying from natural causes that she and her companions "sat up all night, gazing upon him as an object of beauty."[58]

The land itself was blighted by the struggle. The continuing American burning of the Shawnees' towns and crops forced the Indians to rely more on hunting for sustenance. The result was the depletion of wild game throughout the Ohio Valley and the extermination of the entire population of eastern bison within two decades.

In late 1782, the Revolutionary War was ending—at least on two of its three fronts. In the East, the new American government agreed on preliminary peace terms with Britain. A series of American raids on the Cherokees' villages had destroyed the threat in the South. Now the only enemies facing the new republic were the tribes along the Ohio.

In the first week of November, Clark and one thousand mounted men rode up the Great Miami River and spent a week burning Shawnee villages and fields. Only a handful of warriors were killed, but, according to Daniel Boone, the men "entirely destroyed their corn and other fruits, and spread desolation through their country."[59] As was so often the case, patriotism mingled with profit motive. One detachment burned and looted a post operated by a French Canadian trader named Louis Lorimier, carrying off $20,000 in goods and pelts to be divided among the troops.

On September 3, 1783, American diplomats signed the Treaty of Paris with Britain. With the stroke of a pen, everything seemed to have changed. The English turned the Old Northwest over to the new American nation, defining its western boundary as the Mississippi River and setting a northern boundary that included Clark's long-sought objective of Detroit. The British promised to evacuate their posts north of the Ohio "with all convenient speed." If George Rogers's campaigns had achieved nothing else, they prevented the British from claiming the Old Northwest at the negotiating table.

For the tribes, though, nothing changed. The British had signed away the Indians' territory without so much as a word about the natives who had fought alongside them and lived on the lands being transferred. While the struggle for American independence was over, the simultaneous struggle for American empire was continuing. Thousands of settlers were gathering to surge back across the Appalachians, ready to reoccupy Kentucky, a wedge on the white man's map stabbing deep into Indian country. For the Shawnees, the stage for the struggle was moving from their hunting grounds south of the Ohio to their villages and fields north of the river.

There was no room for Indians in Jefferson's empire of liberty. They, after all, had chosen the losing side. During the Revolution, the ambiguous and interdependent accommodations between Indians and whites had given way to a widening chasm. The only choices now available to Indians were to resist, to become "white" at the cost of leaving their tribes, or to be eliminated or removed. Increasing numbers of Shawnees and Delawares chose the last, voluntarily seeking refuge in Spanish territory in present-day southern Missouri.

At the age of thirty, George Rogers Clark was a general without an army. After the Revolution, the cash-poor state of Virginia no longer wanted to pay for a militia to defend its remote western forests. In fact, the Commonwealth had not paid Clark at all for four years and refused to honor the $20,000 in expenses he had assumed on his personal credit in order to feed and clothe his soldiers. At one point, Clark had put up his own land as security to pay for flour needed to feed his men. (The expense vouchers, which had been misplaced, turned up many years later.) Worse, during the war Clark had developed prominent enemies. One was Patrick Henry, whom Jefferson disdained as "all tongue without either head or heart" but whose opposition rankled Clark.[60]

What George Rogers still had, though, was his share of the 150,000 acres Virginia had granted the Illinois Regiment for its campaign. His officers had elected Clark chief surveyor of the new lands, most of them in present-day Indiana and Tennessee. Clark was particularly interested in property on a point of land on the Indiana side of the Falls of the Ohio, where he was granted rights to erect a saw- and gristmill. On July 2, 1783, Virginia governor Benjamin Harrison finally decommissioned Clark, adding his thanks—but not cash—for "wresting so great and valuable a territory out of the hands of the British enemy, repelling the attacks of their savage allies, and carrying on a successful war in the heart of the country."[61]

In the same month the Treaty of Paris was signed, the Clark family gathered in Caroline County for their first reunion since the outbreak of the Revolution. It brought an extraordinary group to the dinner table.

Brigadier General George Rogers was the most celebrated sibling, but Lieutenant Colonel Jonathan had fought at the battles of Brandywine, Paulus Hook, and Monmouth and received a letter of praise from General Washington. John, Jr., a captain, had couriered letters for Washington and had been captured at the Battle of Germantown. He returned ill with tuberculosis contracted on an English prison ship. Brother Edmund had been commissioned a lieutenant at age seventeen and, with Jonathan, had also been held by the British following the fall of Charleston in May 1780. The only absentee was Dicky, who was still serving as an officer with Clark's regiment in the Illinois country.

The Clarks were firmly anchored in Virginia planter society. Males rode in fox chases, gambled at cockfights and shooting contests, and took on the affectations of aristocrats. In his diary, Jonathan recorded going to dances in satin and lace. Women cooked, mended, canned, minded both the children and the enslaved domestics, and attended to churchgoing.

Thirteen-year-old Billy was considered mature enough to stand with Edmund as a co-godfather of Jonathan and his wife Sarah's new daughter, Eleanor. Sister Ann Clark, who had married Owen Gwathmey in 1773, lived nearby. Presiding over the gathering were parents John and Ann, now in their fifties. A friend later described Ann Rogers Clark in her old age as "a majestic woman."[62]

Then, on October 29, 1783, a terrible blow fell. Never fully recovered from his imprisonment at the hands of the British, brother John Clark died at the family homestead at the age of twenty-six. Four days later he was buried.

The next day Jonathan wrote in his diary, "Clear: at Mr. Mason's; set off for Kentucky."[63]

It was a characteristic Clark moment. Wasting not an additional hour to mourn their lost son and brother, the Clarks moved on. John and Ann made plans to move to the Falls of the Ohio. They would settle on a plot George Rogers had surveyed for them on Beargrass Creek, on the hilly east side of Louisville. Now, the day after his brother's funeral, Jonathan was leaving with at least one of the family's slaves—his personal servant Old York—a full year ahead of his parents in order to clear the land for farming.

Meanwhile, with his military career seemingly at an end, George Rogers had continued his regular correspondence with Jefferson. The former governor had renewed his interest in collecting fossil specimens from sites like Big Bone Lick, a sulfur spring on the Ohio south of present-day Cincinnati. At the end of 1783, Jefferson wrote Clark a letter, ostensibly to thank him for a shipment of "shells and seeds." But after only a few sentences, Jefferson suddenly shifted the subject. He was interested in more than collecting fossils. He told Clark that he had learned that the English were raising money "for exploring the country from the Missisipi to California." Further, Jefferson had been sounding out others "in a feeble way" about organizing a similar exploration but doubted that they could raise the money. Then Jefferson all but blurted out to George Rogers a question that must have astonished him: "How would you like to lead such a party?"[64]

CHAPTER THREE

LIEUTENANT BILLY CLARK

1789–1795

With his almost offhand question to George Rogers Clark, Thomas Jefferson had introduced the pattern of military exploration that would prevail in the West for the next century.

The discovery of the continent, Jefferson thought, should not be carried out by lawless traders, settlers, and speculators. Nor should natural scientists or geographers lead the way. The task of securing an empire should be entrusted to military men, equipped to gather scientific and geographical information but ready to impose their will on anyone — natives or Europeans — who tried to stop them. Army surveyors could then lay out a gridwork of sections of 640 acres — a square mile — to await the orderly arrival of farmers.

As a member of the Virginia delegation to the Continental Congress, Jefferson was motivated as much by geopolitical realities as he was by the Enlightenment spirit of inquiry. Just as George Rogers Clark had successfully organized the first displays of American military power across the Appalachians, so could he similarly deal with any foreign or native antagonists he might encounter as the new nation reached across the Mississippi to the Pacific.

Clark himself was not so sanguine. The former general knew only too well the Indians' ability to defend their lands in the face of American expansion. He replied to Jefferson that an exploration of the "western Country" is "what I think we ought to do." But, he said, a large party would "alarm the Indian Nations that they pass through." Instead, he suggested that "three or four young Men" could do the job at "a Trifling Expense" over four or five years. Unwilling to be among the three or four, Clark hinted that he might be willing to serve as a "Superintendant of Indian affairs" once the tribes were brought to heel. But he could no longer afford public service. His goal was to master "the lucrative policy of the world."[1] In other words, it was time to make money.

If Jefferson was disappointed, he left no record. Within six months he sailed to Paris as minister plenipotentiary to France. For his part, George Rogers Clark prepared to make what he hoped would be a fortune from his grant of an "unprecedented Quantity of the finest lands in the Western world."[2] And the rest of the Clarks were bound in earnest for Kentucky.

John Clark began to sell off his holdings in Caroline and Spotsylvania counties. With Ann and their four youngest children—Lucy, Eliza, William, and Fanny—he packed their belongings onto wagons on October 30, 1784, and started the difficult trip to the Ohio country. The image of a pioneer family migrating with all its pots and pans strapped to a wagon can be misleading, however. The Clarks were not economic refugees but rather members of an upwardly mobile elite. Their slaves traveled with them. In her hatbox Ann Clark carried a silver Samuel Wheat teapot, crafted in London in 1761.

Of the two possible routes into the Ohio River valley, the most direct was Daniel Boone's Wilderness Road from the Block House station in southern Virginia across the Cumberland Gap and 195 miles of wilderness to the first Kentucky settlement at Crab Orchard. Travelers crossed five rivers and many streams, always at risk of stumbling upon Indian hunting parties. Wealthier migrants like the Clarks preferred the more roundabout but faster and easier route through northern Virginia and across Maryland on the Nemacolin Trail (later U.S. Highway 40) to Redstone Old Fort on the Monongahela.

As they moved toward Redstone (now Brownsville, Pennsylvania), the Clarks were nearing the Appalachian backcountry they had glimpsed in Albemarle County thirty years earlier. For young William, who had grown up on the tidewater estuary, these rugged ridges were the first mountains he had ever seen. The names of places they passed—Devil's Alley, Shades of Death, Big Grave Creek—hinted at the landscape's violent history and the efforts of migrants to subdue their fears by naming them.

The family planned to buy a flatboat capable of transporting their livestock and anywhere from 20 to 70 tons of goods. But an early winter freeze had already closed the Monongahela by the time the Clarks came over the high bluff above Redstone. They would have to delay their departure until the ice cleared in the following spring.

Despite the numbers of settlers pouring into Kentucky—a thousand flatboats were coming down the Ohio every year—Indians continued to resist the invasion of what they called "a plague of locusts" into their territories.[3] Attacks on the river were frequent, and an occasional macabre keelboat would be found floating downstream with "every person on it dead."[4] One man found an entire newly settled family wiped out on the banks: "The woman had a child in her arms, and it was taken from her when they struck her, and its entrails taken out and wrapped around a sapling before the house."[5] But twelve thousand settlers made it to Kentucky in 1784 alone, and the population of whites and slaves in the bluegrass country exploded from thirty thousand in 1783 to fifty thousand by 1787.

When the Clarks finally descended the Monongahela and entered the Ohio at Pittsburgh, they probably followed a neighbor's warning to "sail all night, unless exceedingly dark" and "stay but a little time at a place."[6] Even when crowded like an ark with people, horses, cows, and sheep, a flatboat or "Kentucky boat" could make 60 to 70 miles a day on high water. The craft drifted past the tributaries that were the principal landmarks on the Ohio—the Muskingum, Little and Great Kanawha, Scioto, Licking, Little and Great Miami.

On March 3, 1785, they reached the mouth of the Kentucky River. A canoe full of Indian men passed nearby, apparently avoiding the well-armed flatboat. The Clarks then stopped at the riverside cabin of Robert and Mary Elliott, whom they had been told to visit. But Mary did not invite the party to her table, so the family camped farther down the river. That same night, as the Clarks learned much later, the Elliotts were assaulted by Indians. Robert Elliott's brother and several workmen were "dreadfully mangled & scalped" and the cabin set afire.[7] Mary and her daughter escaped to tell of the massacre.

The Clark family unloaded at Beargrass Creek, a natural harbor within sight of Louisville, then a bustling hamlet of about a hundred log cabins. The echoing sounds of barking dogs and voices eerily carried for miles across the river, but where the Clarks settled, these were drowned out by the roar of the "immense cataract of water" just downstream at the Falls.[8]

The Clarks built a two-story log structure in the Virginia "I-house" style, with large stone chimneys on the gable ends, overlooking a square mile of land on the south fork of Beargrass Creek. It had pressed-glass windows, unusual for the time. After they added a pantry and a store-room, as well as a springhouse and slave quarters, the farm was big enough to acquire a name: Mulberry Hill.

Farming in Kentucky began with corn but extended to tobacco, hemp, oats, rye, and domestic vegetables like turnips, peas, pumpkins, and sweet potatoes. As in Caroline County, the men worked in the fields harvesting crops, shelling corn, and clearing brush, while the women churned butter, salted beef, smoked pork, spun wool, made soap, and baked bread.

At fifteen, William Clark was midway through two transitions—from boyhood into manhood, and from the comfortable planter society into a violent wilderness. He was tall for his age, a large-boned six-footer who shared his brother George Rogers's red hair, broad face, light blue eyes, flaring eyebrows, and confident manner. He and George Rogers also shared a slight wariness around the corners of their eyes, which gave them a worldly-wise look. Like other Virginia expatriates, William brought with him an admiration for the manly skills of horsemanship and hunt-ing. He was accurate enough a rifle shot to engage in the local sport of "barking squirrels"—firing a bullet at a branch immediately below a perched squirrel, sending it flying.

Proficiency with firearms was necessary. One settler had been killed along Beargrass Creek that year, and brother-in-law William Croghan reported to George Rogers that the tribes had been "Exceding trouble-some &c."[9] The troubles then came home to Mulberry Hill in the form of terrible news: brother Richard, who had served with George Rogers's regiment in the Illinois country, had either drowned on the Little Wabash in February or been killed by Indians. Only his clothes and sad-dle were found, abandoned on the bank.

As the violence mounted, the cry went out in Kentucky for revenge. The British had not pulled back from their frontier posts, as promised, and they continued to incite the tribes against American expansion. The Shawnees had never accepted the agreement made by a handful of Iro-quois at Fort Stanwix near Albany in 1784 to sign away the Shawnees' lands in Ohio. A deliberate confusion over which tribe spoke for which tract of land would prove repeatedly convenient. In similar fashion, the

Delawares, Wyandots, Ojibwas, and Ottawas readily gave away 30 million acres of Shawnee land, nearly half the present state of Ohio.

George Rogers and two other commissioners failed to bring the Shawnees to terms at Fort McIntosh on the Upper Ohio in January 1785. They tried again at Fort Finney at the mouth of the Great Miami (near today's Cincinnati) at the end of 1785. The Shawnees again resisted negotiating, but George Rogers Clark threatened them so convincingly that they arrived amid singing and drumbeating in January 1786. The chiefs began by protesting the Americans' land hunger: "God gave us this country! We do not understand measuring out the lands. It is all ours! You say you have goods for our women and children. You may keep your goods and give them to other nations. We will have none of them."[10]

The Indians presented the commissioners with two wampum belts — one white for peace and one black for war — and asked them to choose. It called for precisely the kind of gesture George Rogers knew how to demonstrate. He contemptuously brushed one of the belts to the floor, and then stood and crushed it under his boot heel. The insult produced a collective gasp from the chiefs — and a signed peace treaty on February 1. Intimidated, the Shawnees for the first time had surrendered lands north of the Ohio.

The peace quickly collapsed when the Miamis along the Wabash said that the chiefs at Fort Finney could not speak for them. Their raids continued. A worried John Clark wrote to Jonathan in Virginia that a family several miles away had been "kild & taken."[11] Neither Congress nor the state of Virginia, which controlled Kentucky, seemed able to respond. Frustrated and frightened, the settlers again turned to George Rogers Clark, calling on him to lead another punitive expedition into the heart of the Indian country. "His name alone would be worth half a regiment," John May wrote to Patrick Henry.[12]

In mid-September, George Rogers gathered 1,200 militiamen at the Falls of the Ohio. He planned a devastating double attack against the Shawnees "to keep them in awe."[13] He would distract the Indians by marching his main force to Vincennes along the buffalo trace. Then a second army under Benjamin Logan would strike directly at the Shawnee towns on the Great Miami.

The result was a fiasco. Clark's undisciplined militia ran short of supplies and was plagued by insubordination, desertions, and near-mutiny. In a decision that would haunt him later, he confiscated a cargo of supplies from Spanish merchants, accusing them of trading illegally. Amid the mounting failure, the old charges of drunkenness were being raised by an ambitious new figure on the scene, James Wilkinson.

After leaving the Continental Army, Wilkinson had come to Kentucky. Ostensibly there to speculate in land and trade, he actually set about continuing a career in conspiracy that is unsurpassed in American history. During the Revolution, he had been implicated in a murky officers' cabal against General Washington. By the mid-1780s, he had arranged for a pension and trade privileges from Spanish authorities in New Orleans in return for his services in the "Spanish Conspiracy," an effort to dislodge Kentucky from the young American republic. Under the guise of speculation, Wilkinson sought and found receptive settlers anxious to ship their goods down the Mississippi to the New Orleans market and willing to give their allegiance not to the flag but to a promise of greater profits. Seeing George Rogers Clark as a rival with ambitions of his own, Wilkinson set about spreading rumors to discredit him.

Meanwhile, Benjamin Logan and his mounted men, who included Daniel Boone and Simon Kenton, swept through the deserted villages on the Upper Miami. Logan reported later that his men burned seven towns, killed ten chiefs, took thirty-two prisoners, and destroyed fifteen thousand bushels of corn, the tribes' entire winter food supply. Lieutenant Ebenezer Denny said that the Shawnees "made no Resistance; the men were literally murdered."

Most disturbing of all was the treatment of Moluntha, an accommodating Mequachake Shawnee chief who had signed the treaty at Fort Finney. Too feeble to join his absent warriors, Moluntha had raised an American flag above his house and walked forward to meet the advancing soldiers, waving a copy of the treaty in his hands. Taken into custody, Moluntha apparently misunderstood a question from Hugh McGary, who asked if the chief had been present at the American defeat at Blue Licks. When Moluntha smiled and nodded affably, the enraged McGary felled him with an axe blow to the head. The old man tried to struggle to his feet, but McGary killed him and took his scalp.

The Clark brothers understandably might have brought the family's military service to a close after the Revolutionary War. John and Richard were dead, Jonathan and Edmund retired, and George Rogers was embittered. But the profession of arms was an honorable one for a gentleman, and the youngest Clark brother, raised on the military exploits of his elders, had yet to make a name for himself.

In the summer of 1789, nineteen-year-old Billy Clark signed up for the Kentucky militia. He joined a volunteer force of 220 mounted men that planned to ride against the Wea tribe's towns on the White river in southern Indiana. This party would be led by a regular army man, Major John Hardin, a thirty-five-year-old Virginia veteran of both Lord Dunmore's War and the Continental Army. With the British vanquished, men like Hardin had moved almost seamlessly from fighting Redcoats in the East to fighting "redskins" in the West.

In the tradition of his older brothers, William Clark was going to be an Indian fighter.

On the 5th of August 1789 we started crost the River Ohio randesvous on Silver Creek. Marched that night about 8 or 9 miles.[14]

With those words, written in his distinctive flowing hand—and with his equally distinctive spelling—William Clark made his first entry in the literature of exploration. Journalizing would become a lifelong habit for him, just as it had been for George Rogers. Enthusiastically, if sometimes repetitively, William reported on the waterways ("this fork is the delatifullest river I ever saw"), the landscape ("the delitefulles plain I ever saw"), and the plant life ("The grass is about 3 foot high with a mixture of butyfull flowers"). His eye was keenly attentive to promising real estate around a mineral spring: "The lick appears to be the best I ever saw. It is large and a fine fresh water and salt water springs running with in a few yards of each other . . . The lick was better than land is gen'ly about licks."

Five days into the expedition, Clark was riding with an advance squad when it stumbled upon several families of Indians camped on a creek. "We fir'd on them," Clark reported. "The other party fired. Rushed on. Kill'd 4 men 4 squaws. Took 2 children 16 horses and 100£ worth of plund'r. We had 2 men wounded."

Even in frontier Kentucky, gunning down four defenseless Indian women did not normally convey bragging rights. But when they reached Vincennes, one of Hardin's men paraded through town, displaying bloody body parts on a stick. The provocation infuriated the post commander, Major John Hamtramck of the regular U.S. Army, a stout man of five feet five who was said to look like a frog when he sat on a horse but was popular with his men. Hamtramck had just finished replacing the old fort with a structure of two-story blockhouses equipped with cannons and encircled by a palisade fourteen feet high. Now he feared that Indians bent on avenging Hardin's raid would wipe it out.

Clark wrote nothing about the gruesome display by Hardin's men at Vincennes, describing instead the village that had been the scene of his brother's greatest victory: "The houses is low and bilt after the French fasion." But already he had the eye of a settler, not a tourist: "It contains about 400 houses and about 3000 soles [souls] on the bank of the Wabash a delitefull river."

Clark reported on just about everything he did. He discovered an Indian cache in "a large holler tree cut in two that would hold 50 bushell," built "2 canoos of bark" to transport wounded men, even "firing off 2 guns" to locate some lost men. Finally, after two weeks in the field, the party rode back through the gnarly hills, now known as the Knobstone Escarpment, that separate southeastern Indiana from the glaciated central and northern parts of the state. They descended at Silver Knobs, "from the top of which may be seen Louisville," and arrived in Clarksville, the tiny community George Rogers had laid out overlooking the Ohio on the Indiana side of the Falls.

A month later, Billy was again on horseback, this time traveling with militiamen searching for Indian war parties that had been raiding in the interior of Kentucky. The most notorious of these incidents was the "Chenoweth massacre." A founding family of Louisville, the Chenoweths lived on Beargrass Creek, near present-day Middletown. While the family and guests were at dinner on July 17, 1789, Indians attacked, killing six and wounding seven. One warrior knocked Peggy Chenoweth to the ground, put his foot on her back, and ripped off her entire scalp. The act of scalping was said to make a distinctive sound, like a sneeze. Peggy somehow survived and covered her bare skull with a knitted cap until she died in 1825.

Billy formed a party with a dozen men, including his cousin William M. Clark and his new brother-in-law, Richard Clough Anderson, husband of his sister Eliza. They rode through the bluegrass country and down the Kentucky River to the Ohio. Along the way, they saw no Indians but killed bear and deer. At Harrodsburg, Billy inspected the ruins of the original pioneer station and stayed with Captain Abraham Chapline, one of George Rogers Clark's old comrades in the Illinois Regiment. Chapline was well known for having survived one of the backcountry's most harrowing experiences. Captured by Indians and forced to run a gauntlet of club-wielding warriors, he survived to be adopted into a Shawnee family on the Upper Miami. He finally escaped and made his way back to Kentucky.

Billy Clark's education continued to broaden. During his stay at Harrodsburg, he was reading and copying from a notebook of "Grammar, History, and Natural Philosophy," part of his informal home-schooling that would continue during his militia service for the next several years. In addition to learning the woodland crafts, he was studying the writings of Aristotle, Cicero, Plutarch, and Pope, as well as astronomy and world history.

There were diversions, too. One was Nelly Slaughter, a relative of George Rogers Clark's friend Colonel George Slaughter. William was a regular visitor at the Slaughter household and expressed disappointment if he missed "seeing the young lady's." On the cold February morning he left Harrodsburg to return to Mulberry Hill, he made his farewells at Nelly's house at sunrise.

The defense of the borderlands was becoming a national issue. Ever since the passage of the Land Ordinance of 1785 and the Northwest Ordinance of 1787, the federal government had acknowledged its responsibility for the Indian lands north of the Ohio. In September 1789, Congress authorized militias to be raised for the defense of the frontiers. But the settlers were now clamoring for the federal government to come directly to their aid in their struggles with the tribes.

Congress had initially been loath to approve a standing army. After he was sworn in, President Washington had only a single seven-hundred-man regiment under his command. But in April 1790, the Continental Congress approved an expansion of the army to 1,216. To lead the first military campaign to be waged by the new United States, Secretary of War Henry Knox appointed Lieutenant Colonel Josiah Harmar.

A Philadelphia Quaker, the thirty-six-year-old Harmar was a gentleman and a snob who traveled with his own supply of Windsor chairs, wines, and cognacs. He had previously failed in the army's earlier efforts to arrest the illegal spread of white settlers across the Appalachians. Now Knox advised Harmar that his task was not to control white incursions on Indian lands but rather "to extirpate, utterly, if possible, the said [Indian] banditti."[15] Harmar agreed; negotiations were over. "The Indians are exceedingly troublesome," he wrote. "I know of nothing that will cure the disorder [other than] the government's raising an army to effectually chastise them—all treaties are in vain."[16]

For the first time, a federal army rather than undisciplined militias would be taking the field against the tribes. In the fall of 1790, Knox and the doomed Arthur St. Clair planned a double assault against the Wea, Shawnee, and Delaware strongholds. Hamtramck would lead a diversionary army north from Vincennes to the Wea villages on the Vermillion and Wabash rivers. Harmar would simultaneously march north from Fort Washington against the stronghold of the Western tribes at Kekionga, called "Miamitown" by the Americans, near present-day Fort Wayne, Indiana.

But instead of mustering in an army of seasoned regulars, Harmar wound up combining an undersupplied contingent of Kentucky and Pennsylvania militia with just three hundred regular troops. One officer wondered if some of the militiamen had ever fired a rifle before. Advancing to Kekionga, the undisciplined and undertrained troops found its three hundred bark cabins deserted. They set to plundering the town and destroying an estimated twenty thousand bushels of corn.

They had been lured into a trap. In a series of carefully orchestrated decoys and ambushes, a confederacy of Shawnees, Miamis, and Weas led by Little Turtle and Blue Jacket attacked the panicking militiamen as they floundered helplessly across streams. By the end of the campaign, Harmar had lost more than two hundred soldiers, an inauspicious beginning for the United States Army. Harmar had already been criticized for indulging himself "to excess in a convivial glass." Now a disgusted President Washington pronounced Harmar "a drunkard."[17]

Like most Americans, Washington preferred to blame army incompetence rather than to admit the strategic prowess and determination of the tribes. It was a misjudgment for which his armies would pay dearly. As Blue Jacket told the British: "We as a people have made no war, but as a people we are determined to meet the approaches of an enemy, who come not to check the insolence of individuals, but as a premeditated design to root us out of our land." He knew why he was fighting: "We and our forefathers and our children were and are bound as men and Indians to defend [this land], which we are determined to do, satisfied we are acting in the cause of justice."[18]

Who now could lead a new American army in the West? Secretary of State Jefferson, who never lost his high regard for George Rogers Clark, wondered if the government might "bring Genl. Clark forward" for another Indian war. "No man alive rated him higher than I did and would again were he to become again what I knew him," he wrote wistfully.[19]

A friend who showed Jefferson's letter to Clark reported that the general became "greatly agitated by the contents, observed that it was friendly, & shed tears."[20]

With Clark incapacitated by alcohol, President Washington's best remaining choices were to be found among what was left of his officer corps from the Continental Army. They were Arthur St. Clair, the gouty governor, and Brigadier General Charles Scott, a darkly handsome, rapier-thin Virginian known for his genteel manners. Both St. Clair and Scott had crossed the Delaware with Washington and fought at the crucial battles of Trenton and Princeton. Both were known to Washington for their fondness for whiskey. In the end, the President overcame his reservations and appointed Major General St. Clair as commander in chief. His mission: to put into the field an American army large enough to crush the Wabash Confederacy once and for all.

William Clark was just the kind of man St. Clair was looking for. But during the severe winter of 1790–'91, Clark was shuttling back and forth between military duties and his expanding family. His sister Lucy had married William Croghan, an Irish-born surveyor who had fought with the Continentals at Brandywine, Germantown, and Monmouth. Croghan built a grand manor for Lucy in Louisville called Locust Grove. In February 1791, Clark's sister Fanny married another Irishman, Dr. James

O'Fallon, a surgeon in the Continental Army who sealed their union by pledging £10,000 to John Clark and guaranteeing another £5,000 and his Charleston estate to his bride.

O'Fallon's wealth was in jeopardy, however. An avid land speculator, he had become enmeshed in a series of ill-fated land schemes initiated by the South Carolina Yazoo Company, variously to start a colony on the Lower Mississippi River or even to break off Louisiana from Spanish rule. O'Fallon had brought George Rogers Clark into his scheme, and Charles Scott had actually considered joining them with a band of 650 armed Kentuckians before cooler heads warned him away from the plan.

O'Fallon's medical practice was no less flamboyant. Treating John and Ann Clark's arthritis, he urged the night-and-day wearing of flannel underwear "of a red, or scarlet color," as well as a daily sprinkling into their socks of "about a Teaspoonful of Salt, finely pounded." Other prescriptions included tinctures of pokeberries, frequent exercise on horseback, chamomile tea, and a daily sponge bath in "the first Runnings of Whiskey from the Still." Presumably the Clarks did not object.

In the spring of 1791, Billy Clark packed his personal firearms and two weeks' worth of provisions, and rode his own horse from Mulberry Hill to the settlement of Frankfort on the Kentucky River. There he mustered into Captain James Brown's company of mounted Kentucky volunteers. They were among 850 militiamen preparing an expedition into Indian country to be commanded by the fifty-one-year-old Charles Scott.

Scott's foray was designed to distract the Indians while St. Clair assembled his American army. Scott planned to lead the Kentuckians to Ouiatenon, a village of the Wea band of Little Turtle's Miami tribe located on the Wabash below today's Lafayette, Indiana. Across the river was a Kickapoo village, and farther north at the mouth of the Tippecanoe River was Kethtippecanunk, a large town crowded with various tribes as well as French traders and British agents.

Scott's mounted men crossed the Ohio at Battle Creek, near present-day Madison, Indiana, and moved north on May 23. The terrain was difficult and the weather worse. In his journal Clark reported "sharp lightning" as the horses crossed countless streambeds with high muddy banks and swamps of white clay, "thick with brush and briers."[21] Scott wrote that the "rain fell in torrents every day, with frequent blasts of wind and thunder storms."

On June 1, they startled a lone Indian on horseback. A detachment under Colonel Hardin galloped after him and unexpectedly rode into a Kickapoo encampment crowded with families. Hardin's men killed six warriors and took more than fifty prisoners, mostly women and children. Meanwhile, Scott's men advanced on Ouiatenon just as its residents were attempting to flee in canoes across the Wabash. Clark's detachment, led by Lieutenant Colonel James Wilkinson, fired on the defenseless Indians and, Scott reported, "destroyed all the savages with which five canoes were crowded."[22]

Clark continued with Wilkinson's men on an eighteen-mile forced march at night to Kethtippecanunk. Arriving just before 11 p.m., they waited until dawn and assaulted the town at all quarters. Clark reported that they "burned and Destroyed 70 Houses," including some "single-roof houses" similar to those of white settlers. The residents, he added, "appeared to be Welthy," since "the town was stockaded" and the plunder included "bear's oil, Kittles plough Carts Salt Sugar Cattle Hogs." The domestic habits of these "savages" appeared to be all but indistinguishable from those of the citizens of Louisville.[23]

With huge plumes of smoke still rising over the burning village, Clark and Wilkinson departed at 6 a.m. to march their forty-one prisoners back to the main army. Scott ordered Ouiatenon set afire as well. He then released sixteen prisoners, giving them a proclamation to be read to all the tribes "living on the waters of the Wabash River." The United States, he said, has "long patiently borne your depredations against their settlements." The Americans could continue to burn their towns, but "they are as merciful as strong." He urged the tribes to "bury the hatchet and smoke the pipe of peace." But, Scott concluded, "should you foolishly persist in your warfare, the sons of war will be let loose against you, and the hatchet will never be buried until your country is desolated, and your people humbled to the dust."[24]

The journey back to the Ohio was difficult. The rains were continuing, flooding the lowlands, and the expedition was running out of food. "The Badness of the Hills and Deepness of the Mud and the Height of the Creeks, together with Brush, exceeds all kinds of Description," Clark lamented. Horses, mired helplessly in the muck, were left behind. The army floundered in confusion fording the White River; three men drowned, along with eight or ten horses.

In his final report on the three-week expedition, Scott carefully said he had not lost a single man "by the enemy" and had killed thirty-two. He further claimed that his troops had refrained from atrocities like scalping corpses—though at the time, the British agent Alexander Mc-Kee reported to his superiors that a war chief of the Weas had been "literally skinned" by the Americans on Scott's mission.[25]

After recrossing the Ohio and turning their prisoners over to the federal troops, three hundred of the Kentucky volunteers accepted an invitation from Colonel John Campbell, a Revolutionary War veteran, to celebrate over a feast of beef, mutton, and whiskey at his home in Louisville.

William Clark was beginning to earn a reputation as a good soldier. He had ventured twice into Indian country and been under fire both times. Other men were impressed with this enterprising young man. "Your brother William is gone out as a cadet with Gen. Scott on the expedition," James O'Fallon wrote to Jonathan Clark. "He is a youth of solid and promising parts, and as brave as Caesar."[26]

On August 1, just six weeks after Scott's Wabash expedition, William again "Randisvoused" with the Kentucky militia.[27] This time, St. Clair had authorized Lieutenant Colonel Wilkinson to mount an expedition of five hundred men to attack Kikiah and other Miami villages near the confluence of the Wabash and Eel (L'Anguille) rivers. They gathered at Fort Washington, a ramshackle post on the north side of the Ohio. It had been jerry-built out of planking stripped from abandoned flatboats that had brought settlers down the river and was painted a garish red, the cheapest and most available color on the frontier. St. Clair had named the little settlement around the fort "Cincinnati" for the Society of the Cincinnati, the Continental Army officers' association.

Wilkinson's expedition was a search-and-destroy mission. But when the soldiers entered Indian country, they found that the tribes had abandoned the Wabash villages. Wilkinson and his men had to settle for burning cornstalks so that the Indians would be "left without horses, home or provision . . . during the impending winter."[28] Clark's brief journal entries over the ensuing days made the strategy brutally clear: "A detachment . . . returned after cutting Down the Corn and burning the

Towns . . . We cut all the Corn Down about 60 or 100 acres in all . . .
Cut down all the corn about 50 acres and Burned the Town about 35
houses . . . Here cut down about 50 acres of Corn."[29] Wilkinson estimated that altogether they destroyed about 430 acres of ripening corn,
"chiefly in the milk."[30]

There was little actual combat. A horseback attack at Kikiah, which
stretched for three miles along the Eel River upstream from today's
Logansport, Indiana, resulted in the deaths of six warriors and two Americans. Wilkinson added almost apologetically that "in the hurry and confusion of the charge . . . two squaws and a child were killed."[31]

Some natural history notes began to pop up in Clark's journal. "A
fowl called the Heath Hen is verry plenty here," he wrote on August 4. At
one point, near the present Illinois border, the party reached the western
edge of the eastern woodlands. There, for the first time, William Clark
found himself gazing with wonder across the "Beautiful" tallgrass
prairies of the West.[32]

The party returned along the buffalo trace that Scott's expedition had
followed two months earlier. On August 20, the men arrived on the north
bank of the Falls of the Ohio. They swam their horses in a single boiling
herd across the half-mile-wide river. The troops then followed in boats,
mustered out, and went home.

Clark was thus unavailable when, two weeks later, the first of Arthur St.
Clair's troops moved north from Ludlow's Station and set to work building the new Fort Hamilton on the banks of the Miami. By early November, the entire army had advanced to the headwaters of the Wabash. On
November 4, St. Clair's forces suffered what would be the most decisive
defeat in the history of the American military.

An appalled George Washington now knew that halfway measures
could not succeed north of the Ohio. The credibility of the federal
government itself was at stake; Congress had launched its first inquiry
into the conduct of the executive branch in the wake of St. Clair's Defeat.
The defense of the frontier would require a professional federal army; local militias would no longer suffice. The army's goal would be not to restrain the settlers, however, but to force the tribes to sue for peace by
crushing them once and for all. In the absence of strong federal action,
Washington thought, the entire trans-Appalachian West could collapse

into a hodgepodge of breakaway colonies, rebellious territories, and land speculators' duchies.

James Wilkinson's detachment had barely finished burying the frozen bodies of St. Clair's soldiers at Mississinewa when the newly forceful Congress, acting under the recently adopted U.S. Constitution, created three additional regular army regiments, increasing the size of the federal force to 5,218. An ardent admirer of Roman military strategy, Secretary of War Knox then reorganized the army as the "Legion of the United States" and divided it into four independent sublegions—each with its own infantry, cavalry, artillery, and rifle units.

Once again, Washington had to find a commander. St. Clair had been cleared by a board of inquiry, but his health and his career were in ruins. George Rogers Clark, past his prime, had been character-assassinated by Wilkinson, who himself was consumed with ambition. Washington thought Scott was "addicted to drinking."[33] His good friend from Virginia, Henry "Light Horse Harry" Lee, was still just a lieutenant colonel. In the end, the President reluctantly overcame his doubts about the "foibles" of yet another veteran of the Continental Army—the controversial Anthony Wayne.[34]

A forty-seven-year-old Pennsylvanian, Wayne appeared to be cut from the same velvet cloak as St. Clair. He was gouty, overweight, vain, and pompous. Like St. Clair, he had fought with distinction during the Revolution, notably at Stony Point and in the campaigns of Brandywine, Germantown, and Valley Forge. After the war, though, he had failed as a plantation owner in Georgia and seen his election to Congress disallowed amid charges of fraud. His famous nickname of "Mad Anthony" (for his supposed temper) was just one of many; some just as aptly called him "Dandy Tony."

Wayne was also a determined and well-prepared soldier; the British had regarded him as one of the most capable officers in the Continental Army. Washington appointed him commander in chief in April 1792. His second in command would be the disappointed James Wilkinson, promoted to brigadier general as a consolation.

Wayne immediately went to Pittsburgh to begin recruiting an army—no easy task after the destruction of the previous American force. Among the first of his new officers was William Clark. Having completed his apprenticeship in the field, Clark had been nominated for an infantry lieutenant's commission by George Washington on March 6, 1792. His pay would be $408 a year. When it was approved by Congress a day later, Clark entered the service of the federal government. It would remain his only employer for the rest of his life.

Clark had spent the early months of 1792 visiting his brother Jonathan and attending to family business in Virginia. As soon as the snow began to clear in the mountains, he outfitted himself in the style appropriate to a young officer: a rifle, powder, razors, knee and shoe buckles, cravats, gloves, a red cape, and a whip. Unlike some, he carried a "Dixinary" to help his phonetic spelling, which was imaginative but not unusual at the time. He rode along the muddy roads to Winchester and the Alleghenies, staying at country inns of varying quality. One "durty disagreeable" house was filled with "rascus" who kept him up all night. At Redstone he constructed his own boat and proceeded down the Monongahela to Pittsburgh and Wheeling.[35]

On May 12, 1792, while Lieutenant Clark was floating somewhere below Wheeling on the Ohio, the American Captain Robert Gray, sailing from Boston on a fur-trading expedition to the Pacific Northwest, piloted his vessel *Columbia* over a sandbar and entered the estuary of an enormous river. He had become the first American to see the Columbia River, and with his voyage established the claim of the United States to Oregon. Americans now knew the full extent of the continent. But no one knew the geography of the interior or the people who lived there.

Two days later, just as the sun set, Clark arrived at Fort Washington to begin his military duties in earnest. Secretary of War Knox had written Wayne to inform him that "a Brother of General [George Rogers] Clarke of Kentucky" had been appointed to Captain John Crawford's rifle company. The new lieutenant had been authorized $300 in expenses to recruit thirty volunteers to the depleted army. "I have no doubt of Lieutenant Clarke's acceptance and from his popular character that he has raised the thirty recruits directed," Knox said.[36]

People were learning to rely on Lieutenant Clark. When Jonathan Clark's wife, Sarah (called Sally), had her fifth child on May 19, the parents named William as a sponsor at her christening. For the second time, he had become a godfather.

Throughout the summer Clark traveled between Fort Washington and other Kentucky posts at Lexington and Louisville—combining recruiting with odd chores, such as delivering $200 cash to Colonel Hardin's wife in Lexington and regularly losing at billiards with his fellow officers (including General Wilkinson). On September 2, he wrote Jonathan that he had "already Inlisted ten men" and expected to fill his quota of thirty soon. But with the Creeks on the south "Killing men and Stealing horses," he was not optimistic that the government could raise an army large enough to defeat the powerful Indian confederacies.[37]

The situation was in fact deteriorating. General Wilkinson had sent Clark's friend John Hardin on a peace mission in September, but Hardin and his companion were assassinated in the Ohio country by a band of Delawares. The attempts to convene a treaty council in Vincennes likewise languished because the Shawnees and the Delawares, flushed with their victory over St. Clair, refused to attend.

In November, Clark was suddenly thrust back into harm's way. He was ordered to lead a detachment to carry military clothing from Fort Steuben, across the Ohio from Louisville, to the renamed Fort Knox at Vincennes. The journey would require traveling 245 miles down the Ohio and another 130 up the serpentine Wabash.

Dispatching his "hors Saddle & Bridle" in advance for the overland return trip from Vincennes, Clark pushed his boat off before dawn in a driving rainstorm on November 29, 1792.[38] He was accompanied by a mixed party of troops and traders that included Pierre Menard, the leading French merchant in Kaskaskia, and Francis Vigo, an Italian-born trader who had delivered essential intelligence to George Rogers Clark before the capture of Vincennes.

William Clark moved down the river amid "freasing ranes," all the while keeping a daily journal. "I went a Shore Killed 6 Turkeys," he noted in the first of many entries recording his hunting excursions.[39] On December 4, hunting at night by moonlight, he killed a buck and a bear.

At the mouth of the Wabash, Clark transferred his cargo to smaller boats to facilitate the upstream journey but had to post guards because the hired French voyageurs "all get Drunk." Ominously, Indians were seen daily: "I saw a number of Indians on the bank to day" (December

10) . . . "passed Indians to day Camp opposite the upper point of an Isle" (December 11) . . . "passed Indians today" (December 12).[40]

Snow was falling when they reached the Grand Rapids of the Wabash, where the river tumbled over an ancient limestone outcropping. The smaller pirogues could force their way over the rapids, but Clark's larger cargo boat became wedged on the rocks. "Snow all this day and night," Clark wrote, "Verry cold Freasing Verry hard." The next day they failed again to move the boats. "Verry cold wind blow made several at[tempt]s to cross the Rapids in Vain." They finally resorted to shuttling the cargo piecemeal over the rapids in flat-bottomed pirogues and then dragging the empty cargo boat over the rocks.[41]

The party pushed on upriver, sometimes clambering into the frigid waters to rock the boats loose or to adjust their loads, all while it was "snowing and verry cold."[42] Finally, at 4:30 p.m. on December 19, the group arrived at Vincennes. The men spread out their cargo on the ground and determined that after a three-week struggle up the icy rivers, they were missing just four pairs of shoes. Two nights later, Lieutenant Clark dined in relative comfort with the same post commander, Major John Hamtramck, who had raged against Hardin's bloodthirsty expeditioners three years earlier.

On Christmas Eve, 1792, Clark and fifty men left for the overland trip to Louisville, following the old buffalo trace that is now Highway 150. Clark would soon become an essential officer in the supply chain linking American outposts north of the Ohio. In February, he escorted General Wilkinson up the Great Miami to Fort Hamilton, a "tegious Disagreea-ble" trip that left most of his sixty men "frosted."[43] He pushed on to the more remote outpost at Fort Jefferson — St. Clair's final base before his disastrous march — traveling through the snowy woods in a horse-drawn sleigh.

Returning by way of Fort Hamilton, Clark noted with interest that a court-martial was proceeding for one Captain John Armstrong. Clark knew Armstrong as an especially interesting individual. A Revolutionary War veteran who had moved on to the Indian campaigns, Armstrong had fought with Harmar and St. Clair and had commanded Fort Steuben. In 1790, Knox and Harmar had sent Armstrong on a secret mission into Spanish territory. The idea was for Armstrong to explore the Missouri River, alone or with a companion in a canoe, "up to its sources." This would have been the first federally financed exploration west of the Mississippi—though it would make do with little equipment. As Knox explained to Harmar, "Pocket compasses would be necessary to their success, & pencils and paper to assist their remarks."[44]

Armstrong had made it as far as St. Louis, gathering information and maps, before being persuaded that he would never get past the Indian tribes on the Missouri. He submitted a bill to the War Department for personal expenses of "70 and 39/90ths dollars" and another $40 for a horse. He was later assigned to Fort Hamilton, where he feuded with Wilkinson, a man not to fall afoul of unadvisedly. Wilkinson soon had Armstrong brought before a court-martial on trumped-up charges ranging from slander to horse thievery.

Back at Fort Washington, Clark was ordered to take a dozen soldiers to the mouth of the Kentucky River, halfway between Cincinnati and Louisville, and build a corn depository there. In early March 1793, he headed downstream in a Kentucky boat and picked out a dry site for the depot above the flooded river bottom. The blockhouses, storage building, and stockade were up within a month. Lieutenant Clark was developing a skill for wilderness construction.

For the rest of the spring, Clark and his men lived a sedentary garrison life, picking up news from families and traders moving down the river. Captain Armstrong passed through, having chosen to resign from the army rather than endure a court-martial verdict. Clark's friend Barrett Tompkins wrote from Caroline County, and in the same mail Clark learned of the kidnapping of two children in Louisville "by the Savage," a pejorative Clark reserved for hostile Indians. When some warriors passing down the river fired on one of his men, Clark dispatched a sergeant and seven riflemen after them, but the men returned a day later with "nothing done."[45]

On June 1, Clark received a letter from General Wayne along with a shipment of five gallons of whiskey. Perhaps not coincidentally, the next day he was "obliged to punish one [man] for neglect of Duty & one for sleaping on his post last night."[46] He did not specify the punishment, but one hundred lashes was the usual sentence. The next day he sent out his men to capture "three deserters discovered coming down the Ohio in a Conoo."[47]

The detachment protecting the corn depository suffered from ill-nesses. Lieutenant Clark was learning wilderness medicine: he "bled" one sick man and "gave him a sweat." He reported on his own ten-day bout with an unspecified malady—"I took a puke verry sick," he recorded on April 15; "I am sick," on April 18; and "I am verry sick," on April 20, marking the onset of episodic intestinal problems that would trouble him the rest of his life.[48]

General Wayne, meanwhile, had drilled his army ceaselessly through the winter of 1792–'93 at a hastily built post near Pittsburgh he called Legionville. He wrote to Knox, "I am also endeavoring to make the rifle-men believe in that arm, the Infantry in heavy buck shots & bayonet, the Dragoons in the Sword, & the Legion in their United Prowess."[49] His army would not repeat the mistakes of the undisciplined militias. In the fall of 1792, seven deserters were executed in public hangings. For lesser offenses, soldiers were whipped or forced to run a gauntlet "through the whole Legion." Wayne was reported to say that he did not want any officers with him unless he had the most unbounded confi-dence in them.

The officers within the Legion were a notoriously fractious group, di-vided by regional rivalries such as between "Tuckahoes" (eastern, or tidewater, Virginians) and "Cohees" (western Virginians). Disputes were typically resolved legally by courts-martial or illegally by duels. Wayne described one affair, between an Ensign Gassaway and a Lieutenant Jenifer, where "it was agreed, that they shou'd stand back to back at a given distance, face, advance & fire—when—& at what distance they, or either of them thought proper. Ensign Gassaway fell."[50]

In May, Wayne moved his army down the Ohio in a huge flotilla of flatboats. The commander in chief rode in a barge called the *Federal*, fes-tooned with gaily painted awnings and silk standards. Reaching Fort Washington, surrounded by the taverns and brothels of Cincinnati, he sniffed the air and judged the place to be "filled with ardent poison and caitiff wretches to dispose of it." Unable to find a suitable spot for his en-campment "except near some dirty village," Wayne built his own head-quarters outside of town and gave it the rueful name of Hobson's Choice.[51]

On June 22, Clark received startling orders from Hobson's Choice. He was to take three armed flatboats loaded with corn, arms, and trade goods down the Ohio to the Mississippi. He and twenty-four men would deliver the goods to a nation of Chickasaw Indians at their villages on the bluffs near today's Memphis. It would be his longest river trip thus far.

A small tribe of about 2,400 people, 500 of them warriors, the Chickasaws occupied a key role on the Lower Mississippi. Thanks to their strategic location controlling river traffic, their chiefs had skillfully played off the European powers against one another for decades. With the British defeated, the Americans and the Spanish were left competing for Chickasaw favors. The English traveler Francis Baily visited Chickasaw Bluffs in 1797 and reported that the tribe was a "well-made handsome race of men" that enjoyed a "good understanding with America, which the latter is obliged to keep up by presents sent annually to them."[52] The Chickasaws, however, were not naive about American motives. Their chief, Ugulayacabe, observed darkly, "We perceive in them the cunning of the Rattle snake who caresses the Squirrel he intends to devour."[53]

Dealing with the Chickasaws could be dangerous, in large part because of the proximity of their tribal enemies. In April 1790, a Major Dougherty was ordered up the Tennessee River on a mission similar to Clark's. He was stopped by a group of Shawnees and Cherokees who approached him under a white flag. They came on board and accepted presents—but upon departing they turned and fired on the American boat, killing or wounding eleven of the fifteen soldiers present.

Handing out extra gills of whiskey—about four ounces each—Clark had his men load the boats in just over twenty-four hours. They moved down the Ohio, paying six dollars to a river pilot to guide them over the Falls. Clark's party floated into the Mississippi on July 3. Wayne had instructed them to travel at night past the Spanish garrison at New Madrid out of concern that the Spaniards might "seize the Arms and Ammunition designed for the Chickasaws."[54] Clark successfully passed unobserved and arrived at the Chickasaw Nation on July 20.

Two days later and several thousand miles to the northwest, Alexander Mackenzie, a Scotsman born in 1762 on the Isle of Lewis in the Outer

Hebrides, stood on a rocky point on King Island, British Columbia, and took a series of astronomical readings. In front of him stretched the Pacific Ocean. After satisfying himself about his location:

> I mixed up some vermilion in melted grease, and inscribed, in large characters, on the South-East face of the rock on which we had slept last night, this brief memorial—"Alexander Mackenzie, from Canada, by land, the twenty-second of July, one thousand seven hundred and ninety-three."[55]

Mackenzie had just become the first European to cross North America, a feat William Clark would not learn of for another decade. On the day that Mackenzie gazed upon the Pacific, Lieutenant Clark was unpacking corn for the Chickasaws.

Two weeks passed. Wayne had still not heard from Clark and was beginning to worry. Wayne knew that the British and Spanish wanted to draw the Chickasaws into "a general confederacy forming against us," and the prospect of the Chickasaws joining the Creeks and Cherokees made him "very uneasy for the fate of Lieutenant Clark." Moreover, he told Knox, if Clark and his men had been killed, the weapons he was taking to the Chickasaws "may eventually be made use of against us."[56]

To his obvious relief, Wayne soon learned that Clark had ridden back safely along the Natchez Trace, bringing with him a band of eight Chickasaw warriors and a chief named Jemmy Underwood whom he had recruited to scout for the Legion. "This young Gentleman has executed his orders . . . with a promptitude & address that does him honor & which merits my highest approbation!"[57] Wayne told Secretary of War Knox.

By the time Clark returned to Hobson's Choice, an Indian war appeared imminent. For most of the year there had been relative calm while the U.S. peace commissioners sent to Niagara by Secretary of War Knox had tried to arrange a treaty council with the Northern tribes. But in August the talks had collapsed: the Shawnees, Delawares, and Miamis were determined to protect their lands north of the Ohio. Writing to James O'Fallon, Wayne blamed the British agent Alexander McKee for inciting the Indians to "repulse every venture of peace."[58]

Now wearing the green-plumed cocked hat of the Fourth Sub-Legion of the United States, Clark went to work delivering supplies to the forts that penetrated into Indian country. In three weeks of good late-summer weather, he ventured seventy miles north to Fort Jefferson, before returning to Fort St. Clair on September 22.

Meanwhile, Wayne's Legion of two thousand men finally began its slow advance north from Hobson's Choice. Unlike Harmar and St. Clair, who had been constantly tangled in the thickets, Wayne could march his army up a broad wagon road he had cut earlier in May. With Knox's warning ringing in his ears that another defeat at the hands of the Indians "would be pernicious in the highest degree to the interests of our country," Wayne proved extraordinarily cautious. His phalanx was preceded, flanked, and followed by advance guards and scouting parties. Every night, the men would clear a seventy-five-acre camp, build a protective log breastworks, and surround it with an abatis of sharply pointed branches.

Clark joined the army as it passed Fort St. Clair, near present-day Eaton, Ohio. Six miles past Fort Jefferson, at the end of the wagon road, Wayne began clearing a winter camp that he called Fort Greenville after his Continental Army friend Nathanael Greene. A sign of Wayne's growing confidence in Clark was that the young lieutenant and his Chicka-saws were assigned to scout the country thirty miles farther north, past the skeleton-strewn site of St. Clair's Defeat, looking for Indian war parties.

Wayne did not want to make St. Clair's fatal mistake of attempting a winter march with dwindling supplies. Deciding to wait for a spring offensive, he ordered his men to begin building huts of the type he and Washington had used at Valley Forge. But long supply lines were already becoming a vulnerability. On the chilly morning of October 17, one of Clark's quartermaster counterparts, Lieutenant John Lowry of the Second Sub-Legion, rode out of Fort St. Clair with twenty wagonloads of Indian corn. As an escort of ninety infantrymen prepared to fall in behind the convoy, an Ottawa war party under Little Otter, waiting for its opportunity, suddenly attacked. With wagons overturning and horses snorting and rearing, most of the men panicked and fled back to the fort. Those who stayed died. Clark grimly wrote in his journal that Lowry was killed, as were "Ensign Boyer & 15 Men . . . about 10 men & 70 horses taken."

Low morale was a problem at Fort Greenville. Wayne's gout attacks had increased, and he was becoming irascible, sentencing two men to death for sleeping on duty. Bickering and dissension flourished; in twelve months, fifteen duels were fought in the Legion. Supplies were running low, in part because Brigadier General Wilkinson was delaying them in order to undermine Wayne. Soon a virulently anti-Wayne clique led by Wilkinson began ridiculing Wayne as "Old Tony" and "Tony Lumpkin."

In November, Wayne ordered Clark and his Chickasaws to escort Wilkinson and a convoy of packhorses back to Fort Washington to procure more supplies. Though Clark was aware of the tension between the two generals, he did not know about Wilkinson's earlier campaign to discredit his brother George Rogers. After spending an uneasy few days at Fort Washington, where the smallpox had arrived, Clark was ordered to deliver two more boatloads of clothing to Vincennes. Along the way, he stopped at Louisville to visit his family, ran the Falls, and by December 15 was at the mouth of the Wabash. His Chickasaw companions continued on to the Mississippi; Clark gave them "20 days Provisions" and started up the Wabash.

It was cold, and his men were unhappy. Two of them deserted. Snow was falling, and thick floes of ice were clogging the river, making the upstream trip agonizingly difficult. Finally, after finding it "impossible to proceed," Clark stopped, and his men pulled their boats ashore.

It was Christmas Day, 1793. The Reign of Terror was raging in France; Marie Antoinette had been guillotined. An epidemic of yellow fever, the worst ever in an American city, had killed five thousand people in Philadelphia. In the Ohio country, Anthony Wayne had led a second burial detachment to the St. Clair battlefield; the soldiers arrived on Christmas to inter the bones and fire a cannon salute to the dead. Wayne chose not to linger, returning to Fort Jefferson in time for a New Year's Day feast of mutton, plum pudding, and ice cream.

William Clark and his men spent Christmas Day shivering, icebound, and watchful on the banks of the Lower Wabash. Clark went ashore to kill two buffalo for food but, embarrassingly, lost a rifle. Clark's detachment finally started moving up the river again, arriving in Vincennes on January 3. It had been a difficult journey. Clark later complained to Jonathan that "it appears that all active & laborous commands fall to me. This last command was not only Labor's but I like to have starved."[59] Fortunately, the next night there was "a Ball in Town," the first of nine he would attend over the next month in a village still flaunting its French flavor.[60]

Indians frequently visited the post, usually accommodating bands of Potawatomis, Weas, and Kickapoos that had not joined the British-led confederacy. In mid-February, a council was convened with the goal of sealing a peace treaty with these tribes and preventing them from aligning with the British and the resisting Northern nations. "At 10 oClock 20 Canoo loaded came with Flags flying," Clark reported on February 19.[61]

High spirits were soon undermined by hard spirits. The Americans customarily dispensed kegs of liquor at councils. On the first evening, Clark said, "the Indians all get drunk and are verry quarrelsome."[62] He did not report on drunkenness among the soldiers, which would not have been unusual.

The council ended peacefully, though not before one intriguing incident. "Some Indians get angry with me and threaten," Clark noted. He did not explain what had provoked them, or how he resolved the problem. But apparently he calmed the situation. A few days later, he seemed relieved to report that "all the Indians clear out."[63]

Once the ice was off the rivers, Clark took his boats back to the Legion. On the way up the Ohio his "flank guard routed several small parties of Ind[ians] . . . but killed none." He spent a week with his family at Mulberry Hill. During this visit, William may have picked up his personal servant, young York, the son of his father's enslaved African-American couple Old York and Rose. In his journal, he merely mentions sending "my boy with two horses."[64]

Clark spent the month of April at Fort Washington, performing staff duties, getting a smallpox "enocholation," and escorting supply convoys to the Ohio country forts. Violence was never far removed:

April 24: "a Man Killed at Whites Station and one wounded, this evening."
April 27: "a rany day T. Killed a Man near F. Hamilton."

In this environment it was never clear whether a dead man was a soldier or a "savage."[65]

In the early morning of May 13, 1794, Lieutenant Clark rode north from Fort Washington in command of a pack train of seven hundred horses escorted by seventy infantrymen and twenty mounted dragoons. About eighteen miles from Cincinnati, Clark was riding near the rear of the mile-long convoy when he heard the high-pitched *pop! pop! pop!* of Indian rifles, identifiable by the low-grade gunpowder sold to them by traders.

Sixty Indians were attacking the advance guard at the head of Clark's procession. Six infantrymen fell dead in the initial fusillade. American soldiers often panicked in the face of an Indian ambush, but Clark's men held firm as the dragoons charged forward. Clark quickly rode up with the rest of the infantrymen, gathered the packhorses, and ordered an ad hoc breastworks built out of baggage packs. In fifteen minutes the battle was over. The Indians hastily retreated, leaving behind a half-dozen rifles, forty blankets, and one fallen warrior, to be scalped by the Americans.

Clark understandably expected to be commended for his courage under fire. But when Wayne issued his account of the attack, he praised "the conduct of Lieut. Turner of the 2d. and Ensign Lee, of the 4th Sub Legions, who with fifteen gallant dragoons charged and defeated three times their number of savages." He went on to acknowledge Clark and his troops "for the rapidity of their march to support the van guard."[66]

To Clark, this was faint praise indeed. He bitterly confided to Jonathan that not only had his leadership been ignored but an officer below his rank and another mere "passenger" had received the "Lorels of that day." If his previous campaign service with Wilkinson had not already made him sympathetic to the anti-Wayne clique in the Legion, this felt oversight made it certain. Clark told Jonathan that he was going to ask for the command of an elite group of riflemen. If refused, he declared, "I will resign."[67]

He did not resign. Instead, Lieutenant Clark accepted a new assignment as quartermaster for the entire Fourth Sub-Legion. At the age of twenty-three, Clark was now in charge of supplying one-quarter of the United States Army on the move through hostile territory.

It was dangerous duty. The Fourth Sub-Legion had been put in charge of Fort Recovery, the army's new forward post, built on the site of St. Clair's defeat. On June 30, an empty pack train had moved barely a quarter mile from the fort when it was attacked by 1,500 Indians and Canadian militia under the command of the Shawnee war chief Blue Jacket. Twenty-two American soldiers were killed and 360 horses captured. But what would have been a clear Indian victory was compromised when the triumphant warriors impulsively assaulted the fort itself. They were beaten back by American sharpshooters and artillery. Seventeen warriors the tribes could ill afford to lose fell dead.

On July 28, Wayne's Legion of the United States began its advance north from Fort Greenville. Soon Wayne expected to be joined by 1,600 mounted Kentucky volunteers led by General Charles Scott. Their goal was to force the waiting tribes into a final confrontation. Lieutenant William Clark, in charge of supplies and a band of Chickasaw scouts, kept one of only a handful of journals to have survived Wayne's campaign.

Clark was not happy. The army moved agonizingly slowly through heavy thickets, gullies, and beds of "Netles more then waist high & miles in length." Horses became hopelessly mired in muddy streambeds. Not until the fifth day did the men emerge into "an open extensive and bountiful" prairie and were cheered by their first view of the entire column in the open.[68]

At the banks of the St. Marys River, Wayne ordered the construction of a fortification he would call Fort Adams. As the timber was being felled, a gigantic tree crashed directly onto the commander's marquee. Wayne, who luckily escaped with superficial injuries, later doubted it had been an accident. Clark, still resentful over Wayne's oversight in May, agreed that there was "so large a field for speculation."[69]

By this time, Clark had fallen increasingly under the influence of Wilkinson—his superior officer, a recent Kentuckian, and a compellingly seductive man—in the rivalries within the Legion. Clark's journal entries grew increasingly sarcastic on the subject of the commander in chief. On August 4, he complained that Wayne's decision to move on from Fort Adams endangered the lives of those left to guard it "in the midst of the Enemys Country, without the Smallest provability of being reinforced."[70] Three days later, as the army approached the large Indian villages at Grand Glaize, at the confluence of the Auglaize and the Maumee, Wilkinson urged a surprise attack. Clark reported on the debate:

> Everybody was flushed with the idea of supprising [the Savage] in the moment of providing for their Wives & Children . . . Genl. Wilkinson suggested the plan to the Comdr in Chief, but it was not his plan nor perhaps his wish to Embrace so probable a means

for Ending the War . . . this was not the first occasion or opportunity, which presented itself to our observant Genl. for some grand stroke of Enterprise, but the Comdr. In Chief rejects all & every of his plans.[71]

The next day, with the element of surprise past, the army arrived at the deserted Grand Glaize villages. The men were astonished at the sight in front of them. Vast fields of corn and vegetables stretched a full seven miles along the Maumee River bottom. Here, at the population center of the confederacy, was "the grand Emporium of the hostile Indians of the West," marveled Wayne.[72] Indians supposedly unable to adapt the white man's farming techniques had in fact built the largest agricultural complex in North America. Smoke was still rising from recently abandoned log cabins, around which Clark noted with admiration fields stretching "as far as the Eye can see . . . covered with the most luxuriant groths of Corn, interspurced with Small Log Cabbins arround all of which you observe theire well cultivated gardens, affording almost every Species of horticultural Vegitables in the greatest abundance."[73]

The army crossed the Maumee and began working its way down the river, toward present-day Toledo, through marshes "sometimes up to waist in mud & water."[74] The British had recently built Fort Miami on American-claimed territory at the Rapids of the Maumee, an act the federal government regarded as an outrageous provocation. Wayne had feinted toward the Indians' western stronghold at Kekionga; now he planned to crush the eastern half of their confederacy beneath the eyes of their British protectors.

In the armies converging at the Maumee Rapids was an array of individuals that, if nothing else, demonstrated the characteristic blurring of alliances and identities on the frontier. With Wayne were not only Wilkinson and Clark but also a future President, William Henry Harrison, serving as Wayne's aide-de-camp, and the future explorer Zebulon Pike, then an adolescent accompanying his army-officer father. Their principal scout was William Wells. As a freckle-faced fourteen-year-old in 1784, Wells had been captured near Louisville by the Shawnees and raised by the tribe. But after fighting with the Shawnees against St. Clair, Wells had decided to switch sides. Clark found him to be an "enterprising young man."[75]

With the Indian army were Blue Jacket and a rising young warrior, Tecumseh, as well as the British agents Alexander McKee and Matthew Elliott. The Tory turncoat Simon Girty, universally despised by the Americans, circulated among the Indians. Their principal translator was George White Eyes, a Delaware who had been educated at the College of New Jersey (later Princeton University) and had returned to his native people. Travelers were astonished to come across young White Eyes reading Greek and Roman classics in the wilderness. However, the confederacy's most experienced strategist, the Miami war chief Little Turtle, had withdrawn, reputedly warning that the Americans were as numerous as "leaves on the trees."

On the rainy morning of August 20, the Legion prepared to engage the enemy. Suffering from a gout attack, Wayne was hoisted into his saddle, an ominous sight to any survivor of St. Clair's Defeat. Clark was on the left flank, leading a column of riflemen. At 7 a.m. the army moved toward the Indians, who had concealed themselves in a jumble of fallen trees blown down by a recent windstorm.

The first shots routed the scouts and advance guard. But even though the Indian attack was "a matter of Surprise to almost every officer," Clark wrote in his journal, this time the entire army did not panic. The dragoons responded by charging through the thinly stretched Indian lines. The Indians attempted to outflank the soldiers on the left, but "Colonel Hamtramck . . . was prepared & gave them so warm a recption as made theire Situation here as disagreeable as that on the Right." Clark and his riflemen drove the enemy back about a mile, suffering only a few losses, while "the Enemy was repulsed with precipation."[76]

In less than an hour the fray was all but over. The Battle of Fallen Timbers was barely a battle at all. Only nine hundred men in the American force of three thousand were actually engaged. The Indians quickly withdrew, leaving forty bodies on the field but carrying away more with them. The Legion lost twenty-six regulars and eight militiamen. The most significant result occurred afterward. The retreating Indians fell back to Fort Miami and tried to enter the stockade. The British commander, Major William Campbell, fearing American reprisals, refused to let them enter. After years of promises of support, the Northern tribes had been abandoned by their Great British Father. Years later, Tecumseh would bitterly remind the English of the day "the gates were shut against us."[77]

Later that day, after the battle, Clark put down "a few observations or relections" about the strategies of both armies. The Indians, he thought, could have broken through the American lines if "they had kept themselves compact and advanced with Judgment." On the other hand, he also thought that Wayne could have won an even more decisive victory had he more adroitly employed Scott's mounted Kentucky volunteers to outflank the Indians and cut off their retreat. "The whole world cannot but be surprised that the Commander in Chief did not availe himself of this advantage," he wrote, "but so far was his Excellency from thus putting an end to this expensive war."[78] It was a remarkably succinct and sophisticated assessment from a twenty-four-year-old.

Over the next three days, Wayne arrayed his army within a pistol-shot of the British garrison, exchanging a series of testy notes with Campbell in a scene reminiscent of George Rogers Clark's earlier confrontation with Hamilton at Vincennes. In the end, neither side wanted to provoke a wider war. Wayne withdrew, instructing his men to burn everything they left behind.

What Clark had called "one of the most beautiful landscapes ever painted" was then turned into a smoking wasteland.[79] The army returned, "cutting down and destroying hundreds of Acres of corn & Burning several large Towns besides small ones," William wrote to Jonathan.[80] An estimated thirty thousand to forty thousand bushels of grain were destroyed, further starving the tribes. "We raised corn like the whites," Little Turtle said later, "but now we are poor hunted deer."[81] George Rogers Clark's slash-and-burn tactics had finally been executed with a vengeance. Wayne's army was employing the same strategy the Virginians had bitterly denounced as barbaric when British Colonel Banastre Tarleton's dragoons swept through Albemarle County in 1781.

Wilkinson continued to enlist Clark in his venomous campaign against Wayne, dining with the young lieutenant and reading him excerpts from his accusations against the commander in chief. Wilkinson, who by this time was a paid secret agent of the Spanish government, called Wayne a "despotic, vain glorious, ignorant general."[82] Soon enough Wilkinson made his charges public, writing to Knox and accusing the commander of high crimes. Knox passed along the charges to Wayne, who replied with a sixteen-page letter defending himself against the "vile assassin Wilkinson."[83]

The usually amicable Clark must have found it awkward negotiating the growing rancor between his commanders. But he had always been good at dealing with difficult people, perhaps an acquired skill for this youngest of six brothers. Then a single incident changed his thinking permanently.

The Legion had moved back to the Forks of the Maumee, where Harmar had met his calamitous defeat nearly four years earlier. Amid the dissension, Wayne started work on what would be known as Fort Wayne. Like other officers, Clark took his turn mounting guard detachments. It could be a harrowing duty. On the return from Fallen Timbers, he had been unnerved hearing "The Savage . . . round my redoubt, late at night, making the most Dreadfull yells Howling like wolves, & crying like owls, which kept me up all night & my Men under arms."[84]

On the night of October 7, Clark was in charge of a guard detail when he failed to establish the password, a mistake he thought could have rendered him "broke & ruined forever." He described it this way:

> The officer of the day visited my guard last night, & I had neglected giving out to my sentinals the Countersign, & approached my Picquet without being challenged. Had this officer known his duty, & had me arrested, I should have been Broke, unquestionably. I can but be astonished to View what a little fault will ruin an officer in the Army.[85]

Whether because of this sobering incident, or because of a larger disillusionment with Wilkinson, Clark abruptly ceased his written criticisms of his commander and never again mentioned Wilkinson in his journal. Two weeks later, on the evening the triumphant army left the completed Fort Wayne, a decidedly less critical Clark "dined with the Commander in Chief by his particular invertation."[86]

As the Legion made its way back toward Fort Greenville under leaden skies, the men were anxious to be out of this cold land. Clark recorded "fowls of passage" flying overhead.[87]

The Legion of the United States marched through the gates of Fort Greenville on the evening of November 2, 1795, to a twenty-four-gun salute from the six-pound cannons. During the fourteen weeks the men were gone, continuing construction had made Fort Greenville the largest American fortress west of the Appalachians. The mile-long palisade enclosed a fifty-acre encampment on a rise of land above a tributary of the Great Miami River, on the site of present-day Greenville, Ohio. Inside was a virtual city—stores, stables, a tannery and slaughterhouse, and several hundred log huts for soldiers. Wayne's quarters included his own well-tended garden. An enormous log Council House, one hundred feet long and covered with a split-shingle roof, had been built for the anticipated treaty talks with the Indians.

The triumphant Wayne ordered up a feast for his troops. Each man was issued a gill of rum to help wash down a dinner of roast venison, beef, mutton, veal, turkey, duck, chicken, raccoon, opossum, pies and preserves, and ice cream. The dinner was followed by a ball, enlivened by the few women present at the fort.

A week later, Billy Clark was officially put in command of his own company of riflemen in the Fourth Sub-Legion. He was now in charge of seventy-five well-trained regulars. But the reassignment did not change his feeling about his long-term prospects. "I have some intentions of resigning and get into some business in Kentucky or on the Mississippi," he wrote his brother Edmund. "I think there is great opening for an extensive successful trade in that River could a man form valuable connections in New Orleans."[88] To his brother Jonathan, he was more blunt: "I am sorry to inform you that the army has become disagreeable to me," he said, "and could I get into any business in a civil capacity I would bid adiew to this unthankful unpolish'd service. I have determined to resign & seek for some more honourable imploymen't for my youthfull days."[89]

What gave Clark pause about leaving the "unthankful unpolish'd service" was the feeling that it would send the wrong signal to leave with "our army crownd with success."[90] The endgame was approaching in the long struggle over the Ohio Valley. A quarter century had passed since George Rogers Clark's first campaign in the Illinois country, two decades since William and his parents had first ventured into Indian country.

After a visit with his family in Kentucky, Lieutenant Clark returned to Fort Greenville in a better humor. He described the fort to his sister Fanny as an amazing "new world—all is gaiety, good humer & Divertion." More than a thousand Indians had arrived and were living in temporary log houses and huts outside the walls of the busy fort. The result was a splendid cacophony. "The eye is constantly entertained with the Splendour of Dress and equipage, and the [ear] with the Sounds of Drums, fifes, Bugles, Trumpets," Clark told Fanny. "The Indians [are] continuerly here in great number and when Drunk (as they are often) Cut a number of antick tricks, Such as are verry amuseing to us."[91]

The whites could cut their own share of antic tricks. One athletic soldier, Robert McClellan, became famous for running downhill and leaping over the top of a wagon said to be eight feet above the ground.

More dangerously, in an apparent effort to differentiate themselves from the "savages," just as Virginia planters did from their slaves, the officers of the Legion increasingly adapted the exaggerated rituals and manners of the elite. Ignoring the rules prohibiting duels, officers engaged in frequent affairs of honor. In one ghastly episode, Lieutenants Bradshaw and Huston squared off and fired at one another. Both fell, mortally wounded. Enlisted men caught sleeping at their picket posts were dragged before execution squads or "hanged by the neck." Chaplain Jones performed last rites. His diary entry for September 11, 1795, succinctly captured a soldier's parallel needs to be mindful of death and to be distracted from it:

> Preached from Matt. 28 and last verse, "Teaching them to observe all things whatsoever I have commanded you, and lo, I am with you always to the end of the world, Amen." N.B.—The number of my lottery ticket is 122A.[92]

The Battle of Fallen Timbers forever extinguished the Indians' dream of confining the Americans to the "Virginia shore" of the Ohio. But the confederacy could not immediately agree on what strategy to follow thereafter. Smaller nations like the Wyandots wanted to negotiate a peace immediately. Pro-British chiefs like Joseph Brant of the Iroquois confederacy urged the Lake Indians to continue to resist. The final course taken would depend on the two most influential leaders, Blue Jacket of the Shawnees and Little Turtle of the Miamis.

The federal government charged Wayne—not previously known for his diplomatic skills—with convening a grand council at Greenville. Reasoning that the defeated Indians were "no more to be trusted than an adder fanged," Wayne ordered "trinkets" for the chiefs and their wives.[93] "Flies are not to be caught with gall or bitter," he remarked. Wayne's figurative language—viewing Indians as snakes and insects—thinly disguised his practical intent.[94] The Legion bayonets, he said, were "the most proper instrument for removing Film from the Eyes—& for opening the Ears of the Savages that has ever yet been discovered."[95]

Unlike previous treaty-makers, he did not invite just a token handful of malleable chiefs to sign away lands they did not control. The Indians arriving at Fort Greenville over the spring and summer of 1795 included the Miamis, Shawnees, Wyandots, and Delawares from the Ohio country; the Ojibwas, Potawatomis, and Ottawas from the North; and the Weas, Piankeshaws, Kickapoos, and Kaskaskias from the Wabash and Illinois country.

Wayne readily adapted the symbolic language and rituals of the chiefs. On June 16, 1795, he opened the council with this speech:

> I have cleared the ground of all brush and rubbish and have opened roads to the east, the west, the north and the south, that all your nations may come in safety, and with ease, to meet me. The ground on which this council-house stands, is unstained with blood, and is pure as the heart of General Washington, the Great Chief of America.[96]

It was an eloquent speech, given to an incomplete audience. Neither Blue Jacket nor Little Turtle had arrived by the day the council opened. Worried, Wayne postponed further talks, awaiting the two influential chiefs. Little Turtle was of particular concern: the Miami chief was widely known not only as a brilliant military strategist but also as a sophisticated negotiator who abstained from alcohol and maintained a "modest and manly" manner.[97] One British officer described him as the "most decent, modest, sensible Indian" he had ever met.[98] John Johnston, the American trader at Fort Wayne, called Little Turtle "the gentleman of his race."[99]

Little Turtle finally arrived on June 23, only to see his wife become ill and die ten days later, a potentially devastating omen to the Indians. Wayne responded by ordering her buried with full military honors, a gesture of respect that impressed the tribes.

When the council reconvened in mid-July, Wayne laid out terms that were not negotiations at all. The Indians were presented with an ultimatum. They would cede to their American "fathers" two-thirds of Ohio, about twenty-five thousand square miles. The new boundary of Indian territory would begin at the mouth of the Kentucky River (where Clark had built his corn depot), run north to Fort Recovery, and then northeast to the Cuyahoga River and Lake Erie, near the present city of Cleveland.

In return, the Indians would receive $25,000 in trade goods—calico shirts, farm tools, trade hatchets, ribbons, combs, mirrors, and blankets—and an annuity of $9,500 a year to be divided among the tribes.

It was a humiliating proposal, with payments that were a pittance, given land values of the time. Some tribes would receive as little as $500 a year. In what now seems a particular irony, the tribes were required to set aside sixteen parcels of land within their remaining territory for U.S. military posts, including 150,000 acres in southern Indiana reserved for the soldiers of George Rogers Clark. In other words, Wayne was demanding that Indians create reservations for American soldiers on their land.

Few Indians, however, could challenge Wayne's terms. After the burning of their fields, many of them had become dependent on the American government for food. Even Blue Jacket had been quieted with a personal $300 annuity that amounted to a de facto bribe. The only objections came from Little Turtle. The Miami war chief rose to speak against giving up lands "where the Great Spirit placed my forefather a long time ago, and charged him not to sell, or part with his lands, but to preserve them for his posterity."[100] But in the end he, too, acquiesced, saying that if he were the last to sign the treaty, he also would be the last to break it.

At some point, while the council fires were still glowing at Fort Greenville, William Clark probably encountered a young ensign who had joined the Second Sub-Legion in May. He was Meriwether Lewis, a gawky twenty-year-old who was four years Clark's junior but had much in common with the lieutenant. Lewis was from an old Virginia family that dated to Sir William Berkeley's cavalier elite. He had lived in Albemarle County and was a family friend of Thomas Jefferson's. Bored with running his late father's plantation, he had enlisted with the Virginia militia sent by President Washington to suppress the anti-excise tax Whiskey Rebellion in western Pennsylvania. Afterward he transferred to the regular army and was sent to Greenville. There he would almost certainly have heard in advance about the likable younger brother of the famous General George Rogers Clark.

The Treaty of Greenville was signed on August 3, 1795, by Wayne and eighty Indian chiefs and agents. A jubilant Wayne then announced that gifts would be distributed to the tribes "and we will have a little drink this evening."[101]

The Indians appeared to think that they had simply exchanged the protection of the British for the equally benign protection of the Americans, which perhaps explains Little Turtle's willingness to acquiesce. The last formal speech of the proceedings came from Massas, an Ojibwa chief. "My people will stretch out their arms towards you," he said to Wayne and his officers, "and when I shall have informed them that you have promised to cherish them as your children, they will rejoice at having acquired a new and so good a father."[102] Few Indians could have realized that while the British wanted their trade but not their land, the Americans coveted their land but not their trade. The boundary line that the Indians regarded as permanent was seen by the Americans as one that could, and would, always be modified with further treaties.

The treaty signed at Greenville was the most important Indian treaty in the nation's history. The immediate result was to bring an end to the brutal Indian war that had lasted thirty years. Along with Jay's Treaty, signed in London in November 1794, the Treaty of Greenville ended British designs on the Old Northwest and opened to settlers the lands stretching from the Appalachians to the Mississippi. The number of Americans in Ohio exploded from approximately 5,000 in 1795 to 230,000 in 1810.

Wayne established at Greenville the endgame for all future relations between Indians and the American government. The first step was white encroachment on lands owned by Indians. Their retaliation would produce demands from settlers for a response from the federal army. After suffering devastating defeats, the Indians would sue for a peace that would be obtained only by ceding more of their lands.

The rituals for conducting treaties were also formed at Greenville. First, invitations would go out with wampum belts for tribes to gather at a designated "council fire." They would be welcomed with gifts "at the woods' edge." The opening ceremony would be a condolence ritual to "cover" the dead. The whites would ascribe favorable weather to the

Great Spirit's blessing upon the treaty. Power relationships would be symbolized by the family rhetoric of "Children" and "Fathers." Indians would eventually agree to land cessions, and after they had affixed their marks, the treaty would end with feasting and dispensing of alcohol. Later, the chiefs would be invited to the eastern cities to view for themselves the awesome evidence of American power.[103]

The principal Indian leaders took up the invitation and traveled east, meeting both President Washington and Vice President John Adams. After his visit to Philadelphia, Little Turtle reflected:

> Here I am deaf and dumb. When I walk through the streets I see every person in his shop employed about something. One makes shoes, another hats, a third sells cloth and everyone lives by his labor. I say to myself, which of all these things can you do? Not one. I can make a bow or an arrow, catch fish, kill game, and go to war, but none of these is of any use here . . . I should be a piece of furniture, useless to my nation, useless to the whites, and useless to myself.[104]

Lieutenant Clark was still pondering his return to civilian life. After the high drama of Fallen Timbers and the Treaty of Greenville, his military career seemed to have peaked, just as his older brother's had after the Illinois campaign. He had already taken military expeditions up and down the Ohio and Wabash rivers, built a fort in the wilderness, fought in three Indian campaigns, and observed the making of a historic treaty. He had learned the finer points of dealing with Indians from the most experienced men in the country, his brother George Rogers and his commander Anthony Wayne. But now, after seven years on the Spanish, English, and Indian frontiers, continued duty in the "unpolish'd service" of a peacetime army was an unappealing prospect. But, like Little Turtle, William Clark wondered if he would be able to find a role for himself in the world of civilians. At just twenty-five, he had every reason to think that the rest of his life could be an anticlimax.

CHAPTER FOUR

SOLDIER AND CITIZEN

1795–1803

It had been a difficult time at Mulberry Hill. George Rogers Clark was increasingly beset by creditors. Sister Fanny, the black-eyed beauty of the family, had separated from her husband, James O'Fallon. When George Rogers was told that O'Fallon had physically abused Fanny, he denounced the doctor as "a Rogue, Rascal and Villain" and attacked him with his walking stick, breaking it over his head.[1] The caning may have contributed to O'Fallon's death a few months later. Fanny became a twenty-two-year-old widow with two small boys, John Julius and Benjamin O'Fallon.

Fanny's difficulties were soon overshadowed. "I can write you no good news," John Clark wrote his son Jonathan on February 9, 1795. "Oh how shall I tel you your <u>Sister Anderson</u> is no more."[2] Eliza Clark Anderson—the eighth of the ten Clark children—had died in January at the age of twenty-six at her nearby home, Soldier's Retreat, of complications following the birth of her fourth child.

William found a way to soldier on. His good nature helped. By the summer, he was writing gossipy letters from Fort Greenville to Fanny about the wife of one Major Shaylor ("of <u>low</u> birth & less breading") and his flirtations with the "<u>Ladees</u> of your Nabouring hood, particularly Miss _____." He did not need to say her name—Fanny surely knew—but she was a heartbreaker: "My long and painfull absence from her Conversation is a Source of the greatest affliction to me." He had come to see romance as a dangerous distraction. "Sensibility (like hers)," he wrote, "can easly conceive the embarisment & distress that this Combat between Love & duty had produced." As for "Miss F_____," Clark wrote, she is "Cruel" and, he guessed, maintained a dozen suitors.[3]

William's infatuations practically extended to Anthony Wayne himself. When Clark's romantic campaigns kept him in Kentucky longer than planned, the commander in chief he and Wilkinson once ridiculed had become an understanding father figure, "a Galant man [who] had some Idea of my Persute [and] treted my inatention as all other good fathers would on the same acasion."[4]

The smitten Lieutenant Clark might have continued his pursuit of the cruel "Miss F_____" but for the intervention of the Spanish government. Tensions had been rising for years along the Lower Mississippi over the efforts of men like James O'Fallon and George Rogers Clark to organize filibustering expeditions into the Spanish-held Upper Louisiana. George Rogers had publicly called for an invasion in 1794, a provocation that required President Washington to issue a proclamation prohibiting armed expeditions against nations with whom the United States was at peace. The United States was not alone, however, in building tensions.

In September 1795, Wayne wrote to George Washington's new Secretary of War, Timothy Pickering, with alarming news. The Spanish had undertaken "an Aggression of a very high & serious nature."[5] Namely, they were building a fort on American territory on the east bank of the Mississippi at Chickasaw Bluffs. From that point, they could control traffic on the Mississippi as well as incite the Chickasaws to join the hostile confederacy of Southern tribes led by the Creeks.

Access to the Lower Mississippi and New Orleans was critical to the expanding American economy west of the Appalachians. In the 1790s, the route to global markets was not the mythical Northwest Passage to the Orient but rather the Southwest Passage down the Ohio and Mississippi to the Gulf of Mexico. With the Indians quelled, farmers in Kentucky and Ohio could ship their goods to European markets far more easily on flatboats through New Orleans than by carting them back over the mountains to the East Coast.

General Wayne could not have known that the Spanish were already aware, thanks to paid informants like James Wilkinson, that George Rogers Clark and other adventurers were continuing to talk about launching a strike against their territories in Louisiana. The struggle for control of the Lower Mississippi was becoming a free-for-all. The Spanish had decided to reinforce their troops on the Mississippi as a precaution against possible invasions from all quarters.

Wayne told Pickering that he intended "to dispatch a flag immediately to the Spanish Commandant to demand by what authority & by whose orders he has thus invaded the Territory of the United States of America."[6] Who better to undertake this delicate mission than the only officer in the American army who had already led an earlier river expedition to the homeland of the Chickasaws?

Lieutenant William Clark left Fort Washington on September 15 in command of a barge crewed by a sergeant, a corporal, and fifteen privates. By September 27, they had traveled 250 miles to the mouth of the Wabash. Two days later, they landed at Fort Massac in a fog so thick Clark "could not see 2 rod[s]."[7] Built a year earlier by Wayne near the ruins of the old French post, Fort Massac was the westernmost outpost of the United States. William repaired his barge and learned from the post commander that the Spanish were not only fortifying the river but, outrageously, impressing Americans out of trading vessels on the Mississippi to work on the new forts—a provocation more common on the high seas.

Clark's barge swung into the Mississippi at noon on October 1. The next day, he wrote in his journal that he "proceeded on," using the phrase he would later make famous. The party moved downstream to within a few hundred yards of New Madrid—once known as L'Anse à la Graisse, or "Cove of Grease," for its abundant bison hunting—the Spanish redoubt on the west bank of the Mississippi he had so carefully avoided on his 1793 trip. Clark was hailed by the Spanish guards and ordered to put to shore.

Instead, Clark moved his barge to an eddy near the bank. A Spanish officer rowed over and issued an invitation to meet with Governor Don Manuel Gayoso de Lemos, the commanding officer in Upper Louisiana. Clark boarded the governor's galley, *La Vigilante*—actually, an armed keelboat—and found himself standing before Gayoso, whose background reflected the polyglot world of Louisiana: Gayoso, a Spanish official, had been educated in England and was married to an American.

"Sir, I am an American officer," Clark began, "and am under orders from the Commander in Chief with a message and letter to the

Commanding officer of the Spanish Troops now at Chickasaw Bluffs, or on the East side of the Mississippi U.S.A."[8]

"I am that person," Gayoso replied. "I command all this upper country—and the Chickasaw Bluffs is under my immediate command."

Clark then presented Gayoso with Wayne's letter demanding to know "by what principles, by what orders, and by what authority" had the Spanish "thus made usurpation into the territory of the U.S. and built a fort therein?"[9]

While awaiting the formal reply to Wayne's letter, Clark struck up a conversation with Gayoso. The governor said that he had purchased the land for the fort from the Chickasaws. Clark asked "whether that was his pretext for building the Fort at that place." Gayoso answered evasively, and with a shrug, "It is a Ministerial business for which I cannot acco[un]t."[10]

The formal reply was handed to Clark at 9 p.m. The lieutenant spent the night aboard the galley, where he "was treated with every politeness by the Governor and his officers."[11] At 10 a.m. the following day, Clark and his men left to a booming salute from Gayoso's cannons echoing across the river. Accompanying them was one of Francis Vigo's trading boats, whose captain later briefed Clark on the fortifications at Chickasaw Bluffs. Poling and rowing their barge upstream for the first time against the "rappid and difficult" Mississippi current, Clark and his men stopped to inspect the ruins of Fort Jefferson, built fifteen years earlier by George Rogers but later occupied by the Chickasaws.[12]

In an odd coincidence, Clark returned to Fort Massac on October 9, 1795, just twenty-four hours after the departure of the French botanist André Michaux from that same place. A friend of Thomas Jefferson's, Michaux had been an unlikely participant in an international contretemps just two years earlier. After George Rogers Clark had proved unavailable, Jefferson had continued to pursue a private or public exploration of the western continent. In Paris, he discussed with the American adventurer John Ledyard an ambitious scheme to cross Russia and the Bering Strait to explore North America from west to east. Ledyard actually made it as far as Siberia in 1788 before he was arrested by Catherine the Great's soldiers and expelled from the country.

Michaux was next to take up Jefferson's dream. A brilliant scientist with an interest in American species—he first classified the crab apple, purple rhododendron, and buttercup—he was commissioned by the

American Philosophical Society in 1792 "to find the shortest & most convenient route of communication between the U.S. & the Pacific ocean, within the temperate latitudes." Along the way, Jefferson explained in his instructions, he should "take notice of the country you pass through, its general face, soil, rivers, mountains, its productions—animal, vegetable, and mineral—so far as they may be new to us, and may also be useful or very curious . . . the names, members, and dwellings of the inhabitants, and such particulars, as you can learn of their history, connection with each other, languages, manners, state of society, and of the arts and commerce among them."[13]

If those assignments were not ambitious enough, Jefferson also wanted Michaux to search for evidence of mammoths and "to learn whether the Lama or Paca of Peru is found in those parts."[14] The botanist was to preserve his notes on animal skins or birch bark. His pay would be $400.

But other games were afoot. On September 17, 1793, Michaux visited George Rogers Clark at Mulberry Hill and handed him a letter from the newly arrived twenty-nine-year-old French minister, Citizen Edmond Charles Genêt. It informed Clark that the Republic of France had appointed him commander of the "Revolutionary and Independent Legion of the Mississippi" with the goal of breaking off Louisiana from Spanish rule.[15] When President Washington learned of this audacious scheme, he ordered Citizen Genêt recalled by the French government, and Michaux's journey was abandoned.

By the time Lieutenant Clark nearly bumped barges with Michaux at Fort Massac two years later, the French botanist had returned to "herborising" on America's rivers. They apparently crossed in the night, heading in opposite directions on the Ohio. Neither man mentions an encounter in his journal—perhaps deliberately, given the embarrassment of the Genêt affair. Just a few months later, Michaux breakfasted with John Clark and George Rogers Clark at Mulberry Hill.[16]

In any event, Clark proceeded on, almost single-handedly supplying more than enough food for his party. Hunting along the shore in one nine-day stretch, he killed eleven bears and wounded another.

Clark reached Fort Washington on November 2 and two days later filed a remarkable report with General Wayne. While he had written down almost nothing of military value during the trip—apparently concerned that his notes might fall into Spanish hands if he were captured—Clark now filled in copious details about the Spanish forces at Chickasaw

Bluffs ("about five hundred men"), their arms ("seventeen Cannon mounted, viz.—three 24 pds. . . . 21 smaller pieces"), and their supporting flotilla ("three gallies and one galliote"). He further described sites for prospective forts at the Chalk Cliffs and the Iron Banks on the Mississippi, south of the Ohio confluence, and the retrieval by the Spanish of eight French cannons from the old Fort de Chartres in the Illinois country. Finally, along with his report, Clark supplied pen-and-ink sketches of both Fort St. Ferdinand at Chickasaw Bluffs and Gayoso's armed galley.[17]

Wayne was delighted with his young lieutenant. Secretary of War Pickering had already said that President Washington had been "pleased" to learn of Clark's mission.[18] Wayne forwarded Clark's report verbatim to Pickering, along with Gayoso's formal reply. As Clark had already discerned, the Spanish governor would argue that he had bought the land for Fort St. Ferdinand directly from the Chickasaws. Wayne tartly commented that by the same logic, the Americans could buy Creek or Choctaw land in the Spanish territories of Louisiana or Florida and build forts there.[19]

At Fort Washington, Lieutenant Clark's reputation could not have been higher. It was not simply that he was the popular younger brother of the celebrated General George Rogers Clark. He was a personal favorite of the two feuding generals, Wayne and Wilkinson, and had somehow managed to give offense to neither. He had led his men on two bold excursions into Spanish territory, the second earning praise from President Washington himself.

By contrast, Ensign Meriwether Lewis was in a mess. Just two days after Clark turned in his meticulous report at Fort Greenville, Lewis was brought before a court-martial at the same post. He had been charged by one Lieutenant Eliott (possibly an army surgeon named John Elliott) with "abruptly, and in an Ungentleman like manner, when intoxicated, entering his House on the 24th of September last, and without provocation insulting him, and disturbing the peace and harmony of a Company of Officers whom he had invited there." Lewis did not seem to know when to leave well enough alone. After Eliott apparently tossed him out, Lewis had "presumed on the same day to send Lieutenant Eliott a Challenge to fight a duell."[20]

The incident irritated Wayne. It was the first court-martial under his command, and he resented it. Though duels were against regulations, Wayne and other commanders tacitly permitted them, preferring that officers find "some other mode of settling their private disputes" than the cumbersome process of a court-martial.[21]

The military court was duly convened, chaired by Major Joseph Shaylor (he of the lowborn wife). Ensign Lewis pleaded not guilty. After a week of testimony he was acquitted "with honor." General Wayne confirmed the verdict and added tartly that he hoped it would be both the first and the last court-martial "of this nature" under his command.[22]

But what now for Ensign Lewis? He clearly could not stay in the same company with Lieutenant Eliott. Wayne must have thought that the excitable Lewis might benefit from serving under the reliable young officer who had just returned from his expedition along the rivers of the West. Lewis was transferred to the Chosen Rifle Company of the Fourth Sub-Legion, commanded by Lieutenant William Clark. Little is known about their relationship then. The early army careers of Lewis and Clark would overlap just a few months, but enough time for Lewis to learn all about Clark's experiences in Indian country.

After a furlough in Kentucky and Virginia, Clark returned to Greenville. There he received a letter from George Rogers, who gave "Billy" some brotherly advice: "If you intend to leave the Army the sooner you can do it with propriety the better, as you have served long enough to qualify yourself for any further military employ which is all you could wish for or at least all the advantage you could expect in the present situation of affairs."

George Rogers then added a postscript: "If you could get y' father a still it would be a good thing."[23]

It's not known whether Billy found a still for his father. But he was evidently ready to take his brother's advice about leaving the army in order to help the family financially. On July 1, 1796, Lieutenant William Clark resigned his commission and returned to Mulberry Hill. He was a civilian for the first time in seven years.

Kentucky was going mad for land. The Continental Army veterans migrating to Kentucky waving their land grants were followed by succeeding waves of speculators waving conflicting land claims and attorneys waving lawsuits. The surveyors' custom of marking out tracts with ephemeral features like buildings and bushes led to overlapping, or "shingled," land claims and voluminous litigation.

Thanks in part to George Rogers's grants of thousands of acres in Indiana and Kentucky, the Clarks were land-rich. Just one of his claims at the mouth of the Tennessee River was for seventy-four thousand acres. The problem was that George Rogers's many creditors were now closing in. Most prominent among them was Laurent Bazadone, a Spanish merchant who had arrived at Vincennes when George Rogers and his men were short on supplies there in 1786. The general's regiment had illegally confiscated Bazadone's goods.

Bazadone's lawsuit was just one of three major actions against George Rogers. He was also being sued by a prominent Kentuckian, Humphrey Marshall, over a contract to sell two large claims of land, and the heirs of Captain William Shannon, a quartermaster in his old regiment. During his 1779 campaign, George Rogers had endorsed vouchers drawn by Shannon in order to supply his army. But the state of Virginia later penuriously refused to pay for either the flour for Clark's men or the general's own salary. "I have given the United States half the territory they possess," George Rogers later wrote bitterly, "and for them to suffer me to remain in poverty, in consequence of it, will not redound much to their honor hereafter."[24]

Since George Rogers was increasingly disabled by alcohol, it fell to the entire Clark family to solve his problems. They divided up the task. Brother Jonathan would lobby for redress with the Virginia state assembly in Richmond, the capital. Brother Edmund would supply ready cash from his gristmill and mercantile businesses in Virginia.

The job of settling the lawsuits fell to brother William. Just over a month after his return from the army, William was on horseback riding through Kentucky, surveying George Rogers's holdings and attempting to extinguish his debts in return for land. In the process, many of the properties were transferred into William's name; this protected them from George's creditors and allowed the younger brother to sell them without complication.

The Clarks were not without assets. The richest 10 percent of Kentuckians in 1800 owned one-third of the land, and the Clarks were firmly placed among this planter elite. Daughter Lucy was living with her husband, William Croghan, in their elegant Georgian manor, Locust Grove, just a few miles from Mulberry Hill. Daughter Fanny had remarried and was now the wife of a wealthy merchant, Charles Mynn Thruston, Sr. She would soon move to his plantation thirty miles upriver.

In addition to land, the family's other significant investment was in human property. Enslaved African-Americans were present in only one of four bluegrass households, though their numbers increased as the forests and canebrakes were cleared and the region moved from mixed farming to a labor-intensive tobacco-based economy. Of Kentucky's total population of 73,677 just before statehood in 1792, some 12,430 were African-American slaves.

Like other tidewater Virginians who settled in Kentucky, the Clarks were convinced that slaves were essential to running a successful plantation. John Clark owned about two dozen slaves at Beargrass Creek, considerably more than the average Kentuckian. Though the phrase "sold down the river" originated in the Ohio Valley, the Clarks chose to view their chattel as fixed rather than liquid assets. They rarely sold slaves and almost never freed them.

William rode throughout the area during a second hard winter, 1796–'97, when temperatures fell to 18 degrees below zero at Cincinnati and the Ohio was frozen over for a full month. By the following summer, however, he had made some progress. On August 18, he wrote Edmund that he was "doing what parts of [George Rogers's] business I could, which I found a verry unfinished Situation." William was planning to go to Vincennes to deal with the Bazadone lawsuit there, "which I fear will go against [George Rogers]." He then added glumly, "After which I shall not [have] Money of my own to attend any longer."[25]

Two days after he wrote Edmund, William set out for Vincennes along the old buffalo trace connecting a string of mineral, or salt, springs. Along the way, he camped with some Delaware Indians along the White River. At Vincennes, then a community of fifty houses along the Wabash, he learned that he would need to push on to visit the lawyer John Rice Jones in the Illinois country opposite St. Louis. George Rogers was delighted with his brother's decision. "I am pleased for two reasons," he told William. "First, you may perhaps do some valuable business and also see a Cuntrey that it may hereafter be of an advantage to you to be acquainted with."[26]

Clark and his companions made it to Kaskaskia in five days, one of which they spent retrieving their runaway horses and riding them bare-back thirty miles back to camp. On September 6, 1797, Clark crossed the Mississippi and stayed as the guest of François Vallé II, the Spanish commandant in Ste. Geneviève, a village founded by the French in the late 1740s. He recrossed to visit Fort de Chartres, once the largest fortification in North America, but by the time of his visit, the fort was occupied only by lizards and foraging deer.

Farther north was Cahokia, a small village in the so-called American Bottom, an alluvial floodplain, three to seven miles wide, that stretched for nearly a hundred miles along the east bank of the Mississippi. With topsoils thirty feet deep, the region had produced huge corn crops annually for a thousand years. The remnants of the ancient Mississippian culture were evident in the six square miles of mounds, the biggest of which covered sixteen acres. As many as forty thousand people had lived there around A.D. 1200, making the complex not only the largest concentration of humans north of Mexico but also larger at the time than London, which had a population of thirty thousand. Clark noticed "the remains of some antent city," but there was little else to hold his attention in Cahokia, a town of "low & mean houses and much stragled."[27]

Of greater interest was the village he viewed across the Mississippi. It was St. Louis, officially Spanish but intensely French in character. A thousand residents—a heady mixture of French Creoles, French Canadians, mixed-race *métis*, Indians, and black slaves—mingled on three principal streets above a low limestone bluff. Clark "was Delighted from the ferry with the Situation of this town . . . commanding a butifull view of the river."[28]

He was warmly welcomed, no doubt because many residents still remembered George Rogers Clark's role assisting in the defense of the village against the British and Indians in 1780. He dined with the Spanish lieutenant governor, Zenon Trudeau, and met the Chouteaus, the French founding family who so dominated the fur trade that they were something like the Medici of the Middle Mississippi.

That night, William went to a ball thrown by the Chouteaus, admiring "all the fine girls & buckish Gentlemen."[29] French dancing was scandalous, since gentlemen put their arms around ladies' waists in public; what was more, local women often applied rose-petal rouge to their cheeks and lampblack to their eyes. William did not get back to his lodgings at Charles Gratiot's house until dawn.

During his visit, Clark would have heard the latest news about the recent excursions up the Missouri River into Indian country. The Spanish had long dreamed of building an empire on the northern rivers as comprehensive as the one they had already established in Mexico and the American Southwest. In 1794, they had supported the trader Jacques Clamorgan in founding the Missouri Company, whose goal was to pry loose the British Canadians' monopoly of the enormous fur trade at the Mandan villages in today's North Dakota.

Between 1794 and 1796, the Missouri Company sent three separate expeditions to the Upper Missouri. The first two, led by Jean Baptiste Truteau and a trader named Lécuyer, were stopped by the Poncas and Arikaras. But the third party, headed by James Mackay, a Scottish fur trader who had taken Spanish citizenship, got as far as northeastern Nebraska. From there Mackay sent on his lieutenant, John Thomas Evans, with the goal of reaching the Pacific. Evans had been backed by Englishmen hoping to find the legendary lost Welsh Indians of Prince Madoc. Evans did not find the Welsh Indians but did travel 1,600 miles upriver to the Mandan villages over the winter of 1796–'97.

Mackay and Evans returned separately to St. Louis just a few weeks before Clark arrived, and descriptions of their discoveries were the current gossip. The former army lieutenant must have been intrigued by what he heard. Mackay and Evans had made the first steps on the ambitious journeys proposed by Thomas Jefferson to George Rogers Clark and André Michaux and by Henry Knox to John Armstrong.

Soon Clark was heading home despite "pressing invertations to stay." Along the way he was delayed by "a violent hed ake" and outbreaks of "several large inflematory sores on my legs & thighs."[30] The infected boils—a chronic problem for Clark—were no doubt exacerbated by many hours on horseback. A few months later, after recovering from "a long and lingering fever," Clark estimated that "I have rode for Bro. George in the course of this year upwards of 3000 miles . . . continually on the pad attempting to save him."[31]

In addition to clearing George's debts, William was helping manage their father's plantation at Mulberry Hill. Their largest cash crop was Virginia-style bulgar tobacco, of which not just the leaves but the entire stalk was harvested and dried. Fortunately for the Clarks, the markets at New

Orleans were once again open. Threatened by war with Britain, Spain had sought to mollify the Americans by reopening their trade. In the Treaty of San Lorenzo in October 1795 (also known as Pinckney's Treaty), Spain granted Americans the right to ship their goods to New Orleans and beyond, without paying duties, and accepted the 31st parallel as the northern border of West Florida, thereby abandoning their claims to the so-called Yazoo Strip on the Lower Mississippi. In effect, Spain was beginning to withdraw from a territory it realized was too large to protect. As its minister Manuel Godoy put it, "You can't put doors on open country."[32]

On March 9, 1798, William hired a crew at the Falls of the Ohio, loaded a flatboat with hogsheads of Clark family tobacco, and pushed off for New Orleans. In a life of journeys, Clark was beginning what would be his longest trip to date. He seemed to anticipate this. As always, he carried a notebook—but in this one he set down more than the usual quotidian entries. In the opening pages he had written a set of maxims, most likely gathered from other sources. Some of them were commonplace-book principles familiar to any follower of the Enlightenment:

> Man cannot make principles, he can only discover them.
> The most formidable weapon against errors of every kind is Reason.
> I believe that religious duties consist in doing justice, loveing mercy, and endeavoring to make our fellow creatures happy.[33]

Another seemed to reflect more personally on his lack of formal schooling:

> Learning does not consist in the Knowledge of Language, but in the knowledge of things to which language *gives* names.

The last in the list could have been Clark's lifelong credo:

> Every person of learning is finally his own teacher.

The boat floated down the river against gusty winds that frequently forced them to tie up and wait out the gales.

March 11: "Wind rose blew & snowed all the evening."
March 14: "Wind rose & obliged us to land."

At Fort Massac, Clark bought a canoe and was joined by four other boats to make up a flotilla. Even in the best circumstances, the Mississippi's currents were a formidable challenge for small craft. When Charles Dickens entered the Mississippi on his American tour forty-four years later, he was appalled at the sight:

An enormous ditch, sometimes two or three miles wide, running liquid mud, six miles an hour: its strong and frothy current choked and obstructed everywhere by huge logs and whole forest trees: now twining themselves together in great rafts, from the interstices of which a sedgy lazy foam works up, to float upon the water's top; now rolling past like monstrous bodies, their tangled roots showing like matted hair; now glancing singly by like giant leeches; and now writhing round and round in the vortex of some small whirlpool, like wounded snakes.[34]

Clark bought a passport at New Madrid to enter Spanish territory, even as his boats continued to struggle against the gusty winds sweeping across the water. On March 23 he wrote, "The wind now verry high obliged us to land—with much Difficuelty & Danger the boates much Scattered."

They passed the first, second, and third Chickasaw Bluffs and navigated the three-mile stretch of swirling currents and rapids called the Devil's Race-Ground. On March 28, they arrived at the newly built Fort Adams, just above the high ground at the fourth bluff. Clark wrote a letter to William Croghan containing the results of the survey he'd made for him at the confluence of the Ohio and the Mississippi. "Capt. Lewis promes to Deliver it," Clark wrote in his journal. "He will set out from [Chickasaw Bluffs] about the 15 or 20 of Apr."[35]

Clark floated on downstream, beset by more foul weather:

March 30: "Raned hard set out early wind rose we continued landed on a Sharp Point a Dangerous part of the river. One Boat far behind and cant get in at the port . . . the bank falling in all night."

March 31: "A violent storm all night it litioned [lightninged] for at least 2 hours incesently as one continued blaze."

Disaster finally came on April 1. Another monstrous wind rose up, driving Clark's canoe into an embedded stump that smashed the bow. The canoe then hit a "sawyer"—a partially submerged tree trunk—which "nearly sunk her." Finally a third trunk "held her fast." In his notebook Clark wrote resignedly, "Here I am at 12 oclock canoo stove."

It got worse. One of the trader's boats, weighed down by its full load of merchandise, was sunk by the same sawyer Clark hit. The surviving flatboats were then driven up against the bank by the raging current, "a very dangerous situation." Surveying his bedraggled men, Clark wrote, "my hands fritened." Not until the next day were they able to dislodge the snagged boat and retrieve a few of the trader's goods that had washed ashore.

They proceeded on downstream, amid driving rains, violent windstorms, thick fogs, and occasional alcoholic hazes. "All the hands Drunk in the contractors boat," Clark tersely noted one day. During the journey, he drew a sequence of freehand maps of the course of the Lower Mississippi that are astonishing in their accuracy and draftsmanship.

As they neared New Orleans, Clark noticed traders' keelboats passing almost every day. Finally, on April 24, he berthed in New Orleans—presumably avoiding the plight of less careful boatmen who, caught in the powerful current, would miss the eddy at the harbor and be swept past the city. Clark rented a warehouse to store his tobacco and successfully located a buyer. With the proceeds from his tobacco sales, Clark paid his men and bought a barrel apiece of sugar and coffee, which he shipped back to Mulberry Hill.

After the harrowing trip downriver, Clark may have hoped for a few balmy weeks in New Orleans, the capital of Louisiana and already the most exotic European city in North America. Enormous poplar trees lined the levee, where Frenchwomen strolled along a raised gravel walk. At the heart of the city was the Place d'Armes, fronted by church and state: the St. Louis Cathedral and the Cabildo, seat of the local government; both had been erected in the past two years. William stayed in Madame Chabot's boardinghouse on Conti Street, whose Irish landlady catered to English and American visitors. He also would have observed in New

Orleans a new, more brutal type of slave society based on the emerging markets for sugar and cotton. These plantation slaves worked in the fields throughout the year, generating enormous profits for their owners.

A week after he arrived, Clark noted in his journal that there was "an uproar about a War with the United States & Spa[i]n France &c." This was the result of the so-called XYZ Affair in Paris—a diplomatic incident that had inflamed anti-French Federalists in the United States and spilled over into an undeclared maritime war. Hundreds of French and American armed merchant ships—privateers—were roaming the seas seizing ships, sailors, and plunder. President John Adams reported that three hundred American vessels had been seized on the high seas by French warships. On May 3, 1798, George Washington had been called out of retirement to command the army, and a new naval department had been authorized.

In the midst of the Quasi-War with France, Clark was making plans to return to the East Coast by sea. On June 19, 1798, the Spanish governor of Louisiana, Gayoso, issued a passport for "Guillermo Clark" to travel from New Orleans to Philadelphia on the schooner *Active*. But delayed perhaps by the uproar with France, or more likely by weather, Clark never did sail on the *Active*. Thirty years later, the ship was involved in one of the most bizarre incidents in nautical history. Anchored in the rich whaling grounds off the Maine coast, the *Active* suddenly began churning through the water with no visible means of propulsion. A whale had become entangled in its anchor chain and towed the vessel to Mount Desert Island, where the dumbfounded crew finally cut the anchor free.

Waiting for another ship, Clark purchased five horses in New Orleans and took them upriver to Natchez in hopes of making some ready cash. At that time, Natchez-Under-the-Hill was the roughest vice district in North America, a gathering place for the flotsam of boatmen, traders, gamblers, and prostitutes coming down the river. The botanist John Bradbury wrote of the town: "There is not, perhaps, in the world a more dissipated place."[36] Here Clark sold the horses at an army camp, played some billiards, and gave nine dollars to "a pore sick man." Two days later, he retreated downriver to New Orleans on a pirogue.

On July 27, Clark boarded a six-gun American vessel, the *Star*, bound for Philadelphia. Escorting it was a two-masted brig carrying eight guns. The two ships departed, passing Spanish ships of war moving up the river, and reached La Balize, the fortified lighthouse the French had built at the entrance to the Mississippi. There they waited for favoring winds to take them across the sandbar at the mouth of the river.

It was a time when suspicions rose quickly. A French privateer with four cannons and fifty men approached and anchored overnight near the *Star*. Clark and the Americans lay awake the entire night, "all prepared" for an attack. But when the morning came without event, Clark and the *Star*'s owner asked permission to board the French vessel. On it they found three American prisoners, sea captains whose ships had been captured. Would the French captain mind if Mr. Clark had breakfast with his countrymen? *Mais non*. It resulted in an extraordinary scene: at this unique confluence of nations and international tensions, Clark sat down at *petit déjeuner* with three captured American captains on a French ship in Spanish waters.

On July 7, the *Star* moved about a mile downstream—an act that generated much alarm on the Spanish galley patrolling the mouth of the river. "We went to shore," Clark said, "and the officer . . . informed us that he had orders to stop us. This information astonish us as we knew of no cause."

The Americans soon learned that they had been accused of "insulting" the commander of La Balize and of making "threats" to the French privateer. Two of their party who had returned to New Orleans to inquire about the cause for the detention were escorted to prison and kept there for twenty-four hours. That gesture evidently satisfied the Spanish, since a letter soon arrived from Governor Gayoso stating that the ship could continue on its voyage, "as the Spanesh Nation is in purfect harmony with the US."

The course the *Star* had charted would take it through the Straits of Florida past Cuba and up the Atlantic seaboard to Delaware Bay. A few days out, a sail appeared to windward. "We all prepared for action," noted Clark, only to learn that the feared French privateer was actually a Spanish ship bound for Havana. Instead of bullets and cannonballs, they encountered storms and heavy seas in the Gulf. Ever succinct, Clark wrote, "I am sick." Other sails appeared and disappeared on the horizon without incident, and eventually the island of Cuba floated through the haze on the southeast.

On September 2, they were approached by an English ship-of-the-line, the brig HMS *Hero*, flying the Union Jack and armed with sixteen cannons and 150 men. A lieutenant climbed aboard and informed the men of the *Star* that they were in the Dry Tortugas, westward of the Florida Keys. Antipathy toward the English ran strong in the Clark family, but in this ever-shifting world of opportunistic empires, the Royal Navy was now helping to protect American shipping against the French. If Clark held any negative opinions about the nation most Americans blamed for the Indian "depredations" north of the Ohio, he did not note them in his journal.

It could have been because he was sick, tired, and hungry. "We are much alarmed about provisions," he wrote, "having consumed the greater part of our stock." So, on September 4, 1798, at latitude 24°28' — a location just off the present-day resort of Islamorada in the Florida Keys — Clark took matters into his own hands: he went deep-sea fishing. During a single day's trolling in an area now famous for sport fish like bonefish and tarpon, he caught "a no. of fish dolfin, skipjacks, grupers snappers &c." The "dolfin" William Clark caught in 1798 is known today as mahimahi, though how it was prepared or appreciated we do not know. The accomplished hunter of deer, bear, and bison did not record his opinion.

The *Star* cleared the Keys shortly before the Caribbean became the scene of the most intense naval action of the undeclared war. On November 20, a French ship seized an American schooner off Guadeloupe. Two months later, the United States Navy's first frigate, *Constellation*, turned its thirty-eight guns against the French *Insurgente*, defeating the larger vessel in an hour-long battle off the island of Nevis.

As the *Star* made its way past the Outer Banks of North Carolina, Clark diagnosed himself "sick" or "verry sick" for thirteen consecutive days, at one point bleakly adding, "Am so reduced can scarcely walk." He may have been seasick, though the evidence suggests something else; Clark later said that he had lived "in bad health" during his civilian years.[37] The ship's men sustained themselves with rainwater collected in sailcloths and with "Sugar Coffee & limes" sent over by a passing schooner.

In late September, the *Star* followed a high tide and favorable winds over the bar at Cape May and entered Delaware Bay. But its destination could no longer be Philadelphia, which had been devastated by an epidemic of yellow fever. Congress had adjourned and hastily departed in

July, and by September 40,000 people had fled the city. Of those who remained, 3,600 died.

Instead, the *Star* docked at New Castle, Delaware, a harbor bustling with forty ships. Among them were the soon-to-be-victorious *Constellation* and a twenty-gun schooner, the *Delaware*, commanded by the already famous Captain Stephen Decatur. Two months earlier, the *Delaware* had seized the French schooner *Croyable* off the New Jersey coast, and now the captured vessel also lay at anchor at New Castle.

Setting foot on land for the first time in nearly six weeks, Clark discovered that New Castle was thronged with refugees from the yellow fever epidemic in Philadelphia. He and a companion hired a horse and buggy to take them to the town of Christiana, Delaware, and on to Elkton, Maryland, and Havre de Grace, on the west bank of the Susquehanna. At 11 p.m., they caught a scheduled stagecoach for Baltimore.

In the winter and spring, coach travel in the new republic was a problematic affair. The previous year, Francis Baily had traveled the same road Clark did in one of the typical coaches of the day, a covered buckboard with twelve passengers crammed onto four seats, all facing forward. "The roads, which in general were very bad, would in some places be impassable, so that we would be obliged to get out and walk a considerable distance, and sometimes to 'put our shoulders to the wheel,'" Baily recalled.[38] He wound up walking six of the twelve miles to Havre de Grace through mud, mire, and pig slop up to his ankles. Still, Baily appreciated the enforced democracy of the road: "The member of congress is placed by the side of the shoemaker who elected him; they fraternize together, and converse with familiarity."[39]

Immediately upon his arrival in Baltimore, however, William Clark found himself thrust into democracy run amok. A congressional election was finishing up, marked by unusual vindictiveness. The incumbent, General Samuel Smith, a hero of the Delaware campaign during the Revolution, had opposed the Alien and Sedition Acts passed earlier that year—an unpopular stand in Federalist Baltimore. His opponent, James Winchester, vehemently castigated Smith while inflaming public opinion against the French.

When the polls opened on election day—Monday, October 1, 1798—the usual politicking, which revolved around free whiskey, barbecues, and rallies, soon degenerated into what Clark called "a riot," with sailors fighting in the streets and one man killed. It was "a horrid seen for an American," he lamented.

The next day was no calmer, but by Wednesday Clark could note that "the opposition not so outrageous as yesterday." Clark's political sentiments were clear enough: he was a Virginian, a Jeffersonian, and a Republican. He admired the French, feared the British, and shared the usual backcountry suspicions of President Adams and Northeasterners. When Smith was finally proclaimed the victor, Clark noted with satisfaction that the general was carried through the torchlit streets for several hours on a chair sprouting laurel branches, "with Shouts Drums & Instruments of all kind playing after him."

Clark spent a leisurely week in Baltimore, boarding at Evans's Tavern, the same place newly elected Vice President Jefferson stayed during his trips from Monticello to Philadelphia. One night he went to the theater. Then, on October 9, he rose at 3 a.m. to catch the coach for the Federal City.

The new nation's capital was a work in progress—only one wing of the Capitol had been built, though "the Presidents house was nearly finished." Clark was delighted with Washington City, "the most elegant situation I ever saw." But he proceeded on to Alexandria and Fredericksburg (where he saw another play), and to his brother Edmund's farm in Spotsylvania, Virginia.

Clark was nearing the end of an eight-month journey in the course of which he had descended the largest river system on the continent, sailed in a tall ship through the Gulf of Mexico and up the Atlantic seaboard, and traveled on stagecoach and horseback across the Appalachians. He had covered about 4,400 miles—a distance, as it happens, more than a thousand miles greater than that from St. Louis to the mouth of the Columbia River. Along the way, he had encountered a potpourri of flatboatmen and Indians on the rivers, French Creoles and Spanish officials in New Orleans, British naval officers on the high seas, and crab-cake politicians in Baltimore.

As he traveled from Virginia to Kentucky, Clark continued to write. But while he was penning the last paragraph on the last page in the journal chronicling his trip, his usually flowing handwriting suddenly tightened and cramped:

Stay a few days at Col. Booths & a few <2> days at Redstone, & at
Wheeling, also Chilacothe. Arrive at my father's the 24 of Dec. at
dusk——

He was unable to bring himself to complete the last sentence. What
he could not write was that on the same day he returned to Mulberry
Hill—Christmas Eve, 1798—his mother, Ann Rogers Clark, had died at
the age of sixty-eight.

William was now the de facto head of the Clark household. His father,
John, was in failing health, and George Rogers was increasingly unteth-
ered by alcohol. "I am sorry to inform you that bro G[eorge] has given up
more to that vice which has been so injurious to him," William wrote to
Jonathan.[40]

Drink and debts combined with politics to push the general to the
family's and the nation's periphery. The previous year, alarmed by the
threat of war with France, George Rogers had traveled to Philadelphia to lobby Congress against a conflict with "the generous nation to
which every American owes his liberty."[41] Instead, the Adams Administration demanded that he either resign his honorary commission from
the French government or leave the country. Faced with imminent
arrest under the Alien and Sedition Acts, George Rogers fled across
the Mississippi to seek temporary refuge with his old friends in Spanish
St. Louis.

On July 29, 1799, John Clark died from "a violent pleurisy."[42]
William had helped his father draw up a will that protected the family's
assets largely by leaving nothing to George Rogers that could be seized
by his creditors. William was the principal benefactor. In August 1799,
he reported holdings that included 3,318 acres of Kentucky land, the
Mulberry Hill house, and an adjacent gristmill.

He also owned twenty-three enslaved African-Americans. In January,
George Rogers had sold five slaves to William, including a man named
Lew and a woman named Venos. From his father's estate William received
"one Negro man named York. Also old York, and his Wife Rose, and their
two Children Nancy and Juba."[43] The others were Molly, France, Tener,
Peter, James, Harry, Cupid, Kitt, Pippo, Ben, Pricilla, Easter, and Dafney.

With the acquisition of land and slaves, William Clark joined Kentucky's landed elite. Only one in twelve Kentuckians owned more than a thousand acres, and planter status was reserved for those with twenty or more slaves. Internal migration, largely from Virginia, had swelled the state's population in 1800 to 221,000. In a single decade, the number of slaves in Kentucky quadrupled to 40,000 as slave labor became increasingly important to the state's hemp- and tobacco-based economy. The landed slave owners dominated the new state's constitutional convention that defeated an anti-slavery plank in 1799.

The distinction between a "good master" and a "severe master"—frequently extolled by Kentucky slaveowners as an essential part of their chivalric code—was often lost on the slaves themselves. In December 1800, Fanny's husband, Charles Thruston, was killed by his slave Luke on his plantation near Westport, Kentucky. Twice widowed but still only twenty-seven, Fanny moved back to Louisville with her two O'Fallon boys and her son and daughter with Thruston.

With his parents dead, his brother disgraced, and his sister widowed, William needed to focus even more on family. The following spring, in May 1801, he departed for another prolonged trip on George Rogers's business. This one took him to Colonel John Armstrong's plantation in the bluegrass region and on the Wilderness Road through the Cumberland Gap into southwestern Virginia. Leaving the watershed of the Tennessee River, he then traveled up Virginia's Great Valley and stopped at Fincastle, a colonial village in the knobby hills that had been the seat of Botetourt County when it extended all the way to the Mississippi.

Clark stayed with his friend William Preston, an army captain with whom he had served under Anthony Wayne. Through Preston, Clark met the first family of Fincastle, the Hancocks. George Hancock had been a colonel in the Virginia Line during the Revolution and twice a U.S. congressman (1793–'97). Preston was then engaged to Colonel Hancock's elder daughter, Caroline, and would marry her the following March.

Clark would have met Caroline's younger sister during this visit. She had been christened Judith, but everyone except her father called her Julia. She was just nine: old enough to be remembered, but too young to make much of an impression on thirty-year-old William Clark. Julia's slightly older first cousin Harriet Kennerly had moved in with the Hancocks after her own mother died. A family story, almost certainly apocryphal, holds that William first encountered Julia and Harriet together when he rescued the two girls from a balky pony they were riding along a country road.

George Rogers's business took William as far as Philadelphia after the yellow fever epidemic subsided. On the way, he passed through Washington City twice in July 1801. The newly elected President Thomas Jefferson was still moving in, after the deadlocked election of 1800 finally ended in the House of Representatives in February. As his personal aide Jefferson had hired his Albemarle County neighbor Meriwether Lewis. A friend of Clark's since their days in Wayne's Legion, Lewis had remained in the army and had been promoted permanently to captain—a rank higher than that of Lieutenant Clark when he mustered out.[44]

In April, Lewis had joined the widowed President in the White House, where Jefferson said they were as cozy as "two mice in a church"[45]—Lewis literally so, since he soon shared the spartan space that would become the East Room with a wheel of cheese that weighed 1,235 pounds. On New Year's Day of 1802, the citizens of Cheshire, Massachusetts, presented to Jefferson this "ebullition of the passion of republicanism," as the President dryly called it. For at least two years, White House staff carved away at the ever-aging wheel.[46]

Lewis continued to stay in touch with Clark from the White House. Just a few weeks before Clark's visit to Washington, Lewis had written to "Mr. Clark" asking for help in locating certificates for two parcels of Ohio land due to Lewis's late stepfather, John Marks, as bounty for his service in the Revolution.[47] That item of business, as much as their friendship, might well have brought the two men together once again during the summer of 1801. If it did, neither recorded the event.

Clark returned to Mulberry Hill to face another shock. The family's gristmill on the South Fork of Beargrass Creek had been "burnt to ashes." All the tools critical to the millwright's operation had been destroyed, along with several hundred bushels of grain. "I am fearful nature intended me for the Sport of fortune," William told brother Jonathan, adding darkly that he wondered about "the cause of the moliscous act."[48]

By this time, Jonathan had decided to move from Virginia and join the rest of the family in Louisville. For all their wealth, the Clarks were ever eager to improve their economic opportunities. As was customary, migrating Virginia planters transported their valuable African-American slaves before the family itself moved. In 1792, Kentucky had been admitted to the Union as a slave state and Eli Whitney had invented the cotton gin. Jonathan's investment in human capital was worth far more in Kentucky than in Virginia, where there was already an ample supply of slave laborers.

William traveled east in December 1801 to take charge of transporting Jonathan's slaves. The trip also enabled him to return to Washington City, his third visit in six months. Again, it is not known if Clark saw Lewis or Jefferson, but it would not have been unusual. Jefferson maintained a busy social schedule, typically holding three dinners for a dozen or more people each week. Clark later said that he "became Acquainted" with Jefferson during his visits to Washington in those years.[49]

Meanwhile, the struggle of empires that William had witnessed in New Orleans was becoming more complicated. Spain, tiring of its efforts to keep the Americans at bay on the east side of the Mississippi, had signed a secret agreement with Napoleon to turn Louisiana over to the French. The Spanish hoped that French Louisiana would become a buffer protecting their holdings in Mexico and Texas from the bumptious Americans. The Treaty of San Ildefonso, signed October 1, 1800, was conditional but would become official in two years.

Jefferson, fearful of losing the right of American shipping through New Orleans, instructed his new minister to France, Robert Livingston, to negotiate against the retrocession of Louisiana. Livingston, a New York judge who had administered the oath of office to President Washington, sailed for France in September with his wife and two grown daughters. In December 1801, the same month Clark passed through Washington, Livingston arrived in Paris. He spoke French poorly, but he must have understood when Napoleon reputedly greeted him at court with the words "You have come to a very corrupt world."[50]

While Livingston went to work in corrupt Paris, William Clark was escorting Jonathan's enslaved African-Americans to Kentucky. The party, which included between thirty and thirty-five slaves, traveled across the Appalachians on terrible, muddy roads in January 1802, "the Coldest I have felt this two winters," William wrote when he arrived at Redstone. It must have been even worse for the slaves on this early version of the Trail of Tears. Clark resorted to giving them "Whiskey frequently" to ward off the chill and to keep them moving to Kentucky.[51]

In July 1802, Jonathan and his family arrived and moved into Trough Spring, the house William had built for them on a tract of land near Mulberry Hill. But all of the Clarks were still struggling with George's debts. William had hired lawyers to help with the Bazadone case, which was in court in Vincennes. Although he had been accepting land from George in exchange for both his services and payments, he was now becoming land-rich and cash-poor. William later estimated that in just over a decade, he had paid out $10,000 on his brother's behalf.

In August 1802, shortly after Jonathan's arrival, William began advertising Mulberry Hill for sale. Ironically, the Clark family was finding it expedient to employ the same strategy in microcosm that the Indian nations resorted to throughout years of contact with European-Americans. In order to raise cash and extinguish debts, they sold their land on the cheap.

In Paris, Robert Livingston was getting nowhere, and Jefferson was getting anxious. In February, Jefferson learned in a letter from Rufus King in London that Napoleon had signed treaties with Spain that gave him control of New Orleans, the Mississippi River, and all of Louisiana. Suddenly France had reasserted its presence in the trans-Mississippi West. Even more alarming, over the summer Jefferson had read Alexander Mackenzie's *Voyages from Montreal*, with its bold call for England to occupy the Pacific Northwest. The rival powers seemed to be coiling and encircling Louisiana.

Then, late in 1802, Jefferson learned that the Spanish had closed New Orleans to American shipping, presumably on French orders. He had written, "The day France takes possession of New Orleans . . . we must marry ourselves to the British fleet and nation."[52] That the Anglophobic Jefferson could be driven into the arms of the British meant that he saw the American right of passage through New Orleans as a national priority. Jefferson instructed Livingston to reopen the entire question of New Orleans at the French court. He also made plans to send James Monroe to Paris as an envoy *extraordinaire*, with the authority to spend up to $10 million to purchase New Orleans and the Floridas from the French.

The evolving international threats renewed Jefferson's old dream of sending an exploration party up the Missouri River to the Pacific. Could there be an alternative to New Orleans as a practical route for American commerce? In December 1802 he asked Lewis to estimate the expenses for such an exploration. Moreover, Jefferson made clear that Lewis would be in charge of any such expedition to the Pacific. For Lewis, it must have been a gratifying moment. A decade earlier, at eighteen, he had volunteered his services to the American Philosophical Society for the assignment that ultimately went to André Michaux. That effort had failed; he was determined that this one would not.

Jefferson also moved to shore up American power on the Lower Mississippi. He asked Secretary of War Henry Dearborn to inquire about old Fort Jefferson, the post George Rogers Clark had built at the confluence of the Ohio and the Mississippi in 1780. Since Lieutenant William Clark had recently visited the site in 1795, Dearborn forwarded Jefferson's request to him. But William diplomatically handed over Dearborn's letter to George Rogers for a response.

The older brother replied directly to the President on December 12, 1802: "It would be necessary for us, at least to have a fortress in this point as a Key to the entrance of the Ohio," he told Jefferson in the course of answering his question about the fort. But then he continued on to give Jefferson a thinly veiled suggestion:

> I will with the greatest pleasure give my bro. William every information in my power on this, or any other point which may be to Service to your Administration. He is well qualified almost for any business. If it should be in your power to confur on him any post of Honor and profit, in this Countrey in which we live, it will exceedingly gratify me.[53]

A month later, on January 18, 1803, Jefferson sent his secret message to Congress asking it to appropriate $2,500 for a voyage of commerce to explore "the only line of easy communication across the continent."[54] Congress approved the measure in February, and by March, Lewis was ordering maps for the expedition.

In Paris, meanwhile, the French minister Charles-Maurice de Talleyrand-Périgord reopened the negotiations over New Orleans on Monday, April 11, 1803, by asking Livingston a stunningly direct question: "What will you give for the whole?"[55]

By "the whole," he meant all of Louisiana. Napoleon's costly war with Toussaint L'Ouverture's rebel army in St. Dominique (present-day Haiti) had led him to abandon his ambition for a Caribbean empire. He was ready to cut his losses. Constitutional scruples notwithstanding, the American diplomats scrambled to close the deal. An agreement was reached in Paris on April 29, and on May 2 the Treaty of Cession was signed, turning Louisiana over from France to the United States for $15 million.

The sale of Louisiana was not the only real-estate deal closed that day west of the Appalachians. In Louisville, William Clark sold to Edmund Clark the 111 acres of land surrounding the gristmill that had burned two years earlier. Unable to find an outside buyer, William had turned to his brothers Edmund and Jonathan to help turn Mulberry Hill into a cash asset. On the day the United States government acquired its western lands, William Clark sold some of his.

In the summer of 1803, the future looked bleak for William. He had paid off many of George Rogers's debts, at the cost of bringing himself to the edge of bankruptcy. The interminable lawsuit filed by the Spanish merchant Bazadone was still mired in court in Vincennes. In June, the Clarks' lawyer Henry Hurst told William that Bazadone was willing to settle under his terms: "one-third in cash, one-third in whiskey, and one-third in land."[56] The suit continued.

Sometime in late 1802, William moved across the Ohio to live with George Rogers at Point of Rocks, near the village the older brother had laid out years ago at the foot of the Falls. George Rogers planned to operate a small stone gristmill on Silver Creek and was already talking about building a canal around the Falls on the Indiana side. They brought several slaves with them, at least one of whom, Ben, was technically "free." In fact, this was a legal charade allowing him to be brought into non-slaveholding territory; on gaining his freedom, he was immediately indentured to Clark for thirty years.[57]

The two brothers built their cabin on a hill with sweeping views up and down the river. It was a simple one-story structure of hewn logs with a stone fireplace. Scattered around the place were many books and also the bones of prehistoric animals George Rogers had gathered upriver at Big Bone Lick. A visitor two years later would note that "General Clark has become frail and rather helpless, but there are the remains of great dignity and manliness in his countenance, person and deportment."[58]

On July 17, 1803, William Clark received a letter from Meriwether Lewis. It was not unexpected. Clark had previously asked Lewis to forward to him some of George Rogers's papers in the possession of Senator Stevens Thomson Mason, a nephew of George Mason's. Senator Mason had died in Philadelphia on May 9, 1803, during Lewis's recent visit to the city.

But in his letter, written from Washington, Lewis raised a new topic. It was one he asked to be held "inviolably secret until I see you." He told Clark that Congress had appropriated money for "exploreing the interior of the continent of North America." The President had put him in charge of this "enterprise." In a matter of weeks, he would be leaving Pittsburgh with "a party of recruits eight or nine in number" to begin the journey. They would travel on the Missouri and Columbia rivers as far as the Western Ocean, where they would obtain passage on a trading vessel to bring them home.[59]

Lewis continued on for several hundred words describing his plans for the trip before writing the sentence that Clark must have been hungering for: "If therefore there is anything under these circumstances, in this enterprise, which would induce you to participate with me in it's fatiegues, it's dangers and it's honors, believe me there is no man on earth with whom I should feel equal pleasure in sharing them as with yourself."

For William Clark, the letter was a prayer answered. For twenty years he had heard talk about such a journey—from his own brother, from his army friend John Armstrong, from the French botanist André Michaux, from James Mackay. His father and his brothers had quested for land in the West; now he would as well. In addition to being promoted to the rank of captain in the army, Lewis said, Clark would be the expedition's co-commander, equal "in all respects" to him.

Clark wrote his reply the next day and got straight to the point in his second sentence: "The enterprise &c. is Such as I have long anticipated and am much pleased with—and as my situation in life will admit of my absence the length of time necessary to accomplish such an undertaking I will cheerfully join you."[60]

William Clark was returning to Native America.

CHAPTER FIVE

"OCIAN IN VIEW! O! THE JOY!"

1803–1806

The heroic story of the Voyage of Western Discovery is well known: the perilous journey up the Mississippi and Missouri in 1803–'04, the harrowing crossing of the Rocky Mountains in 1805, the descent of the Snake and Columbia rivers to the Pacific, and the triumphant return in September of 1806. Along the way, the captains and their party overcame astonishing difficulties: hunger, disease, freezing temperatures, boiling rapids, arduous portages, and furious grizzly bears. They described dozens of Indian tribes and countless plants and animals previously unknown to science. It was a remarkable achievement, full of acts of singular courage, determination, and compassion.

For all its mythic stature, however, the expedition was not a self-contained episode. It was intimately connected to William Clark's earlier experiences on the culturally porous borderlands and to the larger agendas of international empire-building. In the three years of the expedition, Clark would use his proven skills as a leader of men as never before. At the time, a troubling new problem emerged that would dominate the rest of his life: the difficulty of managing a vast territory that the United States owned but did not control.

Without waiting for Lewis's reply, Clark at once set to work to recruit the men needed for the Corps of Discovery. His experiences a decade earlier assessing recruits for Wayne's Legion in the Kentucky backcountry would now pay off. On July 24, 1803—one week before his thirty-third birthday—Clark wrote again to say that he had found several men capable of enduring "those labours & fatigues which will be necessary." Aware of Lewis's patrician acquaintances, Clark made a point of noting that he was not inclined to accept any of the "Gentlemens sons" who had come forward, "as they are not accustomed to labor."[1]

Clark's letters caught up with Lewis in Pittsburgh on July 29. Lewis had set out three weeks earlier from Washington City, stopping in Harpers Ferry to pick up his supplies. While awaiting Clark's answer, and worrying that he might say no, Lewis had arranged for a backup: Lieutenant Moses Hooke, from Fort Fayette, the post built out of the ramparts of the old Fort Pitt.

The idea of promoting Lieutenant Hooke to captain apparently never came up. In fact, none of the official correspondence surrounding the preparations for the expedition indicates that Lewis had been authorized to appoint an officer of any rank higher than lieutenant. Yet Clark had outranked Lewis when they served together in the Legion. Lewis may have felt that in order to attract the older and more experienced man back into service, he would have to offer a promotion—and that he could take care of the details after the fact.

In any event, the arrival of Clark's answer in Pittsburgh brought an early end to the putative expedition of Lewis and Hooke. With an almost audible sigh of relief, Lewis responded to Clark, "I feel myself much gratified with your decision." He went on to endorse Clark's decision to "get rid" of the young gentlemen. He did, however, propose that Clark look into hiring an interpreter named John Conner, "residing among the Delleware Indians on White River." Lewis said that he knew Conner well: "We could not get a person better qualified in every respect than he is, and that it will be advisable to spare no pains to get him."[2]

Lewis had hoped to put his fully loaded keelboat on the Ohio by July 20. It had been a dry summer, and by August the river was falling lower than anyone could remember. An anxious Lewis blamed the shipbuilder for the delay, but his efforts to prod the man got nowhere. "I visit him every day," a frustrated Lewis wrote Jefferson, "and endeavour by every means in my power to hasten the completion of the work."[3] Writing later to Clark, he was less temperate, blaming the "unpardonable negligence and inattention of the boat-builders who, unfortunately for me, were a set of most incorrigible drunkards, and with whom, neither threats, in-treaties nor any other mode of treatment which I could devise had any effect."[4] If nothing else, Lewis made it abundantly clear that he did not suffer fools lightly.

By early September 1803, Lewis was finally on his way downriver in his fifty-five-foot keelboat, which he had lightened for shallow waters by moving some cargo to a smaller pirogue. Another load was sent over the mountains by wagon to meet him on the Ohio at the town of Wheeling. Even so, with barely six inches of water flowing over some sandbars, Lewis and his men had to get out and shovel channels into the gravel for the boats to pass. At least once they resorted to hiring a team of oxen to drag the keelboat over a bar.

Who were the men with Lewis? Though he began keeping a daily journal on August 31, Lewis never named a single member of his crew. There was a river pilot, one "T. Moore," whom Lewis paid $70 to take the keelboat to the Falls of the Ohio. Also aboard were eight recruits de-tached from Lieutenant Hooke's command at Pittsburgh. Among the others were most likely two men who stayed all the way to the Pacific—John Colter and eighteen-year-old George Shannon, the youngest mem-ber of the expedition. The rest of the permanent party would be recruited by Clark at Louisville and from the army posts at Fort Massac and Kaskaskia. If Lewis had opinions about these men, he did not state them.

There was a disconcerting incident at the start. On the first day out of Pittsburgh, Lewis stopped to demonstrate his innovative air rifle to a cu-rious crowd and handed it to a spectator. The weapon accidentally dis-charged, and a woman forty yards away fell to the ground with blood streaming from her head. Fortunately, it turned out to be a surface wound, and she quickly revived. In his journal for that day, Lewis metic-ulously noted that the depth of the wound on her head was about a quar-ter of the diameter of the ball.

The keelboat moved on down the river. Travelers usually described the Ohio as an endless green tunnel, with only an occasional pencil-thin col-umn of smoke rising from an isolated cabin to relieve the sameness. In this dry autumn, however, the riverbanks were colorfully lined with buckeye, sourgum, and sassafras trees whose leaves were already reddening. At Wheeling, Lewis bumped into Thomas Rodney, the eccentric younger brother of Caesar Rodney of Delaware, a signer of the Declaration of Independence. In his journal, Rodney told of visiting "Captain Lewess barge" and observing the marvelous air gun "which fired 22 times at one charge."[5]

Rodney found Lewis to be "a stout young man but not so robust as to look able to fully accomplish his mission." Following Jefferson's instructions for secrecy, Lewis had told Rodney only that he planned to ascend the Mississippi River to Lake of the Woods, in present-day Minnesota. Rodney also thought that Lewis's keelboat was too heavy to fight the Mississippi's currents. Nonetheless, Rodney and his companions took "a parting drink and part of a water mellon on board his boat and then bid him adieu." As Lewis disappeared down the river, Rodney worriedly "waited til I saw him over the first ripple."[6]

At Wheeling, Lewis tried to hire a physician, William Ewing Patterson, son of the scientist Robert Patterson, whom he had consulted in Philadelphia before the journey began. But when Patterson did not show up at the dock by 3 p.m., Lewis departed without him.

Downstream at the Falls of the Ohio, meanwhile, Clark was still looking for "the best woodsmen & Hunters . . . in this part of the Countrey."[7] He continued to reject "Gentlemens sons" but had no trouble finding strong candidates among the desirable pool of unmarried men. He ultimately signed up seven Kentuckians who would be essential to the expedition's success: William Bratton, Joseph and Reubin Field, Charles Floyd, George Gibson, Nathaniel Pryor, and John Shields. Clark apparently did not need to mention to Lewis that also at his side throughout the journey would be an eighth man, his enslaved African-American, York.

John Conner, the interpreter that Lewis wanted to hire, turned out to be unavailable. Conner had claimed that Lewis's letter did not reach him in time and that, regardless, he would not sign on for less than $5,000. But, in direct counterpoint to Lewis's high regard for Conner, Clark shrugged him off: "As this man does not speake any of the languages to the Weste of the Mississippi, I do not think the falur in getting him is verry material."[8]

Lewis was pushing himself harder now and had little patience for inattention to details. On September 9, he gave one of his crewmen, a corporal, "a sharp reprimand . . . for his negligence & inattention with respect to the bread."[9] Yet when two men became so drunk one night they had to be helped aboard the keelboat, Lewis noted the incident but inflicted no punishment.

At the mouth of the Muskingum, he passed Marietta, the first white settlement on the "Indian shore" north of the river. The cool weather raised fogs over the meandering riverbed every morning; moving overhead were flocks of passenger pigeons numbering in the thousands. Lewis observed hundreds of squirrels migrating across the river; his Newfoundland, Seaman, swam out and retrieved several. Lewis "fryed" them for dinner; most taverns in the area served up squirrel stews. On September 16, the fog was so thick that Lewis could not set out until 8 a.m. Even then it was slow going. While his men dragged the keelboat and canoes over sandbars, Lewis walked out on the shore to shoot squirrels. "My men were very much fatigued with this days labour," Lewis wrote. "However I continued until nearly dark when we came too on the Virginia shore."[10]

Two days later, Lewis stopped writing in his journal. It was the first of the inexplicable gaps that, with scattered exceptions, would interrupt his journal-keeping for the rest of the expedition. Perhaps he thought that Jefferson's request to keep a journal applied only to the unexplored territories on and beyond the Upper Missouri. Or perhaps he had already decided to turn over the journalizing to Clark and the sergeants.

On a cloudy Friday, October 14, Lewis floated his keelboat into the natural harbor formed by the mouth of Beargrass Creek, within sight of Louisville. In 1803, it was a settlement of some four hundred residents who lived in a scattering of brick, stone, and frame houses. Its prospect, said one traveler, was "truly delightful. The Ohio here is near a mile wide and is bounded on the opposite side by an open champaign country, where there is a fort kept up for the protection of this infant colony, and called Fort Steuben. About two miles lower down on the opposite shore, is Clarkesville, a little village consisting of about twenty houses."[11] Lewis was never far from reminders of the long legacy of the Clark family on the Ohio.

There are no accounts of the moment Lewis and Clark greeted one another to make their partnership a reality. When he heard that Lewis had arrived, Clark would likely have gone above the Falls to meet him at Beargrass Creek. Recent rain showers had raised the river, so the next day the men seized the opportunity to hire a local pilot to take the keelboat through the Falls, a perilous trip through the "Indian chute" on the north side of the river. At low water the terrifying pounding of the rapids was audible for miles. "The torrent begins to roar," Francis Baily wrote earlier, "and loud-sounding rocks to foam with unabated vigour; then the boat twists its unyielding sides to the forces of the compelling current, and the long-accustomed pilot with dismay exerts himself, and stirs on his associates . . . till at last, escaped from all danger, the vessel (like an arrow from the bow) is propelled with great violence from this Charybdis, and in peace once more possesses the wonted gentle course."[12]

Lewis and Clark tied up their boats at Mill Creek, just below Point of Rocks, and spent nearly eleven days wrapping up paperwork and loading supplies. They swore into service the seven Kentuckians recruited by Clark and two men Lewis recruited on the trip downriver. They may have spent some of the time with William's sister Lucy and her husband, William Croghan, at Locust Grove. Or they could have joined Clark's brother Jonathan and his wife, Sally, at nearby Trough Spring, or gone to the Clark family town house in Louisville, or even camped at William and George Rogers's property at Point of Rocks.

Thomas Rodney caught up with the keelboat in Louisville, and on October 17 the two officers returned the social call Rodney had made in Wheeling. "In the evening Captain Lewis and his companion Captain Clark, son of Genl. Clark, called at our boat to see us and took a glass of wine with us and bid us adieu," Rodney wrote, giving Clark a premature promotion. The next day Rodney barely survived his harrowing descent of the Falls: "For the first time I had a dread of wrecking our boat. The rocks are so cragy, the channil so crooked, and the water so furious and rapid that it requires the utmost care and dexterity to avoid the danger." His boat caught on rocks twice before freeing itself and landing below the Falls.[13]

On Saturday, October 26, a cloudy and rainy autumn day, the expedition's keelboat and canoes were ready to leave from Point of Rocks. The departure would have been late in the day; Clark preferred an afternoon "Hudson's Bay" departure, preventing them from proceeding so far downriver that they could not return the next day if they forgot something. Jonathan Clark noted the event in his diary in his typically laconic style: "Rain at Louisville at Clarksville Capt. Lewis and Capt. Wm. Clark set out on a Western tour."[14] Jonathan joined them as far as his son-in-law's house ten miles downstream, where he disembarked. The captains proceeded on. The tour of Lewis and Clark was under way.

The late autumn was the most pleasant season in the Ohio Valley. A golden haze often lay over the river during Indian summer, giving the sun and moon an apparent smokiness near the horizon. Along the banks were increasing numbers of oaks, ashes, walnuts, hickories, hackberries, locusts, persimmons, and dogwoods. As they gazed over this landscape, the assortment of men aboard the keelboat must have realized that they had little in common other than their upbringing in this western country. Most were not soldiers; most were not rivermen. For William Clark, though, this trip was second nature. He had been leading military expeditions down the Ohio for more than a decade. He saw familiar landmarks like the mouth of the Wabash, which he first visited in the miserable winter of 1792–'93, and Fort Massac, where George Rogers Clark had stowed his canoes in 1778 before his march to the Illinois country.

At the junction of the Ohio and the Mississippi, the party spent almost a week surveying the area and visiting the ruins of Fort Jefferson. Several decades later, Charles Dickens found the area to be "a breeding-place of fever, ague, and death . . . a hotbed of disease, an ugly sepulchre, a grave uncheered by any gleam of promise; a place without one single quality, in earth or air or water, to commend it."[15]

Lewis and Clark were delighted to be there. Clark drew a map of the confluence, the first of over one hundred maps he would draw over the next three years. Lewis, who seemed to steady himself by measuring plants and animals, dissected an enormous catfish, recording the weight of its entrails (14 pounds), span of its opened maw (8 inches), and distance between its eyes (13 inches).

Lewis came down with a fever but had shaken it off by the following morning. Throughout the expedition he remained consistently stoical in the face of pain or illness. Not so Clark. The chronic digestive ailments that had plagued him for years returned on November 16. A week later he was still "indisposed," and the men gave him chicken soup, made from *T. c. pinnatus*, or prairie chicken.[16]

Farther upstream, the men received a hospitable welcome from French residents on both sides of the Mississippi. At Cape Girardeau on the "Spanish shore"—the west side of the river—Lewis went to visit Louis Lorimier, a picturesque French Canadian trader whose thick black hair fell down his back to below his knees. Lewis pronounced Lorimier's half-Shawnee daughter Agatha to be "much the most descent looking feemale I have seen since I left the settlement in Kentuckey."[17] Clark, still ill, did not visit Lorimier—perhaps wisely, since brother

George Rogers Clark's militia had looted and burned Lorimier's trading post on the Great Miami River in 1782.

On November 28, 1803, at Kaskaskia on the Illinois side, Lewis wrote only a single sentence for the date in his journal: "This morning left Capt Clark in charge of the Boat."[18] It would be the end of his daily journal-keeping, save a few random entries, for the next sixteen months. That same day, Clark put down the first of the daily entries he would maintain almost without exception until September 1806.

Lewis had decided to leave the party and travel overland by horseback to St. Louis to begin preparations for the trip up the Missouri. Clark was solely in charge of the men, a responsibility he would shoulder almost without respite for the rest of the Voyage of Discovery.

Clark took the keelboat across the river to Ste. Geneviève, the oldest French village west of the Mississippi. He then pushed on to the Illinois country, passing Fort de Chartres and Cahokia, before choosing a site for the expedition's winter camp. It would be on the American side of the Mississippi opposite the mouth of the Missouri. The party immediately began felling trees for their scattering of cabins.

With Lewis spending most of two full months gathering supplies downriver in Cahokia and in St. Louis, it would fall to Clark to assess and train the men. More recruits had been gathered from the U.S. Army companies at Fort Massac and Kaskaskia. The interpreter they hired at Fort Massac, a half-Shawnee named George Drouillard, arrived with eight more soldiers from Tennessee.

Clark's brother George Rogers was still a legend in both St. Louis and the Illinois country because of his victories over the British. His presence was still tangible. The county clerk and United States postmaster in Cahokia was a Canadian-born trader named John Hay (or Hays). Clark needed Hay's help translating documents, interpreting maps, and smoothing relations with local citizens. In an odd coincidence, Hay may have been the son of Jehu Hay, the British major who was second in command under Henry Hamilton at the siege of Vincennes in 1779. This was the same Major Hay whom George Rogers Clark had threatened to summarily execute and later imprisoned in Virginia.

In the culturally blurred world of the borderlands, though, neither alliances nor enmities were permanent. John Hay became an essential supplier and translator for William and his men. There were other similarly unlikely encounters. Late in December, Clark reported that among several Delaware Indians passing by the camp was "a chief whome I saw at Greenville Treaty."[19] He greeted his former enemy by presenting him with a bottle of whiskey. Then, a few months later, Clark visited a nearby encampment of Sauks and Foxes. He discovered traveling with them the infamous Simon Girty, still remembered for the torture and burning of Colonel William Crawford in 1782. Confronted with a man regarded by most of his countrymen as a traitor and murderer, Clark remarked simply that the sixty-two-year-old Girty "has the Rhumertism verry bad."[20]

Clark was not feeling well himself. In January he fell through some ice on a pond and his feet "had frozen to my Shoes."[21] He reported himself "verry unwell" or "verry sick" fourteen of the next twenty-eight days. Nonetheless, he ran the camp almost single-handedly. Of the 141 days in 1804 the expedition was at what is now known as Camp River Dubois, Lewis was on site for only 36 of them. The rest of the time, he was at St. Louis with the Chouteaus or in Cahokia with Hay and the wealthy fur trader Nicholas Jarrot. Clark was sometimes absent, but not nearly as often.

Clark's initial problem was to bring discipline to the untrained men living in the log huts of Camp River Dubois. On Christmas morning he had bolted awake to the sounds of drunken men firing their rifles into the air. Two of them had a fistfight. A week later John Potts brawled with William Werner "after Dark."[22] On New Year's Day of 1804, a group of local farmers visited the camp and embarrassed Clark by outshooting his men in a marksmanship contest.

Things got worse. When both Lewis and Clark went to a ball in St. Louis and left Sergeant John Ordway in charge of the camp, there was a near-mutiny. Reubin Field refused to take orders from Ordway. John Shields, blacksmith and the oldest man in the party, "excited disorder and faction." Several men who claimed they were going hunting instead went to a "neighboring whiskey shop."[23]

The captains returned to St. Louis for the official ceremonies on March 9–10, 1804, transferring Upper Louisiana to the United States. The officials who carried out the transfer personified the world of fungible loyalties on the frontier. One was Brigadier General James Wilkinson, who a few months earlier had presided in New Orleans at the formal transfer of Louisiana from France to the United States. Wilkinson was still on the Spanish payroll. Another was Captain Amos Stoddard, a Connecticut Yankee who was commander of the U.S. Army artillery company assigned to St. Louis for the transfer. Stoddard would stand in for both France and the United States at the ceremonies in the market square. On March 9, the Spanish flag was lowered and the French tricolor raised. Then, on March 10, the French flag came down and the U.S. flag flew for the first time. When it was over, the new republic had taken possession of the entire western watershed of the Mississippi.

The most prominent absentees at the Three Flags Ceremony were the Indians who actually controlled the lands being transferred. The recorded population of Upper Louisiana in 1803 was 10,350 Euro-Americans and slaves. But the unrecorded population was at least 100,000 Indians belonging to dozens of tribes who dominated the rivers and plains throughout the West. Four thousand people lived in the single agricultural complex at the Mandan-Hidatsa villages, more than in the American capital of Washington City.

The Indians had long done business with the French and the Spanish and were not eager to disrupt their established monopoly of the fur trade. Earlier that week, when Lewis and Clark had entered the quarters of the Spanish commandant, they passed a departing band of Sauk and Fox Indians. Among them was a charismatic young warrior named Makataimeshekiakiak by his people but whom the whites would later come to call Black Hawk. Many years later, Black Hawk would recall that moment with sadness "because we had always heard bad accounts of the Americans from Indians who lived near them!—and we were sorry to lose our Spanish father, who had always treated us with great friendship."[24] Within weeks, Stoddard wrote to Henry Dearborn that the Sauks "certainly do not pay that respect to the United States which is entertained by the other Indians—and in some instances they have assumed a pretty elevated tone."[25]

While Clark was away for the Three Flags Ceremony, the disciplinary problems again boiled over. Shields had opposed orders and threatened Ordway's life; Whitehouse had fought with "F" (Field? Frazer? Floyd?); Newman and Collins had fought each other; either Colter or Collins had loaded his gun to shoot Ordway.

In light of the infractions, Clark needed to send a clearer message than a simple detachment order, no matter how stern. On March 29, he and Lewis convened a court-martial of Colter, Frazer, and Shields. The next day Clark loaded two pistols, just in case of trouble, before reading the verdict before the drawn-up corps. The charges were dismissed, and

Shields and Colter "promised to doe better in future."[26] The light sentence may have reflected Clark's earlier experience of "what a little fault will ruin an officer in the Army." But it had its effect. Shields and Colter would prove to be two of the most valuable members of the expedition.

With the arrival of spring, Clark put the finishing touches on the expedition's logistics. He made the final selection of the men for the permanent party, organizing them into three squads under Sergeants Floyd, Ordway, and Pryor. The permanent party bound for the Pacific would travel in the masted keelboat, which Clark had refitted along the lines of George Rogers Clark's Ohio River galley, adding a flip-up breastworks and mounting a bronze swivel gun on the bow and two buckshot-firing blunderbusses astern. Fully loaded, the fifty-five-foot-long keelboat could carry a cargo of 12 to 14 tons. Six other men and the temporary *engagé* boatmen would bring up two flat-bottomed pirogues, one white and one red. They would eventually decide to spend the first winter at the Mandan Villages, near today's Bismarck, North Dakota. Since the keelboat was too large to proceed farther upstream, Corporal Richard Warfington and a small squad would return with it in the spring to St. Louis.

The men, meanwhile, were training and improving their marksmanship. On April 28 Clark noted with satisfaction that "Several Country men Came to win my mens money, in doing So lost all they had with them."[27]

On April 21, Lewis and Clark went to St. Louis to help Pierre Chouteau arrange to take a party of Osage chiefs to visit Washington City. Four days later, Clark returned by himself to Camp River Dubois to work out the best ways to load the keelboat to face the Missouri's powerful current. Then, on May 8, John Colter came up from St. Louis with a letter from Lewis. It contained Clark's army commission, but it was not for the expected grade of captain in the Corps of Engineers—which the War Department considered "improper"—but rather for the rank of second lieutenant in the artillery.[28] In his accompanying letter, Lewis vowed, almost through clenched teeth, that "it will be best to let none of our party or any other persons know any thing about the grade. You will observe that the grade has no effect upon your compensation, which by G—d, shall be equal to my own."[29]

Clark was obviously disappointed. Yet he agreed to keep his misgivings to himself and to keep his real rank a secret from the men. At camp the next morning, it was back to business as usual. Clark loaded the keelboat, and as twenty oars pulled into the water, it nosed out on the Mississippi for its first trial run.

The relationship of Lewis and Clark had passed its first test. Lewis may have suggested the pretext of Clark's captaincy because it played to both of their strengths. Lewis needed Clark to do the onerous duty of marshaling the men, in which Clark was far more experienced. Lewis would thus be free to invest his time in Indian negotiations and scientific work. The incident also revealed one of the keys to Clark's character. He was willing to compromise in the interest of harmony, without rancor, if he received the recognition he thought was due him. Years later, Clark carefully made clear in the published journals that he and Lewis were equal in every respect during the journey.

By the rainy morning of May 14, 1804, Clark and his men were "fixing for a start." A scattering of local country people — "mail and feemail," Clark wrote — arrived to watch. At 4 p.m. — his usual departure time — William Clark led the three boats of the expedition of western discovery across the Mississippi and into the Missouri River.[30]

The men had begun to bond with Clark during their training at Camp River Dubois. Lewis was frequently absent; if there was a problem, the person to go to for an answer was Clark. At St. Charles, where the expedition stopped to await Lewis's arrival overland from St. Louis, Clark asserted his authority even more convincingly. When three men disobeyed orders and left camp to carouse in the town, Clark convened another court-martial. This time the punishment would get everyone's attention: John Collins received fifty lashes across his bare back at sunset in front of the entire party.

Most of the men barely knew Lewis and had not seen him at all for more than a month. On the expedition's first full day on the Missouri after leaving St. Charles, Lewis left Clark to handle the boats while he walked on the shore, a habit he would continue for the rest of the journey. On the second day out, he was again ashore when, while climbing a bluff above Tavern Cave, he stumbled and nearly plunged to his death.

Like Clark, Lewis was a physically strong six-footer. But he carried himself in a rigid, ungainly manner that was noticed by those who met him. "His person was stiff and without grace," recalled his cousin Peachy Gilmer, a childhood friend, "bowlegged, awkward, formal and almost without flexibility."[31]

In the early months of the journey, the two forces that bound the men of the expedition were the Missouri's current and the captains' authority. Both were getting stronger.

The current of the Missouri River during the spring was faster and more dangerous than that of the Mississippi. It was an immensely powerful brown torrent that could cave in entire riverbanks. Almost without warning, the river could send the heavily laden keelboat wallowing and spinning against treacherous snags. In the worst stretches, the current was strong enough to snap the rawhide ropes, or cordelles, the men used to pull the boats upstream. At one point the keelboat's mast snapped, and at another a storm drove the boat up against an island. Had not the men leaped in unison to one side, pulling on the anchor cable, Clark wrote, it would have "dashed to peces in an Instant."[32]

As the officer in charge of operations, Clark sent sentinels and scouts ahead every time they pulled ashore, and posted guards around the clock. He followed Baron von Steuben's military procedures, setting up an encampment of canvas tents (while they lasted) and at least one bison-hide tipi. On June 29, Collins and Hall were again court-martialed, this time for drunkenness. Clark announced the verdict: fifty lashes for Hall, one hundred lashes for Collins. Two weeks later, the other blacksmith, Alexander Hamilton Willard, was found guilty of sleeping on guard duty: he received one hundred lashes on his bare back, divided over four successive days. Another man, Moses Reed, deserted in August. Clark bluntly told a search party that "if he did not give up Peaceibly to put him to Death."[33] They brought Reed back to run the gauntlet four times through the entire party, who flailed him with switches and ramrods.

Several Canadian traders who encountered the party around this time returned to St. Louis with a report that the men "were much dissatisfied & complained of too regid a discipline."[34] But after John Newman received seventy-five lashes for uttering expressions of a "highly criminal and mutinous nature," the discipline seemed to take hold. No further corporal punishments were inflicted for the remaining two years of the expedition.[35]

During the journey upriver to their winter quarters at Fort Mandan, near present-day Washburn, North Dakota, the captains seemed to share equally the confidence of the men. An indication can be found in the journals of the enlisted men, which offer the only ongoing descriptions of the expedition other than those made by the captains themselves. Three sergeants—Charles Floyd, Patrick Gass, and John Ordway—kept journals, as did one private, Joseph Whitehouse. Floyd's journal ended prematurely with his death on August 20, 1804, and Gass's journal was extensively rewritten and paraphrased by his original publisher in 1807.

The journals of Ordway and Whitehouse thus provide the most reliable accounting of the captains' activities, put down in real time. The number of times each captain was mentioned by name reveals something of their respective roles during the expedition. During the upriver trip to Fort Mandan, for example, Lewis appeared to be slightly more prominent than Clark: Ordway mentioned Lewis by name 64 times and Clark 61 times in 1804. Whitehouse recorded them similarly: Lewis, 69; Clark, 56.

But after the expedition turned west from Fort Mandan in April 1805, there was a subtle shift toward Clark. In the full year of 1805, Ordway mentioned Clark 137 times, Lewis 112 times. Whitehouse wrote about Clark 223 times, and Lewis 220. On closer examination, the journals reveal more striking differences. In May 1805, Ordway singled out Clark 28 times and Lewis just 5 times. Whitehouse similarly wrote about Clark 32 times, Lewis just 6 times.

What was happening in May 1805? After leaving Fort Mandan, the expedition was traveling for the first time into lands previously unmapped by Euro-Americans. Clark's navigational abilities and experience on rivers were more important than ever. Carrying out Jefferson's instructions, Lewis continued to walk on the shore, absorbed as always in recording and measuring flora and fauna. If the men saw Clark as their hands-on boss, it is predictable that they would look first to him—just as a private's top sergeant looms larger in his daily thoughts than any general.

A detailed examination of Whitehouse and Ordway's journals, however, reveals another reason for Clark's preeminence. The expedition had entered the high plains of Montana, rich with big game, and their most active hunter was William Clark.

Here are entries from a single week of Ordway's journal:

May 2: "Capt. Clark & one of the hunters Shot 3 beaver"
May 3: "Capt. Clark . . . killed an Elk"
May 5: "Capt. Clark . . . killed a verry large bair"

May 6: "Capt. Clark killed an Elk"
May 7: "Capt. Clark and one hunter . . . killed 2 buffaloe"
May 9: "Capt. Clark killed 2 buffaloe"

These entries were not atypical. During a single outing on May 11, Clark killed two bison, two deer, and a beaver. In that same month he also killed a bighorn sheep and a wolf (with his espontoon), and wounded a mountain lion.

Perhaps the most remarkable of Clark's hunting exploits was his Missouri River excursion of February 4–13, 1805. Cold and desperate for food during a brutal winter when temperatures sank as low as –40° Fahrenheit, Clark set out on foot with sixteen men, three horses, and two sleighs. They "Descended nearly 60 miles" on the ice-covered river, which was heaving, thawing and refreezing all the way.[36] On the second day Clark "broke thro the ice and got my feet and legs wet." The bottoms of his feet blistered—"walking is painfull to me"—but he pressed on.[37] They killed forty deer, nineteen elk, and three bison bulls, many of them too thin to eat. They packed the meat back on sleighs, only to have one of the return parties accosted by more than a hundred Lakotas, who stole two horses and burned the meat.

If Clark was ever disappointed with his men, he never let it show. The only exception was for the expedition's feckless translator, Toussaint Charbonneau. Descending the Columbia River in October 1805, Clark noted that he had "Some words with Shabono about his duty."[38] For Clark, that was as much irritation as he ever would admit. Lewis was less mild in his criticism:

June 19, 1805: "I rebuked Sharbono severely."
August 11, 1805: "I . . . could not forbare abraiding [Shields and Drouillard] a little for their want of attention and imprudence on this occasion."
August 25, 1805: "I could not forbear speaking to [Charbonneau] with some degree of asperity on this occasion."
April 19, 1806: "I reprimanded [Willard] more severely for this piece of negligence than had been usual with me."

Lewis was uncomfortable with his temper and preferred to think of his outbursts as exceptional. Clark was more matter-of-fact. The difference is revealed in their reporting of the same incident. In August 1805, when Clark's party was coming up the Beaverhead, Charbonneau struck his wife Sacagawea at dinner. Clark wrote only, "I checked our Interpreter for Strikeing his woman at their Dinner." But Lewis, who did not witness the episode, reported it this way: "This evening Charbono struck his Indian Woman for which Capt. C. gave him a severe repremand."[39] What Clark called an almost routine "check" generated in Lewis a much harsher characterization.

Lewis's temper was never far below the surface. In his letter to Clark reporting on his lieutenant's commission, Lewis had gone on to erupt angrily over the activities of the fur trader Manuel Lisa and his partner François Marie Benoit: "Damn Manuel and triply Damn Mr. B. They give me more vexation and trouble than their lives are worth . . . I think them both great scoundrels . . . These gentlemen (no I will scratch it out) these puppies, are not unacquainted with my opinions."[40]

Lewis never hesitated to make known his opinions. At Fort Mandan, the captains encountered Charles McKenzie, a Scottish trader from the British North West Company. McKenzie recorded in his journal the only written impression of the expedition from an outsider. He recalled that the Americans "always treated us with civility and kindness." But, he went on, "it is true, Captain Lewis could not make himself agreeable to us. He could speak fluently and learnedly on all subjects, but his inveterate disposition against the British stained, at least in our eyes, all his eloquence. Captain Clarke was equally well informed, but his conversation was always pleasant, for he seemed to dislike giving offence unnecessarily."[41]

While Lewis was almost eerily oblivious to physical pain—both his and that experienced by others—Clark was sensitive to both. While the men were dragging their canoes up the present Beaverhead River, Clark observed that the task was "emencely laborious men much fatigued and weakened by being continually in the water . . . complain very much of the emence labour they are obliged to undergo & wish much to leave the river." But Clark evidently found a way to empathize, since, as he noted, "I passify them."[42]

Clark's ability to communicate compassion was even more palpable during the last hours of Sergeant Floyd, who apparently died of a ruptured appendix. Floyd "Died with a great deel of Composure," Clark wrote. "Before his death he Said to me, 'I am going away. I want you to write me a

letter . . . This Man at all times gave us proofs of his firmness and Deturmined resolution to doe Service to his Countrey and honor to himself."[43]

Lewis had fewer tools of empathy at his disposal. As the men pushed
and pulled their canoes through the Gates of the Mountains, below today's Helena, Montana, he wrote, "I occasionally encourage them by assisting in the labour of navigating the canoes, and have learned to push a
tolerable good pole."[44] Unable to relate enough to his men to "passify"
them, Lewis did the only thing he could. He joined them.

Clark suffered a variety of physical ailments throughout the journey
and did not hesitate to write about them:

> June 3, 1804: "I have a bad Cold with a Sore throat."
> October 22, 1804: "Rhumetism in my neck . . . I could not move."
> January 4, 1805: "I am very unwell the after part of the Daye."
> September 21, 1805: "I am very sick today and puke which re-
> live me."
> October 6, 1805: "I am taken verry unwell with a paine in the
> bowels & stomach."

Lewis almost never mentions any bodily suffering or pain. When he
was severely wounded by Pierre Cruzatte in a hunting accident, he
passed "a very uncomfortable night" but was soon back to keeping the
world under control by measuring it. On July 29, 1805, Lewis measured
an anthill "10 or 12 inches high."

In his final journal entry, written while lying on his stomach recovering from the gunshot wound, he devoted several hundred words to a pin
cherry, *Prunus pensylvanica*, noting its branch pattern, bark, "peteolate"
leaf, fruit ("globular berry about the size of a buckshot"), stems ("a separate celindric flexable branch peduncle"), and taste ("agreeable ascid
flavour").[45] The discipline required for such attention to detail was rendered poignant by an entry written by Sergeant Ordway two days later:
"Capt. Lewis fainted as Capt. Clark was dressing his wound."[46]

Thomas Jefferson had made it unmistakably clear to Lewis and Clark
that their foremost objective was to find "the direct water communication from sea to sea formed by the bed of the Missouri & perhaps the

Oregon."[47] But in his detailed letter of instructions to Lewis, Jefferson devoted more words to the Indian nations than to any other topic. Not only was Jefferson intensely curious about the tribes, he wanted Lewis and Clark to wean their loyalties away from the despised British traders and enfold them into the orbit of American trade and commerce.

The captains' Indian diplomacy began not on the Lower Missouri, but before they left Camp River Dubois. Indians traveling west from the Illinois River and the Upper Mississippi frequently crossed to the Missouri River on a neck of land just above St. Louis called Portage des Sioux. In late March 1804, Lewis and Clark went to Portage des Sioux with the area's two leading French Creole traders, Auguste Chouteau and his brother-in-law Charles Gratiot. Their goal was to stop a war party of more than one hundred Kickapoos from attacking the nearby Osages, thereby disrupting the profitable fur trade.

Clark had always felt at ease with Indians. He and his brothers, like Daniel Boone, had adopted many of the Indians' ways: they dressed like Indians, hunted like Indians, and knew the vocabulary and rituals of Indian diplomacy. Not surprisingly, the negotiation succeeded. Two days later Clark noted: "The Kickapoos has gone home."[48]

Other tribal negotiations would be more difficult. In September 1804, the expedition came within a heartbeat of being entirely wiped out by a band of the Lakota tribe, sometimes called "Teton Sioux" by the whites. On their way up the Missouri, the captains had faithfully followed the established diplomatic rituals Clark first witnessed at Fort Greenville a decade earlier. A conspicuous display of American power—an armed parade, firings of the air gun—would be followed by speeches and presents.

Armed by both British and American traders, the seminomadic Brulé bands known collectively as the Lakotas were the leading power-brokers on the Missouri. Jefferson had cautioned Lewis about "their immense power" and urged him to make "a friendly impression."[49] In their meeting with the Brulé bands near present-day Pierre, South Dakota, the captains went through their rituals and presented medals to the three principal chiefs—Black Buffalo (Un-tongar-Sarbar), The Partisan (Tortohongar), and Buffalo Medicine (Tar-ton-gar-wa-ker).

Then everything went wrong. Invited aboard the keelboat and offered a quarter glass of whiskey, the Partisan seemed to affect drunkenness.

Clark escorted the chiefs back to their camp on a pirogue. But as they disembarked, several warriors grabbed the anchor cable and the mast, while The Partisan heaped insults on Clark. "His justures were of Such a personal nature I felt my Self Compeled to Draw my Sword," Clark wrote.[50]

Seeing Clark brandish his sword on the shore, Lewis ordered his men on the keelboat under arms and swiveled its bow cannon to face the Indians. The warriors on the bank surrounded Clark and notched their arrows. Everyone froze. Anticipating devastating violence, Black Buffalo then interceded and ordered the young men away from the pirogue. Clark angrily "felt my Self warm & Spoke in verry positive terms."[51] Ordway saw it slightly differently from the boat: "Capt. Clark used moderation with them told them that we must and would go on."[52]

The first crisis of the journey had been narrowly averted. It is impossible to know what would have happened had the places of the captains been reversed—if the more measured Clark had been in the keelboat and the volatile Lewis surrounded by warriors on the shore. Both Black Buffalo and Clark were experienced in warfare and both chose a course of moderation. Lewis had never seen combat. Before the expedition began, Jefferson's Attorney General, Levi Lincoln, had worried about Lewis's headstrong nature. "From my ideas of Capt. Lewis," he warned Jefferson, "he will be much more likely, in case of difficulty, to push too far, than to rec[e]de too soon."[53]

The expedition proceeded upriver to the villages of the Arikaras, the first of the tribes of the High Plains. Clark pronounced them to be "durtey" and "pore," a judgment he consistently made about Indians who had had previous contacts with white men.[54] It would become an article of faith with Clark that contact with Europeans inevitably corrupted native peoples; only the relatively isolated Salishes, Shoshones, and Nez Perces escaped this judgment.

The captains' own journals were beginning to reveal more of the differences between the ways they perceived the world. On the cold morning of October 16, 1804, when the temperature dropped below freezing, Lewis wrote in his journal for the first time in more than a month. In an eerily clinical entry, he described his examination of a hibernating poorwill that he had captured alive: "I run my penknife into it's body under the wing and completely distroyed it's lungs and heart—yet it lived upwards of two hours this fanominon I would not account for unless it proceeded from the want of circulation of the blo[o]d . . . it's weight 1 oz 17 Grains Troy."[55]

Clark was more fascinated with human beings. Like his older brother George Rogers, he was especially drawn to the customs and nature of the tribes. After the expedition arrived at the Mandan villages in November 1804, Clark found himself living in close proximity to Indians for the first time in his life. The complex of earth lodges spread in five villages along the Missouri was the information center of the northern plains. Every fall, hundreds of nomadic peoples gathered to participate in a trading network that reached across much of the interior of the continent. Flint implements from the Knife River villages have been found as far away as Florida.

On the way up the river, Lewis and Clark took extensive notes about the tribes they encountered. During the 146 nights they spent at Fort Mandan, they filled in their information by talking to chiefs like Shehek-shote, Black Cat (Posecopsahe), and Black Moccasin (Omp-se-ha-ra). The result was the written "Estimate of the Eastern Indians," which Clark prepared over the winter and shipped back to Jefferson when the keel-boat returned to St. Louis in April 1805.[56] This remarkable document, in Clark's hand, bears evidence of both Lewis's attention to detail and Clark's facility for spatial organization. It distills an enormous amount of information into seven sheets of paper, which, when pasted together, make a single table about 35 inches by 28 inches. Today we would call it a spreadsheet.

In the "Estimate," Clark painstakingly recorded information about seventy-two different tribal groups, describing in each case their various names, populations, languages, number and location of villages, favored trade goods, types of pelts they hunted, territories they claimed, enemies, and estimated dollar value of their annual trade at the prices then prevailing at both St. Louis and Mickilimackanac. In essence, it was an early-nineteenth-century marketing report.

The grids and tables of the "Estimate" reflected a heroic effort by a man of the Enlightenment, convinced that the world was ultimately knowable, to arrange a complex culture to his liking—orderly, timeless, and predictable. However, the underlying realities on the northern plains were not static and could not be contained in grids. Rather, the size, strength, and relationships of the tribes were constantly changing, influenced by epidemics of disease, evolving trade patterns with Europeans, and shifting allegiances based more on loyalties to villages than to tribes.

Clark's assessment of the Lakotas testified to his frustration with a culture that would not conform to his careful gridwork. The Sioux, he (or perhaps Lewis, originally) wrote with palpable emotion, "are the vilest miscreants of the savage race, and must ever remain the pirates of the Missouri, until such measures are pursued, by our government, as will make them feel a dependence on its will for their supply of merchandise."[57]

When the expedition sent the keelboat back and moved west from Fort Mandan in April 1805, Clark knew more about the Indian nations west of the Mississippi than any living American. He had personally met with twelve of the thirty tribes living on the Great Plains and would eventually encounter a total of fifty different tribes. Yet, as he proceeded into territory uncharted by whites, much of the information he would now need would come from the last two people to join the party—the troublesome French Canadian translator Toussaint Charbonneau and his Lemhi Shoshone wife, whom the explorers called *Sâh-câh-gâh, we â.*

Clark noticed Sacagawea early on. On January 11, 1805, he commented, "the inturpeter oldst wife Sick." She was most likely Sacagawea, who was eight months pregnant at the time. A week later, he ordered York to give her "Some froot stewed and tee" in order to ease a misunderstanding between two interpreters.[58] During Clark's hunting trip down the river, Lewis reported the birth of Sacagawea's son, Jean Baptiste. By the time of the expedition's departure, Clark had become acutely aware of Sacagawea's value as "interpretress" to the Shoshones, the tribe from whom they hoped to buy horses to cross the mountains.[59]

The captains lived in close quarters with the Charbonneau family, sharing the same hide tipi during their encampments. Unlike Clark, Lewis was often dismissive of Sacagawea—"if she has enough to eat and a few trinkets to wear I believe she would be perfectly content anywhere"—and seemed unable to perceive her emotions.[60] Clark took her more seriously. When Clark walked on the shore, it was frequently with Charbonneau and Sacagawea, who would bring him native foods: "In my walk the Squar found & brought me a bush something like the Current, which she said bore a delicious froot."[61]

In mid-June 1805, when Lewis pushed ahead of the party to locate the Great Falls of the Missouri, Clark was preoccupied with Sacagawea, who was apparently suffering from a pelvic inflammation:

June 11, 1805: "The Indian woman verry Sick. I blead her which appeared to be of great service to her."

June 12: "The interpreters wife verry Sick So much so that I move her into the back part of our Covered part of the Perogue which is Cool."

June 14: "The Indian woman complaining all night & excessively bad this morning—her case is Somewhat dangerous."

June 16: "The Indian woman verry bad, & will take no medisin what ever, until her husband finding her out of her Senses, easily prevailed on her to take medison, if she dies it will be the fault of her husband as I am now convinced."[62]

Sacagawea's eventual recovery was due less to Clark's ministerings than to the party's fortuitous arrival at a mineral-rich spring, from which Lewis brought her water.

Clark continued to think of Sacagawea and her child with the kind of familiar affection that led to nicknames. In Clark's journal and letters, Sacagawea became "Janey" and her son Jean Baptiste became "Pomp" or "Pompy." Both diminutives were given to white children and adult slaves in Virginia and Kentucky.[63] When Clark recorded the preferences of the party's members for the location of their camp on the Pacific Coast in the winter of 1805–'06, he dryly noted, "Janey in favour of a place where there is plenty of Potas [wapato]."[64] Lewis recorded no similar endearments for Sacagawea and sometimes referred to her son as "it."

Sacagawea reciprocated Clark's kindness. During the onslaught of ceaseless rains on the Columbia's estuary, Clark became almost despondent:

November 22, 1805: "O! how horriable is the day"
November 28, 1805: "O! how disagreeable is our Situation during this dreadfull weather"

On November 30, Sacagawea found a way to thank Clark for his ministrations during her illness: "The Squar, gave me a piece of Bread to day made of Some flower She has Cearfully kept for her child." But the weather had the last word, since the gift "has unfortunately got wet."[65]

On Christmas Day of 1805, the captains exchanged presents with each other and the party. Clark received "a fleece hosrie Shirt Draws and Socks" from Lewis, a pair of "mockersons" from Whitehouse, and a small Indian basket from Silas Goodrich. From Sacagawea, who could have known little of what this day meant to white men, Clark received "two Dozen white weazils tails," a present given to honor bravery and hunting skill.[66]

Lewis had trained under Benjamin Rush in Philadelphia to be the expedition's doctor. On the westbound journey he provided medical care for the men, dispensing Rush's purgative pills (sometimes called "Thunderbolts"), treating sores and abscesses, and occasionally drawing blood for various ailments. At Fort Mandan, Lewis amputated the frostbitten toes of an Indian boy. But after the expedition crossed the Continental Divide and entered the Columbia Plateau, Clark assumed more and more of the medical duties. Some of his cures seemed to produce amazing results. A man treated for a sore knee, Lewis observed, "soon after recovered and has never ceased to extol the virtues of our medicines and the skill of my friend Capt. C. as a physician."[67] At their winter quarters on the Pacific Coast, Clark gave eyewashes and various cures to visiting Clatsop and Chinook Indians, often in return for food and goods.

By the time of the return trip in 1806, everything had changed. Clark had cemented a formidable reputation as a medicine man, which preceded the party. Indians rode all day to see him. As many as forty or fifty patients greeted Clark every morning. "It was agreed between Capt. C. and myself that he should attend the sick as he was their favorite physician," Lewis acknowledged.[68] A Nez Perce chief who had not walked in five years was carried in on a blanket and placed before Clark. After treating him unsuccessfully for two weeks, the captains lowered him into a sweat pit. By the end of the month he was moving his hands and legs again.

Clark recognized that some of his cures were "deception" carried on in exchange for trade. But, desperate for horses to get them back over the mountains, he reasoned, "We take Care to give them no article which Can possibly injure them, and in many Cases can administer & give Such Medicine & Sergical aid as will effectually restore in Simple cases."[69]

The captains' warm relations with the Nez Perces, especially during the expedition's monthlong layover on the Clearwater River while waiting to recross the Bitterroot Mountains in May and June 1806, contribute to one of the persistent stories about the expedition: that Clark left behind one or more red-haired children with the tribes.

That the enlisted men would consort with native women was a given. Anticipating it, the captains had carried along mercury and other medicines for sexually transmitted diseases. York was especially valued by native women for the magical powers of his skin color, and soldiers of higher rank gained special sexual status as well. The party's top sergeant, John Ordway, precipitated a frightening episode at Fort Mandan when an Indian woman was beaten and stabbed by her husband after she slept with him. To defuse the situation and placate the angry husband, Clark ordered that "no man of the party Should touch his Squar, or the wife of any Indian" and then counseled the man "to take his Squar home and live happily together in future."[70]

What about the captains themselves? Many natives saw sexual relations with the two white chiefs as a way of acquiring their spiritual power. When the powerful Lakotas "offered us women, which we did not except," the Indians saw the white men's refusal as a public affront to the entire tribe.[71] A day later, Clark reported, "they again offered me a young woman and wish me to take her & not Dispise them." Somewhat ambiguously, he then added, "I wavered the Subject."[72]

As the captains traveled farther up the Missouri, the overtures continued. With the Arikaras, Clark observed that the "hansom young Squars . . . peresisted in their civilities."[73] Lewis, who concealed his own sexual feelings behind a self-consciously ornate vocabulary, noted upon meeting the Shoshones that months of abstinence had made the young men in their group "very polite to those Tawney damsels."[74]

The captains had difficulty understanding that among the Indians, sexual relations were a normal and even necessary part of diplomatic and commercial exchanges. When a Clatsop man named Cus-ka-lah offered women to Lewis and Clark on Christmas Eve of 1805, the captains "declined axcepting of, which displeased the whole party verry much—the female part appears to be highly disgusted at our refuseing to axcept of their favours &c."[75]

Five years later, Clark still remembered that episode or a similar incident: "A Claptsop whom I had cured of some disorder brought me out of gratitude his sister—who was anxious to join in her brothers good intentions. She staid two or three days in next room with Chabono's wife. She was quite mortified at being refused," though she declined the overtures of the other men.[76]

The Salishes said that Clark was not so resolute on the outbound journey. In 1890, the Indian agent Peter Ronan talked to an elderly Salish Indian named Ochanee who said that as a girl she had witnessed the arrival of the expedition in 1805 at Ross's Hole in the Bitterroot Valley:

> Captain Clarke took unto himself a Flathead [Salish] woman. One son was the result of this union, and he was baptized after the missionaries came to Bitter Root valley and named Peter Clarke. This half-breed lived to a ripe age, and was well known to many of Montana's early settlers. He died about six years ago [1884] and left a son, who was christened at St. Mary's mission to the name of Zachariah and pronounced Sacalee by the Indians. The latter has a son three years of age, whom it is claimed by the Indians, in direct decent, to be the great grandson of the renowned Captain Clarke.[77]

The captains returned for their second visit with the Nez Perces on the Clearwater River in present-day Idaho in May 1806. While waiting for the snows to clear higher on the Lolo Trail, the members of the expedition passed some of their happiest weeks of the journey. In the warming weather of spring, the captains described feasting, fiddling, dancing, horse races, footraces, quoit-pitching, and rifle shooting. During that time, the captains were also desperate to acquire more horses, anxiously trading everything they could, including buttons cut from their uniforms. At their earlier camps, Lewis and Clark had devoted hundreds of words to describing sexual and gender customs of the natives. But, like Conan Doyle's curious incident of the dog in the nighttime, the curious thing on the Clearwater was what did not happen: on matters of sexuality, the captains suddenly fell silent.[78]

Oral histories of the Nez Perces assert that a yellow-haired son called Tzi-kal-tza was born to Clark and a Nez Perce woman named Daytime Smoke (Halahtookit).[79] This child, called "Clark," is said to have lived long enough to father a daughter named Mary Clark, participate in the Nez Perce War of 1877, and later die on an Oklahoma reservation.

It remains difficult to say with certainty that Clark fathered this child. He was not the only blue-eyed, fair-skinned male in the Corps of Discovery. But given the opportunity of living for a month among the "handsom women" of the Nez Perces, and given the desperate need to exchange good relations for horses, it would have been unusual only if this most agreeable of captains remained celibate.[80]

The captains went up the Missouri armed with the tools needed to impose the order of their civilization on an unknown world. They had a sextant, an octant, a chronometer, compasses, a two-pole surveyor's chain, and a "log line reel" for measuring the speed of the current. They also carried with them all of Jefferson's assumptions about the geography of the West; it would be a mirror image of the East, a place of great rivers flowing to the ocean from low-lying mountains near the coast. Just as the Ohio rose within a short distance of the headwaters of the rivers leading to the Atlantic, so, too, the Missouri's headwaters must lie within a short portage of a great river draining into the Pacific.

Albert Gallatin had asked Nicholas King, the government's surveyor in Washington City, to prepare a map for the explorers in 1803. It would be an amalgam of previous maps by Vancouver, Cook, Mackenzie, Delisle, David Thompson, Andrew Ellicott, and Aaron Arrowsmith. Lewis and Clark had spent the winter at Camp River Dubois studying King's map and new ones given to them by St. Louis fur traders like the Chouteaus and Antoine Soulard. Their chief field cartographer would be William Clark.

Clark described a land he thought was destined to be occupied and controlled. On June 28, at the high ground near the mouth of the Kansas River near present-day Kansas City, Clark gazed on "a butifull place for a fort, good landing place." On July 2, he saw a place where "the Situation appears to be a verry elligable one for a Town," and on August 3 he described Council Bluff as "well Calculated for a fort to Command the Countrey and river."[81] Before leaving Fort Mandan, he would draw up for Jefferson a detailed table listing a dozen "elegable" locations for military forts on the Missouri and Mississippi and the number of soldiers required "to protect the Indian trade and Keep the Savages in peace with the U.S. and each other."[82]

Gazing across the tallgrass prairie on July 4, 1804, Clark had difficulty accepting the idea of such a beautiful landscape not further improved by white settlement:

The Plains of this countrey are covered with a Leek Green Grass, well calculated for the sweetest and most norushing hay—interspersed with Cops [copses] of trees, Spreding ther lofty branchs over Pools Springs or Brooks of fine water. Groops of Shrubs covered with the most delicious froot is to be seen in every direction, and nature appears to have exerted herself to butify the Senery by the variety of flours . . . which Strikes & profumes the Sensation, and amuses the mind.

But Clark felt slightly uneasy "Conjecterng the cause of So magnificient a Senerey in a Countrey thus Situated far removed from the Sivilised world to be enjoyed by nothing but the Buffalo Elk Deer & Bear in which it abounds."[83]

Using dead reckoning and compass readings to keep courses and distances, Clark assembled route maps of the Missouri on fifty sheets of linen paper all the way to Fort Mandan. There he began drawing a larger "connection of the Countrey from what information I have received."[84]

While basing his maps of the Lower and Middle Missouri on country already traveled, Clark faced a problem assembling a "connection" of the uncharted lands that lay ahead. Chiefs like Sheheke drew maps for him, but there already had been indications that Clark and the Indians did not view the landscape in the same manner.

The Indians continued to try to help explain the landscape to Lewis and Clark. On October 13, 1805, Clark had taken down an Arikara story about two stones in the nearby prairie "resembling humane persons & one resembling a Dog . . . those people have a Curious Tredition of those Stones, one was a man in Love, one a Girl whose parents would not let marry, the Dog went to mourn with them all turned to Stone gradually, Commenceing at the feet." The couple fed on grapes, Clark wrote, until they turned completely to stone, "& the woman has a bunch of grapes yet in her hand." Then Clark added, "On the river near the place . . . we obsd. a greater quantity of fine grapes than I ever Saw at one place."[85]

The Indians were describing a storied landscape, one that recorded their oral history with the same fidelity with which books preserved the written stories of Europeans. The maps the Indians drew were not literal representations of the land but more like time lines, narratives in which physical space indicated not distance but the time it took to travel and what might happen to the traveler along the way. An Indian map made no sense without the stories attached to the landscape it described.[86]

In the end, Clark filled in the blank spaces on the map by expanding the places he already knew about. Accordingly, his map vastly increased the drainages of the Missouri and Platte rivers, pushed the Rockies into the Cascades, and collapsed the country between Fort Mandan and the Pacific into a single mountain range and a height of land from which rose all the mighty rivers of the West. It was the dream geography of Jefferson's imagination, with a short portage from sea to sea. It was also a storied landscape.

On their trip upriver from St. Louis in 1804, Lewis and Clark encountered places that had usually been given names by previous travelers. At first, the relatively few names the captains put on the landscape reflected real or fancied features, such as "Cupboard Creek" (June 3) or "Nightingale Creek" (June 4). Tellingly, the first place they named for a person was Floyd's River, in present-day Sioux City, Iowa, for the only member of the Corps of Discovery to die during the expedition.[87]

As they headed west from Fort Mandan in April 1804 into uncharted territory, Lewis and Clark sought to subdue their unspoken fears about these strange new lands by measuring them and by naming them. Indian names vanished, to be replaced by features named for domestic plants (Onion Creek), people (Sharbono's Creek), events (Goose Egg Lake), and days of the week (Sunday Island).

There were some peculiarities. On April 29, 1805, Clark walked three miles up a gentle stream meandering through a "butifull & extencive vallie." In his journal entry for that day he noted, "We call this river Martheys river in honor to the Selebrated M.F."[88]

Who was "the Selebrated M.F."? She was the first woman whose name the two bachelor officers had seen fit to place on the land. She was most likely a woman Clark knew: Martha Fontaine, one of nine daughters of Colonel Aaron Fontaine, a Virginia planter who had migrated to Louisville and operated "Fontaine's Ferry" there. The Fontaine daughters were widely known for their beauty, and Marthey would have been eighteen when William left Louisville. One of her older sisters may have been the "Miss F_____ is Cruel" about whom William had written to Fanny from Fort Greenville in 1795. The two families were certainly close. Marthey's nephew William Fontaine Bullock later married into Jonathan Clark's family.[89]

On May 29, 1805, exactly one month after naming Martheys River, the captains walked up the opposite banks of a "handsome river" flowing into the Missouri in today's Chouteau County. "Capt. Clark . . . has thought proper to call it Big Horn River," Lewis originally wrote.[90] But at some unknown time later Lewis erased "Big Horn" and substituted "Judieths" River. In his remaining references to the river for that date, however, Lewis left "Big Horn" unchanged, as did Clark, both in his journal and on his route map. In fact, the name of the "Judith" River does not appear on any map at all until 1810. Circumstantial evidence suggests that Clark named it not in 1805 for Judith Hancock of Fincastle, whom he had last seen when she was nine, but some time afterward when she had become his wife, Judith ("Julia") Hancock Clark of St. Louis.[91]

The longest-standing relationship within the Corps of Discovery was between Clark and York.

Though York had walked aboard the keelboat with Clark at the Falls of the Ohio and traveled every mile thereafter, the captain's enslaved African-American is nearly invisible in the journals. There are a few glimpses—York sawing timber at Camp River Dubois, York swimming in the Missouri to collect greens for dinner, York giving soup to the dying Sergeant Floyd, and York carelessly leaving his rifle out to be trampled by a bison.

But York was anything but invisible to the Indians. On New Year's Day of 1805, Clark visited a Mandan village where "I ordered my black Servent to Dance which amused the Croud verry much, and Some what astonished them, that So large a man Should be active."[92] On another occasion, perhaps again following Clark's orders to amuse the Indians, York "made himself more terrible in their view than I wished him to Doe as I am told telling them that before I caught him he was wild & lived upon people, young children was verry good eating. Showed them his Strength &c. &c."[93]

Clark wrote that the Arikaras were "much asstonished at my black Servent and Call him the big medison, this nation never Saw a black man before."[94] Clark did not indicate if he found it odd that the man who had the least power and status on the expedition was in the eyes of Indians the most powerful and magical of them all. The Salishes thought that York had been painted with charcoal, perhaps in mourning, and must have been "the bravest of the party." Other Indians called him "the raven's son."[95] Almost all of the tribes sought to acquire his power by offering the sexual favors of their young women.

Talking to Nicholas Biddle years later, Clark noted that the tribes most likely to think of York as "something strange" were those who had seen white Europeans previously but not black men. On the other hand, he added, those tribes who had seen neither Euro-Americans nor African-Americans before, such as the Nez Perces and the Shoshones, "made no difference between white & black."[96] In other words, to tribes unacquainted with Europeans, there was no discernible difference between white men and the black men they enslaved. They were all equally strange.

By the time Clark got to the mouth of the Columbia—and exuberantly noted in his journal, "<u>Ocian in view!</u> O! the joy!"—he had begun to realize that the easy portage he and Lewis hoped to find across the Continental Divide was a chimera.[97] Any new map would have to be adjusted to show this reality. At Fort Clatsop on February 14, 1806, Lewis wrote that "Capt. Clark completed a map of the country through which we have been passing from Fort Mandan to this place."[98] This map was the beginning of an American rethinking of the West. Maps would no longer show a single range of mountains between the Mississippi and the Pacific. They would show that the Rocky Mountains were not a mirror image of the Appalachians but were formidable chains of ridges and valleys stretching from the Black Hills to the Columbia Plateau. The snow-covered peaks that sailors had glimpsed from the Pacific Ocean were not an arm of the Rocky Mountains but an entirely separate range, the Cascades.

"We now discover that we have found the most practicable and navigable passage across the Continent of North America," Lewis wrote, choosing his words carefully.[99] He and Clark knew they had not been sent to find the "most practicable" route across the continent; Jefferson wanted "the direct water communication from sea to sea." On the way home they would have to continue to search for better routes—perhaps along the west-flowing river they reasoned must rise near the headwaters of the Yellowstone and Colorado. Or perhaps Lewis could locate the overland shortcut the Indians had told them about from the Bitterroot Valley to the Missouri River at the Great Falls. To cover more ground, they resolved to split up at Travellers Rest in July 1806: Lewis and a small party would take the northern route, while Clark would investigate the Yellowstone River and its tributaries to the south.

Much of this plan was ill conceived. The mysterious "Multnomah" river they hoped to find was actually a conjectural combination of the Willamette and Snake that reflected the explorers' discredited belief that a single height of land could give rise to the major rivers of the West.[100] Lewis's overland trip proved to be a near-disaster. Removed from Clark's steadying influence, he wound up in a skirmish with a group of young Blackfeet warriors that left one and possibly two of them dead.

Meanwhile, after leaving Lewis on July 3, 1806, Clark had set out for the Yellowstone with twenty men, Sacagawea, a herd of forty-nine horses, one colt, and the seventeen-month-old Pompy. The party divided again, as Sergeant Ordway took a smaller group down the Missouri from Three Forks. Clark's party arrived at the Yellowstone on July 15. They proceeded downstream to a large sandstone formation along the river on which Clark carved his own name but which he called Pompy's Tower. (He named a nearby stream Baptiests Creek.) Not until Clark found himself in a relatively intimate group, without Lewis, did he put the name of Sacagawea's child on the landscape along with those of the rest of the party.[101]

The party had entered the homeland of the Crow Indians. Clark came across a "remarkable" Crow sun-lodge on an island in the river, decorated with buffalo skulls and eagle feathers. But the sure sign of Indian presence came when the group awoke on the morning of July 21 to find its herd of fifty horses diminished by one-half. Over the next week the rest of the herd disappeared.

Clark resolved that he needed to meet with these Indians to impress upon them the power of the United States, to acquire their trade, and to protest the theft of his horses. He drafted a speech to present should he come upon them. It followed the ritualized rhetoric of Indian negotiations he had witnessed at the Treaty of Greenville.

"Children," he began. "The Great Spirit has given a fair and bright day for us to meet together in his View that he may inspect in this all that we say and do."

The assigning of symbolic import to the weather typically opened all Indian talks in the Ohio country. Then came figurative language that would be familiar to the chiefs: "The people in my country is like the grass in your plains noumerous they are also rich and bountifull."

There followed promises that "the Great Chief of all the white people [wishes] that all his read children should be happy . . ."

And then there were appeals to their sympathy: "Children I have been out from my country two winters, I am pore necked and nothing to keep of the rain. When I set out from my country I had a plenty but have given it all to my read children whome I have seen on my way to the Great Lake of the West. And have now nothing."

After sixteen pronouncements and nearly a thousand words, Clark planned to conclude with an invitation for their chiefs to visit the Great Father's "great city," where "you will then see with your own eyes and here with your own years what the white people can do for you. They do not speak with two tongues nor promis what they can't perform."[102]

In his journal, Clark was more direct about his motives. He wanted "to let them See our population and resources &c. which I believe is the Surest garentee of Savage fidelity to any nation that of a Governmnt. possessing the power of punishing promptly every aggression."[103]

Clark never gave this speech. He was unable to find the Indians of the Yellowstone and tell them about their new place in the world as children of an omnipotent white father. He and his group made two twenty-eight-foot dugout canoes, which they lashed together, and floated down the Yellowstone to the Missouri.

The full party reunited on the Missouri on August 12 in present-day Mountrail County, North Dakota. Since Lewis was still incapacitated by the gunshot wound inflicted the previous day by Cruzatte, Clark was fully in charge. With the journey all but completed, John Colter was granted permission to leave and go back upstream with two other fur traders, Joseph Dickson and Forrest Hancock.[104]

On August 18, Clark settled with Toussaint Charbonneau for his services with a sum of $500.33. Charbonneau and his family departed. Then, two days later, Clark wrote Charbonneau an extraordinary letter. "I wish now that I had advised you to come on with me to the Illinois," he said. "You have been a long time with me and have conducted your Self in such a manner as to gain my friendship. Your woman who accompanied you that long dangerous and fatigueing route to the Pacific Ocian and back diserved a greater reward for her attention and services on that rout than we had in our power to give her."

But Clark really wanted to talk about little Jean Baptiste. Clark told Charbonneau about "my fondness for him" and that he would educate

Jean Baptiste "and raise him as my own child." Moreover, "I do not forgit the promise which I made to you and shall now repeat them to you that you may be certain." He told Charbonneau that he would give him land, would furnish him with livestock, would let him visit his family in Montreal, all if he would "leave your little <u>Son Pomp</u> with me." Clark concluded with "anxious expectations of seeing my little dancing boy Baptiest."[105]

Jean Baptiste would not arrive in St. Louis for another three years, but Clark would continue to make similar paternal gestures for the rest of his life. He was intensely loyal to his extended family of brothers, sisters, cousins, nephews, and nieces, and over time he would provide for an ever-increasing entourage of in-laws and friends.

As the expedition continued downstream, groups of fur traders already headed upriver to the riches of the Upper Missouri. One was Clark's athletic army friend Robert McClellan, who had leapt over the wagon at Fort Greenville. McClellan passed around both whiskey and chocolate.

Clark noticed that some things had changed. The restless Missouri River had shifted and shrugged free of its banks: "In places where there was Sand bars in the fall 1804 at this time the main Current passes, and where the current then passed is now a Sand bar. Sand bars which were then naked are now covered with willow Several feet high. The enteranc of Some of the Rivers & Creeks Changed."[106]

And then there were the honeybees.

Going upstream on the Missouri, Clark had seen honeybees at the Osage River, fifty miles beyond the last white settlement at La Charette. But returning downriver two years later, he noticed that the bees had moved farther west, to the mouth of the Kansas River. "They are advancing up the Missouri," he would say later. "We saw them in large numbers."[107]

Chapter Six

THIS WILD COUNTRY

1806–1809

As they hurried toward St. Louis, Lewis and Clark began to realize how much life had gone on without them. On September 3, 1806, in present-day South Dakota, they encountered two boats pushing upriver piled with trade goods. Their owner was James Aird, a Scotsman who worked with the British fur trader Robert Dickson. Aird briefed the captains on news from home, including two surprising and seemingly unrelated events. One was that Aaron Burr had killed Alexander Hamilton in a duel more than two years earlier. More immediately, the new governor of the Territory of Louisiana was none other than General James Wilkinson.

Clark knew Wilkinson's character well from their service together in Charles Scott's and Anthony Wayne's campaigns. But he could not possibly have known the breathtaking extent of Wilkinson's duplicity. Fifteen years earlier, Wilkinson had sought to undermine George Rogers Clark in the Ohio country. Later, as commanding general of the United States Army, Wilkinson had become the secret Agent 13 of the Spanish government, receiving personal payments as large as $10,000 smuggled up the Ohio in barrels of sugar and coffee.

After the Lewis and Clark expedition left St. Louis in 1804, Wilkinson had suggested to his Spanish paymasters that the explorers be arrested. The Spanish launched four such efforts across the High Plains. All of them failed to locate the expedition, though the final attempt, a thousand-man party led by Facundo Melgares, came within a few days' ride of Lewis and Clark on the Lower Missouri. The Pawnees on the Republican River in Kansas later reported that in September 1806 "a large body of

Spanish soldiers arrived at their Village . . . the prarie was covered with them . . . they looked like a flock of blue Birds."[1]

Lewis and Clark were returning amid a maelstrom of international conflict and domestic intrigue. Britain and France were at war, and most Americans thought they themselves would soon be at war with Spain. In the American West, there was no dominant great power; all four were contending. Lieutenant Zebulon Pike, whom Wilkinson had sent on exploratory expeditions in 1805 and 1806–'07, had been turned back by the British on the Upper Mississippi and would soon be arrested by Spanish troops in the Southwest. The Louisiana Purchase appeared to have destabilized the entire region.

Men like Burr and Wilkinson were able to play the power vacuum for personal gain. In 1805, Wilkinson had met with Aaron Burr in St. Louis to discuss a scheme designed to bring a flotilla of twenty-eight flatboats and upwards of one thousand adventurers down the Ohio and Mississippi. Their apparent goal was to create a breakaway republic from Spanish and possibly American lands in the Southwest and West Florida. By early September 1806, Burr was busily traveling through Kentucky and Tennessee, organizing an army of disaffected Federalists and land-seekers. He had little trouble finding recruits. When Lewis and Clark arrived at La Charette, the most advanced American settlement on the Missouri, Clark talked to "the American inhabitants who express great disgust for the governmt of this Territory."[2] The source of their anger was the delay of the new American government in approving land grants previously given out by the Spanish regime.

In the summer of 1806, Wilkinson was ordered by Dearborn to move his U.S. regulars from St. Louis down the Mississippi to Natchez in order to block a Spanish foray into Louisiana. On September 22, as Wilkinson was marching overland to Natchitoches, Lewis and Clark were tying up their boats at Cantonment Bellefontaine, the new post above St. Louis at the mouth of Coldwater Creek. Built by Wilkinson, it was the first American fort west of the Mississippi. The returning explorers were greeted by Wilkinson's wife, Ann Biddle, whom Clark accurately reported to be "in delicate health."[3] Six months later she would be dead.

The next day the Corps of Discovery floated into the Mississippi. Just as he had described the expedition's departure twenty-eight months earlier, Clark once again captured its return in his typically understated language: "Took an early breckfast with Colo. Hunt and Set out decended to the Mississippi and down that river to St. Louis . . . We Suffered the party to fire off their pieces as a Salute to the Town. We were met by all the village and received a harty welcom from it's inhabitants &."[4]

Lewis and Clark pulled up their boats on the banks of a barely sustainable borderland community. St. Louis was isolated and almost entirely dependent on profits from the Indian trade. Nearby tribes like the Osages would exchange fur pelts for manufactured goods, guns, and whiskey. There were no roads to the outside world; the only reliable access was by boat—and even boats could be cut off by ice floes during the winter; in 1804–'05, the Mississippi had frozen over completely. Mail deliveries were so irregular that months would go by without any news at all from the East.

In the streets, though, St. Louis was a global village. The Americans were nominally in charge, but Spanish officials had lingered a full seven months after the Three Flags Ceremony in 1804. The language of choice for most of the 3,500 residents of the District of St. Louis, including the six hundred to seven hundred enslaved African-Americans, was French; church records would be kept in French until the 1830s. The dirt streets were crowded with an assortment of American land-seekers, mixed-race French and Anglo-Indian fur trappers, free blacks, Indians and their *métis* children.

Almost half of all fur trappers married Indian or mixed-race women. These personal liaisons smoothed intercultural relationships. By blending cultures, intermingling one system of expertise with others, the inhabitants equipped themselves to survive in their world of ephemeral and shifting loyalties.

The most prosperous residents were the Chouteaus, members of the old French Creole elite. These Medici of the Mississippi controlled both the fur trade and the Spanish land grants, which had originally been given out by the Spanish colonial authorities to encourage settlers to move across the river. The Chouteaus had adroitly retained their power and acquired additional land through the successive European and American regimes. But now they were rubbing up against land-hungry Americans arriving in increasing numbers after the Louisiana Purchase.

Most of the new arrivals were Virginians and Kentuckians (Kentucky was itself a former Virginia county). They brought with them their slaves and all the supporting strictures. Alarmed by the bloody insurrection in St. Dominique and fearful that the Louisiana Territory could follow the example of the Old Northwest and become free soil, the new citizens were quick to protect the "peculiar institution." Just a few months after Lewis and Clark had headed upriver, the white inhabitants of St. Louis called on Amos Stoddard to demand a legal code to "keep the slaves in their duty according to their Class, in the Respect they owe generally to all Whites, and more especially their masters."[5] The resulting Code of 1804 prohibited slaves from leaving their owner's property without a pass, administering medicine, carrying firearms, hiring themselves out, or being witnesses in a court of law.

The thousands of well-armed Indians surrounding St. Louis could not be dealt with so summarily. Thomas Jefferson had once thought that Louisiana could become an enormous preserve for Eastern Indians, a place where they could be relocated, live independently, and have time to develop the skills necessary to live alongside white people. But in practice, the government acted to make the tribes more dependent on American goods (and less on the hated British traders in Canada). Manufactured goods replaced the Indians' handmade tools, and their artisanal skills atrophied. As the tribes relied increasingly on pelts as their only cash crop, they depleted the wild game on their lands. Eventually their only economic alternative became to trade away their land itself for the tools they needed to survive.

Unlike the French and the British, who sought the Indian's furs but not their land, the Americans were intensely interested in real estate. When the new Louisiana district governor, William Henry Harrison, arrived in St. Louis in the fall of 1804, he seized an opportunity created by the murder of three white settlers on the Cuivre River and summoned several lesser Sauk and Fox chiefs to a council. When the bands arrived, Harrison had them sign a treaty that for the first time extinguished Indian title to lands included in the Louisiana Purchase. Millions of acres in Illinois, Missouri, and Wisconsin were given away for $2,234.50 in goods, a $1,000 annuity, and a promise to establish a new trading post for the tribes at Fort Bellefontaine. Neither Harrison nor the chiefs had been authorized by their respective governments to negotiate a land cession, and at least one Sauk chief, Quashquame (Jumping Fish), later contended that he was drunk when the treaty was signed.

Harrison had put into place the essence of the trading policy Jefferson had urged on him twenty-one months earlier. In a chilling letter Jefferson explained, "We shall push our trading uses, and be glad to see the good and influential Indians . . . run into debt, because we observe when these debts get beyond what the individual can pay, they become willing to lop them off by a cession of land." Jefferson's intent was unequivocally clear: "In this way our settlement will gradually circumscribe and approach the Indians, and they will in time either incorporate with us as citizens of the United States, or remove beyond the Mississippi." It was also pitiless: "The former is certainly the termination of their history most happy for themselves; but, in the whole course of this, it is essential to cultivate their love. As to their fear, we presume that our strength and their weakness is now so visible that they must see we have only to shut our hand to crush them."[6]

Jefferson and his territorial governors were well aware that their ability to obtain concessions from Indians depended on keeping them economically dependent on American trade and free from the influence of their British rivals in Canada. During the time the expedition was away, Wilkinson and Harrison had become increasingly preoccupied with the activities of "Zealous British Partizans" at Michilimackinac, the trading post on the Straits of Mackinac, "from which [they] spread themselves over the North and West of America."[7] Among the most effective were traders like Dickson and Aird, who were willing to give up their rights as British subjects in order to obtain American licenses to trade on the Mississippi.

Because central authority was weak on all sides, loyalties were fungible in this disputed land. Accommodation and compromise were the most practical and effective strategies. Just as trappers took Indian wives to facilitate their cross-cultural transactions, merchants were equally opportunistic in following the flag of convenience. Any soldier, warrior, or merchant who could keep his balance on the shifting middle ground in this environment could succeed.

In order to promote Indian loyalty, European and later the American governments relied increasingly on bringing delegations of chiefs to their capitals, where they would be laden with gifts and presumably awed into acquiescence. Four Mohawks visited London as early as 1710, and an Osage chief was entertained by Louis XV at Versailles in 1725.

Lewis and Clark helped organize several Indian delegations. The first was the group of Osages that Jean Pierre Chouteau escorted to Washington City in the spring of 1804. The group included the aging Osage chief White Hair (Pawhuska), who some claimed acquired his name along with the wig he snatched off a fallen American soldier on St. Clair's battlefield.

In April 1805, Lewis and Clark had sent their keelboat back from Fort Mandan with a cargo of dispatches, journals, specimens — and forty-five chiefs and warriors of the Arikaras, Poncas, Sioux, Omahas, Otoes, and Missouris. The keelboat's arrival at St. Charles a month later was described by a young lawyer visiting from Kentucky:

> Just as we rose from dinner, news Came that Capt. Lewises Barge which had bean Exploring the Mesoori was just Landed. I went on board and Saw a great many Curiosities Such as mocisons Buffaloe Robes Goat Skins Bird and a prairai Dog and the Chief of the Recarreau Indians who was a Very Large fat man Very much pitted with the Small Pox. I Smoked with him as a Brother.[8]

The "Very Large fat man" was Arketarnashar, or Piaheto (Eagle Feather), a chief of the Arikaras. In 1804, Lewis and Clark had named a creek for him in present-day Corson County, South Dakota. After Arketarnashar's departure from St. Charles, he traveled on to Washington City with Captain Amos Stoddard in the autumn of 1805. The other chiefs in the party frequently fell ill, and Arketarnashar himself eventually died on the return trip, an event with ominous implications for relations with the Arikaras.

On January 1, 1806, a day when Lewis and Clark contented themselves with boiled elk, cooked roots, and rainwater at Fort Clatsop, Jefferson welcomed the chiefs to his annual New Year's Day reception at the President's House, paying so much attention to them that the resentful British minister, Anthony Merry, left in a huff after fifteen minutes. Perhaps it was just as well, for Jefferson later informed the chiefs that the Spanish, French, and English were "all gone, never to return again." Instead, he said, Indians should now deal only with Americans, who were "united in one family with our red brethren here." He then backed his point with a barely concealed threat: "We are strong, we are numerous as the stars in the heaven, & we are all gun-men."[9]

His final figure of speech was apt. When Clark replied to Lewis's invitation to join the expedition, he described Jefferson as "that great Chaructor the Main Spring of its action."[10] The metaphor he used was not of the inner workings of a watch, however, but rather of the trigger mechanism of a gun.

Lewis and Clark spent most of the month after their arrival in St. Louis attending celebratory dinners and balls, turning in their supplies and equipment, and mustering out their men. The outside world learned of their return after Clark sent a letter to his brother Jonathan, which was published in a Kentucky newspaper. Never confident of his literary skills, Clark had Lewis draft the letter and then recopied it. On October 10, Clark returned his lieutenant's commission to Secretary of War Dearborn with a terse, two-sentence note in which he wrote that it had "answered the purpose for which it was intended."[11]

On October 21, Lewis and Clark left St. Louis for Washington City on horseback and an accompanying barge that carried the Mandan chief Shehek-shote with his wife and son, Pierre Chouteau and a delegation of Osage chiefs, York, Sergeant Ordway, and the interpreters René Jesseaume (with his wife and two children) and François Labiche. Two weeks later, Jonathan Clark of Louisville noted in his diary "a little Rain—Captains Lewis & Clark arrived at the Falls on their return from the Pacific Ocean after an absence of a little more than three years."[12]

William Clark was home. The day he arrived, he went to Louisville and equipped himself at Fitzhugh and Rose, the dry-goods store operated by his sister Fanny's new husband, Dennis Fitzhugh, her first cousin once removed. On November 8, the captains attended a family celebration at Lucy Clark Croghan's Georgian manor house, Locust Grove. The upstairs ballroom, with its French floral wallpaper, would have been filled with the proliferating nieces and nephews of William's siblings Jonathan, Ann Gwathmey, and Fanny O'Fallon Thruston Fitzhugh. William's bachelor brother Edmund and Richard Clough Anderson, the widower husband of sister Eliza, and his children were all likely present.

Looming over everyone was fifty-four-year-old George Rogers Clark, a frail but still formidable presence. The previous year, Josiah Espy had noted "the remains of great dignity and manliness in his countenance, person and deportment" and fancied a resemblance to George Washington.[13] The men of George Rogers's Illinois Regiment regularly visited their general at Point of Rocks, and in 1805 the Miami chief Little Turtle stopped by with William Wells on his way home from a treaty council at Vincennes. An eyewitness to the meeting later recalled, "When introduced, the Turtle said, 'General, we have met often in war—never before in peace. I perceive that you, like myself, are getting old. We must be content that it is so—sit at our fireside & smoke our pipes while our young men carry on the affairs of our people.'"[14]

For twenty years, George Rogers Clark had been the consultant of choice for anyone planning a military expedition down the Ohio and Mississippi. Aaron Burr had visited Clark at Point of Rocks while recruiting men for his expedition. Afterward, Burr is said to have remarked that he'd never met a man "of so much natural capacity & general knowledge as George Rogers Clark."[15]

Lewis left Louisville on November 11 with most of the traveling party, including the chiefs. The group split up at Frankfort, with Chouteau and the Osage chiefs going directly east to Washington City while Lewis took a southerly route through the Cumberland Gap. He would then go down Virginia's Great Valley and spend Christmas with his family outside Charlottesville. His visit would prove brief, for Washington and an audience with a President eager for news awaited him.

Meanwhile, Aaron Burr arrived at Louisville on November 27, 1806.[16] Clark was still there; Burr would certainly have wanted to interview him about his expedition into the formerly Spanish lands. But if Burr met with William, or saw George Rogers, no one kept a record of it. Few people at the time kept evidence of any potentially incriminating contact with Burr. In any event, Burr's plans were beginning to unravel. Seeking to extricate himself, Wilkinson had denounced Burr in two letters to Jefferson. When Jefferson received Wilkinson's letters at the White House on November 25, he issued a presidential proclamation for Burr's arrest.

Clark did not leave the Falls until mid-December, traveling overland with York to the Cumberland Gap. After only a few days, though, he was cold and saddle-sore enough to send York back to Louisville with instructions to buy corduroy or dark velvet for a pair of sherryvallies—trousers that buttoned on the outside seam of each leg to cover other garments while riding.

Lewis's goal was to see the President in Washington, but Clark had a more pressing destination: Fincastle, Virginia. There he visited his army friend Major William Preston and his wife, Caroline, certainly arriving in time for the double wedding on December 23, 1806, of Caroline's sister Mary Hancock to John Griffin and her cousin Harriet Kennerly to John Radford. Caroline's younger sister, Julia Hancock, had just turned fifteen, mature enough to catch the eye of William Clark.

Meanwhile, Lewis arrived in Washington City on December 28 for his long-anticipated reunion with Jefferson. The President greeted Sheheke and the Osage chiefs—careful to do so on separate occasions, though all the chiefs came to the annual New Year's Day reception at the President's House. A presidential gala had been planned for the captains, but it had to be postponed while Clark lingered in Virginia.

In a public ceremony in Fincastle on January 8, Clark endured the fulsome praise of the citizens. ("You have navigated bold & unknown rivers, traversed Mountains, which had never before been impressed with the footsteps of civilized man, and surmounted every obstacle, which climate, Nature or ferocious Savages could throw in your way.")[17] In reply, Clark modestly attributed his success "to a singular interposition of providence, and not to the wisdom of those who commanded the expedition."[18]

Clark finally arrived in Washington more than a week after Jefferson had gone ahead with the postponed testimonial dinner. But he was not too late to enjoy the social scene. "I have become quit[e] a gallant and somewhat taken with the fair creatures," he reported.[19] He was less enthusiastic about the awkward evening he spent with "the god of War," Henry Dearborn, the Secretary of War who had denied his promotion to captain in 1803.[20]

Jefferson had proposed to reward Clark now with a lieutenant colonel's commission in the U.S. infantry, but Congress rejected the nomination. The army's bureaucrats said that he could not be promoted over the heads of more senior officers. But Clark felt "gratified" nonetheless by the Senate's assurance that any other such appointment would be confirmed.[21] It was soon coming. In the first weeks of March 1807, Lewis was appointed governor of the Louisiana Territory, and Clark was named brigadier general of the territorial militia and principal U.S. Indian agent. Lewis and Clark would remain together, headquartered in St. Louis. Dearborn gave Clark a salary of $1,500 a year. Moreover, Clark and

Lewis would each receive double pay for their time in the expedition, along with 1,600 acres of land in Louisiana.

At noon on March 11, Clark left Washington to return to Fincastle, this time to visit the Hancocks at their 295-acre estate, Santillane, on the outskirts of town. William had already told Jonathan to tell his wife "that I have an object in view that I flatter my Self will Extort from her that old promis." How long-standing a promise is unknown; not so Clark's readiness to celebrate. "It is almost time to put up the Chickens & ducks to fatten and prepare Sugar and plumbs for the pies," he wrote.[22]

By March 15, the "object in view" was within his grasp. Thirty-six-year-old William Clark was formally engaged to Julia Hancock, fifteen. She had light brown hair and blue eyes and was strikingly pretty. Lewis's brother Reuben met Julia later that year and described her as "charming" and "very handsome."[23]

Clark wrote a teasing letter to Lewis with the news: "I have made an[d] attacked most vigorously, we have come to terms, and a delivery is to be made first of January [1808] . . . when I shall be in possession highly pleasing to my self." Clark went on to note his alarming discovery that Julia's father, Colonel and former congressman George Hancock, was not a fellow Jeffersonian but rather a Federalist, "which I did not know until the other day. I took him to be a good plain republican. At all events I will hope to introduce some substantial sincere republicanism into some branch of the family about January."[24]

With his wedding plans set, Clark returned to St. Louis in April 1807 to take up his new duties as head of the militia and principal Indian agent. He was overseeing trade and relations with Indians spread over an enormous area, extending from New Madrid and the Arkansas River in the south, to Illinois and the Great Lakes in the north, to the entire Missouri River watershed in the west. Only the Osages remained, for the time being, under the supervision of their longtime agent, Pierre Chouteau.

His thinly spread Indian Office staff of twenty agents, interpreters, and blacksmiths was overwhelmed by problems arriving every day. The Sauks and Foxes were already protesting Harrison's Treaty of 1804, arguing that the chiefs who signed it were not authorized to make land cessions. The Kickapoos, Delawares, and Shawnees were complaining about encroachments of white settlers on their lands, particularly in the rich lead-mining districts around Ste. Geneviève and present-day Dubuque, Iowa.

White Hair and his Great Osages told Clark that the Spanish from the Southwest were constantly trying to recruit them to turn on the Americans. Clark heard similar reports that the British on the Upper Mississippi were redoubling their own efforts to control the Indian trade. For their part, the Indians were surely trying to play the various powers against one another, and it worked. In his first report to Dearborn, Clark said he feared "all the rich furs and peltries with which the Teritory abounds will fall into the hands of British Merchents who will take them immediately to Montreal."[25]

The leading trade item on the northern rivers was the beaver pelt, valued not for its protective outer coat but for its luxuriant undercoat, which was processed to make felt for hats. In the early years of the fur trade, beaver pelts were in far greater demand than buffalo robes, bearskins, or deerskins. Tens of millions of beavers lived on virtually all the rivers and streams west of the Mississippi, though Indians had already begun to deplete their numbers in response to European demand. As early as 1804, Lewis and Clark had noted extensive beaver lodges on the Niobrara River "but none of the animals themselves."[26]

The first entrepreneur to act on Lewis and Clark's reports of an abundance of beavers near the Rocky Mountains was Manuel Lisa, the resourceful trader who had helped outfit the expedition in 1804. Born in New Orleans to Spanish or Cuban parents, Lisa had operated a trading post in Vincennes before crossing the Mississippi to St. Louis in 1799. A few years later, he successfully challenged the Chouteau brothers' monopoly of the Osage trade, winning the exclusive license from the Spanish authorities. But his monopoly left along with the Spanish, and now Lisa found himself having to deal with the Americans. Wilkinson, who could recognize sheer ambition better than most, called Lisa an untrustworthy "Black Spaniard."[27]

Fluent in both European and Indian cultures—he would later take a beautiful Omaha wife named Mitain—the thirty-four-year-old Lisa organized a large trading and trapping venture up the Missouri to the Rocky Mountains. On April 17, 1807, he departed with George Drouillard and fifty to sixty men, including two other recently discharged members of the Lewis and Clark expedition, John Potts and Peter Weiser. At the mouth of the Platte they were joined by John Colter, on his way down-river from his trapping expedition with Dickson and Hancock. Lisa and his men went on to the mouth of the Yellowstone and Big Horn rivers, where they erected a trading post that would be known as Fort Raymond. The American occupation of the Great Plains had begun.

Meanwhile, Clark had put one of the expedition's reliable sergeants, Nathaniel Pryor, in charge of a group to return Sheheke and his family to the Mandan villages on the Upper Missouri. Now promoted to ensign, Pryor left St. Louis in late May with a joint military-commercial party of sixteen soldiers under his command and thirty-two traders directed by Auguste Pierre Chouteau, the eldest son of Pierre. Traveling with them was a separate group of twenty-two soldiers and traders escorting fifteen visiting Sioux chiefs to their villages near present-day Omaha. Given that the once-fearful Sioux were "highly pleased with the presents & treatment which they have received," Clark foresaw little difficulty in taking Sheheke past them to the Mandan villages.[28]

Of greater concern was the hostility of pro-British tribes on the Upper Mississippi and Great Lakes. Beaded belts of wampum, conveying ceremonial messages of war, were rapidly circulating from one tribe to another. "A spirit is prevailing, by no means pacific," said one report from Michilimackinac. There were increasing rumors of the attempts of the Shawnee Prophet, Tenskwatawa, and his older brother Tecumseh to forge a pan-Indian confederacy in the Old Northwest. This nativist movement drew its energy from animosity toward the Americans. In May 1807, a chief named Le Maiouitinong (The Trout) gave a speech in which he claimed to be a conduit of God's own word:

> I am the father of the English, of the French, of the Spaniards, and of the Indians. I created the first man, who was the common father of all these people, as well as yourselves; and it is through him, whom I have awaked from his long sleep, that I now address you. But the Americans I did not make. They are not my children, but the children of the evil spirit. They grew from the scum of the great water, when it was troubled by the evil spirit, and the froth was driven into the woods by a strong east wind. They are numerous, but I hate them.[29]

Against this threatening backdrop, Clark was beginning to see problems in his job description. For matters of territorial administration, he reported to the Secretary of State. But for Indian affairs, he reported to the Secretary of War. Moreover, both were often at odds with the local authorities. For example, his responsibilities included appointing all Indian subagents and "factors" operating government stores trading with the tribes. But he had less control over the licensed private traders in his territory. His old army friend Robert McClellan had been authorized by Wilkinson to arrest unlicensed traders and seize their goods. But when McClellan did exactly that on the Missouri to an unlicensed trader named Francis Hortis, a grand jury refused to prosecute. Instead, McClellan was arrested for seizing Hortis's goods. Clark was outraged. He was caught between the legal requirements of federal authority and the fiercely independent local jurisdictions. He wrote to Dearborn that "the principal I fear will be established in this Country that no punishment can be expected for an infringment of the present Laws regulateing Indian intercourse."[30]

While reorganizing the militia to bolster the territorial capital's "feeble defence," Clark remained convinced that the causes of Indian hostility lay less with avaricious traders or encroaching settlers than with the unseen but pernicious "<u>Spanish</u> or <u>British</u> influence." He advocated building forts in the Indian country both to intimidate the tribes and to guarantee control of foreign agents.[31]

By the summer, though, Clark's thoughts were beginning to turn elsewhere. In June, he left in his desk a draft of a money order on which he had doodled the names "Julia Hancock" and "Julia Clark" and her future "JC" monogram. In August, he was on his way eastward.

Before he got to Virginia, however, Clark had agreed to do a favor for the President. Thomas Jefferson continued to be fascinated by the reports of the huge fossil beds at Big Bone Lick on the Ohio. For thousands of years, bison, elk, deer, and other ungulates had congregated and died there, leaving their fossilized bones bleaching in the marl around the Lick. Early British traders like George Croghan, the uncle of Clark's brother-in-law William Croghan, had already recovered fossilized bones there. Of particular interest to Jefferson were the enormous tusks, jawbones, and teeth found bleaching in the sun. Perhaps they belonged to an ancestral elephant, a herbivore rendered extinct by climate changes. But Jefferson hoped that they belonged instead to a giant carnivore, a creature previously unknown to natural philosophers. The confirmation of this American *incognitum*, Jefferson thought, would indisputably refute the insulting theories of the French naturalist Georges Louis Leclerc de Buffon that the species in the New World were not as evolved as those in Europe.

In the 1780s, Jefferson had twice asked George Rogers Clark to collect specimens at Big Bone Lick; one such request was in a letter hand-carried by Daniel Boone. George Rogers was unable to procure the bones but correctly told Jefferson he was skeptical that they belonged to a carnivore. (They in fact belonged to a leaf-eating Pleistocene elephant of the extinct genus *Mammuthus*.)

In 1803, Meriwether Lewis had stopped on his trip down the Ohio and gathered several hundred pounds of bones for Jefferson, including an immense fifteen-foot mammoth tusk. But Lewis's collection was lost in a shipwreck on the Lower Mississippi. A cargo of ten more crates shipped later to Jefferson from Cincinnati by Dr. William Goforth was instead redirected to England and sold by a swindler named Thomas Ashe. Jefferson's hopes that Lewis and Clark would find fossil elephants or living mammoths near the Rocky Mountains had also proved fruitless.

In desperation, Jefferson turned to Clark, offering to pay him privately for any bones he could gather for the American Philosophical Society's fossil collection.

Clark arrived at the Lick on Sunday, September 6. The next day, he and ten hired men started digging into the marsh. Looking over his shoulder, Clark would have seen a possible distraction: his brother George Rogers, finally on the verge of fulfilling Jefferson's request of twenty-six years earlier—but not fully equipped to help. "Brother G.____ D[runk] and has given me some uneaseness but he appears to be more thoughtfull to day," William wrote Jonathan.[32]

The work was disagreeable. The Lick had been picked over so thoroughly that the remaining bones were embedded, and they crumbled when exposed to air. Sulfurous vapors from the fetid muck and nearby salt-making furnaces aggravated William's rheumatism. On September 20, he wrote the President that he'd spent two weeks "searching for the bones of the Mammoth without meeting with as much suckess as I expected."[33] A few weeks later, though, Clark packed more than three hundred fossil bones and teeth into ten crates to ship by flatboat to New Orleans and then by schooner to Washington.

Clark was modest about his expertise. In his accompanying report, he told Jefferson that "having no treatis on Comparritive Anatomy, I am compelled to make use of the Most Common terms." He then went on to write an eleven-page description to Jefferson that was detailed enough to help naturalists of the day differentiate the fossils of mammoths from those of the previously unknown mastodons.

Shortly after returning briefly to Louisville, Clark received a letter from Ensign Pryor with alarming news about his excursion to return Sheheke to his village. Pryor's fleet had been stopped on the Missouri by a well-armed army of 650 Arikaras, the once-friendly tribe that had treated Lewis and Clark so warmly during their expedition. Angered by the death of their chief Arketarnashar during his trip to Washington in April 1806, the Arikaras planned to plunder the boats and murder Sheheke. Pryor suspected, probably unfairly, that Manuel Lisa had informed the Arikaras of the Mandan chief's imminent arrival when he had been similarly threatened by the tribe several weeks earlier.

Pryor instructed Sheheke to conceal himself in the hold of the keel-boat, and a standoff ensued. But when a white man was clubbed to the ground, a fierce gun battle erupted that lasted for an hour. Outnumbered, Pryor was forced to retreat downstream to St. Louis with Sheheke still aboard. Three of his men had been killed and several wounded, including the expedition member George Shannon, whose leg would eventually be amputated. Pryor told Clark that it would require a force of at least four hundred soldiers to get past the Sioux and Arikaras and "even one thousand men might fail in the attempt."[34]

Clark left Louisville and proceeded on to Virginia. On January 5, 1808, he presented himself before the Botetourt County Clerk in Fincastle, Virginia, and asked for a marriage certificate. With him were William Preston, who paid the $150 marriage bond, and his future father-in-law, George Hancock, who signed his permission for the wedding of his underage daughter "Judith" (as she was named in the documents). Later that day William Clark—who already had sponsored two godchildren and had more than thirty nieces and nephews—finally became a husband. The ceremony would have been the biggest event in the picturesque county seat since Clark himself had been toasted by the citizens of Fincastle as a returning national hero almost a year earlier to the day.

The newlyweds spent two months waiting for the ice to clear on the Ohio and packing up Julia's things for her new life. She later asked Jonathan's wife to send cooking essentials like sage to "this wild Country" in the West.[35] She would be transporting all the finery of planter society, including a piano, the first ever seen in St. Louis. By mid-March, they were headed west, a caravan of carriages and wagons escorted by York and several Hancock slaves, including a woman named Molly and her family. They would have taken either the southern route through the Cumberland Gap or the Midland Trail turnpike, a new road across present-day West Virginia to the Ohio River at Huntington.

In either case, travel on frontier roads was a spine-jarring, tooth-loosening experience. Wagons and carriages rumbled over washboard roads built of "corduroy," split trees laid side by side with the flat sides down. Stumps were often left in the middle of the road, and low tree limbs could knock a careless driver off his perch. Coaches would ford countless streams, bogs, and sinkholes. Accidents were frequent. One man claimed to have been overturned more than a dozen times in three years traveling between Cincinnati and Cleveland. George Washington's carriage once sank so hopelessly into a mud hole on the way to Mount Vernon that the President of the United States had to be extricated with ropes and planks. A stagecoach's horses would be changed every fourteen or sixteen miles while travelers refreshed themselves at a tavern.

On the new road—a better choice given their load of furnishings— William and Julia's party would have made their way to Old Sweet Springs, 30 miles northwest of Fincastle, and picked up the Midland Trail turnpike at Crow's Tavern. The next stop would be White Sulphur Springs, the largest spa in Virginia. Following the route of today's U.S. 60, they would pass Lewisburg, Rainelle, and Charleston on their way to Huntington. It was another 220 miles by flatboat downriver to the Falls of the Ohio.

By mid-April, the newlyweds were in Louisville. They caught up with friends and family and former expedition members. One was Reubin Field, who had recently married the daughter of his brother Joseph, who was also on the expedition but had been killed soon afterward. His niece had become his wife. At Louisville, William and Julia's party gained a new member—Clark's own niece Ann Clark Anderson, a daughter of his late sister, Eliza, and her husband, Richard Clough Anderson. At eighteen, Ann — often called "Nancy" — would be Julia's traveling companion into the strange new land across the Mississippi. Her presence would be especially welcome in the coming months, since Julia was now pregnant.

Clark transferred their personal furnishings into the flatboats, along with a load of merchandise for the government trading-house and cantonment at Bellefontaine. He sent back to Jefferson "the skin of the sheep of the Rocky Mountains" and a grizzly hide to display in his Indian Hall at Monticello. He separately boxed up three additional crates of fossils left over from Big Bone Lick to ship to Jefferson by way of New Orleans.[36]

On June 2, Clark left Louisville and descended the Ohio to the mouth of the Cumberland River. From there he sent his horses, carriage, and wagon overland to Kaskaskia with York and two other family slaves, James and Easter. They were accompanied by Joseph Charless, an Irishborn printer who, with financial backing from both Lewis and Clark, was planning to start the first newspaper west of the Mississippi. He founded the *Missouri Gazette* in July 1808.

Meriwether Lewis, who had finally arrived in St. Louis a full year after he had been appointed governor of the Territory of Louisiana, was busily preparing for his friend's arrival. He had rented a French colonial house from John Campbell, the new subagent for Indians on the Upper Mississippi. Built in the characteristic French *poteaux en terre* style of logs planted upright in the ground and chinked with a filling of grass, clay, and stone, the house offered two fireplaces, four downstairs rooms, an office, a stable, a nearby well, a fenced-in garden, and a wraparound porch.

In a warm letter to "My dear friend," Lewis proposed sharing the quarters with the newlyweds and noted that if there was not sufficient room he could move out. He then added a teasing, if typically strained, Lewisian reference to William's earlier description of "the goods" he would be bringing to St. Louis. "I must halt here," Lewis wrote, "and ask you if the matrimonial dictionary affords no term more appropriate than that of goods, alias merchandize, for that dear and interesting part of the creation? It is very well Genl., I shall tell madam of your want of Gallantry; and the triumph too of detection will be more compleat when it is recollected what a musty, fusty, rusty old bachelor I am."[37]

Lewis was still feeling the sting of his own romantic disappointments.

On his trip west, he had visited Fincastle and fallen for a beautiful woman, Letitia Breckenridge. Two days later, she fled not only Lewis's overtures but the town itself. She eventually married in Richmond the following summer.

Ready to be the gallant host to his friend and his new wife, Lewis had arranged for Ensign Pryor to meet Clark at Fort Massac with two keelboats and twenty-five soldiers and *engagés*. In their company, Clark transferred his cargo to the keelboats and headed up the Mississippi to St. Louis.

The stir in town was immediate. "Genl. Clark and his family have arrived," reported one enthusiastic citizen, "and bring with them the beautiful and accomplished Miss Anderson, a niece of the Genl. Great agitation In St. Louis among the bachelors, to prevent fatal consequences a Town meeting has been proposed for the purpose of disposing of her by lot, no meeting has yet been had."[38]

Clark had other concerns. He matter-of-factly reported to Jonathan that during the river trip from Louisville "We lost Nan[c]y's Child, and Bens horse"—pairing the loss of a slave child and a domestic animal in a single sentence.[39] Since there was strong demand for slave labor in the territory, he immediately began hiring out some of his enslaved African-Americans. Others he set to work for his family. "Ben is making hay, York is employed in prunng[?] wood, attending the garden, Horses, &c. &c.," he told Jonathan.[40]

Then, in an aside, Clark added that Venos, his cook, had become "a very good wench Since She had about fifty." By that he meant fifty lashes of the whip. "Indeed, I have been obliged [to] whip almost all my people. And they are now beginning to think that it is best to do better and not Cry hard when I am compelled to use the whip. They have been troublesome but are not so now."

In the code of Virginia slave owners, the use of the whip could be an admission of failure. Perhaps the master was unable to control his human property effectively; perhaps the slaves were "incorrigible" and unfortunately required correction. Clark believed he was "compelled" to use the whip. What Clark could not acknowledge was that in the same journey in which he brought his new wife to St. Louis he had divided the families of the slaves traveling with him. Slaves often retaliated with the only means available to them, the partial or complete withdrawal of their labor.

Soon after his arrival in St. Louis, Clark found himself similarly vexed by the other non-Europeans in his world. "I am much pestered with Indians," he told Jonathan.[41] The two buildings he had rented to use as an Indian Council Room and place of business were teeming with more than one hundred Sauks, Foxes, and Iowas who had come to St. Louis to witness the trials of three warriors accused of murdering traders near St. Louis. With only 250 regular troops protecting the city from thousands of Indians in the vicinity, Clark and Lewis were careful not to excite the Indians, despite popular sentiment in favor of punishing the tribes. In the spirit of calming a potentially explosive set of circumstances, the *Missouri Gazette* assured, "The governor and the general appear to be well acquainted with the motives that have the entire dominion over the hearts of the Indians."[42]

Lewis was actually becoming even more frustrated with the tribes. He erupted to Secretary of War Dearborn that the Great Osages "have cast off all allegiance to the United States" and no longer accepted the authority of their chief, Pawhuska. "War appears to me inevitable with these people," he said. "I have taken the last measure for peace."[43]

Worried that the bellicose Lewis might act rashly, President Jefferson wrote to remind him that "commerce is the great engine by which we are to coerce them, & not war."[44] Moreover, Jefferson was already putting into place the mechanism by which the "great engine" of commerce would be brought to bear on even the most recalcitrant Indians. It would be implemented through a chain of government "factories," or trading posts, placed deep into Indian country. These were intended to pull the tribes from the thrall of Spanish and British traders.

The problem was that as long as traders circulated freely among the Indians, supplying them with guns and ammunition in exchange for peltries, the tribes would continue to be well armed and independent. On the other hand, if the government could strictly license traders and confine their activities to the factories, it could both police the traders and force the Indians into economic dependency on the United States.

Jefferson's policy was designed to attract those tribes who had yet to accept the "protection" of the American government. West of the Mississippi it meant appealing to the Osages, Kansas, Pawnees, Omahas, and other tribes Jefferson considered "inclined to the Spaniards" and who "have not yet had time to know our dispositions." Near the Great Lakes, it meant wresting the Sauks and Foxes, Winnebagos, Iowas, and Potawatomis from the influence of British traders in Canada. "Those on this side of the Missipi will soon be entirely with us if we pursue our course steadily," Jefferson told Lewis.[45]

The first and most important of the tribes to subdue were the Osages. The largest tribe, and the closest to St. Louis, the Osages had controlled trade on the Lower Missouri for a half century. Armed by the French and Spanish with *fusées*, or trade muskets, they had kept rival tribes like the Quapaws, Sauks, Shawnees, Chickasaws, Sioux, Comanches, and Iowas at bay while providing the Europeans with a rich supply of buffalo robes and dressed skins of deer, elk, bear, and beaver. Their warriors were expert hunters, well known for their physical strength and great height. Many exceeded six feet—and they seemed even taller with their heads plucked of all hair except for their bristling roaches. Jefferson described the 1804 Osage delegation as "the most gigantic men we have ever seen."[46] Washington Irving later called them "Romans . . . the finest looking Indians . . . in the West."[47]

Of the five bands of Osages, the two most dominant were the Great Osages on the Marais des Cygnes (Marsh of Swans), led by Pawhuska, and the Little Osages on the Osage River in southwestern Missouri, led by Walk-in-Rain. In a letter to Dearborn, Clark differentiated the "friendly and well disposd" Little Osages from the "vicious and obscene" Great Osages.[48] Another large and determinedly independent band of Osages lived farther west on the Verdigris, a branch of the Arkansas River in present-day Oklahoma.

The government resolved to close the factory and cantonment at Bellefontaine and to divide its trade goods between two new locations: one at the Osage villages in present-day southwestern Missouri, the other on the Mississippi near the mouth of the Des Moines River. "As soon as our factories on the Missouri & Misipi can be in activity," Jefferson said, "they will have more powerful effects than so many armies."[49]

The boast, however, was premature. First a military force would need to go into Osage country to build the new fort and factory. The question was, who would lead it?

Set out from St. Charles, at half past 11 oClock a.m. and proceeded on, passed Several branches of the Dardan Creek a
branch of the Mississippi through a Butifull high rolling Country
intersperced with plains of high grass . . .[50]

It was August 24, 1808. William Clark was leading his second military expedition into the trans-Mississippi West. The double column of
eighty mounted riflemen, called dragoons, left St. Charles for Fire
Prairie, a high plain overlooking the Missouri River, three hundred miles
from its mouth, deep in the heart of Osage country. Captain Eli Clemson had left two weeks ahead of Clark to take six keelboats of supplies up
the river. Clark would ride overland with the dragoons, guided by Captain Nathan Boone, the twenty-six-year-old son of Daniel Boone.

Fire Prairie was named for the Indian practice of burning the grasses
to create meadows and improve hunting conditions. Clark had noticed
its advantageous location on his first voyage up the Missouri in 1804. He
arrived four years later as darkness fell on the evening of September 4. In
his journal, he recorded that he was even more delighted this time with
the "elegant" situation of the high bluff commanding a long sweep of the
river. It offered access to the villages of the Great and Little Osages, ample game, and open fields.

Waking early the next morning, Clark ordered the boats unloaded and
the site cleared for the post. He had designed a triangular fort with blockhouses, similar to the plan of Fort Mandan in 1804. But these untrained
men were not the Corps of Discovery. "Militia work reluctantly & much
difficulty to get them to do anything," Clark complained.[51]

Clark dispatched Nathan Boone and an interpreter named Paul
Loise (the half-Osage son of either Auguste or Pierre Chouteau) to sum-
mon the tribes to Fire Prairie. Within a week, seventy-five Indians
appeared, led by the chiefs Pawhuska of the Great Osages and Walk-in-
Rain of the Little Osages. Clark "informed them that they had been in
frequent habits of committing Theft Murder and Robory on the Citizens
of the U.S." He said that "an under Standing must take place" to put a
stop to such acts before he left Fire Prairie just three days later.[52]

Clark then produced a treaty that he had drawn up the previous
night. He proposed that a line be drawn from Fire Prairie south to the
Arkansas River "and all the land South of that line to be given up by the
Osages to the U.S. for ever." That cession, added to two others Clark

proposed, would be the largest made by Indians to the United States since the Treaty of Greenville; they totaled 82,000 square miles, most of the present state of Missouri and half of Arkansas. The compensation ultimately given the Indians would amount to one-sixth of one cent per acre.

Clark handed copies of the treaty to the Osage bands and instructed them "if any [objection] Dwelt on their minds to speak it & not be bashfull." They raised no complaint. To the contrary, he reported later, they assured him "they would do it with pleasure . . . that I was doing them a great Service."[53] That evening the Indians joined in ceremonial dances and singing. Clark, suffering from dysentery, lay awake all night listening to the celebration.

The next day, in a ceremony modeled on the Treaty of Greenville, 120 Osages gathered on the banks of the Missouri, four or five miles above Fire Prairie. After the signing, cannons were fired and each chief received gifts of twelve *fusées*, one hundred pounds of gunpowder, two hundred pounds of lead, and twelve twists of tobacco.

There were significant underlying differences between the Treaty of 1808 and the ones signed at Greenville in 1795. One was that many principal chiefs, including the influential Big Soldier of the Osages, were not among the signers in 1808. Another was that the Osages had not been defeated militarily. Indeed, to what degree they understood or even intended to fully honor the treaty is questionable. In exchange for promises of American trade and protection, they were giving away the empire of furs that was the economic base of their culture. In return, they received $1,400 in gifts, a $1,800 annuity, the services of a blacksmith, some farm tools, and the use of a gristmill. Perhaps anticipating future criticism, Clark told Dearborn that "no unfair means had been taken on my part to induce the Osage to seed to the United States such an extencive Country for what is conceived here to be so small a Compensation."[54]

The treaty collapsed almost immediately. Three days after Clark returned to St. Louis, Pierre Chouteau told Lewis that the Osages were complaining of being "deceived" at Fire Prairie. Lewis met with the Osages, who said they had not intended to convey land ownership to the United States but rather thought they were merely extending hunting rights to their land. Moreover, they said that the compliant Pawhuska did not represent their nation at the treaty.

Lewis was convinced that "the Indians were urged to make those objections by some white person," a suspicion that appeared to be borne out when Pierre Chouteau asked him to include an article in a revised treaty confirming the Osages' previous award to him and his interpreter of 25,500 acres of choice land within the cession. Lewis promptly refused on the grounds that "if the Indians are permitted to bestow lands on such individuals as they may think proper, the meanest interpreter in our employment will soon acquire a princely fortune at the expense of the United States."[55]

Lewis redrew the treaty with almost identical terms and sent Pierre Chouteau back to the Osages with orders to accept no changes in the signed treaty. Clark fully agreed with Lewis's assessment and was all the more convinced that Chouteau had attempted to sabotage the earlier version in order to preserve his personal land claims. Lewis told Jefferson he found it "extremely difficult and embarrassing" to deal with the growing acrimony between Clark and Chouteau, given their mutual "want of cordiality and confidence."[56]

The failure of the Osage treaty he drafted made Clark anxious about negotiating further treaties with Indian nations without specific instructions or guidance from his government. Yet such guidance would rarely be forthcoming or timely: it still took forty-two days for a letter to reach St. Louis from Washington. In a rare moment of introspection, Clark confessed his concerns to Jonathan. "It is too much for one man like me to do," he wrote in his draft of the letter, adding that "the pie must have a new Crust and more crumbs put in by partcular fingers."[57] In other words, if he was going to take on the difficult task of extinguishing Indian land titles single-handedly, without guidance, he needed to be paid more for his labors.

Acquiring financial security had been a priority for the Clarks ever since George Rogers's debts almost ruined the family. "I assure you that the married State makes me look about my Self and excites a disposition to accoumilate a little for a future day," William told Jonathan.[58] As early as 1794, he had described to his brother Edmund his dream of building a mercantile business on the Mississippi River. Now, in St. Louis as the government official in charge of the Indian trade, Clark saw his opportunity to combine public service with private profit.

His proven skills involved leading men, not making money. Nonetheless, he envisaged a far-flung trading enterprise that would buy merchandise cheaply in Baltimore or Washington and ship it down the Ohio on flatboats. The goods would be stocked in Louisville, from where they could be sent on to the main retail store in St. Louis. Government barges could be used, upon availability. Clark pointed out that the plan required two stores, so he could restock faster than his competitors—otherwise, he noted, "my principal plan will be k[n]ocked in the head."[59]

Clark hoped to go into business with his brother Edmund and his nephew John Hite Clark, Jonathan's eldest son, who were operating a store in Louisville. "It is now the time to Speek candidly to each other," he wrote to John. "Let us Say what we Can do, what we wish to be done & what we will do, for my part I have Said what I Could do, I will to be Connected with you[r] uncle Edmond & yourself equally in a S[t]ore at Louisville and this place." Promoted to a position of influence and newly married, Clark felt the joint pressures of need and opportunity. "I must be doing Something, and I know of nothing which appears So certain as mercantile business, and no time is to be lost."[60]

While waiting to start his trade business, Clark was struggling to manage his investment in human property. His relationship with York was becoming fractious. His lifelong companion was chafing over the separation from his wife. In the fall, Clark gave York permission to accompany the beautiful and accomplished (but still unwed) Ann Anderson on her return to Louisville. York remained a few weeks afterward to visit his wife, but Clark refused to let him stay longer and hire himself out. "He is Serviceable to me at this place, and I am determined not to Sell him, to gratify him," he told Jonathan. "If any attempt is made by York to run off . . . I wish him Sent to New Orleans and Sold, or hired out to Some Severe master."[61]

A month later, Clark had grown so exasperated with York that it took Lewis's intervention to prevent him from selling York down the river: "Govr. Lewis has insisted on my only hireing him out in Kentucky which perhaps will be best . . . I do not wish him again in this Country until he applies himself to Come and give over that wife of his."[62]

Clark remained "vexed and perplexed" by the unwillingness of both Indians and enslaved blacks to conform to his way of life. He complained that his slaves "wish to go on [in] the old way, Steel a little take a little, lie a little, Scolw a little pout a little, deceive a little, quarrel a little and attempt to Smile, but it will not all answer."[63] He wondered to Jonathan about selling "all the Old Stock except Ben." Irritated by the "capers" of one of his father's former slaves, Easter, Clark gave her what he termed "a verry genteel whipping"—and then worried that he would have to pay her midwife's fee when she gave birth four days later.[64] He gave up completely on Scippio and Juba, placing this advertisement in the *Missouri Gazette* on February 22, 1809: "I wish to SELL two likely NEGRO MEN, for Cash. WILLIAM CLARK."

The Mississippi froze over completely in the winter of 1808–'09. Children skated and sleighed, and townspeople drove wagons and horses across the ice to the Illinois bank. A full two months went by without any mail or newspapers from the East; William laid in cords of firewood and killed "19 fat Hogs" for his provisions. He and Julia had moved out of the quarters Lewis had rented for them—which were converted into Webster's Eagle Tavern—and purchased a one-acre lot near the center of town with an apple grove and a stone wall facing the river. "It answers my purpose," said Clark, "as Commerce is my Object."[65]

Nine months pregnant and homesick, Julia "takes a little cry and amuses herself again with her domestic concerns," William reported.[66] Then, on January 10, 1809, she gave birth to their first child, a boy. The delighted father pronounced him to be "a stout portly fellow"—but after eleven days still had not decided on his name.[67] The new parents may have been given pause by the long Clark tradition of naming firstborn sons either "John" or "Jonathan." When the baby was christened by the Catholic bishop Benedict Flaget, he was given neither of those names.[68] The boy would instead be Meriwether Lewis Clark, in honor of his godfather, formally fusing the two names that had already become inseparable. He would be called simply "Lewis."

In the early months of 1809, Clark turned again to his most pressing public obligation, to send the Mandan chief back to his tribe. Sheheke's safe return was both a national obligation and a practical necessity to prevent the Upper Missouri tribes from aligning with the British. Moreover, Clark and Lewis saw a way to organize the trip that would combine government policy with their own increasing interest in the private fur trade.

Manuel Lisa had returned from his 1807–'08 expedition with a rich supply of peltries and promises of far greater profits to be reaped in the fur trade near the Rocky Mountains. In March, Lisa joined with Clark and a consortium of leading citizens to form a commercial fur-trading venture called the St. Louis Missouri Fur Company. The other partners included Pierre Chouteau and his son Auguste Pierre, the Kaskaskia merchants Pierre Menard and William Morrison, Andrew Henry, Sylvestre Labbadie, Wilkinson's nephew Benjamin Wilkinson, and Lewis's brother Reuben Lewis, whom Clark had appointed a subagent to Indians on the Missouri River. Clark's dual role as both government Indian agent and private Indian trader was not unusual—the British operated similarly—but it began to generate criticism from other entrepreneurs.

Governor Lewis then contracted the federal government to pay $7,000 to the St. Louis Missouri Fur Company to guarantee the success-ful return of Sheheke to his home. With most of the company's start-up costs covered, Lisa planned a bifurcated expedition. An armed force of 125 men, including 40 members of the militia, would escort the chief. A parallel commercial group of 150 fur traders and *engagés* would build trading posts and forts on the Upper Missouri. Clark would act as the company's St. Louis agent. He made plans to build a commercial ware-house on his property and use it to supply both government factories and private traders. He would also receive the furs shipped down the river in packs, airing and beating them to remove moths and worms and sending them on to New Orleans and markets in the East. "I have not the Smalest doubt of Suckcess," said Clark, who bought one share in the new company and tried to sell others to his brothers.[69]

The construction of Fort Osage had cleared the Missouri River for American traders, but Indian resistance remained intense on the Upper Mississippi. British merchants from the Michilimackinac Company still dominated trade with the tribes and used their influence against the Americans. The U.S. agent at Prairie du Chien, John Campbell, who had rented his St. Louis house to William and Julia, was killed in a duel with the British trader Redford Crawford. The *Missouri Gazette* reported afterward that Crawford had "grossly insulted" Campbell as a means of instigating the duel in order to kill him.[70]

In the spring, rumors swept down the river that the Shawnee brothers Tecumseh and Tenskwatawa were renewing their efforts to organize the

Northern tribes in opposition to the Americans. A worried Clark wrote to Dearborn that "The Indian prophets have been industriously employed . . . attempting to seduce the Kickapoos, Saukeys, and other bands of Indians residing on the Mississippi and Illinois river, to <u>war</u> against the frontiers of this country."[71]

Clark began preparing for the worst. The new Fort Bellevue (later Fort Madison), built on the Mississippi near today's Iowa-Missouri border, proved to be so poorly defended that Clark guessed that the Indians "could with great ease <u>jump</u> over" its pickets.[72] In April the government trader stationed there wrote nervously that the entire nation of Sauks was camped directly across the river from him. Clark and Indiana governor William Henry Harrison both braced for a Sauk attack they predicted would soon result from "the British interference with our Indian affairs in this country."[73] Apparently, they could not imagine that the Indian nations would want to organize a resistance on their own, without help and instigation from Europeans.

Clark and Lewis responded to growing public alarm by calling up the local militias. The decision was not welcomed by local citizens, who wanted the regular army to come to their defense. Even before then, Lewis had made himself unpopular among the newly arrived Americans by attempting to evict those whites who had settled illegally on Indian lands. Further, some inhabitants began to question the propriety of the two highest-ranking officials in the territory assigning public funds to a company they owned. Rudolphe Tillier, the former factor at Fort Bellefontaine, asked Madison, "Is it proper for the public service that the U.S. officers as a Governor or a Super Intendant of Indian Affairs & U.S. Factor should take any share in Mercantile and private concerns[?]"[74]

While Clark was able to deal effectively with the government bureaucracies and even gain influence during a crisis, Lewis's political base seemed to be eroding. Lewis's biggest problem was his relationship with his second in command, Territorial Secretary Frederick Bates. Appointed by Jefferson, Bates had served competently as acting governor for a year while awaiting Lewis's arrival in St. Louis. He drafted a set of laws for the Louisiana Territory that became the first American book published west of the Mississippi, and he busily set about sorting through the overlapping Spanish land claims.

But the men were almost too much alike. They were both stiff, slightly humorless, punctilious Virginia bachelors. Both were nonplussed by the lively French Creole society of St. Louis. "Our Balls are gay, spirited and social," Bates wrote to his brother. "The French Ladies dance with inimitable grace but rather too much in the style of actresses . . . to me they would be more interesting with a greater show of modesty and correctness of manners."[75]

Their relations soured on their first working day together—Lewis ordered Bates to hand him a full report in writing on Indian affairs—and soon grew worse. Bates wanted to promote hunting, trading, and settling by whites in Indian country; Lewis wanted to restrict hunting, trading, and settling until the Indians were brought to heel. "We differ in everything; but we will be honest and frank in our intercourse," Bates wrote his brother Richard. "I lament the unpopularity of the Governor; but he has brought it on himself by harsh and mistaken measures. He is inflexible in error."[76]

Soon the two men were no longer speaking, except on matters of public business. A particularly embarrassing scene resulted when they encountered one another at a ball in St. Louis. Bates described it to his brother: "[Lewis] drew his chair close to mine—There was a pause in the conversation—I availed myself of it—arose and walked to the other side of the room. The dances were now commencing. He also rose— evidently in passion, retired into an adjoining room and sent a servant for General Clark, who refused to ask me out as he foresaw that a Battle must have been the consequence."[77]

Despite all his formidable gifts of compromise, Clark was unable to broker an accommodation between the two men. Lewis began steering more and more official business away from Bates to Clark, while Bates continued to criticize Lewis's policies and appointments. "His habits are altogether military," said Bates. "He never can I think succeed in any other profession."[78]

Lewis was beginning to show signs of strain. In the late spring, as Chouteau and Lisa prepared to return Sheheke to his native people, Lewis gave them a letter of instruction that was startlingly vindictive. All the tribes should be treated in a friendly manner, Lewis said, except for the Arikaras. They should be "severely Punished," even if it were necessary "to exterpate that abandoned Nation." Lewis told Chouteau to force the Arikaras to turn over the warriors who had killed the men of Pryor's party. If the tribe did not produce those particular individuals, it should be made to deliver an "equivalent number." Then, Lewis said, those hostages should be "shot in the presence of the nation."[79]

The parties under Chouteau and Lisa left in separate groups in May and June. Though depleted by numerous desertions, they joined at Fort Osage to make a combined force of 150 soldiers, traders, Indians, Creole boatmen, and free blacks. One keelboat of Americans was commanded by Reuben Lewis. It was the largest expedition to ascend the Missouri to that date.

Lewis's relationships with his superiors in Washington City were deteriorating. Jefferson had already written Lewis several mildly chastising letters about his delay in preparing his journals for publication. But Jefferson was out of office, and Frederick Bates had the ear of the new Administration of President James Madison.

In August 1809, Lewis received a devastating letter from Madison's new Secretary of War, William Eustis. Eustis began by complaining that the government had not been consulted in advance about Chouteau's mission. Specifically, he objected that the contract with the St. Louis Missouri Fur Company combined "commercial as well as military objects," that "the object & destination of this Force is unknown," and that it was commanded by an official who had originally been appointed to a different position. (Pierre Chouteau was agent to the Osage Indians.)[80]

Then came the coup de grâce. Eustis stated that the government would not honor the additional payments Lewis had made to Chouteau and others for expenses beyond the $7,000 already contracted. News of the rejection of Lewis's bills had the immediate effect of precipitating a run by the governor's creditors on all of his debts, which were considerable because he had borrowed heavily to buy land in the region. Unable to raise the cash to pay his creditors, Lewis was pushed into near-insolvency.

On August 18, 1809—his thirty-fifth birthday—the deeply distressed Lewis replied to Eustis that he would travel to Washington to clear his name. "Be assured Sir, that my Country can never make 'A Burr' out of me," he said, reflecting his and the nation's continued preoccupation with the western conspiracy. "She may reduce me to Poverty; but she can never sever my Attachment from her."[81]

Before he departed, Lewis gave Clark and two other friends the power of attorney to settle his loans by selling off his property holdings. Like George Rogers Clark previously, Lewis was resorting to the measures Jefferson had hoped would be forced on the Indians: he was selling off his land in order to lop off his debts.

By this time, rumors had reached St. Louis that Lewis would not be reappointed as governor, and many people thought he would not be back. "He is a good man, but a very improvident one," said one friend. "I apprehend he will not return."[82]

It had been a difficult time for many of the men of the Corps of Discovery. Even Clark was chastised by Eustis, who vacated a half-dozen appointments in the Indian Office, including one given to one of the expedition's blacksmiths, Alexander Willard. The reliable George Drouillard had been jailed after Lisa's expedition and charged with murder for shooting a deserter who later died. (Drouillard was found not guilty after a jury deliberation of fifteen minutes.) Some of the men immediately cashed in the land grants they received as rewards from the government. The lawyer William C. Carr purchased one grant of 320 acres "lately issued by the Secretary of War to the followers of Lewis & Clark." He paid for the land not with cash, however. The price was one slave.[83]

After Eustis told Clark that "it does not appear to be necessary that the expense attending our Relations with the Indians in the Territory of Louisiana should be four times as much as the whole expense of supporting its civil government," Clark decided that he, too, needed to pay a visit to Washington.[84] He would travel a different route from Lewis's in order to take his wife and infant son to visit her family in Virginia.

Clark would be haunted by his final meetings with Lewis. He told Jonathan that on August 25 his friend had expressed his distress "in Such terms as to Cause a Cempothy which is not yet off." Yet, Clark assured his brother, "I do not beleve there was ever an honester man in Louisiana nor one who had pureor motives than Govr. Lewis." Ever hopeful, he predicted, "I think all will be right and he will return with flying Colours to this Country."[85]

Lewis left St. Louis on September 4, four days after the recalcitrant Osage band on the Arkansas River finally signed the 1808 treaty. Clark observed with satisfaction that it would "extinguish the Indian title to more than 200 miles square of the finest country in Louisiana."[86]

Meanwhile, Clark was making arrangements for his own trip. He finished relocating his family to his new house and dispatched a government boat to New Orleans loaded with packs of shaved deerskins and hatters' furs from the factories at Fort Osage and Fort Madison.

A warm letter arrived from Jefferson, who wrote from Monticello to thank Clark for his donation of mastodon bones that "have given to my collection of Indian curiosities an importance much beyond what I had ever counted on." Jefferson added a note of congratulations to Clark on his growing family: "While some may think it will render you less active in the service of the world, those who take a sincere interest in your personal happiness, and who know that by a law of our nature we cannot be happy without the endearing connections of a family, will rejoice for your sake as I do. The world has, of right no further claims on yourself & Govr. Lewis, but such as you may voluntarily render according to your convenience or as they may make it your interest."[87] The contrast with Madison and Eustis's attitude could not have been sharper.

On September 21, a festive crowd had gathered in St. Louis to witness the public hanging of a convicted murderer. A week later, Clark began his overland trip east, riding alongside a carriage with Julia and their eight-month-old son. They were accompanied by a slave couple, Scott and Chloe, and their daughter Rachel. Although York had returned to St. Louis, he no longer traveled with his owner. In May, Clark reported that York was "insolent and Sulky. I gave him a Severe trouncing the other day."[88] Later, he sent York to the "Caleboos" for an unnamed offense. After again threatening to sell or hire out York, Clark complained, "I cant Sell negrows here for money."[89]

Public accommodations on territorial roads were rough and egalitarian. Most homeowners on the principal routes boarded travelers to supplement their income. A high official might share a room with the innkeeper and his wife. Outside of Kaskaskia, the scene of George Rogers Clark's first triumph in 1778, William and Julia found no food at all at one boardinghouse. So the man who had once hunted grizzlies killed two chickens. "Mrs. Clark & Cloe Cooked a good Brackfast, and we proceeded on," Clark wrote in his pocket journal.[90] They sometimes stayed with friends. Clark was popular in the Illinois Territory, and in April the citi-

zens of St. Clair County, Illinois, had petitioned the President to name
him their governor.

They crossed the Ohio at Shawneetown and visited Jonathan's
daughter Nelly and her husband, Benjamin Temple, in Russellville, in
today's Logan County, Kentucky. During the visit, Julia took down
Nelly's recipe for "green Sweet Meats":

> Let your [cu]cumbers of muskmelons (or such fruit as you wish)
> lay in salt water until they turn yallow. Then boil them in spring
> water until they Cook plump. If they will not green as deep as you
> want them throw a small bit of alum in while boiling. Have your
> cirrup ready to lay them in before they get cold or else they will all
> draw up. The ginger must be soaked well before it is put in.[91]

After encountering "many familys all going to Louisiana," the party
arrived at Jonathan's house above the Falls of the Ohio at sunset on October 12.[92] It was a bittersweet reunion. The previous March, brother
George Rogers Clark had stumbled and fallen insensate near a burning
fireplace at his cabin at Point of Rocks. No one really knew whether he
had been blind drunk or had suffered a stroke. But his badly burned right
leg had become gangrenous. On March 25, George Rogers had been
carried to Dr. Richard Ferguson in Louisville, who amputated his leg
above the knee. Believing that martial music might distract him during
the operation, members of George Rogers's regiment gathered outside
and played "Yankee Doodle" while the old soldier purportedly "kept
time by humming the tune."[93]

William and Julia spent two weeks visiting Jonathan and his family at
Trough Spring and the Croghans at Locust Grove (to which George
Rogers had moved). They may also have visited John James Audubon,
then living in Louisville with his family. By October 26, though, the cou-
ple had repaired their often-broken carriage and continued their journey.
They were traveling on a road familiar to Clark from the days of his mili-
tia campaigns. They went first to Colonel Richard Anderson's house,
Soldier's Retreat, in Middletown, and then headed for Frankfort.

During a stopover at Shelbyville, William picked up a copy of a
Frankfort newspaper, the *Argus of Western America*. His breath stopped.

Meriwether Lewis was dead.

The newspaper said he had cut his throat with a knife.

Clark somehow pressed on to John Shannon's tavern, near Peytona in today's Shelby County. There, in a pub room crowded with drunks, he wrote an anguished letter to Jonathan: *"I fear O! I fear the waight of his mind has over come him, what will become of ~~my~~ his paprs?"*[94]

CHAPTER SEVEN

LIFE WITHOUT LEWIS

1809–1813

After leaving St. Louis in early September 1809, Meriwether Lewis made his way slowly down the Mississippi to the fourth Chickasaw Bluff and Fort Pickering. He was in terrible condition, drinking heavily and taking pills laced with laudanum, an opiate. He had scrawled a will into his notebook, leaving his landholdings (his only assets) to his mother, Lucy Marks.

When his boat arrived at the fort on September 15, the crewmen informed the commanding officer, Captain Gilbert Russell, that Lewis had twice tried to kill himself. Russell ordered Lewis detained until his health improved.

The next day, Lewis wrote a semicoherent letter to President James Madison, explaining his intention to travel overland to Washington on the Natchez Trace, by way of Nashville, rather than risk being stopped by British warships on a sea voyage from New Orleans. His once-precise handwriting was large and loopy, riddled with strikeouts and misspellings. James Neelly, the agent to the Chickasaw Nation, found Lewis to be "in Very bad health."[1]

After two weeks of rest, Lewis seemed to have recovered. On September 29, he left Fort Pickering accompanied by his personal servant, John Pernier, who had previously worked for Jefferson, as well as Neelly and his servant. A few days later, though, Neelly observed that Lewis again "appeared at times deranged in mind."[2] He was talking deliriously about his protested drafts and, as Clark reported later, had gotten the idea that "he herd me Comeing on, and said he was certain [I would] over take him, that I had herd of his Situation and would Come to his releaf."[3]

What Lewis could not have known was that during the week he was at Fort Pickering, Pierre Chouteau had finally delivered Sheheke safely to his people at the Mandan villages on the Upper Missouri. Ironically, the mission that had precipitated Lewis's difficulties had at last been completed.

On the evening of October 10, Lewis arrived at Grinder's "Stand" (the local term for an inn), about seventy miles south of Nashville. Sometime after midnight he fired two bullets with his pistols. One grazed his skull and the other penetrated his chest. "I have done the business," he told Mrs. Grinder. He died shortly after dawn on the eleventh.

It was suicide. That was the unequivocal testimony from the scene by Neelly, Pernier, and Mrs. Grinder. Clark immediately came to the same conclusion, as did Jefferson.[4] Historians and writers have since sought to assign Lewis's suicide to the depressive effects of diseases ranging from alcoholism or malaria to syphilis acquired from the Lemhi Shoshones. Others attribute it to lifelong bipolar illness.

What is remarkable, regardless, is how much Lewis accomplished in the face of his problems. For the final six years of his life, Lewis found in William Clark the necessary mediator between his brilliant but remote personality and a world he could measure but not grasp. Clark had already performed a similar service for another dysfunctional national hero, his older brother George Rogers. Lewis's isolation became more pronounced during the expedition's return, with the result that Clark assumed more and more of the daily leadership. Perhaps when Lewis first arranged for them all to reside under the same roof in St. Louis, he had hoped things might continue as they always had. But when Clark committed himself to a new partner, his wife, Julia, Lewis was left without his stabilizing center.

As Clark and his family continued on their trip east, he encountered his brother-in-law Dennis Fitzhugh coming the other way. Fitzhugh confirmed the report that had given Clark "much uneasiness": Lewis had ended his life. Disturbed by news that was "a turble Stroke to me in every respect," Clark did what he had always done: he put the tragedy behind him and began to work on the task at hand.[5] In this case, that meant taking over the preparation and publication of the long-delayed book that would confirm the accomplishments of the Voyage of Discovery.

From the road, Clark wrote to a magistrate friend to make sure Lewis's traveling trunks, which contained the only set of their journals, would be secured. He asked Jonathan to forward the disturbing last letter he had received from Lewis in Louisville, since "it will be of great Service to me." (It has never been located.) But William acknowledged to Jonathan that he was in a quandary about how to proceed further: "I do not know what I Shall do abut the publication of the Book. It will require funds which I have not at present."[6]

Friends were already beginning to ask if he would replace Lewis as governor of Louisiana, but Clark could not countenance reporting to Secretary of War Eustis, "a green pompous new englandr," whom he blamed for his friend's troubles.[7]

Their carriage rattled on through the night, over the Cumberland Gap and Clinch Mountain on what Clark dryly noted was "what they Call a turnpike road, for which pleasant traveling I payed 162½ cents."[8] Snow was now falling in the mountains. At one stop, fearing that little Lewis might acquire whooping cough from his hosts' children, Clark applied a folk remedy of tying a string around his son's neck. On November 21, the Clarks happily discovered that George Hancock had ridden forty miles up the road to meet his daughter, son-in-law, and new grandson and escort them to his new country estate, Fotheringay, south of present-day Roanoke. It was Julia's eighteenth birthday. She had not seen her Virginia home in eighteen months.

Clark knew that he needed to talk to Jefferson as soon as possible. The former President had already been told by the publisher that "Govr. Lewis never furnished us with a line" of the journals.[9] Leaving Julia and Lewis at her parents' principal estate, Santillane, in Fincastle, Clark made his way to Charlottesville. First came a sad visit to the Lewis family farm at Locust Hill. Lucy Marks was not there, but "I shewed young Mr. Mark's [Lewis's half-brother John Marks] all the letters I had about his Brothers situation and told him my opinion on that subject. He distressed."[10] (Lewis's brother Reuben, an Indian subagent on the Upper Missouri, would not learn of Meriwether's death for at least another year.)

The next day, Clark made the long ride up the mountain to Monticello. Although he dined with Jefferson and stayed all night, in his journal entry for that day Clark described the ensuing conversation with what even for him was unusual brevity. He wrote only that he and Jefferson "spoke much on the afs of Gov. Lewis &c&c&c."[11]

The "&c&c&c" had everything to do with the publication of the journals. Clark must have told Jefferson that Lewis had indicated nothing to him about his failure to begin his narrative of the expedition. Moreover, Clark did not know what arrangements Lewis may have made about preserving their scientific, ethnographic, and cartographic discoveries. He would have told Jefferson that he did not think he had the literary skills to write the narrative himself. Finally, he would have said that he could not afford to pay for the publication single-handedly. What should he do?

Jefferson told Clark that he first needed to locate the journals and the scientific materials. Perhaps the American Philosophical Society in Philadelphia could help. Then they would have to hire a writer. The onetime President said he could not write the book himself; he was sixty-six years old and preoccupied with his affairs at Monticello. It would be up to William Clark to bring to the public the story of his and Captain Lewis's tour to the Pacific.

At 11 a.m. the next day, Clark rode down the hill from Monticello. Instead of proceeding directly to Washington, as originally planned, he went to Richmond, where he met Lewis's cousin William D. Meriwether, the executor of Lewis's estate. Meriwether agreed that Clark could separate the expeditionary papers from Lewis's personal belongings. Clark also met with William Wirt, a well-known lawyer and writer (and a future U.S. Attorney General). Clark inquired if Wirt would be able to undertake the editing of the journals.

Before receiving Wirt's answer, Clark left Richmond on December 13 and rode all night in the rain to visit relatives near his childhood home in Caroline County. By then the trip had become his first prolonged absence from his wife and son, and he missed them. The long journey from St. Louis to the East, which included sixty-one separate overnight stops, had brought him emotionally closer to Julia. In his notebook, Clark had begun to refer to her as "my Dear wife" and wrote a note to himself that a husband must treat her with "tenderness" and "be faithful to her love; give up my heart to her in confidence and obliterate her cares."[12]

Julia herself had entered more practical reminders in her husband's notebook. She wrote out a shopping list for William to use in the eastern cities, which included "one fashionable dress any thing but thin Muslin" and "1 dark silk shall [shawl] as large as possible." Then she wrote out a request for "necklace and bracelets of linked hair. If you would have JHC put in gold letters in the clasps it would be much handsomer. This is the shape . . ." Then, like any other wife instructing a clueless husband, she sketched a drawing of a braided hair necklace, with a label stating, "This is hair."[13]

Clark arrived in Washington City on December 18. After ordering new clothes from a local tailor, he paid a call on the "green pompous new englandr" himself, William Eustis. Clark stoutly defended Lewis's conduct to the Secretary of War, extracting from him a belated assertion that "the Govr. had not lost the Confidence of the Government."[14]

Clark spent the holidays in Washington, lobbying Congress for a pension for brother George Rogers (which was later granted by Virginia) and financial assistance for the publication of the journals (which it declined). He met with President Madison and found to his pleasure "I am rather a faverite." But to his brother Jonathan he confided his disdain for William Simmons, the War Department accountant who had protested Lewis's invoices and "who I treat like a puppy—as he is." Around this time, Madison and Eustis apparently sounded out Clark about replacing Lewis as territorial governor, but he had no appetite for the political battles that had wounded his friend. "I am afraid, and Cannot Consent," he said. "I do not think myself Calculated to meet the Storms which might be expected."[15]

A few days after New Year's 1810, Clark went to the President's House to meet with Isaac Coles, Jefferson's last personal secretary, who had retained the position under President Madison. They opened Lewis's trunks and carefully separated his personal items ("Two striped summer coats") from the papers ("Sixteen Note books bound in red morocco with clasps") that made up most of the expedition journals.[16]

With the manuscripts in hand, Clark set out for Philadelphia, deeply worried that his fears that "nothing has been done" would be borne out. On the way he jotted down a to-do list: "If man can be got to go to St. Louis with me to write the journal & price . . . The price of engraving animals Inds. & Maps Papeer & other expenses . . . Get some one to write the scientific part & natural history—Botany, Mineralogy & Zoology."[17]

In Philadelphia, Clark was able to track down a few items Lewis had left there—original specimens of some plants, birds, animals, and rocks—as well as drawings Lewis had commissioned of the falls of the Missouri and of the Columbia. Clark sat for a portrait by Charles Willson Peale, just as Lewis had done in the summer of 1807. The differences between the portraits are interesting: Lewis is shown in a three-quarters view, gazing past the viewer, without eye contact. The redheaded Clark turns to face the viewer directly, but with a worried look around his eyes.

The scientist Benjamin Smith Barton told Clark he would edit the sections dealing with botany and zoology. Ferdinand Rudolph Hassler, a Swiss instructor of mathematics at West Point, would do the necessary calculations to correct the captains' observations of longitude and latitude. As for the all-important narrative, Clark was still counting on William Wirt, "as I believe him one of the first writers in this Country."[18]

Some felt that "General Clark" (as he was now known for his militia rank) was too modest. Charles Willson Peale wrote to his son, "I would rather Clark had undertaken to have wrote the whole himself and then have put it into the hands of some person of talents to brush it up, but I found that the General was too diffident of his abilities. I would rather see a single narrative with such observations as I am sure Clark could have made on the different Nations of Savages & things, which the Notes taken by Capt. Lewis probably passed over unnoticed."[19]

During his visit to Philadelphia, Clark met a man who could not have been more different from himself. Just twenty-four years old, Nicholas Biddle was an aristocrat, a Federalist, and a Philadelphian. Blessed with chestnut hair and Byronic good looks, he was known as the handsomest man in Philadelphia and possibly the most brilliant. He had entered the University of Pennsylvania at the age of ten and graduated at fifteen from the College of New Jersey (later Princeton) as valedictorian of the Class of 1801. He grew up in a Federalist household; his father, Charles Biddle, had given refuge to the fleeing Aaron Burr following his duel with Hamilton.

While Lewis and Clark were pushing and pulling their keelboat up the Missouri in 1804, Biddle had sailed to Paris as personal secretary to John Armstrong, the U.S. minister to France. He traveled to Florence, Rome, and Athens and learned languages well enough to lecture at

Cambridge on the differences between classical Greek and the modern vernacular. When he returned to Philadelphia, Biddle set up a busy law practice while contributing essays to Joseph Dennie's *Port Folio*, a prominent weekly journal.

It's not known who introduced Clark and Biddle. Surely Jefferson had heard of Biddle's growing literary reputation, but Biddle had not yet joined the American Philosophical Society. The Philadelphia aristocrat first corresponded with the former President in December 1809, shortly after Clark left Monticello, but on another subject. It is most likely that Clark was introduced to Biddle not by Jefferson but by Benjamin Barton or his book's contracted publisher, John Conrad. Regardless, Clark was so impressed with Biddle that, even while awaiting Wirt's response, he raised with Biddle the possibility of his "writing my Western Tour &c."

Soon after he returned to Fincastle, Clark wrote Biddle with the news that Wirt had indeed turned down the project. "I have calculated on your writing for me," he said to Biddle. "Cant you Come to this place where I have my Books & memorandums and stay with me a week or two; read over & make yourself thirly acquainted with every thing which may not be explained in the Journals?"[20]

Biddle at first declined, explaining in a four-sentence letter, "I have neither health nor leisure to do sufficient justice to the fruits of your enterprise and ingenuity."[21] But ten days later, after talking to both Barton and Conrad, Biddle changed his mind. He told Clark that he would be willing to take on the project after all. He would catch the stagecoach to Fincastle in less than a week.

Biddle spent three weeks in Fincastle, interviewing Clark at Santillane. Julia would have helped entertain him, as would have little Lewis, now a toddler, the same age as Pompy during the expedition. The two men worked almost constantly, as Biddle peppered Clark with questions:

Tell me more about the "barking squirrels."
What are the customs of the Minitarees?
What exactly did you say to the Sioux chief to "touch his pride"?
Did both Indian men and women have the venereal?
Are there oysters on the Pacific coast?
How do Indian mothers flatten the heads of their babies?

Does York have a wife? Were all the tribes equally astonished by
him?

Biddle's meticulous notes show that his editorial prodding helped fill in the
drama and detail behind many of the best-known incidents during the expedition, ranging from Sacagawea's dramatic reunion with her Shoshone
family to the consternation of a Hidatsa chief upon first seeing York.

Clark patiently answered question after question as Biddle filled up
his notebooks. On April 14, Biddle left for Philadelphia, taking with him
the astronomical and scientific materials and several pocket journals
from the expedition. Several months later, he mailed another fusillade of
twenty follow-up questions:

Are the band of the Tetons which you met called by the French
bois roulé which may allude to their smoking rolled wood, or *bois
brulé* burnt woods? It is of some consequence to be accurate.[22]

After Biddle left Fincastle, Clark was ready to take his family back to
St. Louis. Six months had passed since the night Lewis had fired two lead
balls into himself at Grinder's Stand. In that time, working with almost
no prior information, Clark had successfully revived the moribund publication project. He had located the journals and navigational data, met
with the publisher, put Benjamin Barton to work on the scientific as-
pects, found Biddle and briefed him extensively about the journey. Now
he could leave.

On the way back to St. Louis, Clark stopped in Louisville and dispatched George Shannon to Philadelphia to help Biddle further with
his editing. Shannon had been the youngest man on the expedition,
but Clark thought highly of him. He has "a sincere and undisguised
heart," Clark told Biddle, in an interesting choice of words. After losing his leg following the disastrous first attempt to return Sheheke to
his nation—he would evermore be known as "Peg-Leg Shannon"—
Shannon had pursued legal studies in Kentucky and would go on to a
career in jurisprudence.

The boat trip from Louisville to St. Louis was nightmarish. Descending the Ohio, Clark's little entourage ran into headwinds, soaring summer
heat, and shallow-running river water. At the junction with the Mississippi,

the travelers lightened their keelboat by sending the carriage and horses overland and hired laborers to help pull and pole the boat upriver. There were "tormenting musketeers" and violent storms with "trees and banks falling in different directions about us," Clark said, in phrases that could have been lifted from his journals. But not this one: "Rachel fell between boats and drowned." Rachel was the baby daughter of the family's enslaved couple, Scott and Chloe. Julia became so disheartened by the difficult trip that she feared she would never be able to leave St. Louis again.[23]

The Clarks returned to a territorial capital that was nearing the heyday of the fur trade. John Jacob Astor had organized the American Fur Company and was preparing his assault on the North West Company. In a romanticized passage written years later, Washington Irving described the period this way:

> Here were to be seen about the river banks, the hectoring, extravagant, bragging boatmen of the Mississippi, with the gay grimacing, singing, good-humored Canadian voyageurs. Vagrant Indians, of various tribes, loitered about the streets. Now and then, a stark Kentucky hunter, in leathren hunting-dress, with rifle on shoulder and knife in belt, strode along. Here and there were new brick houses and shops, just set up by bustling, driving and eager men of traffic from the Atlantic States; while on the other hand the old French mansions, with open casements, still retained the easy, indolent air of the original colonists; and now and then the scraping of a fiddle, a strain of an ancient French song, or the sound of billiard balls, showed that the happy Gallic turn for gayety and amusement still lingered about the place.[24]

Irving did not mention the hundreds of slaves and free blacks whose labor was essential to the St. Louis economy.

Frederick Bates was now acting governor, though in April President Madison had appointed Benjamin Howard, Clark's friend and Kentucky congressman, to replace Lewis. (Howard would not arrive to take office until September and was frequently absent from the territory.) Within a few days of his return, Clark learned that during his absence Bates had filed unnamed complaints about him with the War Department. "I am at Some loss to determine how to act with this little animale whome I had mistaken as my friend," he scathingly told Jonathan.[25] Typically, however, Clark found a way to work with Bates, though "I have neither love nor respect for him."[26]

Government business in St. Louis was dominated by a familiar issue: the increasingly bitter conflict between American settlers and Indians over land they shared. Atrocities were common on both sides. In July, the *Louisiana Gazette* reported that the expedition's reliable hunter, George Drouillard, had been killed and cut to pieces near Manuel Lisa's outpost at the Three Forks of the Missouri. A postal rider making the weekly delivery from Vincennes was slain. On July 20, four members of a party led by Captain William Cole near Boone's Lick were ambushed and killed by a band of Potawatomis.

Indians also continued their deadly campaigns against one another. Clark reported to Eustis that he had succeeded in stopping a force of Shawnees, Delawares, and Cherokees from attacking the Osages. All of these Indians were American trading partners. On the other hand, he saw the uses of allowing unfriendly Indians to kill one another. When the Kickapoos were preparing for war with the British-controlled Winnebagos, Clark told Eustis, "I have made no exertion to divert the Kickapoos from their object; thinking it might be bad policy at this time; as universial peace among the Indians would most probably be, a signal for war with us."[27]

Reports continued to flow into St. Louis about the Shawnee brothers Tecumseh and Tenskwatawa. The younger brother, originally named Lalawethika, was one of triplets born near present-day Springfield, Ohio, after his father's death at the Battle of Point Pleasant. Neglected by his mother, who favored Tecumseh, and blinded in one eye in a childhood accident, he fell into alcoholism. But a vision experienced during a whiskey-induced coma led him to give up alcohol and to preach a spiritual doctrine based on restoring traditional Shawnee lifeways. He changed his name to Tenskwatawa (The Open Door to Heaven). A portrait painted in 1824 of the Shawnee Prophet, as he was known, inaccurately suggests a menacing personality.

No portrait was ever made of the handsome and charismatic older brother, Tecumseh. Those who met him were uniformly impressed: "One of the finest-looking men I ever saw," said a Clark relative who observed Tecumseh at the time. "About six feet high, straight with large fine features and altogether a daring, bold-looking fellow."[28] As a young warrior, he had fought with Blue Jacket against Anthony Wayne at the Battle of Fallen Timbers. He also advocated a pan-Indian confederacy based on renouncing the white man's influence and preventing the tribes from agreeing to any further land cessions. Tecumseh began circulating through the Old Northwest, seeking to unify Great Lakes tribes like the Sauks and Foxes, Menominees, and Winnebagos. Soon reports began coming back to Clark that the British were heaping gifts on the Indians, supplying them "liberally with everything they stood in want of."[29]

Tecumseh and Tenskwatawa established a village called Prophetstown on Tippecanoe Creek in Indiana, where as many as three thousand Indians from several tribes were gathered. In August, Tecumseh and seventy-five warriors met with Indiana governor William Henry Harrison at his home in Vincennes. In a celebrated incident, Tecumseh refused to join Harrison on his platform, explaining, "The earth was the most proper place for the Indians."[30] The meeting ended acrimoniously as Tecumseh and his followers stormed out of the council after Harrison denied that the Indians were one nation or owned the land in common. After all, had not the Great Spirit given them different tongues?

Other tribes were more compliant. Clark met with Gomo, the principal chief of the Potawatomis, who blamed the recent violence against settlers on the Prophet's influence over a breakaway Potawatomi band led by Main Poc (Withered Hand). "I have no father to whom I have paid any attention but yourself," Gomo assured Clark. "I have been advised several times to raise the tomahawk, [but] I shall hold you by the hand." In return, Gomo wanted his own needs attended to: "I hope you will extend your goodness and give me a gun to kill some meat on my way home, and a little of your milk to raise the drooping spirits of my village on my return to them."[31]

The American government's policy of controlling the Indians was built around commerce and liberal applications of the "white man's milk," usually corn-based whiskey. The hope was that the network of government-subsidized trading posts, or "factories," would lure the Indians from the influence of the British and undercut the private traders. Moreover, as Jefferson had argued, if the Indians became economically dependent on the factories, the factories would assist in extinguishing Indian land titles as the Indians sold their lands to lop off their debts.

The factories created economic opportunities for merchants who supplied Indians with manufactured goods. No one was more aware of this opportunity than Clark, who as a new husband and father in 1810 was concerned about his financial future. "My head is full of mercantile business here," he told his nephew John Hite Clark.[32] Given an additional responsibility as St. Louis agent for the federal Office of Indian Trade, Clark was responsible for ordering supplies for the factories and then collecting and selling the furs and pelts received from the tribes. He could steer business to the St. Louis Missouri Fur Company, but it was struggling and issuing calls for additional cash from its investors. "It is too late to repint of my bargain when things are going badly," William concluded to his brother Edmund. "It is time to Scuffle and try to get out of the dificuelty."[33]

In the meantime, he continued to mix his personal investments with government business. In September, Clark wrote to Secretary of War Eustis urging that the army establish a garrison and factory at Prairie du Chien (literally, "dog prairie"), the large Indian trading center three hundred miles up the Mississippi near the mouth of the Wisconsin River. Every year, upwards of nine thousand Indians came to Prairie du Chien to trade with one another and with British traders from Canada. Clark saw great value "in Checking British influence and preventing illicit trade." Moreover, he knew precisely the right person to run the new factory: "Mr. Denis Fitzhugh, a Gentleman of my Acquaintance." What Clark did not tell Eustis was that the gentleman of his acquaintance was also his brother-in-law and prospective business partner.[34]

He was not without lighter thoughts. Learning that John Hite Clark had been smitten by a woman, Clark gave out some advice to the lovelorn: "I know whin a man is in that way his mind is bend on the Object of his admoration and he thinks every attention he can pay to the fair Object, is Scerce Sufficient to Shew the arder of his passion. [M]an in that State of mind deserves not only pity but the applaus of his friend[s]."[35]

The manly code that had been so much a part of Clark's world in Virginia and Kentucky had also migrated to the territory. On Christmas Day of 1810, Clark personally delivered a challenge to a duel to a lawyer in St. Louis named James Graham. Clark was acting as the second to Dr. Bernard Gaines Farrar, the Virginia-born surgeon at Fort Bellefontaine and later the first American physician in private practice west of the Mississippi. The odd affair began because Farrar had previously carried a challenge to Graham from a third man, army lieutenant John Campbell, after a dispute growing out of a card game. But when Graham spurned Campbell's challenge on the grounds that the officer was not a gentleman, Farrar concluded that as Campbell's designated representative, he, too, had been equally insulted.

The arrangements were made in Clark's office. The men then rowed through ice floes on the Mississippi to a sandbar later known as Bloody Island, directly opposite St. Louis. Standing ten paces apart, or about sixty feet, they fired three times. Farrar hit Graham each time—"Close shooting for such a young man," Clark wrote admiringly—grievously wounding him.[36] Dr. Farrar, who would have presented only his side to his adversary so as to minimize the target, was struck by a single bullet to the buttocks. The seconds halted the affair because of Graham's loss of blood, but the lawyer died from his wounds several months later. Afterward, the *Louisiana Gazette* criticized the "barbarous custom, hooted at by civilized society," and Clark found himself "vexed" by an accusation that he had given surreptitious hand signals to help Farrar gain the first shot.

At this point in his life, Clark was juggling two different but related projects: publishing his account of meeting Indians in the West, and fighting them on the Mississippi. In December 1810, Clark replied to a further list of questions from Nicholas Biddle on topics ranging from a game played by Indians ("it resembles Billiards very much") to the names different tribes gave to the Missouri River ("Most called it Troubled water").[37] With his letter he enclosed what he called "a large Connected Map" he had finished that month. Intended to accompany Biddle's narrative, this new map, wrote Clark, "is much more Correct than any which has been before published."[38]

That was an understatement. Clark's finished map of 1810 was a cartographic masterpiece, a remarkably accurate rendering of the inner continent of North America. During the expedition, he had made fifty route maps, on large sheets of linen paper, and dozens of smaller maps. As early as Camp River Dubois, Clark had begun sketching a comprehensive, or "connected," map of the entire Missouri River drainage. He compiled the route maps into two large maps during the winters at Fort

Mandan and Fort Clatsop. After the expedition, Clark gathered more information from trappers like Drouillard and John Colter and military explorers like Zebulon Pike.

The completed map that Clark sent to Biddle stretched four feet wide and more than two feet deep. It depicted the multiple ranges of the Rocky Mountain chain and outlying ranges like the Black Hills. Clark showed all of the major rivers traveled by the Expedition, as well as places they had not seen, such as Yellowstone Lake (which he called "Lake Eustis"). The vast empty canvas on previous maps was now filled in with distinct regions—the tallgrass and shortgrass prairies, the Columbia Plain and Basin, the Northern Rockies and the Coast Ranges.

Parts of the map still reflected Jeffersonian preconceptions. The Central Rockies were compressed into a few hundred miles, and the headwaters of the major rivers of the West—the Yellowstone, Big Horn, Platte, Arkansas, Rio Grande, Colorado, Snake, and Willamette ("Multnomah")—all rose from a single height of land barely fifty miles on a side. More important, though, the landscape viewed through Clark's steady blue eyes showed no short overland passage across the Continental Divide to the Pacific. No one would find a Northwest Passage along the Missouri River.[39]

Clark maintained an abiding interest in describing the natural world as well as mapping it. When the Scottish-English botanist John Bradbury visited Clark in St. Louis in 1810, he was struck that his host was "more intelligent in Natural History than from his few opportunities of intercourse might be expected."[40] Bradbury gathered specimens around St. Louis until March 1811, when he started up the Missouri with Wilson Price Hunt and the overland Astorian expedition. On the way upriver, he met Daniel Boone, then seventy-six but still going on spring hunts, and Clark's fellow expedition member John Colter, who had married and settled near La Charette. Bradbury became the first to record Colter's extraordinary tale of being attacked by Blackfeet Indians while trapping beaver near Three Forks. His companion John Potts was killed, and Colter was stripped naked and forced to run for his life. Eluding his pursuers, Colter made his way across two hundred miles of prickly pear cactus and prairie to Fort Manuel Lisa on the Yellowstone.

As he continued up the river, Bradbury noted that "Bees have spread over this continent in a degree, and with a celerity so nearly corresponding with that of the Anglo-Americans, that it has given rise to a belief, both amongst the Indians and the Whites, that bees are their precursors, and that to whatever part they go the white people will follow. I am of the opinion that . . . it is as impossible to stop the progress of the one as of the other."[41]

Following close behind Hunt and Bradbury on the Missouri were not only bees but a St. Louis Missouri Fur Company keelboat rigged with sails and led by Manuel Lisa. Lisa was distrusted by mountain men, probably because of his Spanish origins, but he quickly won the admiration of a traveler he had taken aboard, Henry Marie Brackenridge, a lawyer with a literary talent. Lisa was "a man of a bold and daring character," Brackenridge wrote in his journal. "There is no one better acquainted with the Indian character and trade, and few are his equals in preserving indefatigable industry."[42] As Lisa's keelboat vigorously pursued Hunt's group, in order to combine with it for greater security, Brackenridge observed that along the way Lisa took great pleasure in reading *Don Quixote* in Spanish.

Brackenridge also preserved in his journal the last written impression of Sacagawea. "We had on board a Frenchman named Charboneau, with his wife, an Indian woman of the Snake nation," he noted. "The woman, a good creature, of a mild and gentle disposition, greatly attached to the whites, whose manners and dress she tries to imitate."[43] Sacagawea and Charbonneau had just delivered their son Jean Baptiste ("Pomp") to Clark for his education. Although the boy apparently never lived in Clark's personal household, he was baptized in St. Louis and matriculated at a parochial school run by a Baptist minister.

William began to invest in additional land, including buying a single lot from Alexander McNair for $1,500. It was the precise amount of the annuity given to the Osages a few years earlier for millions of acres of their lands.

The Clark household was beginning to fill up. Young Lewis was running through the streets beating his drum, and Julia was pregnant with her second child. Moreover, Clark had become a surrogate father to his nephews John and Benjamin O'Fallon, the sons of his sister Fanny by her first husband. Both O'Fallon boys had moved to St. Louis to live with the Clarks and receive their education.

A half-dozen or more slaves also lived under the Clark roof. Whites in St. Louis devoted much of their energy to keeping their Indian and black populations under control. In early 1811, reports swept up the Mississippi of a slave rebellion near Natchez. Between 150 and 500 black field hands left their plantations in St. John Parish and marched toward New Orleans in what became the largest slave uprising in U.S. history. The white citizens, fearing a repeat of Toussaint L'Ouverture's revolution in St. Dominique, were terrified. It took an impromptu force of regular troops and Louisiana militia, which included free men of color, to stop the rebellion in a battle near present-day Kenner, Louisiana. Twenty-one of the slave leaders were later executed.

The uprising stirred widespread panic among the white population. William's father-in-law, George Hancock, wrote from Fincastle with news that a fire in a hemp warehouse had stirred "apprehension that the Negroes about here had intended a massacre of the Whites . . . It was expected to have been attempted [this month] when 5 negroes were hung here for the Murder of their Masters." Interestingly, the plot Hancock claimed that the slaves were planning—"to Set fire to the Town & while the citizens were engaged in extinguishing the fire the Negroes were to seize on the arms &c"—was the same one colonial New Yorkers had accused their slaves of hatching as early as 1712.[44]

Later that year, John O'Fallon wrote Clark from Louisville that he had inquired about York, who was now living there and had been hired out to various masters. York's conduct had been excellent, O'Fallon reported, but he had been poorly clothed and "appeared wretched under the fear that he has incurred your displeasure and which he despairs he will ever remove. I am confident he sorely repant of whatever miscounduct of his that might have lead to such a breach and moreover has considered amended and in fine deem it not inreasonable to recommend his situation to your consideration."[45] No reply from Clark has been found.

Meanwhile, tensions were increasing in the Upper Mississippi Valley as the independent tribes located along the Illinois, Rock, and Wisconsin rivers continued to adroitly play the competing American and British interests against each other. The surge of Americans to the West following Lewis and Clark's expedition had simply bypassed these Great Lakes tribes, leaving them as free agents in the contest for empire. Nicholas Boilvin reported that the tribes gathering at Prairie du Chien "complain that their American Father does not take sufficient care of them" and that the British had told them that "their american father is So poor, that if it was not for their Old English father, they would not have a Single blanket to cover themselves." More ominously, he stated, "soon their English father will declare war against the Americans, and will again take under his protection his beloved red children."[46]

Boilvin had replaced John Campbell as subagent at Prairie du Chien after Campbell was killed in his duel. His instructions, as laid out by Secretary of War Eustis, were a model of Jeffersonian ideals: he was to "conciliate the friendship of the Indians generally towards the United States." He was to "prevent the use of ardent spirits among the Indians." He was to promote the "Arts of Agriculture and domestic manufactures" among the Indians. In short, he was to convert the Indians into Jefferson's beloved if idealized yeoman farmers.[47]

That agenda would have seemed far-fetched to George Sibley, the factor at Fort Osage, as he contended with the numerous tribes who traditionally viewed the powerful Osages as even more dangerous competitors than the newly arrived Americans. Sibley told Clark that the Osages had been attacked by the Iowas, Otoes, Sioux, and Potawatomis. He reported that these tribes "have Robbed them of their horses, and murdered their People, insulted the benevolent and just policy of the U.S. and have nearly, if not quite, compelled them to the last Resort, the tomahawk and Scalping Knife."[48]

The Osages' patience ended when they apprehended an Iowa spy on their lands in April 1811. The hapless warrior was instantly cut into at least fifty pieces. That night Sibley, a stylish dresser who insisted on wearing silk vests every day, was awakened from a sound sleep to find his bedchamber crowded with excited Osages flourishing the bleeding, decapitated head of the Iowa warrior over the foot of his bed.

Sibley and Clark encouraged their Osage allies to retaliate with raids against the Iowas on their northern borders. At the same time, they sought to protect the Osages' western flanks on the Great Plains. That spring Sibley visited tribes farther west and painstakingly signed a series of peace treaties with the Pawnees and Kansas. He reported being treated with "the utmost friendship and respect" and even noted that American flags were flying on some lodges.[49]

One tribe seemed to get it right from the start. These were the migrant Shawnees who had moved from their original homes in the Ohio Valley to a cluster of communities near present-day Cape Girardeau in the Missouri boot heel. Unlike more militant Shawnees such as Tecumseh and the Prophet, or those who had fought George Rogers Clark on the Ohio, these peaceful, agrarian Indians sought to live quietly alongside the whites. Indians who lived acquiescently with Americans were repaid with William Clark's sympathy. Clark wrote directly to President Madison to urge that they be granted a permanent tract "where the White people might not encroach on them . . . and where the white people will not be permited to sell them spirituous Liquors." Clark pointed out that his ability to protect them was limited, since "nine out of ten of the Indian Traders have no respect for our Laws."[50]

The response Clark received from his superiors in Washington said nothing about the plight of these powerless Shawnees on the Mississippi. Instead, the Administration granted a tract of nine square miles to an entirely different band of Shawnees on the Meramec River. The reason for the generous treatment of the Meramec Shawnees? They were working lead mines. Early industrialized Shawnees were more acceptable to the government than the Indian versions of Jefferson's yeoman farmers. Here, Eustis told Clark, "the whites must be forbidden to intrude on such Territory as may be designed for the Indians, and if necessary may be expelled according to law."[51]

Along the Mississippi and in the Illinois country, meanwhile, more and more settlers were being killed by more militant tribes. Clark warned Eustis of "the rooted enmity of the Prophet to the United States, and his determination to commence hostility as soon as he thinks himself sufficiently strong." Clark recommended that farmers build blockhouses and band together into stations similar to those erected by George Rogers Clark in Kentucky a generation earlier. "I am inclined to believe that the crisis is fast approaching," he concluded.[52]

The *Louisiana Gazette* was particularly alarmed about the absence of white preparedness, noting that only one in every four householders in Illinois even owned a rifle: "We have every reason to expect a general attack as soon as the corn is ripe enough for food."[53]

Who, then, would rid the borderlands of the Indian threat? The most aggressive public official west of the Appalachians was the Indian territorial governor, William Henry Harrison. Three years younger than Clark,

Harrison was a college-educated Virginian who originally studied medicine in Philadelphia. He had joined the army, served with Lewis and Clark in Anthony Wayne's campaign, and was present at both Fallen Timbers and the signing of the Treaty of Greenville. A patrician in both background and bearing, he had constructed an enormous brick mansion called Grouseland on the outskirts of Vincennes.

Beginning with the Treaty of Fort Wayne in 1803, Harrison had methodically extinguished Indian claims to tens of millions of acres of their homelands east of the Mississippi. His 1809 treaty at Fort Wayne had itself turned three million acres in Indiana over to the United States in return for trade goods worth $7,000 and an annuity of $1,750.

Harrison proposed that an American army be formed to march up the Wabash to eliminate the Prophet's "banditti" for good. In the fall of 1811, he was pressing for immediate action, in order to further prevent the British from cynically arming the Indians against the Americans. "It is impossible to ascribe this profusion [of weapons and supplies] to any other motive than that of instigating the Indians to take up the tomahawk," he said. "It cannot be to secure their trade, for all the peltries collected on the waters of the Wabash, in one year, if sold in the London market would not pay the freight of the goods which have been given to the Indians."[54]

When Tecumseh passed through Vincennes on the way to enlist the Southern tribes in his confederacy, Harrison seized the opportunity created by the leader's absence from Prophetstown. Acting on his own initiative, Harrison moved up the Wabash into Indian-owned lands with a thousand regulars and militia, including three of Clark's young nephews: John O'Fallon, George Croghan, and George Gwathmey. It was the largest campaign the American military had mounted against Indians since Anthony Wayne's march to Fallen Timbers in 1794.

Camped on Tippecanoe Creek at dawn on November 7, the Americans were suddenly attacked by Indian warriors who were apparently provoked when sentries fired upon several young Winnebago men. The army beat off the attack, and the two-hour battle ended with 188 Americans killed or wounded, and approximately the same number of Indian casualties. But when Harrison's men advanced and burned Prophetstown the next day, the Americans gained at least a psychological victory.

Harrison claimed that his invasion of Indian territory had ended the terror east of the Mississippi. Clark agreed, telling Eustis that the Prophet would now be treated as "an imposter" by his own people, who themselves "will be pursued in every direction, caught, and punished."[55]

The actual result was almost the opposite. Harrison's march dispersed the most militant warriors throughout the region as they prepared for the next phase in their long war against the American invaders. Tenskwatawa retained much of his influence. Tippecanoe has been called the first engagement of the War of 1812—though it was in truth a continuation of the war for independence that the Indians had fought separately but parallel to the conflict between the Americans and the British. The Indian war in the West was as distinct from the War of 1812 as George Rogers Clark's Illinois campaign was from Bunker Hill.

While Clark was attempting to woo the Indians from avaricious British traders, he was also seeking to turn a profit himself. Pursuing his private trade with retailers and merchants, he purchased goods from distant markets in the East for shipment to the government factories. In the spring of 1811, a Louisville hatter named Henry Duncan sent Clark barrels of whiskey, gunpowder, and tobacco with instructions to "procure for me all the muskrat skins you can," or at least two thousand pelts.[56]

The fur trade was an integral part of the growing national and international market. When two of Manuel Lisa's barges came down the Missouri loaded with furs in late July, the *Louisiana Gazette* wrote bullishly that "A well organized company on the Missouri will be able to draw immense wealth, from the incalculable resources of that vast country."[57] Clark told George Shannon that he had purchased $8,700 in goods and urged Shannon to "join me in trade at this place."[58] Shannon didn't jump at the chance, and a few weeks later a discouraged Clark feared he would have to carry the entire risk himself. He told Jonathan, "I am getting a little tired of mercantile business and if I do not get Such a person to join as I wish Shall Sell out."[59]

Nicholas Biddle had spent most of the previous year waking up at 5 a.m. and working on the journals seven or eight hours a day, often with George Shannon at his elbow. On July 8, 1811, Biddle wrote to Clark with the news that the manuscript was all but finished. He had cropped Clark's map to fit and was "now ready to put the work to the press." He then raised a delicate matter: "It is the exact relative situation in point of rank & command between Captain Lewis & yourself." Biddle had noticed that Congress had differentiated their ranks in its act compensating them. In an earlier draft of the same letter, Biddle put the matter more bluntly: "I am very desirous of having that matter settled, so as to prevent the possibility of any unpleasant reflections in future on the part of the friends of either of you."[60]

Clark's reply was instant and unequivocal. The two men were "equal in every point of view." Clark admitted that "I did not think myself very well treated as I did not get the appointment which was promised me," but said he had never mentioned the matter to anyone and asked Biddle to say nothing about it himself.[61] The obvious corroborating witness was Thomas Jefferson, but if Lewis had in fact asked Jefferson that Clark receive a captain's commission, the President never made note of it. To the contrary, Jefferson persisted in calling the expedition "Capt. Lewis's Tour" long after it was over. In 1803, he had nominated Lewis—but not Clark—to membership in the American Philosophical Society. To Jefferson, Clark was a loyal and successful second in command.

A few months later, with his Lewis and Clark project apparently completed, Biddle married a young Philadelphia woman, Jane Craig, at her family's country home, Andalusia, on the Delaware River. Clark's own family was growing as well. "I have another Son, a great rough red headed fellow who is now four days old," he wrote to Jonathan.[62] The redheaded fellow inherited his father's melanocortin 1 receptor but not his name: he was christened William Preston Clark, in honor of Clark's friend William Preston, who was then visiting from Virginia.

Just two months later, William received a severe blow. His eldest brother, Jonathan, had always been a revered father figure to him. The first of the ten Clark siblings, Jonathan was twenty years older than William to the day (they shared the same August 1 birthday). The brothers' correspondence reflected their close relationship, with William frequently asking Jonathan for advice or to "ride over" from Louisville to visit him in St. Louis. (He apparently never did.) But Jonathan, who had gotten wet at the launching of a schooner at Louisville, fell ill and died in what the family called "an apoplectic fit" on November 25, 1811.[63]

Jonathan was the wealthiest of all the Clarks. His estate listed fifty-six slaves by name, including two called "Janey." The slaves were valued at $11,555, an enormous sum at the time. Among the household items left to Jonathan's six children were nine Windsor chairs, one backgammon table, and a library that included works by Cicero, Virgil, Erasmus, and Tobias Smollett. There was also "1 whip."[64]

Among William's prospective business partners in Louisville was the young John James Audubon. In 1811, Audubon had formed a partnership with his brother-in-law Thomas W. Bakewell in a commission merchandising enterprise based in New Orleans. At about 2 a.m. on December 16, Audubon was riding across the Big Barrens, a large grassland in western Kentucky, when his horse suddenly stopped, froze, and splayed out its legs as if walking on a smooth sheet of ice. "At that instant all the shrubs and trees began to move from their very roots," Audubon recalled. "The ground rose and fell in successive furrows, like the ruffled waters of a lake."

At that same moment, the steamboat *New Orleans*, the first steam-powered boat ever to run on western waters, was on its trial voyage down the Ohio. The *New Orleans*, built in Pittsburgh by Nicholas Roosevelt, great-uncle of Theodore Roosevelt, and Robert Fulton, had been launched just a few weeks earlier. Aboard was a skeleton crew, along with Roosevelt, his wife, Lydia, and their newborn son. Below the Falls of the Ohio, the crew noticed trees and bushes along the shore beginning to heave and wave silently, even though it was a windless night. Alarmed at the sight of riverbanks caving in, the steamboatmen tied up on an island, only to discover in the morning that the sandbar had vanished and their mooring line plunged straight into the water, drawn as tightly as a violin string. They hurriedly cut the vessel free.

Both Audubon and the Roosevelts were near the epicenter of one of the largest earthquakes in history and the biggest ever recorded in North America. It was the first in a series of three immense quakes in 1811–'12 — and as many as two thousand smaller ones — that were felt across the entire eastern United States and as far away as Quebec City. Stone walls cracked in St. Louis. Church bells rang out in Charleston. Seismologists estimate their intensity as 8.4 to 8.7 on the Richter scale, compared with 6.6 for the 1906 San Francisco earthquake.[65]

The closest town to the epicenter was New Madrid. Clark had traveled to New Madrid sixteen years earlier on his military mission to protest the Spanish fortifications. Now the Cove of Grease was a scene of Goyaesque horrors. Clark's friend John Bradbury was on his way down the Mississippi and had tied up near the second Chickasaw Bluff when he was jolted awake by a "most tremendous noise . . . All nature seemed running into chaos," he wrote, "as wild fowl fled, trees snapped and river banks rumbled into the water."[66] Empty boats drifted by, disconcertingly, carrying neither passengers nor cargo. The ground quivered like "the flesh of a beef just killed," as one person put it. In the town of New Madrid, Lorenzo Dow heard "the screams of the affrighted inhabitants running to and fro, not knowing where to go, or what to do—the cries of the fowls and beasts of every species—the cracking of trees falling, and the roaring of the Mississippi."[67]

Throughout the New Madrid seismic zone, "sand blows" erupted, spouting mud and debris into the air. The Mississippi's waters, filled with masses of oleaginous foam, surged back up creeks. Briefly the entire river seemed to flow backward, creating a temporary waterfall whose roaring could be heard as far as New Madrid itself. (The falls quickly disappeared as its sand and mud base washed away.)

In Louisville, George Heinrich Crist was knocked out of his bed by the first shock wave, which was accompanied by a roaring "I thught would leave us deaf if we lived . . . all you cold hear was screams from people and animals. It was the worst thing I have ever witnessed." In darkness so complete "you could not see nothng," Crist sought in vain for support. "You should not hold onto nothing neither man or woman was strong enough—the shaking would knock you lose like knocking hi-cror nuts out of a tree."[68]

Writing about the earthquake a few months later, Clark observed that New Madrid had been "nearly depopulated" in the aftermath. St. Louis had escaped with minimal damage, and "one chimney was thrown down in the American Bottom [the alluvial plain on the east side of the Mississippi]."[69]

Many Americans thought the upheaval was related to another extraordinary natural phenomenon that year. In March, an enormous comet had appeared low in the southern sky. Over the following weeks, it steadily brightened, and by September the Great Comet of 1811 was seen around the world, with its tail stretching 17 degrees across the sky and with a head looking, from Earth, as large in diameter as the sun. Farmers who first saw the steamboat *New Orleans* on the Ohio belching flames and sparks into the nighttime sky were convinced that the comet had fallen into the river.

Indians and some whites interpreted the earthquake and the comet as divine signals, said to be predicted by Tecumseh after the Battle of Tippecanoe. The entire continent seemed unnerved. In one of the more bizarre episodes of an unsettling year, two of Thomas Jefferson's nephews, Lilburn and Isham Lewis, were charged with killing a slave in Kentucky on the night of the first earthquake after the body's decapitated head rolled into view during an aftershock seven weeks later. Anyone looking for dark omens found ample material in the closing months of 1811.

> Mr. Dickson and those British traders who are also Agents who have smuggled an emince quantity of goods through [Green Bay] could be caught on their return as they go out in the Spring— This description of people grasp at every means in their power to wave the affections of the Indians from any thing that is American.[70]

With those words written to Secretary of War Eustis, Clark acknowledged not only the general threat posed by the British traders but also the particular influence of the man who would become both his antagonist and his real-life doppelganger.

Born in Dumfries, Scotland, Robert Dickson was a tall, robust redhead with a full, florid face, an engaging manner, and a commanding presence. He had come to North America with two brothers in the 1780s and entered the fur trade at Michilimackinac. He had married an Indian woman, Totowin, the sister of a chief of the Dakota Sioux, or Santees. But unlike most traders, he had remained faithful to his Indian wife and lived with her in a post he built on Lake Traverse, on the border between present-day Minnesota and South Dakota. He was known for his intelligence, fairness, and compassion. The Dakotas, who trusted him more than any other European, called him Mascotapah, or "Red-Hair Man."

More than a thousand traders worked the northern waters on their fleets of *canots de maître*, but Dickson was by far the best known. At home in two worlds, he was a member of Montreal's elite Beaver Club but also spoke the Sioux languages, as well as Ojibwa and French, all with a Scottish burr. On his expedition up the Mississippi in 1805, Zebulon Pike met Dickson—but might have been describing William Clark when he called the trader "a gentleman of commercial knowledge and possessing much geographical knowledge of the western country and of open, frank manners."[71]

Dickson had first formed a partnership with James Aird, whom Clark had met in 1806 on his return from the Pacific. He later started his own Robert Dickson and Company and then the Michilimackinac Company. In 1807, Louisiana's acting governor, Frederick Bates, had issued Dickson an exclusive license to trade with the Nakota Sioux and Iowas.

Dickson traveled to St. Louis frequently, and on at least one occasion he brought in an Indian accused of murder and turned him over for trial. He was revered by the Indians and constantly urged them not to kill and take scalps, saying that the greater warriors took and saved prisoners rather than destroying them. Dickson also remained fiercely loyal to the British Crown. He had acted as a second for Redford Crawford in his duel with John Campbell at Prairie du Chien and chafed at the restrictions the American government sought to put on British traders.

At the outset of 1812, William Clark saw Dickson and his colleagues as the instigators of a campaign of terror in the Mississippi Valley. Early in January Clark learned that a party of one hundred Winnebagos, seeking revenge for their losses at Tippecanoe, had attacked the lead-smelting furnace on the Galena River. Two whites were "butchered in a most horrid manner," though the proprietors, George Hunt and Nathaniel Pryor, claimed they were English and escaped with their Indian wives.[72] (Pryor, the trusted expedition sergeant, had resigned from the army in 1810.)

A few weeks later, Indians fired on another expedition member, Alexander Willard, who was carrying messages for Clark on a sleigh down the frozen Mississippi. Willard had just discovered the bodies of nine members of a single family named O'Neal, murdered on the Mississippi above St. Louis. "The Winnebagoes are Deturmined for War," Clark told his superiors.[73] Concluding that the destruction of Prophetstown had not quelled the tribes, Clark and the Louisiana territorial governor, Benjamin Howard, urged that a military campaign be mounted in the spring to cut off the Indians from their British suppliers.

But who would fight the war? A total of 240 regular army troops were scattered thinly among the U.S. garrisons at Forts Osage, Madison, and Bellefontaine. Another 2,000 adult males were available for militia duty. Facing them were potentially as many as 4,400 warriors who lived near enough to St. Louis to join a confederacy should Tecumseh's efforts prove successful.

William Henry Harrison knew just the man to help organize the territory's defenses. "At a time like this when the Government is no doubt in search of Military talents," he wrote to the Secretary of War, "I think it my duty to mention to you Genl Wm Clark of St. Louis. I have long known this gentleman having served with him in the army & I have never known one to whom the observation . . . is more applicable—that he came a soldier out of his mothers womb."[74]

Clark knew something had to be done. He and Howard met with Ninian Edwards in St. Louis and told the Illinois governor that "a formidable combination of Indians will be effected and that a bloody war must ensure; more murders committed; the Prophet is regaining his influence."[75]

The mood in the army garrisons was equally grim. John Johnston, the factor at Fort Madison, wrote that his post was surrounded by so many hostile Indians that American scouting parties were afraid to venture more than two hundred yards outside its walls. "I believe every man of us will perish," he said.[76] An army captain at Fort Wayne observed, "Some say if we have a British war we shall have an Indian war . . . but I have every reason to believe we shall have an Indian war this spring, whether we have a British war or not."[77]

In this unstable environment, the St. Louis Missouri Fur Company was not prospering. In 1811, it had brought in furs worth $20,000, but the aggressive Blackfeet had cut off the trappers from their rich hunting grounds at the Forks of the Missouri, and a fire at its depot at Cedar Island cost the company $15,000 in furs. Clark and his partners decided to liquidate their original enterprise and form a renamed Missouri Fur Company with $50,000 in capital. Clark would be president of the board; Manuel Lisa was put in charge of trading. The new company began operations in May, when Lisa left for the Upper Missouri with two keelboats, accompanied by Clark's bookkeeper, John C. Luttig.

At the same time, Clark and Howard began to shore up the territory's defenses in the early part of 1812. Daniel Boone's son Nathan patrolled the countryside with his militia company of sixty mounted rangers. The *Louisiana Gazette* called them "as fine a body of hardy woodsmen as ever took the field."[78] In March, Howard and Boone's Rangers went 120 miles up the Mississippi to build a new post, Fort Mason, at the mouth of the Jeffreon (present-day Fabius) River, a site thought to be more defensible than Fort Madison.

In April, Clark convened several dozen chiefs, warriors, women, and children from the recalcitrant bands on the Illinois River in St. Louis. He then played what had always been the government's trump card in impressing Indians: he told them he would take them to Washington. On May 5, Clark left St. Louis with a large entourage that included twenty-nine chiefs and warriors from the Great and Little Osages, Shawnees, and Delawares; three Indian women; several interpreters; and Maurice Blondeau, the subagent for the Sauks and Foxes. In addition, he was taking Julia and his two sons back to Virginia, where they could sit out the renewed hostilities on the Mississippi in safety. Accompanying them was Clark's nineteen-year-old nephew, John O'Fallon.

On June 18, as Clark's group moved up the Ohio, the U.S. Congress stunned the world by declaring war on Great Britain. The European continent was enmeshed in the protracted Napoleonic Wars that pitted Britain, Russia, Austria, and Prussia against an expansionist France and its justly feared Grande Armée. In the months before America's declaration, Britain, spread thin by its military commitments, had begun impressing American seamen and disrupting American commerce bound for France. The United States, however, was not choosing sides in the great European struggle. Indeed, the Senate fell only two votes short of also declaring war on France.

The first declaration of war under the U.S. Constitution was unpopular from the start. Every Federalist in the Senate voted against it, but the Republican Henry Clay and his "War Hawks" had prevailed. Full of nationalist ardor, they were ready to annex Canada, if necessary, in order to restore American honor on the high seas and put an end to the British-instigated Indian "depredations" on the Mississippi and in Florida.

The real issues in the West were land and trade. The *Louisiana Gazette* estimated that Indian trade on the Upper Mississippi was worth $100,000 annually in lead, furs, and pelts.[79] Even though the Louisiana Purchase had been signed almost a decade earlier, the Americans still had no secure title to its lands, with British and Indians controlling the Northwest and the Spanish in the Southwest continuing to insist that the purchase covered only a narrow strip of land west of the Mississippi.

The day after war was declared, the Secretary of War sent a circular letter to all territorial governors and agents advising them to spare no expense in keeping the Indians "quiet and friendly."[80] In St. Louis, that instruction seemed too little and too late. Governor Howard replied to the Secretary of War that the Indians would be upon them as soon as the corn ripened. Then the news arrived that the unprepared American commanders at Michilimackinac—who had never been told of the declaration of war—had surrendered without a fight to a British force of Dakota Sioux, Winnebagos, and Menominees.

The leader of the British force was none other than Robert Dickson. He gave generous terms: the merchant ships in the harbor would be turned over to the British, but the Americans in the garrison would keep their private property and be allowed a month to depart from the island. Dickson noted with some satisfaction that the Indians "all returned to their Canoes, and not one drop either of mans or animals Blood was spilt."[81]

With the capture of Michilimackinac, and the surrender of Detroit a month later to a force also recruited by Dickson, the Great Lakes had become a British pond. The way down the Mississippi to St. Louis lay all but undefended. As the St. Louis merchant Christian Wilt put it: "If Mackinaw is taken it will encourage the Indians to ravage the frontiers."[82]

Clark continued up the Ohio with his delegation of chiefs. Sick with one of his frequent fevers, he wrote ahead to George Shannon, asking his friend to meet him in Pittsburgh with carriages, harnesses, and teams of horses for the overland trip to Washington. At Hagerstown, Maryland, the group divided. John O'Fallon escorted Julia and the boys south to Fincastle, while William and the chiefs proceeded directly to Washington City.

The arrival of the chiefs touched off an uproar in the capital. They attracted curious crowds to their quarters at Davis's Hotel on Pennsylvania Avenue and Sixth Street. They dined with President Madison at the White House. They attended the theater. Clark ordered new boots for the chiefs from the Office of Indian Trade. The *National Intelligencer* found the chiefs—among them the Osages Big Soldier and Clermont— "very respectable . . . remarkable for their gigantic figures and fine proportion of their forms."[83]

Clark's discussions with the War Department were centered on the losses of Michilimackinac and the continued activities of Dickson. "I fear for the effects which this may produce on the Indians, who may be prepared for action," Clark wrote to Ninian Edwards.[84] It was a prescient judgment. That same week, American soldiers abandoning Fort Dearborn at present-day Chicago were all but wiped out by an Indian attack; among the dead was William Wells, the famous scout who had first fought with the tribes against St. Clair and then changed sides to join the Americans at Fallen Timbers.

During his trip east, Clark had received dismaying news from Biddle: the publisher they had contracted to print the journals, John Conrad, had gone out of business. But Biddle had already found a replacement, Samuel Bradford, "one of the best booksellers here."[85] Clark could not conceal his disappointment—"I think we might have expected from him some intimation of his situation which would have prevented a delay"— but, as always, he moved on.[86] Clark offered Biddle one-half of his share of the book's profits if he would see it through publication. (Clark later designated Lewis's share to go to Lewis's mother, Lucy Marks.) By then, Biddle had begun a political career in the Pennsylvania legislature and had no time. He turned over the task of completing the editing of the journals to Paul Allen, one of his colleagues at *Port Folio*, for which he would pay Allen $500.

Clark returned to St. Louis in mid-November, after an absence of six months, to find the territory in turmoil. Even before he arrived, he had been forced to request a company of military recruits to escort him and protect his chiefs—not from rival tribes but from vindictive settlers. Informed daily of yet another American setback, if not debacle, the citizens were outraged at the lack of support from Washington. William Hull, the American general who surrendered Detroit, was burned in effigy in the streets of St. Louis.

The name of the territory itself had been changed. Louisiana was now the Territory of Missouri, a result of the earlier admission of the District of Orleans to the Union as the state of Louisiana. Missouri was elevated to a second-class territorial government, allowing its citizens to elect their own territorial assembly and to send a nonvoting delegate to the U.S. Congress. With the new government came regional jealousies and rivalries, many of them pitting Clark and the French Creole establishment in St. Louis against newly arrived land speculators and settlers from the southern counties. In the first election for Missouri's delegate to Congress in 1812, Clark's friend Edward Hempstead ran as the Creole candidate and defeated the populist postmaster Rufus Easton.

Clark was just as committed to land speculation as were his newly arrived countrymen. He and his extended family maintained their large land investments in Kentucky and Indiana, dating back to George Rogers Clark's land grant, and William had steadily built his own land grant into significant holdings in the St. Louis area.

Now all of these holdings seemed threatened. As the violence spread and commerce crawled to a halt, Illinois Governor Ninian Edwards predicted that up to one-half of the residents of his territory might leave and return to the east. Convinced that Missouri was in danger of "a total overthrow" at the hands of the British and Indians, Howard worked with Clark to plan an offensive against the tribes and then left for Kentucky in November 1812.[87]

With Howard's departure, and the ice on the rivers reducing mail deliveries from Washington to once every two months, Clark finished the military plan on his own authority. He would send an army into Indian country as far up the Mississippi as Prairie du Chien—the "Metropolis of British traders," as Howard had put it.[88] The army would be supported by two armed galleys. Clark contracted Major Christy to convert the Indian Department's keelboats into gunboats fitted with cannons and capable of holding forty to fifty men apiece. He and Howard were so convinced the government would supply the necessary troops—they asked for four thousand—that they ordered a thousand barrels of pickled pork for the quartermaster's future larder.

They received fewer troops than they needed and far more pickled pork than they would ever eat. But with the boat construction under way, Clark decided to return to Virginia in December and "proceed on as far as Philadelphia, to push the publication of Lewis & Clarks Tour, which has been neglected two years—caused by my absence so far on Publick business, and the falue of a Buck seller whom I had employed to Carry it on after Govr Lewis Death."[89]

As Clark headed back east, the frontier's other red-headed man was still busy with his own public business on the Canadian front. The previous summer, Robert Dickson had dispatched the rising Sauk warrior Black Hawk to Chicago and Detroit with five hundred men. Black Hawk later recalled that Dickson "had been ordered to lay waste the country around St. Louis, but that he had been a trader on the Mississippi for many years, had always been kindly treated and could not consent to send brave men to murder women and children. There were no soldiers there to fight, but where he was going to send us there were a number of soldiers, and if we defeated them, the Mississippi country should be ours."[90] By the time Black Hawk arrived at Chicago and Detroit, though, the Americans had already been defeated. The British military aim achieved, Dickson had also accomplished his goal of deflecting the Indians from attacking border settlements.

Dickson went to Montreal in the fall, where British General Isaac Brock appointed him Superintendent of the Indians for the Western Department, a job precisely analogous to that held by William Clark in the United States. Dickson then made an astonishing return trip of 1,500 miles from Montreal back to Prairie du Chien in three winter months. His hope was to free British trade from American interference and "throw off the Shackles that have so long fettered us."[91]

The War of 1812 continued to be an American disaster. Secretary of War Eustis, a Harvard-educated surgeon who had tended to the wounded at Bunker Hill, resigned in December 1812 even as the setbacks mounted. On January 22, 1813, an American army under General James Winchester was wiped out by a combined British and Indian force on the river Raisin, south of Detroit. The battle, fought on icy ground, was an eerie reprise of St. Clair's Defeat, twenty-two years earlier and 150 miles to the south. Of the 934 American soldiers who fought at the river Raisin, more than 900 were killed or captured.

The surviving Americans later charged that many of the defenseless wounded had been slaughtered after the battle. John O'Fallon wrote to his mother, Fanny, that 180 men in his company had been killed during the campaign and that "a greater degree of inhumanities and savage barbarity never was before evinced by a civilized nation." Decades of Indian anger over the encroachments on their lands were surging to the surface. "The Indians were so unrestrained in acts of barbarity that they were let loose upon the wounded who had been placed in houses and after butchering them consumed their houses reducing to ashes them all."[92]

Throughout the winter of 1812–'13 many Americans thought they would have to abandon their lands in the Louisiana Purchase. The Indian subagent Thomas Forsyth told Clark that settlers in St. Louis were selling their properties and moving out. The newspaper editor Joseph Charless advised the government that "a great number of families are preparing to remove into Kentucky and Tennessee as soon as the weather will permit. These consist generally of the most respectable of our popu-

WILLIAM CLARK

Clark organized the defense of Missouri Territory as governor and brigadier general of the militia during the War of 1812. (Joseph Bush/Filson Historical Society, Louisville, Kentucky)

George Rogers Clark, William's older brother by eighteen years, organized a daring campaign to capture the Old Northwest during the American Revolution. He was Thomas Jefferson's original choice to lead an expedition to the Pacific.

Fort Washington, the future site of Cincinnati, was Clark's headquarters during the Indian wars on the Ohio. It was sketched in 1790 by Captain Jonathan Heart, who was killed the following year leading a bayonet charge at St. Clair's Defeat. (Ohio Historical Society)

The Battle of Fallen Timbers was a turning point in the Indian wars and made Anthony Wayne the first hero of the new United States Army. Lieutenant Billy Clark fought with a rifle company on the left flank. (Granger Collection, New York)

The scheming General James Wilkinson drew Clark into his intrigues against Anthony Wayne and later urged the Spanish to arrest both Lewis and Clark. (C. W. Peale/Independence National Historical Park)

In 1791, gouty Scottish-born General Arthur St. Clair led a force of regulars and ragtag enlistees into one of the greatest disasters in U.S. military history. (Granger Collection, New York)

Although George Washington worried that Anthony Wayne was "a brave general and nothing else," Wayne carefully prepared the Legion of the United States for its decisive defeat of the Ohio Indian confederacy. He later assigned Clark to lead military missions down the Ohio and Mississippi rivers. (Edward Savage/Collection of the New-York Historical Society)

The artist-illustrator Howard Chandler Christy's heroically realized tableau of the Treaty of Fort Greenville, painted in 1945, romanticized the participants. The triumphant Wayne and the acquiescent Little Turtle (holding a wampum belt) dominate the scene. To the right of Wayne are Clark and William Henry Harrison. Meriwether Lewis stands behind The Sun (the chief signing the treaty), and William Wells (in buckskin, to the right of Little Turtle) is the translator. Among the Indians are the Shawnees Blue Jacket (seated behind Little Turtle, with head turned) and Buckongahelas (to the left of Wells, on his knees, with arms folded). (Ohio Historical Society)

Clark never lost faith in his "worthy friend" Meriwether Lewis. Charles Willson Peale painted the recently returned hero in 1807; Lewis committed suicide two years later. (Granger Collection, New York)

Thomas Jefferson had an abiding interest in Indians—as long as they did not stand in the way of the expanding republic. "They will either incorporate with us as citizens of the United States," he said, "or remove beyond the Mississippi." (C. W. Peale/ Granger Collection, New York)

Sergeant Patrick Gass's 1807 book about the Lewis and Clark expedition was the first to be published. The 1810 edition depicted Clark and his men in felt caps shooting bears at a reassuringly (and rarely achieved) safe distance. (Gass Journal/ Granger Collection, New York)

Published in 1814, Clark's "Map of Lewis and Clark's Track" redefined the American view of the West for an entire generation. It remains one of the most influential maps ever drawn of the western continent. (Corbis)

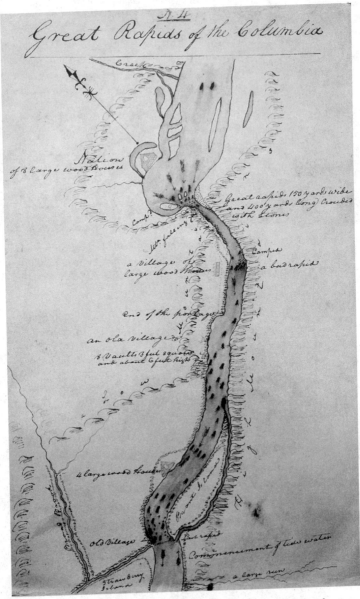

Great Rapids of the Columbia

Clark's detailed route maps, prepared using land sighting and dead reckoning, were remarkably accurate. At the Indian salmon fishery at the Cascades of the Columbia, he recorded a landscape crowded with new and ancient villages. But the detailed information regarding Indian dwellings was largely omitted from the larger composite maps, which inaccurately suggested an empty wilderness. (Missouri History Museum, St. Louis)

Clark described the bird *Nucifraga columbiana*, commonly called Clark's nutcracker, near the Continental Divide on August 22, 1805. Other species named for Clark include *Clarkia pulchella*, a flowering plant commonly known as ragged robin or elkhorn, and *Oncorhynchus clarki*, the cutthroat trout. (John James Audubon/Audubon Society)

Lewis bought four compasses in Philadelphia before the expedition. After returning, Clark presented this one to a military friend. It remains the only authenticated scientific or navigational item actually carried on the journey. (National Museum of American History, Smithsonian Institution)

Married at sixteen, Julia Hancock Clark moved with William to the remote town of St. Louis and bore five children. Her death in 1820 at the age of twenty-eight was a severe blow. (John W. Jarvis/Missouri History Museum, St. Louis)

Clark's second marriage, to Julia's widowed first cousin Harriet Radford, was a happy one. This silhouette was passed down through her family. (Missouri History Museum, St. Louis)

Nicholas Biddle, reputed to be the handsomest man in Philadelphia, edited the long-delayed journals and helped prepare them for publication in 1814. In his later career, he became Andrew Jackson's antagonist as president of the powerful Bank of the United States. (Andalusia Foundation)

Spanish-born Manuel Lisa helped outfit Lewis and Clark before the expedition and went on to become the dominant entrepreneur in the early Missouri River fur trade. (Missouri History Museum, St. Louis)

Meriwether Lewis Clark was said to bear a strong resemblance to his father. One of his own six sons, Meriwether Lewis Clark, Jr. (seated at far right in this 1854 photograph), went on to found Churchill Downs and the Kentucky Derby—and, like his father's namesake, died by suicide. (Filson Historical Society, Louisville, Kentucky)

The Omaha Chief Big Elk (Ongpatonga) delivered a celebrated oration at the 1815 Council of Portage des Sioux that reassured whites by suggesting that he accepted the inevitable destruction of Indian cultures. (Charles Bird King/Gilcrease Museum, Tulsa, Oklahoma)

Sheheke (also known as Shehek-shote) was chief of the Mandan village closest to Lewis and Clark's winter camp in 1804–05. He later accompanied the captains to Washington and met Thomas Jefferson. Attempts to return Sheheke to his native village precipitated the first armed battles between Americans and the Plains Indians. (Saint-Mémin/American Philosophical Society)

As federal commissioners at the 1825 Grand Council at Prairie du Chien, Clark and Lewis Cass addressed thousands of Indians from a raised platform. The land boundaries defined by the treaty put the framework in place for the eventual removal of the tribes. (James Otto Lewis/Bancroft Library, University of California, Berkeley)

Clark issued passports for passengers on steamboats like the *Yellow Stone*, the first to travel to the Upper Missouri. In 1833, the Swiss artist Karl Bodmer depicted crewmen cordelling small boats that were carrying cargo off the steamboat, which had been driven onto a sandbar by the powerful current. (Historical Picture Archive/Corbis)

Black Hawk's career paralleled that of Clark for more than thirty years. The two men died just a month apart. (Property of the Westervelt Company and displayed in the Westervelt-Warner Museum of American Art, Tuscaloosa, Alabama)

Thomas McKenney called Keokuk "a magnificent savage. Bold, enterprising, and impulsive." Unlike Clark, who was never photographed, the Sauk chief lived long enough to pose for this daguerreotype in 1847. (Thomas Easterly/Missouri History Museum, St. Louis)

The so-called Black Hawk War ended at the Battle of Bad Axe, when Indians fleeing across the Mississippi were massacred by American soldiers firing from the steamboat *Warrior*. (Granger Collection, New York)

In 1838, Robert E. Lee, then a young lieutenant in the Army Corps of Engineers, rented a cottage on Clark's property in St. Louis. Clark served seven presidents, from Washington to Van Buren, and lived long enough to have personally known many of the eventual leaders of the Civil War. (William E. West/ Washington Custis Lee Collection, Washington and Lee University)

Clark posed for an awkward portrait in his militia uniform sometime after 1820. Tragedies in his family and the stresses of his job were beginning to affect his health. (Missouri History Museum, St. Louis)

lation."[93] Charless stopped printing reports of Indian movements in order to prevent further panic.

Rumors abounded. The feared Robert Dickson was said to be everywhere. Frederick Bates reported that Dickson was planning an assault from the Upper Mississippi. Alexander McNair heard that Dickson was collecting a large body of Indians at Prairie du Chien. Horatio Stark said he was at Rock River. Maurice Blondeau said that the British had landed at Chicago and that Dickson was assembling the "Puants and Follavoine" (Winnebagos and Menominees) at Green Bay.

The Committee of Safety in St. Louis met and decided to build a ten-foot-tall stockade around the town; each citizen would be in charge of erecting up to one hundred yards of pickets. There was talk about repairing the old Spanish fortifications last used in 1780. The army began to make plans to pull back from its garrisons at Fort Osage and Fort Mason.

Frederick Bates, returning during Howard's absence to his familiar role as acting governor, concluded that the people of St. Louis "were never, in our times, in such a state of alarm as they are at present." He then suggested "an extraordinary expedient" to calm the public: the Americans would arm the friendly Osage Indians to fight the Mississippi tribes on their behalf.[94] Pierre Chouteau soon wrote to the new Secretary of War, John Armstrong, agreeing that a militia of the Osages, a "resolute and constant friend to the united States . . . deserve our confidence and ought to be considered as our most solid defence."[95]

The Osages volunteered 500 men to fight alongside the Americans against their traditional enemies on the Mississippi. Chouteau chose 260 of "their principal chiefs and best warriors" and started to bring them to St. Louis. But when he reached the mouth of the Osage River, he was stunned to receive instructions from Governor Howard not only contravening Bates's order but asking that he negotiate a repeal of the 1808 treaty article mandating a government factory at Fort Osage.

Howard explained that even though he favored sending tribes to attack one another as "not only Justifiable but good policy," the stationing of armed Indians inside frontier settlements would frighten the residents and violate the government's official position. However, he added, the Great Father would no longer be a peacekeeper: "You may say to them that they are now at liberty to avenge [injuries received from Indians of the Mississippi]."[96]

Chouteau swallowed hard, but "after the greatest difficulty"—and the liberal bestowing of presents and promises—he persuaded the Osages to return to their villages.

By this time, Benjamin Howard made it clear that he had tired of the territorial governorship and would prefer a military command. Aware of Howard's wishes, Territorial Delegate Edward Hempstead wrote to President Madison and recommended that he appoint Clark to the governorship—"He is I presume too well known to the Government to require further recommendations."[97] A month later, Secretary of State Monroe sent Howard a blank commission appointing an unnamed person as governor of the Missouri Territory. He instructed Howard to fill in his name if he wished to be reappointed governor. But if he chose instead to accept a military commission, he was to fill in the name of "William Clarke."

In Washington, Clark met with the new Secretary of War, John Armstrong, and finally received an official order to convert the Indian Department keelboats into gunboats for the offensive, which would need to be delayed until the following year. In Philadelphia, he gave Biddle a power of attorney to negotiate with a new publisher, Bradford & Inskeep. Julia, who had been ill, paid a visit to the famous Dr. Philip S. Physick, who was also Thomas Jefferson's physician. Before Clark left, he picked up from the cartographer Samuel Lewis the original manuscript of his master map of the West.

When the ice finally cleared from the rivers in the spring of 1813, Clark returned to St. Louis. Julia and the boys accompanied him as far as Louisville, where they would stay until the fall. Clark traveled the last leg of the journey alone. When he arrived in St. Louis on July 1, 1813, after having been away from his territorial post for twelve of the previous thirteen months, he was welcomed as the new governor of the Missouri Territory.

Benjamin Howard had in fact chosen to accept command of the Eighth Military District, and on June 16, 1813, President Madison appointed Clark to a three-year term. His salary was $2,000 a year. Clark was taking command of a territory that was on a wartime footing. His old job as Agent for Indian Affairs West of the Mississippi had been collapsed into his new responsibilities. He would be in charge of all the business of the Indian Office as well as the territorial administration. He would have direct command of the territorial militia and, until Howard arrived, all U.S. regular army troops west of the Mississippi.

Clark's skills were well suited for many of his new responsibilities. He knew how to organize military units—both as militias and in the regular army—and how to command men in the field. He was just as experienced in dealing with Indians; he was deeply familiar with what he called "the Indian character." Other responsibilities would put new demands on him. Now he would have to master the delicate art of working with federal officials in Washington and pleasing the stubbornly independent citizens in the territory. His friend Meriwether Lewis had struggled with both jobs. Three years had passed since Clark himself worried that he was not "Calculated to meet the Storms which might be expected." But now he felt up to the task.

At the age of forty-two, William Clark had become the most powerful American in the West.

CHAPTER EIGHT

TERRITORIAL GOVERNOR

1813–1820

The white settlers of the Missouri Territory were under siege. The day before Clark was sworn in, a detachment of army rangers was attacked at Fort Mason on the Mississippi; four were killed. The *Missouri Gazette* stopped its presses in August to print a rumor that somewhere between six hundred and three thousand hostile warriors were roaming and pillaging in St. Charles County. The vulnerable Fort Madison on the Mississippi was besieged by British and Indian forces throughout the summer. Starving, the American soldiers had finally dug a trench at night and crawled from the fort to the river, where they piled into boats and fled downstream, leaving the post in flames.

Clark and his Indian agents needed to act. They devised a two-pronged response. Their first effort would be to protect their western flanks by shoring up relations with still-friendly Missouri River tribes like the Osages. "Their Steady adherence to us entitles them to every accommodation that we can conveniently afford them," the subagent George Sibley said. "I think it is our best policy to keep up the influence of Trade over them, by means of which they may be Retained as friends and kept out of the reach of the intrigues of the Hostile Indians & British agents."[1] Sibley reopened the Osage factory at Arrow Rock, near today's Boonville, Missouri. Before Sibley left in September, the two men carried out their own arms trade: Sibley sold a sword and a pair of pistols to Clark for $21. Clark sold Sibley a brass-barreled blunderbuss for $16.

The second part of the military response was to launch at last the armed expedition up the Mississippi that Clark and Howard had been planning for two years. Its initial component was the conspicuously visible construction of the armed gunboats at St. Louis. "The hostile Indians would hear of it," Clark reasoned, "and magnify its size and importance."[2] General Howard then marched some 1,300 men up the Illinois River to the site of present-day Peoria, where he built a fort he named for George Rogers Clark, "the veteran who traversed this territory when almost unknown to Any American."[3] He mounted and fired a six-pound cannon in a further effort to intimidate the tribes.

Clark next sought to isolate the pro-British Sauks and Foxes by relocating friendlier bands of the same tribes west of the Mississippi. When these bands arrived near St. Louis, descending the river in 155 canoes in late September, Clark gave them food and promises of trade in return for their moving to Osage lands on the Missouri, a step he assured his superiors "will secure nearly 1,000 Warriors from joining the British party."[4]

Although Sauks were their traditional enemies, the Osages did not immediately protest the relocation; they were preoccupied with a new tribal enemy, emigrating Cherokees who had been likewise guaranteed lands west of the Mississippi by the American government. Sibley tried unsuccessfully to persuade the Osages to move farther west to the Arkansas River in order to make room for the Cherokees. Told of the failed negotiations, Clark noted wryly to Sibley that the Osages were saying that "a friend of theirs advised them not to make peace with the Cherokees who were no better than the Virginians."[5]

The armed displays by the Americans on the Mississippi—along with the arrival of fall—brought a temporary respite in the hostilities. Meanwhile, good news concerning America's military fortunes against the British arrived at last from the East. Oliver Hazard Perry's victory over the British fleet on Lake Erie was celebrated with a "general illumination" in St. Louis as cheering citizens dragged a flaming canoe through the streets.

Then a few weeks later came dramatic news: Tecumseh himself had been killed at the Battle of the Thames River in Ontario on October 5, 1813. William Henry Harrison led an army of about 3,500, including 1,000 mounted volunteers from Kentucky, against a retreating British force of 400 regulars and 1,000 Indians. Richard Mentor Johnson, a thirty-two-year-old Kentucky congressman and one of the War Hawks who had provoked the conflict with Britain, later ran for Vice President on the claim that he had personally killed Tecumseh. The warrior's body was never found, but Clark later interviewed Indians present at the battle who seemed to verify Johnson's account.

With the end of the war seemingly near, Clark went to Louisville to retrieve Julia and the boys. He reported to Colonel Hancock that "Judith"—the name only her father used—"has been very industrious . . . she has dried several bushels of peaches apples & cherries made 30 gallons of excellent Bounce [brandy] and as many preserves as will last us a year." But due to what he called "the clumsy state of part of my family"—in other words, Julia was once again pregnant—they would travel to St. Louis not by horseback or carriage but rather on a keelboat equipped with a private room and fireplace.[6]

Meanwhile, Nicholas Biddle and Paul Allen had been pushing forward the long-delayed publication of the journals. Biddle had signed the printing contract with Bradford & Inskeep, and Allen had solicited from Jefferson a biographical sketch of Lewis to relieve what he called the "dullness" of the journals. As for Clark, Jefferson explained that he was not familiar enough with the general's early life to write a similar biography of him, so only Lewis's was completed.

In March, Biddle gave Clark the welcome news that "the Travels are published . . . Henceforward you may sleep upon your fame which must last as long as books can endure." In a remarkably graceful gesture, Biddle, who had recently lost both his son and his beloved mother-in-law, added that he would not accept any compensation for his work. As he explained to Clark, "I am content that my trouble in the business should be recompensated only by the pleasure which attended it, and also the satisfaction of making your acquaintance, which I shall always value."[7]

Fewer than 1,500 copies were published of the two-volume *History of the Expedition under the Command of Captains Lewis and Clark*. It was priced at $6; Biddle's name did not appear in it. (The title page said only, "Prepared for the press by Paul Allen, Esquire.") It sold poorly, probably because of the seven-year delay since the expedition as well as the distraction of the war with Britain.

Over the winter, the war that was expected to end in fact escalated. Britain's redheaded Indian agent, Robert Dickson, was busily arming the Northern tribes on the Upper Mississippi. "Shold the Americans have come up you will endeavor by all means to get the Indians to drive them down again," he instructed an officer in the British Indian Department.[8] Dickson vowed to "make an example" of pro-American Indians and predicted that "St. Louis might be taken this spring with 5 or 600 men." With such a success, he was certain "The Scoundrel American Democrats will be obliged to go on their knees to Britain."[9]

St. Louisans were bracing for Dickson's onslaught. "We have heard of Mr. Dickson's threats as well as his boastings a long time ago," said one newspaper columnist. "For the last six months it has been no unusual thing for our wives and children to start from their sleep under the dreadful imagination that he was thundering at their doors."[10]

On New Year's Day of 1814, Julia gave birth in St. Louis to the Clarks' first daughter, another redhead. They named her Mary Margaret, after both Julia's sister and her mother. But the new mother was not at ease in the feebly defended frontier community. "I am afraid we shall have some trouble in the spring with the Indians," she wrote her brother. "God only knows what our fate is to be."[11]

Through his use of paid Indian spies, Clark was well aware of Dickson's activities. "The noted Robert Dickson is with the Sacs, keeping alive that assendency which the British has gained over those Tribes," he informed Secretary of War Armstrong.[12] Many of the violent incidents near St. Louis were blamed on Dickson's influence with the Sauks. In April, two farmers were shot and mutilated at Boonslick, and a Captain Cooper was killed at his hearth by an Indian who poked a hole through a log wall and fired a shot into the house.

"Those savage bands between Lake Michigan & the Mississippi, we must Consider as our Enemies," Clark concluded.[13] Now even the compliant Osages were coming under suspicion. When Sibley told Clark of Osage "depredations" (in a letter carried by the father of the future mountain man Jim Bridger), Clark, oddly echoing Dickson's similar warning, replied that "an example must be made of them, and the sooner the better."[14]

What Clark and his countrymen rarely acknowledged was that settlers usually came under attack only after moving into Indian lands they did not own. The Sauks were still bitter over Harrison's 1804 treaty that had appropriated millions of acres of their land. When four hundred American families settled north of the Missouri on land claimed by the Sauks and Iowas, Clark found an imaginative solution. Rather than remove the trespassers, he had the proposed boundaries of St. Charles County redrawn "to include this rich and flourishing settlement, and some of the best lands in the Territory."[15]

In February, as the attacks continued, the anxious residents of St. Louis called a town meeting to protest the federal government's failure to provide for their defense. For Clark, it must have seemed a replay of his brother George Rogers's experiences a generation earlier in Kentucky's frontier stations. By May, the news arrived of Andrew Jackson's near-massacre of the Creeks at Horseshoe Bend, Alabama. At least 850 of the war party known as the Red Sticks were killed—a count the soldiers confirmed by cutting off the noses of the dead warriors. Soon the *Missouri Gazette* was thundering, "The BLOOD of our citizens cry aloud for VENGEANCE. The general cry is let the north as well as the south be JACKSONIZED!!!"[16]

Clark was at last ready to launch his military strike up the Mississippi into the heart of Dickson's trading network. "The British will not relinquish the Indian Trade, unless we possess the northern lake & passes," he said. "Whoever enjoys the Trade of the Indians will have the controal of their affections & power."[17] Specifically, Clark believed that the key to the Upper Mississippi was Dickson's headquarters at Prairie du Chien, "a very important point for the U.S. either in peace or War." He argued that "it should be taken possession of as Soon as it is practicable."[18]

When Clark learned that Dickson had crossed from Green Bay to the Mississippi with five large boats "loaded with goods Amunition &c. as presents for the Indians; and is at the time raising a large Indian force," he decided it was time to act.[19] On his own authority, Clark recruited 150 men to serve as a short-term militia for three months. The men, who would make up the crews of the gunboat expedition up the Mississippi, would be paid $20 a month directly out of the Indian fund. It was an unauthorized expenditure that, if rejected, could have been as disastrous for William as similar expenses of expediency had been for both George Rogers Clark and Meriwether Lewis.

In early May 1814, Clark headed up the Mississippi with a flotilla of five armed keelboats and two hundred soldiers. Among the officers were militia lieutenants George Hancock Kennerly and James Kennerly. The Kennerly brothers were the Virginia-born first cousins of Clark's wife, Julia. George was Clark's aide-de-camp, and James had recently opened a store with Clark's nephew John O'Fallon, selling pickled pork, beef, and flour. John's brother, Ben O'Fallon, followed the military party in a supply boat loaded with provisions.

Clark's stated goal was to "flusterate the plans of Mr. Dickson." The Secretary of War had approved the campaign but remained skeptical. "I cannot believe in the wisdom of establishing a post 600 miles in the enemy's country," John Armstrong noted on the letter he received from Clark. "Once established it must be supported & at an enormous expence."[20]

On June 2, Clark and his troops arrived at Prairie du Chien to find it deserted but for a small contingent of Winnebago Indians. Dickson had learned of the American expedition and departed for Michilimackinac three weeks earlier with three hundred of his Indian troops; the British commander left to defend the trading post had also disappeared. Clark's men confiscated nine or ten trunks of Dickson's records and promptly announced that the papers proved that the Scotsman was indeed a "hair-buyer" who rewarded Indians bringing in scalps. The accounts showed one Indian was paid "5 carrots of tobacco; 6 lbs. Powder; 6lb. Ball" for an American scalp.[21] The British military commander William McKay later scoffed over "that most gallant action of having stormed & taken two old trunks belonging to R. Dickson Esq." McKay's minimizing the number of trunks taken did little to conceal the barb of his comments: "A grand prize for Gov. Clark . . . This will be a good acquisition to the Governor who I presume will have them exposed for sale in his store for the purpose of pasting windows."[22]

For their part, the British complained of "horrible cruelties" by "these relentless Assassins," as they termed the Americans, whose "appetite for encroachment grows by what it feeds upon & can never be satisfied." The commander at Michilimackinac passed along a particularly gruesome version of Clark's behavior recounted by an Indian named Tête du Chien: "This Ruffian [Clark] on taking Prairie des Chiens, captured eight Indians of the Winnebago Nation; they cajoled them at first with affected kindness, set provisions before them; & in the act of eating treacherously fell upon them & murdered seven in cold blood—the eighth escaped to be the sad historian of their horrible fate." In an amplified version of the events, the British commander went on to report, "[Clark] shut [four others] up in a log house, & afterwards shot them thro' between the logs."[23]

This solitary account was never verified. Clark did report, however, that twenty Winnebago prisoners had "made their escape in the dark night, from a Strong Guard under a heavy fire, Several of them wounded & dead."[24]

In any event, the Americans had atrocity stories of their own to report. "How will the English government and their agent Robert Dickson (a native of Scotland) appear to the world, when it has announced that he suborned a Sac warrior to assassinate governor Clark while in council at Prairie de Chien?" asked *Niles' Weekly Register.* "This Indian rose and occupied the attention of the assemblage with a harangue of trifling import, that his eye were fixed upon the governor as if riveted to the object—at that moment the governor shifted his sword from an unhandy position to across his knees, when the savage retired to his seat."[25] What lent both atrocity tales credibility to their listeners was the long legacy of violence in the borderlands.

Having rid Prairie du Chien of Winnebagos, Clark located a commanding site overlooking the village and set his men to work building a triangular fortification that would be named Fort Shelby (after the governor of Kentucky). A day later, he was heading back downriver, leaving behind two gunboats and a small garrison of 135 soldiers under the direction of Lieutenant Joseph Perkins and the two Kennerly brothers.

On June 13, Clark arrived triumphantly in St. Louis with news of "the fortunate results of that hazardous enterprise."[26] With the new fort erected, and the soldiers there "anxious for a visit from Dickson and his red troops," Clark and his friends gathered for a celebratory banquet at William Christy's Missouri Hotel.[27] Here, they raised toasts to "the late expedition [which] has cleansed [Prairie du Chien] of spies and traitors."[28]

It did not take long for the American soldiers at Prairie du Chien to receive a visit from Dickson's "red troops." In the morning of July 17, they were startled to see a combined force of at least 650 Indians, British regulars, and Michigan Fencibles (a militia of Canadian trappers) arrayed in the prairie three miles away. Dickson had raised what amounted to a private army to retake Fort Shelby. The Americans were vastly outnumbered, but Perkins refused a demand for unconditional surrender. A cannon erupted from one of the gunboats, which the besieging British had commandeered. The other American gunboat, the *Governor Clark*, returned fire but was driven downstream and, to the dismay of the defenders of Fort Shelby, never returned.

The siege lasted fifty-four hours. Finally, on the evening of July 19, Perkins and the Kennerlys realized that they were out of ammunition, water, and medicine—and could see Indians digging tunnels toward the fort. George Kennerly carried out a white flag, and a surrender was agreed upon on the morning of the twentieth. McKay, the British commander, agreed to protect the Americans from the vengeful Winnebagos and to give the soldiers a boat to return to St. Louis, under a promise to never again take up arms against Britain (a typical condition of prisoner releases of the time).

Meanwhile, another battle erupted down the Mississippi at the Rock River Rapids, at today's Davenport-Moline. An American expedition bringing reinforcements upriver arrived at the Sauk and Fox villages in three keelboats and two trading boats. Its commander, Lieutenant John Campbell, judged the Indians to be "friendly and well disposed." He was wrong. The next day his expedition was attacked by Black Hawk and his warriors. The Sauks killed sixteen American soldiers, captured a trading boat, and appeared ready to annihilate the rest of Campbell's troops. But, in a bizarre coincidence, the gunboat *Governor Clark*, fleeing downriver from Prairie du Chien, floated into the middle of the ongoing battle. As the gunboat provided cover, Campbell's soldiers clambered into the remaining boats and retreated in humiliation to St. Louis, arriving on July 30, 1814. Lieutenant Perkins and the soldiers captured at the Fort Shelby debacle landed a few days later. The expedition that at first drew toasts of triumph had ended in a fiasco.

Clark came under severe criticism. Secretary of War Armstrong's concerns about the risk of building a fort deep in enemy territory seemed to have been borne out. But Clark was not without supporters. "Some blame Governor Clark for the manifold disasters which have occurred," said the *Missouri Gazette*. "We would ask in the name of common sense how can he be liable to censure who has nothing more to do in the defence of the country than to order out such portions of the militia as may be demanded of him."[29]

Ordered back to St. Louis, General Benjamin Howard organized a punitive expedition against Black Hawk's Sauks and Foxes. On August 22, Major Zachary Taylor packed four hundred men into eight boats and headed upriver. Taylor and his troops built a fortification at the Des Moines River they called Fort Johnson. They proceeded on to Saukenuk, Black Hawk's village at the mouth of the Rock River. There they were greeted by devastating cannonades from the six-pounder and three-pounder captured at Fort Shelby. Stunned, they were sent reeling back to St. Louis. Fort Johnson was later burned and abandoned.

August 1814 was the blackest month of the war for Americans. A British expeditionary force landed on Chesapeake Bay and burned all of Washington's public buildings. Clark's dashing young nephew Lieutenant Colonel George Croghan led an effort to recapture the British garrison at Michilimackinac on the Great Lakes that failed utterly. Most Americans in the West believed that their feebly defended "frontier" would inevitably be lost. The St. Louis merchant Christian Wilt wrote that he could not see "what is to prevent the [Spanish and British] & Indians from overwhelming this Country." The only solution, he thought, would be to kill "every Indian from here to the Rocky Mountains."[30] The factor and subagent George Sibley was no more sanguine, saying, "This territory is being very seriously threatened with invasion by an immense savage force . . . We have suffered pretty severly in this quarter I assure you, and I fear shall suffer much more."[31]

At this grim moment, Governor Clark decided to embrace the solution the federal government had previously disdained. He would arm the Indian tribes against one another.

In August, Clark sent the friendly Shawnees and Delawares to attack the pro-British tribes to the north and made plans to encourage the Osages to do the same. George Sibley would now use his warehouse of trade goods to encourage tribes to go to war instead of keeping the peace. Sibley explained to his brother, "We are now about to employ the Osagez to take up the War Club against those Indians who are Hostile to us, to effort which I have agreed to stand paymaster."[32]

Neutralizing the powerful tribes on the Upper Missouri was crucial to the war effort. "Those Missouri Tribes must either be engaged for us;

or they will be opposed to us without doubt," Clark told Armstrong.[33] He appointed Manuel Lisa and Pierre Chouteau's son Auguste Pierre as special Indian agents and gave them $4,300 in gifts "for the purpose of engaging those Tribes in Offensive operations against the Enemies of the United States; particularly the Tribes on the Mississippi who are too numerous for our thin population to oppose."[34]

Lisa's participation was particularly important. Even though he had made $9,000 on his last trading expedition, the Missouri Fur Company had reorganized during the war and Lisa had been forced out. Yet he remained the trader with the most influence over the powerful Nakota Sioux of the Middle Missouri. Charged with instructions from Clark, Lisa went up the Missouri and persuaded the Omahas and various Nakota Sioux bands to cross to the St. Peter's River in present-day Minnesota and attack the Iowas and the Dakotas, or Sioux of the Lakes. The strategic feint worked. Forced to defend their northern flanks, the Upper Mississippi tribes never were able to mount a direct attack on St. Louis.

Clark, understandably, was feeling the pressure. "I assure you that I have had my hands full in the Territory," he wrote worriedly to Biddle. "An emence number of Indians & som of British to oppose & but fiew men to stand their post, our small force has had a great deel of fighting on very unequal terms."[35] He said that he had finally borrowed a copy of his journals but had not even had time to read it. In September, there was worse news: Clark's friend Brigadier General Howard suddenly fell ill and died, leaving the regular army garrison at Fort Bellefontaine without its commander.

Clark was also concerned about his family. Julia's "Breast continues to be sore & enlargens," he told Biddle. "I am apprehensive it will terminate in a Cancer."[36] Another trip to her Philadelphia doctor seemed necessary. Later in the year, Clark complained to his brother Edmund that he had not heard from him and that "it hurts me a little to find my friends have so soon forgotten me." In an inquiry that revealed much about his priorities, he asked Edmund about, first, "the horse I left at Mr. Gwathmeys" and, second, "my negrow man York."[37] After this letter, York disappeared completely from Clark's correspondence.

Once again, the winter brought a respite in the Indian wars. In October 1814, Clark organized Missouri's first territorial militia; its members included Auguste Chouteau, the businessman William H. Ashley, Manuel Lisa, and the eighty-year-old Daniel Boone.[38] Rumors were beginning to arrive that a peace might be negotiated at Ghent in Belgium, where American and British negotiators had been meeting since June. Dickson made the most of one report that the American negotiators had flatly rejected a British proposal to create an Indian buffer state between the Ohio River and the Great Lakes. Here was proof positive, Dickson told his Indian allies, that only the British were their true friends.

Then, early in the year, electrifying news arrived in St. Louis. In a two-hour battle at New Orleans in the misty early hours of January 8, 1815, General Andrew Jackson's Tennessee and Kentucky sharpshooters had won an overwhelming victory against the British army that had defeated Napoleon. The carnage had been terrible. The British had foolishly attempted a frontal assault in closed ranks against Americans entrenched behind parapets. Of their men, 2,036 were killed or wounded; 13 Americans had been killed, and 58 were missing or wounded.

In St. Louis, cannons were fired, windows illuminated, and a solemn High Mass and Te Deum celebrated at the Catholic church. It was one of the few significant American land victories of the entire war—and it had no effect on the outcome. The war had already ended with the signing of the Treaty of Ghent on December 24.

Secretary of War James Monroe at once sent Clark and the other territorial governors a copy of the peace treaty. Even though the British and Indians had taken control of the Great Lakes and the Upper Mississippi during the war, the treaty required that national boundaries be returned to *status quo ante bellum*—precisely the same as before the war began. The British would have to withdraw from their conquered territory and return Prairie du Chien and Michilimackinac to the Americans. Moreover, the American negotiators had also agreed to "put an end to all Hostilities with the Indian Tribes with whom [the United States] might be at War . . . and to restore to such Tribes all the rights and privileges to which they were entitled previous to the war."[39]

Who would tell the Indians? Monroe appointed Clark, along with Auguste Chouteau and Ninian Edwards, as commissioners plenipotentiary of the United States. They were instructed to convene the tribes to "such place or places, as you may appoint for the purposes of concluding the proposed treaty of Peace and amity between the United States and all those Tribes." Monroe told the commissioners that the treaties should not deal with land cessions or other such topics. Instead, "it is thought proper to confine this Treaty to the sole object of peace."[40]

The Western Indians had little reason to cooperate. They had neither signed the Treaty of Ghent nor been defeated militarily by the Americans. In fact, Dickson and the British army captain Andrew Bulger had just convened an enormous council of Indian warriors at Prairie du Chien in April and were preparing to launch a decisive *coup de main* down the Mississippi. Bulger was convinced that "the Spaniards are certainly coming to St. Louis by way of the Missouri, and that they are cussedly afraid at St. Louis."[41]

Dickson and Bulger were appropriately astonished when the gunboat *Governor Clark* arrived at Rock River bearing news of the Treaty of Ghent. They tried to soften the blow to the Indians that their Great British Father had once again abandoned them, but militant chiefs like Black Hawk were furious. He had already dispatched advance raiding parties down the Mississippi, and it was too late to call them back.

In the months after the Treaty of Ghent, the Indian war in the West entered its strangest and bloodiest phase. Indian war parties freely roamed the region, while American defenders were prohibited by treaty from any offensive attacks. In just one month, Clark wrote to Monroe, "eight parties of the hostile Indians from above Rocky River, have visited the frontiers of this territory and killed ten men. One of those parties, a few days ago, attacked a small French village, on the Missouri [Cote Sans Dessein], in which there was about 200 souls. They killed four men, plundered the houses, and burnt down part of the town. The inhabitants shut themselves up in two small forts, which they had built in the town for security." Clearly concerned with the lingering constraints imposed by the recently signed treaty, Clark told his superiors that only an offensive response was apt to quell the Indian violence: "I am under some apprehention that it will be necessary to cut off the Rocky River Tribes before we shall be at peace."[42]

Another Sauk war party attacked the Ramsay family at the settlement of Femme Osage, killing three children and severely wounding both parents. Four days later, in present-day Lincoln County, Missouri, four American rangers were killed by fifty warriors led by Black Hawk. When American soldiers counterattacked, the Indians barricaded themselves in a sinkhole "and perfectly secured themselves from the powerful exertions of our troops."[43] Among the soldiers at the Battle of the Sink Hole was

Clark's athletic army friend Robert McClellan, who had returned in 1813 with John Jacob Astor's overland expedition that had founded Astoria at the mouth of the Columbia.

Scalped bodies were regularly found floating down the Missouri from the undefended territory. Local citizens were alternately outraged and panicked over the government's failure to punish the Indians. "Very few days elapse without unfolding some horrid deed," said the *Missouri Gazette*, "a family cut off, travelers shot and cut to pieces on the frontiers or in the neighborhood of our villages; the thing is passed off as a matter of course, until the news of another massacre arrives." No longer sympathetic to beleaguered public officials, the editor Joseph Charless barely concealed his disdain for Clark and the military for their supposed indifference: "Another pinch of snuff is taken, and the affair is forgotten." His words crackling with sarcasm, Charless wondered if St. Louis's problem was that "it affords more amusement than the dull employment of protecting our border people from the tomahawk and scalping knife."[44]

In this increasingly acidulous atmosphere, Clark and the commissioners prepared to negotiate what seemed to be irreconcilable interests. The outraged citizens of the territory wanted the Indians who had terrorized them to be nothing short of exterminated. Yet Clark was charged by Monroe to invite the same tribes to what would be the first great treaty council ever held west of the Mississippi. The citizens wanted revenge; Clark was under orders to offer the olive branch. It would be impossible to please both sides.

The first task was to select a suitable site. Clark and the commissioners settled on the tiny village of Portage des Sioux, nestled on an alluvial floodplain stretching seventy miles long and five miles wide at the confluence of the Mississippi and Missouri rivers. Portage des Sioux was already well known as a shortcut between the rivers.

It was also something of a tourist attraction. Travelers emerging from the thickets of the eastern hardwood forests were often taken to Portage des Sioux for their first glimpse of one of the most celebrated sights on the continent—the tallgrass prairie of North America.

"The first time a stranger comes in view of this prairie," wrote Timothy Flint after his initial visit, "a scene strikes him that will never be forgotten. I observed the cottonwood trees to be immensely tall, rising like Corinthian columns, enwrapped with a luxuriant wreathing of ivy, and the bignonia radicans, with his splendid, trumpet-shaped flowers, displayed them glittering in the sun, quite on the summits of the trees." Flint reported that the prairie itself was a glorious spectacle, "sweet from a recent shower and lit by a brilliant sun . . . Extending beyond the reach of the eye, and presenting millions of flowers of every scent and hue, [it] seemed an immense flower-garden . . ."[45]

Traveler after traveler reacted similarly. Henry Vest Bingham, the father of the painter George Caleb Bingham, called it "one of the most Delightfull prospects In the world."[46] William Campbell Preston was struck speechless by "what everybody talked about . . . the almost boundless extent and inconceivable magnificence of the scene . . . nothing can be more strikingly beautiful."[47] "To those who have never seen any of these prairies," wrote Henry Brackenridge, "it is very difficult to convey any just idea of them. Perhaps the comparison to smooth, green sea is the best." But he quickly concluded that this was insufficient. "After gazing for an hour, I still continued to experience an unsatiated delight in contemplating the rich and magnificent scene . . . In some places there stands a solitary tree, of cottonwood or walnut, of enormous size, but, from the distance, diminished to a shrub. A hundred thousand acres of the finest land are under the eye at once, and yet in all this space there is but one little cultivated spot to be seen."[48]

These rhapsodic descriptions were about something other than aesthetics, however. They reflected the discerning judgments of future settlers gazing over real estate that was fertile, available, and breathtakingly plentiful.

To Clark, Portage des Sioux offered more prosaic advantages: it was accessible to tribes coming down the rivers, it was far enough from St. Louis to keep threatening Indians at a distance, and it could be readily defended.

The commissioners dispatched invitations to thirty-seven different tribes to gather at Portage des Sioux on July 6. Lisa would bring the Missouri River tribes, and Thomas Forsyth would notify the Illinois River bands. But the Sauks and Foxes at Rock River remained intransigent: they killed one of the messengers on the Mississippi and stopped others bound for Prairie du Chien. The *Missouri Gazette* reported that the

British Captain Duncan Graham — "deputy scalping master general" — had armed the tribe with ten barrels of gunpowder and twenty *fusées* "as a reward for their services in butchering helpless women and children on the frontiers."[49]

Clark's aide George Hancock Kennerly eventually volunteered to take the invitations to the tribes at Prairie du Chien the back way, traveling up the Missouri River and then eastward across present-day Iowa. It was a courageous undertaking, for the commissioners were in no doubt "that it is the intention of those tribes to continue the war, and that nothing less than a vigorous display of military force can change their disposition."[50]

In June, Manuel Lisa returned to St. Louis with the first of the Indians to arrive, forty-three chiefs from the Upper Missouri. Among the group were several chiefs Clark had met originally in 1804 during the Voyage of Discovery, including the Brulé Lakota chiefs Black Buffalo and The Partisan. "These chiefs . . . are anxious to make war on the Sacks and other hostile Indians, and have actually killed several Iaways a few weeks ago," the *Missouri Gazette* reported approvingly.[51] The Sioux chiefs got straight to the point in a preliminary council with Clark. "We are not like those nations that receive your presents and put them under their blankets and then turn their backs on you," said one. "Put something sharp into our hands that we may help ourselves and by so doing help you."[52]

Though they intended to begin the actual treaty-making on July 6, Clark and the commissioners waited another four days, allowing more tribes to gather. A few Sauks and Foxes arrived, but their principal men, Keokuk and Black Hawk, were not present. Instead, the Sauks had sent what Clark called "a Considerable number of the most insignificant & contemptible persons." Moreover, "we . . . have reasons to believe that their principal chiefs & warriors continue to cherish the most inveterate & deadly hostility towards the American people & govt."[53]

Clark opened the council on July 10 to the sounds of rolling drums amid a visual panorama of clashing cultures on the prairie. The U.S. regulars had lined up their one hundred tents in precise rows. Patrolling the rivers were the armed galleys *Governor Clark* and *Commodore Perry*. Surrounding the Americans was the colorful panoply of dwellings and canoes of some two thousand Native Americans, all reflecting their distinct tribal customs. Eastern tribes like the Kickapoos and the Potawatomis built bark- or mat-covered lodges and traveled in graceful white birch canoes. The mounted nomads of the plains erected bison-hide tipis and used heavier dugout canoes suitable for the Missouri's powerful current.

A July heat wave had sent afternoon temperatures into the mid-nineties when Clark opened the proceedings. Standing in the shade of a brush arbor, he addressed the tribes individually, giving "a luminous view of the conduct of the different nations of Indians before and during the late war with the British." Pointedly waiting to address the group of Sauks and Foxes last, he informed them of the benevolent intentions of the Great Father in Washington and "his wish to bury the tomahawk and forget past transactions."[54] But after the olive branch came the sword: if their principal chiefs did not arrive in thirty days, Clark said, there would be war.

At those words, the tribal enemies of the Sauks and Foxes—the Shawnees, Delawares, Sioux, and Omahas—leaped to their feet with "vehement cries of applause, which much appaled the Sac's and Kickapoos."[55] By the next morning, the few Sauks and Foxes present had vanished upriver.

The treaty-making commenced, despite a potential catastrophe when the chief Black Buffalo suddenly died. The Lakotas might well have seen his death as a disturbing omen. But, in a gesture recalling Anthony Wayne's respectful burial of Little Turtle's wife at the Treaty of Greenville, Clark gave Black Buffalo a full military funeral, with pageantry and rifle salutes. Tensions eased. The mood shifted even more favorably when the Omaha chief Big Elk (Ongpatonga) delivered what proved to be a celebrated eulogy over Black Buffalo's grave:

What is past and cannot be prevented should not be grieved for. Be not discouraged or displeased then, that in visiting your father here, you have lost your chief . . . this would have attended you perhaps at your own village. Five times have I visited this land and never returned with sorrow or pain. Misfortunes do not flourish, particularly in our path. They grow every where. What a misfortune for me, that I could not have died this day, instead of the chief that lies before us. The trifling loss my nation would have sustained in my death would have been doubly paid for by the honors of my burial. They would have wiped off every thing like regret. Instead of being covered with the cloud of sorrow, my warriors would have felt the sun-shine of joy in their hearts . . . Chief of the Warriors—Your labors have not been vain—Your attention shall not be forgotten. My nation shall know the respect that is paid over the dead.[56]

The *Missouri Gazette* reprinted Big Elk's speech, which later appeared nationally in *Niles' Weekly Register*. Most Americans considered it a moving example of Indian oratory. Big Elk had told whites what they wanted to believe: wise Indians recognized the superiority of Euro-American civilization and would embrace it even at the moment of their death. Big Elk had memorably articulated the myth of the noble savage, proud of his traditional culture but freely accepting his tragic fate. The inevitability of Big Elk's doom relieved whites of any guilt for his demise; responsibility for it was replaced with a comforting paternalism.

Clark, for one, was well aware that Indians knew how to tell whites what they wanted to hear. Timothy Flint recalled meeting a visiting chief "of singular mildness of countenance and manner" who spoke "in a very insinuating style." He observed to Clark that "he was the only Indian I had ever seen, who appeared to have mildness and mercy in his countenance." Clark replied that the man was a flatterer and that under his gentle demeanor "were concealed uncommon degrees of cunning, courage, revenge, and cruelty; that in fact he had been the most bloody and troublesome partisan against us, during the war, of the whole tribe."[57]

Almost unique among American officials of his generation, who saw all Indians as undifferentiated "savages," Clark had a sophisticated grasp of the differences among Native Americans, both individuals and the various tribes. He was familiar with their cultures and, even though he relied entirely on interpreters, was able to speak to them in their richly allusive vocabularies. Clark was at heart paternalistic: he wanted to help his "red children" to submit to the will of their Great Father. If they did not, he would be as stern and punitive as his brother George Rogers had been. The problem was that by merely sitting down with Indians, he put himself at odds with the territory's vengeful citizenry.

Clark led the commissioners through painstaking negotiations with each of the individual tribes assembled at Portage des Sioux. On July 18, the Potawatomis and Piankashaws of Illinois pledged "peace and friendship" with the United States. Four Sioux bands—the Tetons (Brulé

Lakotas), Sioux of the Lakes (Dakotas), Sioux of St. Peter's River (Dakotas), and Yanktons (Nakotas)—signed on July 19. Then Waanowrabai, who was the grandson of the celebrated chief Blackbird, and Big Elk signed for the Omahas on the twentieth.

Clark's son Lewis played nearby when Big Elk addressed a speech specifically to the governor. "My father," Big Elk said. "Since I have been here you have treated me well—you treat me as my little brother. [*Here he pointed to Gov. Clark's little son who passed near him.*] You take me in your hand and protect me from injury." But, he went on, there were other white men, by whom he meant American and British traders, "who live among us and give my young men bad advice, they have wives with us; they divide the bands; they often tell my young men that such a place is a better place for a village, and to make a difficulty among us."[58]

Then Big Elk said that he could not even wear the peace medal Clark had given him for fear of being attacked by the British and the younger Indians in their league. "These whites have taken the medal from my neck and told me it was no more than dung—But if it were British it would be something." He went on to tell Clark, "I have bad young men as well as yourself. When I am away the whites go out to kill the buffalowe and catch the beaver. If my young men kill one of them do not blame me." Big Elk appealed to Clark's self-interest: "I do not want hunters to kill those animals the Great spirit gave us to depend on. I wish to preserve these animals for food for my people so that we shall be able to make your traders glad and they will come down and make you glad."[59]

But while cooperation was the ideal, in its absence injury would beget injury. "What would you think," he asked Clark, "to see one take your women in the streets and violate them? The whites at our village take the women or braves and violate them in open day . . . I have been obliged to give all I have to cover the injury. I did this in order to save them, as I thought those whites were your children. But in future I shall not interfere."[60]

By July 22, seven tribes had "touched the quill," scorching their seals into the parchment with hot ceremonial pipes. Clark then adjourned the council to await the end of the thirty-day deadline he had given for the remaining Sauks and Foxes to arrive and to learn if George Kennerly would bring in more tribes from the north. Clark remained convinced that the pro-British bands on the Upper Mississippi would be brought to agreement only "at the point of the bayonet." In the meantime, he ordered the militia to be held in readiness to avoid further "melancholy and horrid scenes of murders, rapine, and violence."[61]

Violence was never far below the surface on the borderlands. During Clark's protracted council seeking peace among the tribes, General Daniel Bissell, the territorial military commander, cudgeled another officer nearly to death at nearby Austin's Tavern. Andrew McNair and Robert McClellan had to forcibly drag off Bissell, who was still raging and firing his pistol into the floorboards. Most men carried concealed pistols and dirks. Visitors remarked on the fact that if a dirk fell clattering to a ballroom floor during a dance, the women present barely took notice. When the *Gazette*'s editor, Joseph Charless, encountered his rival politician-publisher, William Carr, at the post office, Carr spit into his face and brandished a pistol at him.

Men in the Clark family continued to participate in the southern gentleman's *code duello*. In 1816, George Kennerly was wounded in a duel with Henry Geyer, a future U.S. senator. Two years later Clark matter-of-factly noted that "Ben [O'Fallon] has in a duel shot a Lut. in the mouth."[62] While Clark was sometimes called on to intervene to prevent duels, there is no evidence that he participated in them himself, beyond his seconding of Dr. Farrar in 1810.

Slavery was also an intimate part of the family's southern-based code. In the same month as Bissell's attack on his fellow officer, Clark's nephew Benjamin O'Fallon posted a newspaper notice offering a $20 reward for the return of Juba, a twenty-four-year-old slave Clark had inherited from his father. "He is very apt to stammer considerably when spoken to," O'Fallon said, a telling comment about the treatment of slaves.[63] Juba's brother was York, but the family tie offered no advantage. After he was recaptured, Juba was sent to Louisville and sold on the steps of the courthouse.

At the end of September, the commissioners sent home the last 150 Indians remaining at Portage des Sioux. By then they had signed thirteen separate treaties with the tribes and distributed $20,000 in gifts to seal the agreements. The commissioners' instructions had been limited to "peace and friendship," but they found it difficult to pass up a land bargain. When the Piankashaws and Iowas made "spontaneous" offers to sell land that "would be a valuable acquisition," the commissioners told the War Department that "it might be very advisable to accede to their proposition."[64] Surprisingly, the Madison Administration said no; those cessions could come later.

During the long summer at Portage des Sioux, three of the most independent northern tribes—the Foxes, Kickapoos, and Iowas—finally arrived and signed treaties. The Great and Little Osages, Kansas, and Sauks of the Missouri followed. The commissioners reported satisfactory negotiations with the Delawares and Shawnees, two Eastern tribes that already had been pushed across the Mississippi. Those tribes and those Cherokees who had already emigrated to Arkansas complained about white encroachment on their lands. Because of the "uncommon sobriety and general good conduct of those Indians" and "the progress of civilization among them," the commissioners said, "we feel it our duty to recommend them to the benevolence as well as to the justice of our Government."[65]

But some issues remained unresolved. The Southwestern Chippewas (Ojibwas), Menominees, and Winnebagos had not sent a single person to Portage des Sioux. As for the Sauks of Rock River, the so-called British Band, the commissioners said, they "not only most explicitly refused to treat with us, but manifested without disguise their opposition to the view of our government, and committed many of the most wanton depredations upon the frontier, even after the treaty commenced. Their conduct has been so outrageous and improper . . . good policy requires that they should be compelled to make some restitution at least."[66] In other words, the Rock River Sauks had so vigorously resisted the appropriation of their homelands that they deserved further punishment.

The United States Senate ratified the Portage des Sioux treaties on December 26, 1815. For the first time, tribes on the Upper Mississippi and Great Plains had pledged peace and placed themselves under the exclusive jurisdiction of the American government. Nonetheless, the pressures on those tribes would soon increase. In a candid letter to the Secretary of War, Illinois governor Ninian Edwards outlined the strategy:

Every dictate of good policy recommends the utmost liberality, (for a few years at least) towards the Indians of the Illinois river, & those who live between Lake Michagan & the Mississippi river—

Nothing less, can wean them from British influences to which they, more than any other Indians, in these Territories have long been devoted—Peace with them is more important than with any others, because their proximity to our frontiers enables them to do us most injury—Their hostility would at once put an end to the surveying, or occupying of the military lands . . . If they can be kept in a good humor for two or three years, the growth of our population, by the appeals it will then make to their fears, will prevent all future danger.[67]

Edwards was bluntly stating that the American goal was to acquire Indian land. If that meant mollifying the Sauks and Foxes until they were inevitably outnumbered, that was a small price to pay. What was absent from his reasoning was the usual argument that it was all for the benefit of the savages.

Contrary to the fears of the commissioners, the British began to pull back their traders after the war. With most of the Indian nations pacified, and the British departing, for the first time in its young history the United States controlled navigation on the entire Mississippi River from its headwaters to its mouth. In the years to come, the conversation between the U.S. government and Indians would not be over their resistance or their rights but increasingly over their removal. But for now, Clark believed he could act as a moderating influence in the long struggle over Indian land: the Indians would not be allowed to keep all that they once had, but neither would the settlers be allowed to take as much as they wanted.

The immediate consequence of the end of the War of 1812—and the halt in the parallel Indian resistance—was an explosion in migration across the Mississippi. Settlers who had hesitated to move during the war were now heading west by the thousands. In six years after 1814, the population of the Missouri Territory grew from 25,000 to 65,000. Many of the newcomers were Virginians and Kentuckians who brought slaves with them. Cotton plantations began to spring up in the lowlands south of St. Louis near Cape Girardeau.

A new merchant class was beginning to arise in St. Louis. Charles Latrobe found the city "overrun by the speculative New Englanders." Moreover, he wrote, "A new town has, in fact, sprung up by the side of the old one . . . It is amusing to see a European to step aside from the hurry and bustle of the upper streets, full of pale, scheming faces, depressed brows, and busy fingers, to the quiet quarters of the lower division." It was only in Old World neighborhoods where you found the "odd little coffee houses with the homely billiard tables . . . cosy balconies and settees."[68]

The pressure to turn over ceded Indian lands to these ambitious new settlers was intense. Government surveyors hurriedly spread out to divide the land into sections of 640 acres and quarter-sections of 160 acres—to be put up for public auction. But many newcomers could not wait. Hunters and settlers began flooding onto unoccupied U.S. and Indian lands. The Indian agents struggled to keep angry tribes and invading whites safely apart. At the center of the whirlwind stood Clark.

The ground was beginning to shift beneath his feet. In the years during and immediately after the expedition, Clark's exceptional skills of leadership and military organization were used to their best advantage. He lived in a borderlands culture where whites and Indians shared equal powers. He could find ways to accommodate and work with the powerful Indian nations west of the Mississippi. He could plan and build forts and factories in the Missouri backcountry. The landscape of contesting national interests—British, Spanish, Indian, American—was one he and his brothers had known all their lives.

But with the end of both the War of 1812 and the accompanying threat of an Indian-British alliance, the federal government had less incentive to accommodate the tribes. The primary goal of the factory system—to keep the trade and loyalty of the tribes away from the British—was not necessary on the Lower Missouri. To the contrary, many citizens regarded the quasi-monopolistic factory system as an obstacle to the unimpeded westward sweep of American commerce.[69]

In his administrative job, Clark would need a new set of skills: the ability to show leadership in territorial politics and a willingness to confront a new type of interest group. Agents like William Lovely, a Revolutionary War veteran placed in charge of the migrating Cherokees, protested the excesses of white hunters, who slaughtered thousands of bison for their tallow, or oil. "Their minds are warped," he told Clark. "The Tallowing, in my opinion is Destructive to Buffaloes Race which must soon be Destroyd; They kill the Buffalo & Leave the Carcass which might Sustain the hunting tribes of Indians."[70] By 1815, the hunting grounds of the Osages had become so depleted that they found it necessary to travel up to six hundred miles in search of bison.

Clark was still struggling to find a balance between his conflicting constituencies: his remote federal superiors in Washington, the land-hungry citizens of his territory, and the Indians he was supposed to protect. In December 1815, Clark finally announced that the intrusions of "white persons" onto Indian lands would no longer be permitted. "Our government, founded in justice will effectually extend its protection to the Native inhabitants within its limits," he said. What was more, he was ready to use the militia to evict trespassing whites, should they fail to leave on their own.[71]

The decision created a furor. Clark had already been criticized for rewarding the Indians at Portage des Sioux with $20,000 in presents. In the eyes of the citizenry he was now further siding with the "savages," perversely protecting terrorists while threatening to use the force of arms against peaceful settlers. "We do not want W Clark our Governor any longer," wrote a disdainful John Heath, a rural lawyer and salt-maker, adding, "I have no doubt this would be freely subscribed by nine tenths of the Territory."[72] Clark's friend Alexander McNair, the recorder of land titles, speculated, probably accurately, that not even five militiamen would be willing to march against the intruders on public lands.

On Christmas Day of 1815, Clark appealed for support from his superiors in Washington. President Madison obliged with an anti-squatter proclamation of his own to ease Clark's "difficulties and embarrassments." The President denounced the intrusions of "lawless adventurers" and asserted that "premature occupancy of the public lands can be viewed only as an invasion of the sovereign rights of the United States" and would be vigorously suppressed.[73] But by mid-March, even Madison had backed away from this political lightning rod and signed a law permitting settlers to remain on public lands until they were put up for sale.

While dealing with illegal settlers posed a delicate problem for Clark, he was well aware that the thriving population was ultimately an opportunity for him. "The tide of imigration is bending it's course up the Missouri," he told Biddle. "The only obsticle is the want of Lands to purchase."[74] He formed a partnership with Charles Lucas to quietly buy up land warrants issued by the federal government to victims of the New Madrid earthquakes. In April 1816, he purchased half of a city block on Main Street from Auguste Chouteau for $4,500. He had an old stone building on the site torn down and began to build what would be the Clark family compound. By the time the buildings were finished in 1818, there would be a two-story brick town house facing west, a two-room cottage behind it, and assorted stables and outhouses.

Attached to the town house was a long, low building with a room about a hundred feet long. This was Clark's Indian Agency Council Room, where he met with tribes visiting St. Louis. Lining the Council Room's walls were cabinets of curiosities, an array of Indian and natural artifacts that included items Clark had collected during the expedition and amplified over the years. The first description of what became known as Clark's Indian Museum comes from the Virginian William Campbell Preston (no relation to Clark's army friend), who visited St. Louis in 1816:

> The Governor's large council chamber was adorned with a profuse and almost gorgeous display of ornamented and painted buffalo robes, numerous strings of wampum, every variety of work of porcupine quills, skins, horns, claws, and bird skins, numerous and large Calumets, arms of all sorts, saddles, bridles, spears, powder horns, plumes, red blankets and flags.

Preston was impressed with the way that the forty-six-year-old Clark attracted trust and respect. He was, Preston said, "that most benevolent and intelligent gentleman, a man of primitive and heroic character, made up of firmness and tenderness." Physically, he was of "a remarkable fair complexion with gray locks and light blue eyes, hence the epithet, 'White Chief.'"

During Preston's visit, the long-awaited delegation of chiefs from the Rock River Sauks had finally arrived in St. Louis for treaty-making. Preston's description of the ensuing council is the only surviving account of Clark's negotiating technique:

> In the center of the hall was a large long table, at one end of which sat the governor with a sword laying before him, and a large

pipe in his hand. He wore the military hat and the regimentals of the army.

As [the chiefs] came in the Governor uttered no word nor made any salutation. Regarding them with a fixed and stern countenance he half unsheathed his sword and said: "Well, what have you to say?" . . . There was a long pause; the interpreter whispered that they expected a pipe to be lit, but the Governor was imperturbable. At length a chief past middle life, rolled up in a long buffalo robe, having a red feather in his hair and his face very much painted, rose and said, "White Chief, we have come down to have a friendly talk with you. There is no more war in our hearts—(a general grunt) We are poor and needy, cold and hungry. We want something to eat, and ammunition to hunt game or we shall starve next winter. We will behave like dutiful children and never again molest our white brethren."

"Who are you, you rascal!" exclaimed the Governor interrupting him—"I think I know you."

"I am," said the speaker, "the first man who broke into the settlement on the breaking out of the last war. I killed and scalped two women and a child. Here are the scalps," (taking them out of his pouch) . . . "Here is my war path," said he, unfolding his robe upon the interior of which was rudely painted in red a long road, with bloody hands splotched along it, and at the end a picture of a conflagration . . . "Small as I seem to you to be I am a great warrior, a very great man, most as great as you. I have taken a great many scalps, stolen a great many horses with bridles and saddles—but now we are beaten and I give up. I have come down to beg peace, and flints and powder that I may hunt deer and buffalo. I have come down as softly as the dew falls at night, but if you refuse these presents the next time I will come like the Missouri in flood. Our horses have trod so gently that not a spark has been struck. If you refuse these presents I will come down like a prairie on fire."[75]

The chiefs then asked for a pipe to be passed, but Clark refused, calling them "rogues, liars, and murderers." The Indians left "with a sorrowful aspect." Clark had made his point by dealing only from strength. He then called two of the chiefs back and, after reprimanding them for bringing "that rascal with you on a peace visit," gave them flints and powder.

One of the grateful chiefs then gave a farewell address to Clark. Preston reported that he had never seen a more elegant speaker. "His gesture was free and graceful, dignified and deliberate . . . there was a pathos in the tone of his voice and his manner which one would have understood even without the very appropriate and pregnant words which the Interpreter rendered at the end of each sentence."[76]

The treaty that was eventually signed with the Rock River Sauks and Foxes required them to recognize Harrison's despised Treaty of 1804. But instead of inflicting "the severest chastisement upon them," as the treaty put it, the United States, "being always disposed to pursue the most liberal and humane policy towards the Indian tribes within their territory," would prefer "their reclamation by peaceful measures."[77]

Meanwhile, in Philadelphia, the publication of the expedition journals was again foundering. Shortly after the volumes had been printed, the publisher, Bradford & Inskeep, went bankrupt, like its predecessor. Biddle informed Clark that the accumulated expenses and Paul Allen's fee of $500 would wipe out any profits. "The trade of bookselling has been of late years a very ruinous one," he explained, consoling Clark with the thought that "nothing can deprive you of the glory acquired by that expedition & I hope you will be able to indemnify yourself for the disappointment by judicious management in your young & thriving country."[78] Five months later, Clark still had not received his personal copy of the journals.

If there was any good news, it was that the Clark family was growing. Apparently Julia's suspected cancer had stabilized; in May 1816, she gave birth to her fourth child and third son. He was named George Rogers Hancock Clark, in honor of the increasingly frail George Rogers Clark, who had suffered a stroke and was living as an invalid under the care of his family at Locust Grove.

The end of the protracted Indian war—and the rise of a merchant class drawn by newly opened markets—stimulated political factionalism in the territory. Arrayed on one side was the old order of Creole families and fur traders, with their American allies such as Clark, Thomas Hart Benton, Edward Hempstead, and John Scott. Opposed to this "Junto" (as Joseph Charless caustically labeled it in the *Missouri Gazette*) were populists such as Rufus Easton, John B. C. Lucas, William Russell, and David Barton. The Junto faction favored honoring the old Spanish land grants, while the newcomers advocated the auction of public lands, the removal of Indians, and a vigorous market capitalism. Both sides adamantly opposed any restrictions on slavery and slaveholders.

The breach was visible as early as 1814. In the second election for a territorial delegate to Congress, the new American settlers defeated the Creole establishment and sent the former postmaster, Rufus Easton, to Washington. Two years later, Easton, a New Englander, was opposed for reelection by Clark's friend John Scott, a feisty Virginia-born lawyer from Ste. Geneviève. Angered by an opposition broadside, Scott challenged J.B.C. Lucas's son Charles to a duel. It was averted only after Clark and others intervened.

The election was a virtual dead heat. An early count showed Scott with 1,816 votes to Easton's 1,801. On September 19, Governor Clark proclaimed Scott to be the winner by 15 votes. But he had certified the vote before the election judges had validated a late-arriving group of disputed ballots from the town of Cote Sans Dessein that Scott himself had delivered on horseback. Charless erupted with a series of anti-Clark editorials in the *Missouri Gazette*, accusing him of "willful violations of law and principle" and "egregious errors." Charless railed that "the truth can no longer be smothered by official juggling and cabinet intrigue."[79]

Clark admitted to Biddle that he had "to contend now with a little news paper abuse for my political course."[80] To Jefferson, he stoutly defended his performance as governor, though he acknowledged, "I have succeed in the worst of times with more approbation than I had expected. Lately a Small and disappointed party has sprung up determined to vex & Teaze the executive."[81]

Both Easton and Scott traveled to Washington to make their case to be seated in Congress as the territory's sole nonvoting delegate. A House committee initially ruled in favor of Easton, but after a floor debate the full body ordered a new election. Both candidates decided to run again, and Clark set the election date for Monday, August 4, 1817.

The result was another imbroglio. Scott won by four hundred votes, but the heavy-handed campaign tactics of the Junto generated more controversy. On the day of the election, an armed detachment of pro-Scott soldiers from Fort Bellefontaine set up a canvassing table immediately outside the polling place bedecked with signs for "John Scott." They began handing out free glasses of whiskey and port to Scott voters and insulting anyone thought to favor Easton. Clark came to vote, reportedly announcing loudly afterward that he had cast his ballot for Scott.

Among the officers present was Clark's nephew John O'Fallon, who was not a legal resident but had set about to defend his uncle from those people spreading "the most scurrilous and abusive calumnies" against "his fair and unsullied character." When O'Fallon noticed Dr. Robert Simpson, a frequent public critic of Clark, at the polling place, he deliberately jostled Simpson and asked if he took it as an insult. "No, sir, I assure you I do not," Simpson replied. O'Fallon then snapped, "Sir, I intended it as an insult."[82]

Simpson tried to let the incident pass, though he had cocked his pistol in his pocket, since "My first impulse was to shoot him on the spot." Two days later, O'Fallon again bumped into Simpson on the street and called him a coward and a liar. This time Simpson fired his pistol at O'Fallon, though the powder flashed in the pan. O'Fallon retaliated by giving Simpson what he called "a complete cudgeling" with his cane, chasing him through an alley to his house.

Simpson published his version of the incident in the sympathetic *Missouri Gazette*, in which he pronounced the "elective franchise completely destroyed, and the public voice controlled and overawed by a combination of executive and military indulgence." The source of the travesty, he charged, was Governor Clark, who had attempted "to convert his high office into a political machine."[83]

On that same election day, another incident with more serious consequences took place between two of the town's most prominent lawyers. One was Charles Lucas, the popular son of Judge J.B.C. Lucas, who was the U.S. Attorney for Missouri Territory. The other was the voluble Thomas Hart Benton, who had recently moved to St. Louis from Tennessee after wounding Andrew Jackson in a street brawl. He quickly found favor with the Junto.

The two men were already courtroom rivals over land-claims issues when, on election day, Lucas challenged Benton at the polling place to prove that he had paid the taxes required for voting. Benton said that he would not answer to a "puppy." A week later, both men went to Bloody Island at dawn to settle the dispute. Standing thirty feet apart, they fired simultaneously. Benton was slightly wounded in the knee, but the younger man suffered a serious wound to the throat. With blood pouring from his neck, Lucas said that he was satisfied with the outcome. But Benton later insisted on another meeting after hearing reports that the Lucases had accused him of fleeing from Tennessee to escape criminal prosecution.

In the second duel, the men stood a murderous ten feet apart. Benton fired his ball squarely into Lucas's chest. As he lay dying, Lucas shook Benton's hand and forgave him. But Benton was labeled a villain by the *Missouri Gazette* for participating in the "infernal practice of dueling [which] has taken off this morning one of the first characters of our country."[84] Lucas's sister Anne was so fearful of Benton that she moved outside of St. Louis in order to avoid seeing him on the streets. Lucas's father spent the rest of his life denouncing Benton as an assassin who had deliberately provoked the duel to eliminate a political rival.

At the end of November 1817, Clark may well have wanted to travel to Washington, D.C., simply to escape the territory's poisonous atmospherics. But he had a practical reason as well. While the departing President, James Madison, had appointed him to a second three-year term as governor, Clark had not yet officially called on the Administration of the recently elected President Monroe. He needed to discuss Indian policy with the two strong-willed personalities he would now answer to: Secretary of War John C. Calhoun, a charismatic South Carolinian, and Secretary of State John Quincy Adams, a flinty New Englander.

Clark spent more than a month in the capital. He briefed Calhoun on the effectiveness—or lack of it—of the government's management of the 73,750 Indians under his supervision. Clark argued that the government's Indian policy needed to be drastically overhauled to give the Indian agents the legal power to detect unlicensed trade, to evict squatters, and to stop the smuggling of alcohol into Indian country. Most important, he felt that the factory system could not effectively influence the most distant tribes. Instead, he urged the creation of a powerful commercial company, protected by the government, that, as he had argued earlier, would "sweep the whole of the valuable fur trade of the Missouri and Mississippi; expel all of the petty (though now very powerful) British traders; and bring into our markets immense quantities of the most valuable furs and peltries." Trade, Clark said, echoing Jefferson's words, "is the great <u>lever</u> by which to direct the policy and conduct of the Indian tribes towards the United States."[85] (Such a powerful enterprise would eventually arise, not as a government-sponsored monopoly, however, but rather as John Jacob Astor's American Fur Company.)

Another agenda item for Clark was the continuing relocation of Eastern tribes across the Mississippi. Clark's job was to acquire land from the Western tribes that could then be provided to the dislocated tribes from the East. The predictable result was a series of bitter conflicts. The Osages, who thought they were ceding land to whites, suddenly found that their new neighbors were the hated Cherokees. The Lakota Sioux on the Missouri were equally dismayed to discover bands of relocated Sauks and Foxes infringing on their hunting grounds.

Over the previous year, Clark had supervised a series of land purchases designed to free up more land for the migrating tribes. The most significant of the cessions were made by the Osages. The government had long urged the Cherokees to move from their Georgia territories so their land could be converted into cotton plantations. By 1816, some six thousand Cherokees had moved into Osage territory on the Arkansas River.

The Osages had been persuaded to give up three million acres of their hunting grounds in return for an annuity arranged by the Cherokee agent, William Lovely (the so-called Lovely's Purchase). Now the government wanted to give millions more acres of Osage land ceded in the Treaty of 1808 to the Cherokees in exchange for their remaining holdings in Georgia and Tennessee.

The Osages protested that the land was still theirs. Exactly what the Osages had ceded to the United States over numerous agreements was not precisely clear, and certainly the tribe had not anticipated that its lands would be handed over to its historic enemies. But Clark believed that the educated, acculturated Cherokees made their case eloquently. It contained "a most masterly view of their situation totally unrivalled by any thing we have ever heard from an Indian . . . they spoke several days in succession and certainly supported their claim with astonishing ability."[86]

Clark and the commissioners tried to settle the dispute by sending out surveyors to draw boundary lines demarcating the land they believed the Osages had already ceded in negotiations. The surveyors returned with the news that "the Osage cession is very considerably larger than was supposed either by ourselves or by the Indians."[87] In the end, the new boundaries would eventually push the once-powerful Osages all but out of the present state of Missouri.

In October 1817, the Cherokees attacked an isolated Osage village and killed or captured 138 inhabitants, mostly women and children. While Clark had sought to prevent the war, he had been so angered by the Osage resistance to the cessions that he concluded that the conflict was not necessarily a bad thing and could even produce "a favourable effect."[88] As he explained, "Experience has proved to me that a General peace amongst the Indian Tribes is a Signal for difficulties with the whites."

Clark also told his superiors that he needed to monitor British influence over the contentious Rock River Sauks and other militant tribes on the Upper Mississippi. Benjamin O'Fallon had been appointed a special Indian agent at Prairie du Chien, where he had been "keeping a watchful eye over the feelings of the Indians and the disposition and conduct of the faithless Mackinac traders." As O'Fallon put it, "It will be a vain struggle to attempt the change of the treacherous savage, so long as unprincipald British Traders are permited to trade within our Territory."[89]

To the bumptious O'Fallon, the most treacherous of the British traders was "the famous Dickson," the "villain" who was telling the Indians "to keep bright and sharp the scalping knife and tomahawk."[90] When he encountered Dickson on the Upper Mississippi in 1818, O'Fallon pronounced him to be illegally trading on American soil, took the British subject prisoner, and brought him shackled in irons to St. Louis. Dickson was turned over to Clark. The two rivals must have had an interesting conversation before Clark released the trader, sending him back to Canada.[91]

During his return from Washington in March 1818, Clark learned in Louisville that his brother George Rogers Clark had died at Locust

Grove a month earlier. It would have been an emotional moment. George Rogers was the family's Achilles—the charismatic flawed hero who had first led the Clark family across the Appalachians into the West. Since brother Edmund had died the previous year, William, the youngest, was now the last survivor of the six illustrious Clark brothers.

After an absence of almost five months, Clark arrived in St. Louis in April to find the city booming. The federal government had finally begun to auction off the public lands in the territory. The availability of cheap land, which could be purchased on credit, touched off a speculative mania. Properties worth $30 in 1817 would hit $2,000 just two years later. The previous summer the first steamboat to pass the mouth of the Ohio, the *Pike*, had docked in St. Louis. Suddenly markets on the East Coast were weeks away instead of months. St. Louis was thriving with about five thousand residents, forty merchants, and dozens of tradesmen, saloon-keepers, hoteliers, doctors, lawyers—and slaves.

The ambitious new merchants and speculators had little use for the whist-playing Creole elite and their conservative American friends. "Governor Clark is as unpopular as it is possible for a man to be," said William Russell.[92] Judge Lucas, profoundly embittered over the loss of his son, willfully placed himself in "an open war" with Clark and the Junto.[93] Lucas blocked political appointments for "the governor's Creatures" and eventually denounced Clark to Secretary of State Adams in an extraordinary ad hominem attack:

> This William Clark has nothing to recommend him personally, except his trip to the Pacific Ocean. He knew so little of his duty as Indian agent as to be publicly concerned in Indian trade, and was actually President of a Fur Company and trading up the Missouri in 1808 and 1809 whilst he was an Indian agent. He also kept Indian goods for sale at his store in St. Louis.[94]

Lucas criticized the wartime Prairie du Chien expedition as a boondoggle for Benjamin O'Fallon, who supplied goods to the troops, and complained that the Indian Office jobs "are filled with [Clark's] nephews, brothers-in-law or other friends and dependents."

The nepotism charge was not without justice. When Clark informed Secretary of War Crawford that he had appointed Benjamin O'Fallon a special Indian agent to the Northern tribes, he described him simply as

"This young Gentleman a native of Kentucky who has been recommended to you by gentlemen of high respectability in this Territory."[95] What he did not say at the time was that O'Fallon was his nephew and virtual adopted son who had lived under his roof since the age of fourteen. During his trip to Washington, Clark had lobbied unsuccessfully for a political appointment for his other nephew, John O'Fallon.

Kinship ties were vital to Clark. After Lovely's death, he appointed Meriwether Lewis's brother Reuben as Indian agent for the Cherokees. When the government later needed an Indian agent for the Upper Missouri tribes, he recommended that the appointment go to either Benjamin O'Fallon, his nephew, or to George Hancock Kennerly, his wife's cousin. Both eventually got jobs. John O'Fallon ruefully acknowledged Clark's success when he told his mother that his own job search had failed because the government had thought it "improper that too many appointments should be bestowed on a family."[96]

It was not surprising that Clark sometimes found himself out of step in the political world. He had carried into preindustrial Missouri a set of values that originated in the more genteel eighteenth-century Kentucky and Virginia. As the territory expanded and the Indian threat diminished, the kind of casual nepotism that was conventional during the regime of the Creole elite was less accepted by the ambitious new mercantile class in St. Louis.

Again preoccupied with his wife's poor health—Julia was both pregnant and "dangerously ill"—Clark may have been oblivious to the activities of his political enemies. Judge Lucas began to build a dossier on Clark, in which he recorded the governor's missteps dating back to the ill-fated Treaty of 1808 with the Osages. Among its entries were papers demonstrating that Clark had concealed his speculation in the New Madrid land warrants and had sought to pressure civil authorities under his supervision into supporting John Scott in the recent election.

Unlike most of his contemporaries, Lucas believed that there was room for both whites and Indians in the territory. He thought that Clark had "a disposition for officiousness" and unfairly purchased Indian land "below value" from tribes that were unrepresented at the treaty councils. "The immense extent of soil allows a compatibility of interests," Lucas wrote. While arguing for better treatment of the Indians, Lucas recognized that in the long run their fate would be the same. "If like wild plants [the Indians] must decay and disappear at the approach of civilization and its concomitant agriculture let it be without violence or fault of our own," he wrote. "Let it not be said that whilst we have asserted . . . the religious civil and political liberty which was denied to our Ancestors in Europe and had induced them to emigrate to the wilds of America, we have in turn retailed injustices and oppression and ground down the ignorant aborigines into annihilation."[97]

After his return to St. Louis, Clark had little opportunity to enjoy the fine spring weather. Julia was so ill that he told George Sibley he could "only absent myself for a fiew minutes at a time."[98] In the first week of July, she gave birth to their fifth child, a boy they named John Julius. The baby suffered from a birth defect, with symptoms resembling spina bifida. Julia was only twenty-seven, but her health was failing, probably from progressive breast cancer. Three months later, William reported that she still could not walk without assistance.

Over the summer, Clark and Auguste Chouteau signed "peace and friendship" treaties with several bands of Middle Missouri tribes, including the Grand Pawnees, the Noisy Pawnees, the Republican Pawnees, and the Omahas. Amity with these "warlike and powerful" tribes was necessary, Clark said, because they not only controlled the Missouri River trade but, in the event of an American war with Spain — tensions continued along the southwestern borders — "might be sent down in force upon our extended western frontier."[99]

During these negotiations, Clark complained that he had "not time scarcly to think," but visitors found him unfailingly welcoming.[100] Henry Vest Bingham judged Clark to be "a verry Civil polite Gentleman altho he must be Much plaughed by the Visits of Strangers; he politely Invited us to use his office to Do any writings that we wished and Said the Door was always open at an Early hour in the morning we Could he said use his paper Maps & to ascertain the Situation of the Country."[101]

Secretary of War Calhoun instructed Clark that his next goal must be to stop the fighting among the Cherokee, Osage, and Quapaw tribes. Calhoun wanted these treaties to turn over as much land as possible to the Cherokees, "as the President is anxious to hold out every inducement to the Cherokees and the other Southern nations, to emigrate to the West of the Mississippi."[102] Calhoun authorized Clark and Auguste Chouteau to spend up to $3,000 to reward the tribes for their cooperation.

The Quapaws came in first, signing a treaty in St. Louis on August 24, 1818, that ceded 30 million acres in the present states of Arkansas and Oklahoma for trade goods worth $4,000 and an annuity of $1,000. Clark and Chouteau signed, along with a dozen Quapaw chiefs. Among the witnesses listed on the treaty document were the names of two small boys: M. Lewis Clark, age nine, and William P. Clark, age six.

A month later, Clark reported with obvious satisfaction that he had "with much difficulty succeeded in bringing about a peace between the Osages and Cherokees." Neither of the warring tribes, he said, would accept a treaty that was not made in his presence. Consequently, delegations from both had come to St. Louis. The Osages had ceded a sixty-mile-wide swath "of very fine land," which, together with the Quapaw cession, "places an immense Country at the disposal of the United States."[103]

Monroe and Calhoun had good reason to be pleased with their territorial governor. His political problems notwithstanding, Clark had all but single-handedly extinguished most of the Indian titles in two future states—Missouri and Arkansas—for a total of 51 million acres. Moreover, the recent signing of the Treaty of St. Mary's near Lake Erie meant that the once-powerful tribes north of the Ohio—the Delawares, Miamis, Weas, Potawatomis, Shawnees, and Wyandots—could be relocated across the Mississippi. Their new home would be the land Clark had acquired from the Osages and Quapaws.

The road looked just as clear to white settlers. In 1819, the *St. Louis Enquirer* reported that four hundred to five hundred families were crossing the Mississippi every day to move onto land cleared by Clark's treaties with the Osages. The territory's white population was more than forty-five thousand, easily enough to qualify it for statehood.

Despite the increased trappings of development from the East, St. Louis was still a roistering frontier town, divided between the rough-hewn American and French Canadian keelboatmen on the wharf and the educated French families and American lawyers and doctors who lived above the limestone bluffs. The future mountain man Jim Beckwourth, the mixed-race son of a slave, roamed the streets, as did the young Jim Bridger.

Most celebrated of all was Mike Fink, the Ohio boatman, who was not yet the "ring-tailed roarer, half-alligator, half-man" of legend but rather "a large heavy slow-spoken, slow-moving quiet man with a dark sallow countenance."[104] By 1821, though, Fink's reputation for braggadocio had grown so large that he had the distinction of being portrayed as a minor character in Alphonso Wetmore's St. Louis production of *The Pedlar* while he was still alive. Two years later, after shooting a man in the forehead in a William Tell–like stunt, he was killed in retaliation at the mouth of the Yellowstone and Missouri.

Perhaps the most unusual figure in St. Louis was Jean Baptiste Charbonneau—"Pompy," the *métis* son of Toussaint Charbonneau and Sacagawea—the youngest member of the Voyage of Discovery. Clark had legally adopted Baptiste (as he was called) and his sister Lisette after Sacagawea's death in December 1812 at Fort Manuel. Fulfilling his promise to educate the boy, Clark enrolled Baptiste as a ward of the Indian Office at Mr. Welch's school at the corner of Third and Market. Clark's accounts from the time show expenses charged to the government of $16.37 "for two quarters' tuition of J.B. Charbonneau, a half-Indian boy, and firewood and ink."[105] Sacagawea's fifteen-year-old son was reading Roman history and wearing corduroys purchased from James Kennerly's store.

Everyone thought St. Louis would be the "future seat of empire," as Henry Rowe Schoolcraft put it. In late 1817, residents had begun to draw up the first petitions for Missouri statehood, and in January 1818 territorial delegate John Scott presented the citizens' petitions to Congress. In November 1818 the Missouri territorial legislature passed a resolution "praying" for statehood. A month later, Henry Clay introduced the bill for Missouri statehood on the floor of Congress. But when James Tallmadge of New York offered an amendment prohibiting the importation of more slaves into Missouri and freeing all children of slave parents at the age of twenty-five, Clay and the slaveholding Southerners were outraged—and the battle was joined.

Missouri's prosperity brought increased demand for slaves. In 1818, the English traveler Henry Bradshaw Fearson recorded seeing fourteen flatboats on the Mississippi filled with slaves being exported from Kentucky.

Clark continued to purchase slaves and hire out those he owned, in both St. Louis and Louisville. With freedom available across the river in Illinois, Missourians managed their slaves strictly; an 1818 law decreed that any slaves found on the streets between 9 p.m. and dawn could be whipped.

In April 1818, the New England missionary the Reverend John Mason Peck met with Clark and discussed with him the condition of St. Louis's slaves. According to Peck, "The Governor, alluding to the scenes of dancing, drunkenness, and fighting on the Sabbath . . . stated that the preceding summer he had to call out a military company three times to suppress riots among this class." Clark went on to tell Peck that "the character of the Negroes in general was a tolerably correct index to that of the white population among whom they resided. They were characteristic for imitation, and quick in catching the living manner, and quite successful in cultivating the low vices of the superiors."[106]

Slavery was an issue within the Missouri Territory only to the extent that political candidates competed over who were its most ardent supporters. Only one family in ten actually owned slaves, but many held out hopes that they would someday. In 1819, the citizens of St. Louis passed a resolution asserting that the end of slavery in Missouri would be "equally contrary to the rights of the State, and to the welfare of the slaves themselves."[107]

Although Clark had convened the territorial legislature in the fall of 1818, he was not present for the passage of the statehood resolution. Just nine days after moving into the new brick house he had built next to the Indian Agency Council Room, the governor left St. Louis on October 20 to take his family to Louisville. Julia had again fallen ill, and Clark hoped a visit with her sister Caroline Hancock Preston and his sister Fanny Clark Fitzhugh would restore her health.

His frequent absences from St. Louis were becoming a political liability. "I have been told, that some of the Legislative body have been grumbling about your not being here when they met," Thomas Forsyth wrote to Clark. "It is said by some people in this place that you make yourself very easy about this Territory or the people in it as you are working to be appointed Superintendent of Indian Affairs, as soon as we go into a State Government. My answer to one, whom I heard mention this, was, that I hope withal my heart it would take place, this answer astonished him."[108]

Julia's trip to Louisville did not help. She spent three weeks confined to her bed. William entertained the children, taking the older boys to see a play, buying cakes and toys for Mary, and indulging in oranges, oysters, and "seegars" for himself. In his notebook, he regularly recorded gifts ranging from $1 to $12 that he gave to beggars.

Clark returned to St. Louis in March to find himself once again mired in territorial politics. The newspaper editor Joseph Charless had flown into a rage upon learning that his *Missouri Gazette* would no longer be given the lucrative contract to print the territorial laws. The decision was probably made by Scott, but Charless blamed both men. "To be stript of employment because I differed in opinion with Governor Clark and Mr. Scott is not to be submitted to silently & without a struggle," he said.[109] Charless retaliated with a scathing news item reporting the suicide of a Clark family slave originally from Louisville. "Scipio, the Negro who nursed Governor Clark, shot himself through the head this morning," Charless explained privately to Judge Lucas. "Clark was about sending him to Orleans, on board the steam boat which sailed today, in order to convert his old companion into cash, but the generous Negro preferred death to parting with an ungrateful master."[110]

After passing just eight weeks in St. Louis, Clark returned to Louisville. He picked up Julia and took his family to Virginia by way of the Cumberland Gap. They spent the month of July at Fotheringay, the 598-acre Hancock country estate on a branch of the Roanoke River, near present-day Elliston, Virginia. The older boys Lewis and William were sent to boarding school nearby. Clark and Julia then took a recommendation from President Monroe and embarked on a two-month restorative tour of Virginia's mineral springs—Sorrell Springs, Salt Sulphur Springs, Red Sulphur Springs, and Sweet Springs. Exhausted (not surprisingly), Julia collapsed and had to be physically carried in a bed back to Fincastle. "For three weeks [I] expected every day she would die," said Clark, who turned to a folk remedy: "I commenced the use of the fumes of Tar thro' a tube, which has produced the most favourable effects."[111]

Encouraged by his wife's apparent recovery, Clark went on to Washington to visit President Monroe and Secretary of War Calhoun. After spending the Christmas holidays at Fotheringay, he left Julia and the children in Virginia and made his way back to St. Louis, arriving on March 19, 1820. He had been away from his territorial post for the past ten months and twenty of the previous twenty-eight.

During Clark's absence, Missouri had continued its campaign for state-hood. The national debate over permitting slavery in newly admitted states had been tabled, if not resolved, by Henry Clay's Missouri Compromise. Missouri would be admitted as a slave state and Maine would be admitted as a free state, thus preserving the balance between slave and free states at twelve apiece. Slavery would be prohibited in the territories north of latitude 36°30'. Earlier that month, Monroe had signed the Missouri Enabling Act, calling for citizens to elect delegates to a convention to write the new state constitution.

Monroe had reappointed Clark to a third term as the territory's chief executive, but his tenure would end as soon as the new state elected its first governor. Would he run? Clark was not interested. In January he drafted, but apparently never sent, a letter to a newspaper explaining his decision:

> Having been frequently spoken to on subject of standing a [poll] for Governor of the new State by Gentlemen from different points of this Territory and often solicited by my particular friends to offer for that [position] I must . . . tender my greatful acknowledgements to those of my friends and fellow citizens who have a desire for my continuing to serve in the capacity of Governor, and regret that the peculiar situation of my family now in the State of Virginia demanding my immediate attention, will deprive me of the satisfaction of tendering my services in execution of the duties of Chief Magistrate of the new State of Missouri.[112]

Clark's friend Alexander McNair, a Pennsylvania Federalist, announced that he would run. McNair was an affable militia officer who was well liked for tolerating squatters while running the territorial land office. The St. Louis caucus initially supported him because of his fervent opposition to any restrictions on slavery. But when McNair took more populist stands during the constitutional convention, the Junto withdrew its support and turned to Clark. By mid-February, with Julia's health apparently improving, Clark had changed his mind and decided to run.

It was a bitter campaign, fought largely in the columns of the rival newspapers, the pro-McNair *Missouri Gazette* and the pro-Clark *St. Louis Enquirer*. Joseph Charless denounced Clark and "a few nabobs selected by a secret caucus" and even editorialized against slavery, an unpopular position in a state that did not elect a single candidate to its constitutional convention who favored any restrictions on slaveholding. For his efforts, Charless was assaulted on the street on May 19 by Isaac Henry, one of the avidly pro-slavery editors of the *Enquirer*.

By early July, Clark felt he needed to return to Virginia to be with Julia. He departed on July 3, leaving behind a campaign statement that the *St. Louis Enquirer* would run, in full, each week before the election on August 29. Clark made a case largely distinguished by its modesty. "The choice of a Governor is your business and not mine," he wrote, "and so far as my fitness for that place may be the subject of enquiry, that matter may be discussed as well in my absence as in my presence." He went on to cite his long residence in the area, his friendship with "the old inhabitants and early settlers," and his career in public service that had begun under George Washington.[113]

Charless responded with a barrage of mordant editorials in the *Missouri Gazette*, charging Clark with having "deserted his post, and having been repeatedly absent," adding, "The attention and care which Mr. Clark owes to his family cannot be an apology." That Clark had spent long months away from his post was certainly true, but to this factual accusation Charless added misrepresentations: "I cannot admire a person who turns into a sinecure an office to which not many important duties are attached; and who pockets public money without earning it."[114] In later editorials, Charless improbably accused Clark of deserting the territory during the War of 1812 in order to be in Washington, D.C., to attend to his Spanish land claims.

Clark was defended by the town's other two newspapers. When the accusations resurfaced that Clark sided with Indians over settlers, the *St. Louis Enquirer* noted that if he were blamed for "undue partiality for the Indians . . . That he treats these unfortunate people with mildness and humanity is not denied. It is his duty to do so."[115] The *Missouri Intelligencer* praised his "dignity of character, that suavity of manner, that sterling integrity, that intuitive knowledge of the human character." He was, the newspaper concluded, "the poor man's friend."[116]

The governor left the election debate behind as he hurried on to Virginia. He had gone on from Louisville the day before the news arrived that Julia Hancock Clark had died at Fotheringay on June 27, 1820. She was just twenty-eight. By the time Clark finally arrived in Fotheringay, he was informed that Julia's father, George Hancock, had also died three weeks after the death of his daughter. The patriarch had suffered an "apoplectic fit," probably a stroke. A double funeral was held for father and daughter in the parlor of Fotheringay; they were later buried in the family's mausoleum on a hillside overlooking the valley. In his notebook, Clark noted that he "paid for Mrs. C's coffin $20."[117]

By this time, the governor's friends in St. Louis were worried about his neglected campaign. "The election is getting very warm," John O'Fallon observed. "McNair is making the greatest exertions in the tippling shops of this place."[118] O'Fallon published and distributed a pamphlet summarizing Clark's life and achievements, but by mid-August he was despairing. "Uncle William will not be elected," he wrote to his stepfather, Dennis Fitzhugh. "His opponent will have a handsome majority. They accuse Gov. Clark of being friendly to the Indians, being still & reserved and unhospitable."[119]

In its final days, the campaign turned particularly vicious. Clark's enemies accused him of complicity in the recent failure of the Bank of St. Louis, of trading with Indians during the war, and of having an Indian wife and a mixed-race child who was being educated at public expense in St. Louis (presumably a reference to Jean Baptiste Charbonneau). Clark was said to be, moreover, a pawn of "the Virginia dynasty," a man who "possesses a compound of gloss and borrowed manners, which give him the appearance of what is termed in Europe, *a provincial gentleman.*"[120] For their part, Clark's supporters tried to label McNair as an anti-slavery "restrictionist"—the most damning charge that could be brought against any territorial politician.

In the end, the election was not even close. McNair won by 3,920 votes, gathering 6,576 votes to Clark's 2,656. Clark lost every county in the new state, usually by a 2-to-1 margin.

Why did Clark lose? At one level, the election was less about the governorship itself than a referendum on the old territorial elite. Clark was convincingly defeated because a new ideology was ascendant in Missouri. It was robustly democratic, rural, expansionist, anti-federal, and rabidly opposed to accommodating the region's Native Americans. Clark's personal qualities paled beside the widespread conviction that he put the interests of Indians and the despised federal government ahead of those of Missouri's own citizens. Missourians wanted to keep their slaves and get rid of the Indians. Thomas Hart Benton, who won his Senate seat in the same election, well understood the implications. "To remove the Indians," he later wrote, "would make room for the spread of slaves."[121]

On the day of the election, William Clark was traveling in Kentucky with his three youngest children and three slaves—Berry, Anthony, and Litty—somewhere east of Louisville. Three weeks later, he crossed the Mississippi to St. Louis. It was September 19, which, as it happened, was the same day Alexander McNair was taking the oath of office at the new three-story Missouri Hotel, the finest in the West. Clark did not attend the ceremony. Instead, he went to the brick house he and Julia had just built at Main and Vine. Julia's jewelry, linens, and clothing were still where she had left them packed into trunks and drawers.

At the age of fifty, Clark was a widower with five children and uncertain prospects. But he at once set to work to replenish the family's larder, purchasing beef, bacon, flour, fish, potatoes, butter, bread, milk, apples, wood, nuts, knives and forks, cups and saucers, plates, dishes, tumblers, coffee, brown sugar, and tea. He spent a dollar on "toys by William."[122] As he had been so many times before, William Clark was ready to proceed on.

CHAPTER NINE

"THE RED-HEADED CHIEF"

1820–1829

In March of 1821, Missouri entered the Union as the twenty-fourth state and the largest of all in raw land. Immigrants—whites, blacks, and Indians—were pouring across the Mississippi. Newspapers reported between four hundred and five hundred families arriving in St. Louis every day. Meanwhile, an earlier generation was departing. In August 1820 the indefatigable Manuel Lisa, who had traveled up the Missouri more times than anyone, died in the unlikely location of his bed. A month later, Daniel Boone died at the age of eighty-six at his son Nathan's house on the Missouri River.

Clark was preparing for a transition in his life in the midst of a transition in the life of the territory. The fur trade was booming, as were land sales in Missouri. As a result, pressures were growing on the remaining Indians in Missouri and beyond. Merchants in St. Louis were shipping enormous quantities of goods to markets in the East and in Europe. The force of the market economy was now reaching farther and farther west.

Given the stakes, it was not surprising that the United States Army had returned to the High Plains for the first time since the Lewis and Clark expedition. In March 1818, the charismatic thirty-six-year-old Secretary of War, John C. Calhoun, concluded that the best way to send a message to Indians and the British about American power would be to fortify the wilderness. Calhoun envisioned a chain of forts stretching like a string of pearls along the northern border with Canada.

It was a plan that drew directly on the vision for garrisoning the west that Clark had outlined at Fort Mandan during the winter of 1804–'05. Clark had estimated that a dozen forts and a force of seven hundred officers and soldiers would be enough to control the continent and keep the British at bay. He had outlined the staffing down to the number of buglers required. The military goals of the expedition would now be realized.

In 1820, the reach of the American military stopped at Fort Bellefontaine at St. Louis and Fort Crawford at Prairie du Chien. Calhoun proposed building forts on the Upper Mississippi at the mouth of the St. Peter's (now Minnesota) River and at the Falls of the St. Marys between Lake Huron and Lake Superior. But the most dramatic gesture would be sending the flag 1,800 miles up the Missouri to the mouth of the Yellowstone River. "The glory of planting the American flag at a point so distant, on so noble a river, will not be unfelt," Calhoun predicted. "The world will behold in it the mighty growth of our republic, which but a few years since, was limited by the Allegheny; but now is ready to push its civilization and laws to the western confines of the continent."[1]

In the aftermath of the financial Panic of 1819, however, Congress lacked funds for Calhoun's ambitious plan. Instead, what became known as the Yellowstone expedition evolved into three separate journeys: an Upper Mississippi excursion led by Colonel Henry Leavenworth, a military expedition up the Missouri commanded by Colonel Henry Atkinson, and a scientific party also on the Missouri led by Major Stephen H. Long.

The first phase of the military expedition began on September 1, 1818, when a battalion of 350 men left Fort Bellefontaine and began poling and pulling keelboats up the Missouri. Clark used his maps and memory to help plan the expedition, and its sutler, the man responsible for providing all supplies not explicitly requisitioned by the army, was his nephew, Captain John O'Fallon. Clark had recommended that they push as far as the Mandan villages or Council Bluff, where he had spent his thirty-fourth birthday in 1804 waiting to meet the Oto and Missouri Indians. Instead, the party traveled just four hundred miles and made its winter camp at Cow Island, just above present-day Leavenworth, Kansas.

The next summer, Colonel Atkinson intended to bring the full Sixth Infantry Regiment of about 1,100 men up the river to join the group at Cow Island. He contracted a fleet of five steamboats, the first to travel on the Missouri, to carry his soldiers. But the steamboats were poorly made: one did not reach St. Louis at all, two broke down before reaching the mouth of the Missouri, and a third gave out soon afterward. With each successive breakdown, the soldiers transferred into keelboats in order to keep moving.

The only steamboat that succeeded in getting within a few miles of Council Bluff was not one of Atkinson's vessels but rather the *Western Engineer*, Stephen Long's stern-wheeler with a fanciful dragon painted on its smokestack. Traveling with Long was Clark's other nephew, Benjamin O'Fallon. On Clark's recommendation, O'Fallon had been appointed a special Indian agent for the Upper Missouri tribes, charged with treating the Indians "with kindness and firmness" and with dealing with the "foreign or illicit traders who either have or may desire the monopoly of the fur trade."[2]

Atkinson and his men unloaded their cargo at Council Bluff, just north of today's Omaha, on September 19, 1819. It was the same spot that Clark had identified fourteen years earlier as "a very proper place for a trading establishment and fortification."[3] Cantonment Missouri, as it was then called, was situated on an unhealthy river bottom: more than one-tenth of the men died of disease and malnutrition during a disastrous first winter. After the entire camp was flooded during the spring, it was moved to higher ground. Renamed Fort Atkinson, it was constructed as a massive wooden fortress, two hundred yards on a side. With eight blockhouses and quarters for a thousand soldiers, Fort Atkinson was the largest and westernmost outpost of the United States Army.

In the spring of 1820, Stephen Long took a group of fifteen soldiers and scientists from his own camp, just below Fort Atkinson, and headed up the Platte River to the Front Range of the Rockies. He returned down the Arkansas River with a map and a label—"Great American Desert"—that would inaccurately characterize the prairies east of the Rockies for years. (Long later led the 1823 exploration that fixed where the 49th parallel crosses the Red River on the present-day Minnesota–North Dakota border.)

Both O'Fallons soon returned to St. Louis. Benjamin told Clark that Atkinson's outpost "could not fail to produce the most favourable impression of our strength and capacity to punish such as might presume to insult us."[4] Atkinson was promoted to brevet (or temporary) brigadier general and transferred back to St. Louis. His replacement was Colonel Henry Leavenworth, a Connecticut Yankee and veteran of the War of

1812 whose recent expedition up the Mississippi had resulted in the construction of Fort Snelling on a site that is now one mile east of the Minneapolis–St. Paul airport.

Although no longer governor, Clark had been asked by Calhoun to stay on as Superintendent of Indian Affairs "as you have heretofore done . . . until you are relieved."[5] It was a blessing. As territorial governor, Clark had struggled with an impossible conflict. His job was to reconcile the interests of two incompatible groups: as governor he represented the expansionist American settlers; as Indian superintendent, he was to protect the treaty-given rights of Native Americans.

As superintendent, he was charged only with keeping the Indians at peace and protecting them from the pernicious influence of illegal traders and settlers. While his core view did not change—Indians needed to be removed from the corrupting influence of whites for as many as thirty years while they gradually and peacefully learned the ways of Euro-American culture—his correspondence and actions began to reflect his narrower responsibilities: no longer accountable politically to an increasingly rapacious citizenry, Clark could afford to view the declining welfare of the Indians with increasing sympathy and concern.

At home, Clark was an active single father. The three older boys— Lewis, William, and George—lived in St. Louis with him. He bought oranges and cakes for them, took them to traveling circuses, and entertained them at weekly performances at the local theater. The youngest boy, Julius—or "Julias," as his family usually spelled his name, after his mother's—had remained in Virginia with the Hancocks. He was a lively child, but his birth defect had led to speech and hearing difficulties.

Clark's six-year-old daughter, the redheaded Mary Margaret, lived in Louisville with the families of her aunts Caroline Hancock Preston and Lucy Clark Croghan. Clark was devoted to his only daughter. "Dear Papa," she wrote, "I hope you are well. I want to see you, and my Brothers. Kiss them for me. I am a good Girl, and will learn my Book." Clark filed away her letter after carefully noting that it had been "Answered by all the boys."[6]

Surrounding Clark's immediate family was an ever-blooming houseful of relatives. Two of Julia's cousins from Fincastle, James and George

Kennerly, operated a store out of the first floor of Clark's brick house. A third Kennerly brother, Augustin, worked as a clerk in the Indian Office. Their sisters Harriet and Elizabeth visited from Virginia. Clark's O'Fallon nephews were virtually surrogate sons. His niece Ann ("Nancy") Clark Thruston, Fanny's daughter, had moved to St. Louis as the wife of the mercurial Dr. Bernard Farrar. Jean Baptiste Charbonneau—Sacagawea's "little dancing boy" Pomp—still lived in town. Clark had continued to pay for Jean Baptiste's education, as he had promised Charbonneau. The half-Indian youth lived in a boardinghouse across the street, but if he ever visited the Clark household, it was not noted.

Clark's household did encompass the parallel families of enslaved African-Americans, who divided their time between the Clark compound in town and his nearby farm, Marais Castor (Beaver Pond), a few miles to the west. On Christmas Day of 1820, Clark's first without Julia, he bought presents for the boys and also for his black servants: Anthony, Chloe, Berry, Ben, Allen, Ebenene (Ebony), Nancy, Rosalle (Rosalie), and Henry. Clark frequently rented out his domestic slaves to other families in St. Louis and Louisville when he was out of town.

Clark celebrated that bittersweet Christmas with a new friend, a wealthy Englishman named William Stokes. Stokes had recently arrived with his wife, Ann, and his half-sister Harriet Stokes. William Stokes had flaunted enough money around town to attract the attention of local businessmen, including Missouri's newly elected lieutenant governor, William H. Ashley, who was looking for investors in his new fur-trading and trapping expedition. Captain John O'Fallon, meanwhile, had courted Harriet Stokes and made plans to marry her.

But life in the borderlands was nothing if not unpredictable. After O'Fallon married Harriet the following April, he received startling news from his stepfather, Dennis Fitzhugh. Posting a letter from the steamboat *Calhoun* on the Ohio, Fitzhugh reported that another passenger on the *Calhoun* was an Englishwoman named Marianne Stokes, who was on her way to St. Louis. Marianne had told Fitzhugh that she was William Stokes's legal wife and that the woman in St. Louis with her estranged husband was actually his mistress, Ann Smith. Moreover, Fitzhugh said, Marianne "is a sensible, well informed woman, talks much and talks good sense," who "laments on your account that she is to break in on the Tranquillity of the Family."[7]

Marianne had in fact married Stokes in 1802 in London. Five years later, they were legally separated. Ignoring his obligation to pay her an annuity of £100, Stokes departed for the American West with the woman he was now calling his wife. Outraged, Marianne pursued Stokes across the Atlantic and across half a continent. When she got to St. Louis, she sued him for abandonment; Stokes countered by charging her with living in "a state of adultery" and being "the mistress of different men." The scandal played out within two years. Stokes's mistress, Ann Smith, committed suicide by poison, and, disgraced, he died at the house of his brother-in-law, John O'Fallon. Marianne Stokes returned vindicated to London. But Stokes would find no peace in the grave. Fifty years later, excavators accidentally unearthed his burial site in St. Louis and dumped his remains into a landfill.[8]

Against this discordant backdrop, Clark continued to toil away in the Indian Office, using its funds to assist the burgeoning numbers of Indians now crossing the Mississippi in their almost desperate efforts to stay west of the advancing lines of white settlement. In a single week in 1821, Clark's office paid the fees to transport 222 Indian families and 264 horses across the Mississippi on Sam Wiggins's new steam-powered ferry.

The superintendent continued to struggle with ambiguities within his official responsibilities. Was he in charge of the Indians only in the state of Missouri? What about the Indians who lived in the "immence tract of Country" west of Missouri?[9] Who would manage them? An abrupt reply came from Secretary of War Calhoun. The government was pulling back on its costs, and "the Dept. does not think itself authorized to continue your services as Superintendent of Indian affairs, longer than may be necessary to wind up the public business committed to your charge."[10] Two months later Calhoun added, almost apologetically, "The Department is well satisfied with the manner both as to judgment and economy in which the business of your superintendence has always been transacted; and it will be happy to avail itself of the patriotic offer which you have made of your services on any future occasion wherein your knowledge and experience would be useful."[11]

Calhoun's reassurances meant little to Clark at the time. There was a more serious problem. Mary Margaret had fallen dangerously ill, and her father hastily left for Louisville to be with her. "Genl. Clark has been at Mrs. Preston's for some time, attending to his daughter, who is extremely ill, not expected to recover," wrote one family member.[12] Mary Margaret died on October 15, 1821, at the home of her aunt Caroline.

In a span of sixteen months, Clark had lost both his wife and his only daughter. At Louisville, he dolefully noted expenses for Mary's two doctors ($80), and then "Mecidine" ($8.25), "Shrouds etc" ($14.75), "Toomstones" ($35), and finally "Parson &c." ($10).[13] "I sympathize most sensibly for the irreparable loss of Uncle Wm.," John O'Fallon wrote to Dennis Fitzhugh. "I am gratified to hear that he bears it so well. I fear he will not spend the evening of his life as serenely as he desires."

O'Fallon's concerns included his uncle's financial plight. The recent failure of the Bank of St. Louis, of which Clark was a director, had been another business disappointment. "It will, I apprehend, hurt him more than he is aware of," O'Fallon said. "I wish he could get something from the Genl Govt to contribute to his support." In O'Fallon's view, Clark was relying too heavily on poor advice from people such as the Kennerly brothers, "whose want of judgment have embarrassed them."[14]

Clark had returned to St. Louis from Louisville by early November. Sometime in the course of that year he had begun to see more of Julia's widowed first cousin, Harriet Kennerly Radford. Harriet was a tall, attractive woman with a fair complexion and dark eyes and hair. Her mother, Mary Hancock Kennerly, was the sister of Julia's father, George Hancock. After Mary died in childbirth with Harriet, the Kennerly children had been raised in the Hancock household. The family would later say that Harriet was the other girl on the pony when William Clark met Julia. What is certain is that Clark attended Harriet's wedding to John Radford in Fincastle in December 1806. After Radford was killed by a wild boar in Kentucky in 1817, Harriet moved to St. Louis with her three small children to be with her three brothers.

Seventeen months after his wife's death, William Clark married Harriet Radford. The Reverend Salmon Giddings, founder of the first Presbyterian church in St. Louis, performed the service at James Kennerly's house on Wednesday, November 28, 1821. Overnight the Clark household increased by four—Harriet and her children, William, Mary, and John—not counting the slaves she brought to the union. John O'Fallon soon reported that he found Clark to be in good spirits in a marriage that "will contribute much to his comfort and happiness"—this despite the fact that O'Fallon judged Harriet to be an indifferent housekeeper compared with the fastidious Julia.[15]

The fur trade, which had languished during the War of 1812 and the economic slump afterward, was beginning to revive. The establishment of Fort Atkinson gave traders confidence to return to the Lower and Middle Missouri. After Manuel Lisa's death, the Missouri Fur Company reorganized with Joshua Pilcher as its field manager. Men like Pilcher and William Ashley were beginning to dream about returning to the beaver-rich waters controlled by the Blackfeet on the Upper Missouri. The British seemed to have conceded the Middle Missouri and Upper Mississippi to the Americans. Even Clark's hated British rival, Robert Dickson, had quietly moved to Lord Thomas Selkirk's community on the north-flowing Red River. (Dickson died in 1823 on Drummond Island in northern Lake Huron.)

When Mexico won its independence from Spain in 1821, a promising new trading route opened up. On July 25 of that year, William Becknell placed a notice in the *Missouri Intelligencer* recruiting "a company of men destined to the westwards." Six weeks later, he and his group were the first American traders to travel from Boon's Lick (present-day Franklin, Missouri) to Fort Osage and across the southwestern plains to Santa Fe. Within a few years, hundreds of independent traders flooded down the Santa Fe Trail, and they returned with one-quarter of all the fur-trade revenues in the West. Clark was an involved consumer, noting to himself, "The Spanish Blankets are made by the Navarho tribe who reside SW. of Santa Fee, and live better than the Spaniards."[16]

The most significant change of all, however, was the attack on the governmental factory system led by the fur-trading interests, especially John Jacob Astor's American Fur Company. The fur traders had always despised the factory system, which was in effect a government-sponsored monopoly. Its purposes had been twofold: first, to lure Indians away from the influence of British traders by selling goods below market prices, and second, to enable the Indians to trap their own lands peacefully free from the inflammatory presence of liquor-and-arms-toting unlicensed traders.

Some of the factories succeeded. George Sibley ran a busy fur trade at Fort Osage that collected thirty-three thousand deerskins in 1819. But a successful factory just engendered more hostility from the large fur companies and private traders, who saw it as a hindrance to their own potential business. Other factories offered wares inferior to and often more expensive than the manufactured goods supplied by the British. The result was that some Indians continued to take their trade to British posts. At the same time, the federal government was unable to effectively stop unlicensed American traders from entering Indian lands. George Sibley observed that "the game is very sensibly diminishing in the country" and the Osages "are more and more dependent upon the Traders, and consequently more and more debased and degraded."[17]

Calhoun likewise passed on to the President Clark's view that after contact with white society, the Indians "lose the lofty spirit and heroic courage of the savage state, without acquiring the virtues which belong to the civilized. Depressed in spirit, and debauched in morals, they dwindle away through a wretched existence, a nuisance to the surrounding country."[18]

Calhoun's argument represented an early articulation of the rationale for the federal government's removal policy. The wretched state of the Indians, it was argued, proved that the factories had failed to protect them from being debauched by traders. Since the Indians could not be assimilated as Jeffersonian yeoman farmers, they would have to be removed for their own protection.

But in the early 1820s, this argument went just far enough to justify removing the factories. When the bellicose Thomas Hart Benton, who had become a U.S. senator from Missouri, added his voice to those of Astor and Ramsay Crooks, the head of the American Fur Company's western department, the factories were doomed. Benton rammed through Congress a bill on March 3, 1821, that would eliminate the factories in May of the following year.

What was not settled was how to administer Indian relations after the flimsy leverage supplied by the factories was removed. Who would tell the Osages, for instance, that the factory their Great Father had promised by treaty to keep at their villages in perpetuity would be removed the next year? Who would license traders who wanted to go west of Missouri and Arkansas? Who would control the importation of liquor into Indian country? Who would supervise the Indian agents and pay out the annuities promised to the tribes?

The answer was soon coming. In the same law abolishing the factories, Congress created a new position of United States Superintendent of Indian Affairs at St. Louis. The person appointed by Monroe and Calhoun to fill it could only be William Clark.

In his new job, Clark gained discretionary powers that exceeded those of the territorial governorship. Reporting only to the President and Secretary of War, Clark was charged with issuing licenses and passports to all traders and travelers in Indian country, calling on the U.S. Army to arrest lawbreakers, negotiating treaties, establishing tribal boundaries, arbitrating disputes, and managing fifteen agencies and ten subagencies and a field force of agents, interpreters, blacksmiths, and clerks. His realm encompassed a geographical area as large as the then-existing United States and included thirty-six Indian nations—all of the tribes west of the Mississippi and some who lived on both sides of the river in Illinois and Wisconsin.

The demise of the factory system unleashed a buccaneering orgy of independent investing and adventuring into the fur country. In September 1822, the *St. Louis Enquirer* reported that "great activity has prevailed" in the fur trade since the end of the factory system. "Those formerly engaged in it have increased their capital and extended their enterprise, many new firms have engaged in it, and others are preparing to do so. It is computed that a thousand men, chiefly from this place, are now employed in this trade on the waters of the Missouri, and half that number on the Upper Mississippi."[19] The one man best positioned to govern—and profit from—this renewed activity was William Clark.

The most prized pelt on the rivers of North America was the beaver, *Castor canadensis*. Millions of beaver once lived on streams across the continent, but by the 1820s Indians and Europeans had depleted most of their population east of the Mississippi. The European economic invasion of the West began with the lust for beaver pelts, not bison robes. Indians who controlled the richest beaver waters were best positioned to acquire firearms and whiskey from the whites. The highest-quality beaver furs came from the coldest waters; those procured along the northern reaches of the Missouri were the most coveted of all. For that reason, tribes along the Upper Missouri were especially vigilant in controlling access to the enormous beaver grounds at the river's headwaters in present-day Montana. One single beaver dam on the Jefferson River was about two thousand feet long.

Before the 1820s, beavers were taken crudely—by clubbing them, ripping open their dens, draining ponds, or shooting them with muskets. But the invention of the steel trap in 1823 revolutionized the trade. A trapper typically set out his traps at nightfall and harvested them in the morning. Each trap, baited and scented with castor oil, was placed in shallow water and anchored by a chain to a pole hammered into the shore. Once trapped and unable to surface, a beaver usually died from drowning, not from the blow of the trap's jaws.

After carefully skinning the animal, which typically weighed from 35 to 60 pounds, the trapper would scrape the pelt and stretch it on a willow hoop to dry. The dried pelts were then pressed into 100-pound packs for shipment to St. Louis. Along the way, the packs would frequently be opened, aired out, and beaten to remove insects. From St. Louis, they would be sent on by boats to eastern ports and Europe. A trapper received $5 or $6 per pound for his pelts in 1820, making a single pack worth about $9,000 today.[20]

Hatters shaved off the beaver's coarse outercoat—the so-called guard hairs—to collect the velvety undercoat, or "duvet." This was treated with mercury nitrate and then shaped, singed, trimmed, dyed, steamed, brushed, blocked, and decorated. The result could be a soldier's cocked hat or a gentleman's topper.[21]

TO

ENTERPRISING YOUNG MEN

The subscriber wishes to engage ONE HUNDRED MEN, to ascend the river Missouri to its sources, there to be employed for one, two or three years—For particulars, enquire of Major Andrew Henry, near the Lead Mines, in the County of Washington (who will ascend with and command the party) or to the subscriber at St. Louis.   WM. H. ASHLEY.

The advertisement placed by William Ashley in St. Louis newspapers in February and March 1822 marked the opening of the mountain-man era in the Rockies. A friend of Clark's, Ashley was a Piedmont Virginian who had become a successful lead-and-gunpowder entrepreneur in Missouri's Cape Girardeau district. During the War of 1812, he had been a popular militia general, and as Missouri's new lieutenant governor he did nothing to dampen his reputation for flamboyance. He would prance through the streets of St. Louis on a white stallion with a pack of baying foxhounds at its heels.

Now Ashley and his partner Andrew Henry, who had spent a decade in the western ranges, were planning to organize an expedition to the mouth of the Yellowstone that would be unlike any other. Instead of relying on Indian hunters, as did other traders, they intended to bypass the irritating middlemen: they would send out their own brigade of independent trappers and hunters to bring in the furs.

Trapping and hunting by whites on Indian-owned land had been illegal for decades, but Ashley had influential friends. Assisted by Missouri's entire congressional delegation—Congressman John Scott and Senators Benton and Barton—Ashley applied directly to Calhoun for a license that specified trading but said nothing about hunting or trapping. It was promptly granted, with no explicit restrictions. Benjamin O'Fallon, the Indian agent who had just escorted a delegation of chiefs to Washington, was aghast. He warned Calhoun that if Ashley's party were to trap and hunt in Indian territory "nothing is better Calculated to alarm and disturb the harmony so happily existing between us and the Indians in the vicinity of the Council Bluffs . . . hunting and trapping should be prohibited and our traders confined alone to a fair and equitable trade with them."[22] O'Fallon was concerned less about the rights of the Indians than about keeping them quiescent for the benefit of white traders.

By this time, Clark had assumed the responsibilities of his superintendency. Contradicting his nephew, he reassured Calhoun that Ashley and Henry would "cultivate the friendship" of the tribes and that their license "will not produce any disturbance among the Indian tribes with whome we have much intercourse."[23] If he was aware of their intent to trap and hunt on Indian land—and he almost certainly was—Clark did not mention it. Policies had changed, and obstacles to white trappers and traders were to be removed. Even though he had once supported the factory system, he was now charged with dismantling it.

Ashley and Hunt were financially allied with Clark's fur-trading interests in St. Louis. One of Ashley's creditors was Clark's nephew John O'Fallon, who was Benjamin's brother but far less worried about disturbing the Indians. Moreover, the entire town supported an enterprise whose acknowledged goal, as the *St. Louis Enquirer* put it, was "to trap and hunt" in a region "which contains a wealth in *Furs* not surpassed by the mines of Peru."[24]

Among the recruits who answered Ashley's initial newspaper notice were men who would gain almost mythic stature in the West, including Jim Bridger, Mike Fink, Thomas Fitzpatrick, and Jedediah Smith. The twenty-three-year-old Smith's remarkably literate journal of the trip opened by observing the unmistakable harbinger of settlements advancing up the Missouri: "The Country was well stocked with Bees . . . we frequently had a plentiful supply of honey."[25]

Henry's party left first, followed by Ashley, who had to return for re-supplies after one of his keelboat masts snagged an overhanging tree limb and overturned, spilling the boat's entire cargo. The two groups made the 1,600-mile journey in one hundred days to the mouth of the Yellowstone, where they erected Fort Henry (later Fort Union). In the late fall, Henry's men pushed on to trap beaver on the Musselshell and Yellowstone rivers, while Ashley returned down the ice-choked river to St. Louis with his packs of beaver pelts loaded into a large pirogue. Reporting on Ashley's arrival to Calhoun, Clark lamented once again that the military had not followed his 1805 proposal to build forts on the Missouri at the mouth of the Yellowstone and Great Falls in order to create a show of force that would "greatly assist our traders in that upper country."[26]

Clark granted Ashley his second license to "trade" with the Indians on March 12, 1823. That same day Ashley met his two keelboats, the *Rocky Mountains* and *Yellow Stone Packet*, at St. Charles and promptly headed up the river with another group of seventy *engagés* and "St. Louis gumboes" recruited from "grog Shops and other sinks of degradation." As Clark knew well, these men were recruited not to trade but to trap. Outside of St. Charles, they raided local henhouses for food, hiding pigs and chickens in their furled sails when the farmers came searching. One Shakespeare-reading journal-keeper, James Clyman, observed dryly that "Fallstafs' Battallion was genteel in comparison."[27]

Cordelling their keelboats with rawhide ropes, or sailing with favorable winds, Ashley and his little brigade made it to Fort Atkinson in May. Ahead were the Arikara villages, the stockaded stronghold of the earth-lodge-dwelling tribe that had turned back Ensign Pryor and Sheheke in 1807. Ashley was apprehensive; he knew that the son of the Arikara chief Grey Eyes had been killed a few weeks earlier in a skirmish at the Missouri Fur Company post at Cedar Island. But Ashley also needed to buy forty or fifty horses to replace those that Henry had lost the previous year.

On May 30, Ashley arrived opposite the Arikara villages and went ashore to parlay with the chiefs. By the evening of June 1, he had purchased nineteen horses and was preparing to proceed upriver in the morning. But then, at 3:30 a.m., pandemonium erupted. Violating orders, two of his men had slipped into the village in search of women. One of them, Aaron Stephens, had become embroiled in a dispute. His eyes had been gouged out, and he had been decapitated.

At dawn, some six hundred Indians opened up their "London Fuzils" in a deafening fusillade against Ashley's ninety men, helplessly pinned on a sandbar across the river. Returning fire amid the whinnying of their panicked horses, the men splashed and scrambled into the keelboats and cut their cables. But in fifteen minutes, a dozen men had been killed and eleven wounded, including "Willis," a free black. Three more men would die later. Downriver, they buried the dead at a makeshift camp; Smith gave a prayer. Smith and a Canadian then volunteered to make their way overland to inform Henry, still waiting for reinforcements at the mouth of the Yellowstone, about the disaster.

On June 18, the *Yellow Stone Packet* arrived at Fort Atkinson bearing forty-three of Ashley's wounded and frightened men who had refused to stay with Ashley at the mouth of the Cheyenne River. Colonel Henry Leavenworth, the fort's commander, and Benjamin O'Fallon, the Indian agent, were stunned by the news of the attack. O'Fallon harangued the deserting men for their "shame" at having left "the A'rickaras mangling the bodies and decorating themselves with the reeking scalps of 14 of your Comrads."[28]

That was just a rhetorical warm-up for the now-vengeful O'Fallon. He told Clark that "those inhuman monsters" would be made to atone for "the most shocking outrage to the feelings of humanity ever witnessed by Civilized men — unexampled in the annuals of the world."[29] To Ashley he vowed, "The blood of A'rickarars must run from many vital veins . . . or the fur trade of the upper Missouri is suspended for a long time."[30]

Determined to avenge Ashley's humiliation, Leavenworth rode out of Fort Atkinson on June 22 with 230 gray-jacketed soldiers from the Sixth Infantry Regiment. He called them the Missouri Legion. Following him on the river were supply boats carrying two six-pound cannons, the heaviest armaments in the West. Leavenworth was known as a cautious and careful commander, but these atmospherics were freighted with vengeance. The Missouri Fur Company's Joshua Pilcher, acting as

Indian agent on the campaign, soon joined the Missouri Legion with a rag-tag force of some forty private traders and two more keelboats. Moving up to the mouth of the Teton River, Leavenworth recruited about five hundred warriors from various Lakota Sioux bands—the Oglalas, Sicangus (Brulés), Hunkpapas, Itazipos (Sans Arcs), Oohenumpas (Two Kettles), and Minneconjous. There he finally joined Ashley and his remaining men, who had been camped for a month waiting for reinforcements.

Leavenworth's march was the opening episode in the armed struggle between the U.S. Army and the Plains Indians that lasted the rest of the nineteenth century. However, most Americans on the scene were unwilling to credit the Indians with the organizational resourcefulness to defend their own land. They were persuaded that attacks farther north by the Blackfeet on a Missouri Fur Company expedition and Andrew Henry's men at the Yellowstone could only have been instigated by the British. "I was in hopes that the british Indian traders had some bounds to their rapacity," O'Fallon wrote to Clark. But "like the greedy wolf, not satisfied with the flesh, they quarrel over the bones."[31] Clark agreed, telling Calhoun, "If this hostile Tribe are not Chastized and the British Traders driven from the Missouri, it is apprehended that they will become more hostile, and other Tribes will be incouraged to follow their example, and in that case, no Trader will be safe in their persons or property above the influence of the Troops at Council Bluffs."[32]

Leavenworth and his columns arrived at the Arikara villages on the morning of August 9. The Lakotas broke ranks and rode pell-mell toward the town, driving the women and children inside. The ensuing skirmish ended with a scattering of casualties on both sides. By the next morning, Leavenworth's cannons had arrived on the keelboats, and the artillerymen began lobbing shells into the Indian compound. One blast killed the Arikara chief Grey Eyes.

The villages were completely surrounded by Leavenworth's troops, the chanting Lakota warriors, Pilcher's men, and the remnants of Ashley's brigade. But, inexplicably to Pilcher and many of the officers, Leavenworth called off the attack. He was running low on ammunition and was worried about the loyalty of the Lakotas. Instead, he asked that the Arikara chiefs come forward to negotiate an end to the battle. The translator for their meeting was a man familiar to both sides: Toussaint Charbonneau.

The Arikara chief Little Soldier, terrified of the American army, promptly agreed to terms. Ashley was delighted; his boats could now proceed up the Missouri. But Pilcher angrily refused to smoke the peace pipe or shake hands with the chiefs, arguing that only by crushing the Arikaras could they be permanently subdued. The Lakotas agreed and left, expressing their disgust at the cowardly American troops for failing to fight on.

Leavenworth was a soldier willing to look beyond the immediate solution of violence. "My officers generally and all the men were anxious to charge upon the towns," he reflected in his official report. "I felt that my situation was a disagreeable and unpleasant one. It appeared to me that my reputation, and the honor and brilliancy of the expedition required that I should gratify my troops, and make a charge." On the other hand, he was beginning to realize the limits of retaliation: "If we succeeded in our charge, all that we could expect was to drive the Indians from their villages and perhaps kill a few more of them: The remainder would be left in the Country in a confirmed state of hostility to every white man."[33]

The next morning, Leavenworth and his colleagues were stunned to discover that the Arikaras had disappeared overnight. The Indians had escaped further sanctions. On August 15, the Missouri Legion departed for Fort Atkinson amid increasing acrimony between Leavenworth and the traders. As they left, the Missouri Fur Company's Angus McDonald and a companion insolently burned the Arikara villages. Such destruction would have been standard procedure for George Rogers Clark's militia, but it infuriated Leavenworth, who accused Pilcher of deliberately trying to sabotage the possibility of peace with the tribe. On his part, Pilcher bitterly denounced Leavenworth in a public letter, saying, "You have by the imbecility of your conduct and operations, created and left impossible barriers."[34]

The campaign against the Arikaras ignited a national debate. Politicians and newspaper editors railed against Ashley's provocations. "These hunters in defiance of the law, enter the Indian country, put to hazard the peace of the frontiers, and involve the United States in a distant and expensive war," said the Detroit Gazette.[35] Leavenworth wrote to Atkinson to point out that Ashley's "<u>trapping</u> business is carried on under a license to <u>trade</u>." It was, he said, "a palpable and plain violation of the letter, spirit and meaning of the law" and "a violation of the rights of a poor miserable set of savages whose only means of support is thus destroyed contrary to the benign policy of our government."[36] Leavenworth's complaint clearly applied to the man who issued the license, William Clark.

The government policy would soon become less benign. Once again citing the supposed British threat, Clark renewed his case to Calhoun for a dramatic display of American force. "I am under [the] impression that the punishment of the Ricaras by Col Leavenworth will have a very good effect, if pursued by a show of troops on the Upper Missouri next spring," Clark said. But, he warned, "If a large force is not sent up the Missouri next year I shall be under apprehensions that no good effect will result from the late punishment inflicted upon the Ricaras, the Souix will be presumtious and our upper Trade[r]s may be drove down below the Mandans." In that case, he concluded, the issue would once again become the economic struggle of empires between the British and the Americans over the trade of the Arikaras, Blackfeet, and neighboring tribes. They "will depend entirely upon the b[r]itish for supplies," he said, "and is it probable that we shall ever get possession of the upper Missouri again on as easy terms as we can now keep it?"[37]

The following March, Clark warned Secretary of War Calhoun that the United States was at risk of losing the entire trade above the Big Bend of the Missouri, "which has already produced considerable wealth to the British traders."[38] He said that the British would ship 63,300 pounds of beaver pelts out of the Columbia Basin that spring alone and that their yearly revenues would be $190,000—worth about $3.4 million today.

The less Anglophobic Leavenworth agreed that a military force should be sent up the Missouri—to restrain not the British and Indians, however, but American trappers. "The reports which are circulated on the subject of the instigation of our Indians to acts of hostility by British traders appears to us to be not well founded," he said. "It is not seen why American traders should not enjoy the friendship and confidence of the Indians as well as the British traders, unless it is because the latter never trap and hunt the beaver, but give the Indians a fair equivalent in articles necessary for them." Action was urgently needed, Leavenworth said, because "the game of all sorts is fast receding. . . . The time is not far distant (especially if trapping and hunting by white men Continues) when the means of subsistence for those poor wretches will be entirely exhausted. The subject is too gloomy to dwell upon."[39]

Even though the British had given up their aspirations to the fur trade on the Middle Missouri—the stretch between the Mandan villages and the Platte—they remained determined to keep the Americans out of the still-disputed Pacific Northwest and Upper Rockies. The British governor George Simpson sent Hudson's Bay trappers into the Upper Snake and Salmon drainages with instructions to eliminate the beaver along the Continental Divide and create what he called a "fur desert" to keep American trappers out of the Columbia Basin. This variation of a scorched-earth policy was ultimately devastating to tribes like the Blackfeet that depended on trading beaver skins for manufactured goods.

Clark and Thomas Hart Benton continued to press for a military expedition up the Missouri. On May 25, 1824, President Monroe signed a bill that created a Bureau of Indian Affairs as part of the War Department and appropriated $10,000 for an Indian peace commission to the Upper Missouri. The joint commissioners would be General Henry Atkinson and special Indian agent Benjamin O'Fallon.

Atkinson's immediate need was to transport 450 infantrymen from St. Louis to Council Bluff. In the twenty years since Lewis and Clark had navigated the Missouri, almost no one else had done it as successfully. "The Missouri River is four times as bad to navigate as the Mississippi," said the river pilot John Cummins, "owing to the strength of the water, the many sandbars, changing of the channel, falling in of the banks; the many logs, snags, and roots, and many of them concealed under water, and the water being so muddy that they cannot be seen, which subjects boats very often to run on them, and be greatly delayed, and sometimes destroyed."[40]

Unwilling to risk steamboats after the mishaps of the 1819 Missouri expedition, Atkinson turned to a novel craft he had observed in Louisville: the wheel boat. A keelboat rigged with paddle wheels on each side, the wheel boat was propelled mechanically by horses or men walking on a treadmill. Atkinson modified the design so that the wheels would be powered by twenty men on seats, pulling and pushing on crossbars.

In St. Louis, Atkinson converted four keelboats, adding the man-powered wheel mechanisms, and gave them names fur traders could appreciate: *Beaver, Mink, Muskrat,* and *Raccoon.* On September 17, 1824, the wharf at St. Louis was crowded with spectators as the troops, commanded by thirty-year-old Major Stephen Watts Kearny, boarded the boats and churned upriver. Within four days, they were forced to put out cordelling ropes to pull the boats, but by early November the party had reached Fort Atkinson.

Once the ice cleared the following May, an enlarged armada of eight wheel boats headed up to the mouth of the Yellowstone, supported by a detachment of mounted rangers on the shore. By all measures, the expedition was a success. Treaties were signed with twelve tribes and bands—the Poncas, Lakotas (Tetons), Yanktons, Yanktonais, Oglalas, Saones, Cheyennes, Hunkpapas, Arikaras, Mandans, Minitarees (Hidatsas), and Crows. Toussaint Charbonneau once again served as translator, and Clark's new brother-in-law George Hancock Kennerly was the expedition's sutler. Each treaty-signing ended with an awe-inducing military parade, the firing of cannons, and the distribution of whiskey. The ceremonies could have been scripted by Lewis and Clark, or even Anthony Wayne.

The only rancorous notes came from Benjamin O'Fallon, who continued to inveigh against the "Continued robeing and butchering of our people by the Indians" and the "dark designing sycophants" who protect them.[41] He denounced Atkinson and Leavenworth's conciliatory tactics, and during a council with the Crows he became so enraged that he clubbed two chiefs over the head with a musket.

The commissioners were hardly more amicable toward one another. George Kennerly reported that during a dinner argument, O'Fallon and Atkinson flew into rages, "mutually seized, one a knife, and other a fork, and made the attempt to stab." Kennerly headed off bloodshed only by throwing himself between the combatants. Describing the incident later to his brother James, Kennerly confessed his embarrassment that O'Fallon was the "nephew of the man whomn I look up to as a Father."[42]

A few months later, basking in the warmth of a banquet celebrating the return of the expedition to St. Louis, Atkinson and O'Fallon could overlook their differences. Not a single man had died on the journey. No evidence had been found of British agents on the Missouri. Moreover, William Ashley had joined them at the mouth of the Yellowstone with an astonishing story. Determined to bypass the belligerent Upper Missouri Indians, Ashley had made his way up the Platte River in the fall of 1824 with twenty-five trappers and a train of packhorses. Then, the following July, Ashley's men and a brigade of free trappers held the first mountain-man rendezvous on the Green River at Henry's Fork, in present-day Wyoming.

Ashley reaped a fortune in furs and floated down the Big Horn and Yellowstone rivers to the Missouri with a hundred packs of beaver loaded into bull-boats made from bison hides. Two historic achievements were behind him. He had established the system of mountain-man rendezvous that would free fur traders from company trading posts on the Missouri. In addition, Ashley and his men had rediscovered South Pass, an ascent over the Continental Divide gentle enough for wagons to use. Suddenly the struggle for control of the Upper Missouri had become irrelevant. An empire of fur beyond the Rockies was within easy reach of St. Louis.

Prosperity and steamboats were both arriving in St. Louis. Boats were docking daily from Louisville and New Orleans, filling the waterfront with activity. They had already depleted the riparian woodlands along the Mississippi: a steamboat typically burned between twenty-five or thirty cords of wood every twenty-four running hours; a fur-trapping post consumed about a thousand cords a year. A St. Louis newspaper reported that the pall of smoke over St. Louis was "in some instances so dense as to render it necessary to use candles at midday. Rain in passing through it has been so discolored as to stain everything with which it came into contact, like ink."[43]

The most prominent citizen of St. Louis was William Clark. Memories of the bitter election campaign of 1820 were beginning to fade. He owned a traveling carriage and a lightweight "Dearborn" carriage that he used for weekly trips to his Marais Castor farm. He was a trustee of the town and co-founder of the first school system. He owned a pew in the Roman Catholic church, co-chartered the first Episcopal church west of the Mississippi, and bought a new hat to wear on Easter Sunday. At the same time, he was just as apt to gather with his friends to play whist, smoke cigars, and sip his favorite port and Madeira wines. In June 1821, Clark paid the painter Chester Harding $20 for several portraits, apparently executed during the gubernatorial campaign the previous year.

His museum of Indian curiosities was becoming a renowned attraction to traveling dignitaries. One such visitor was a German aristocrat, Paul Wilhelm, Duke of Württemberg, who in the spring of 1823 described the museum and Clark's meeting with a group of Potawatomis. Paul Wilhelm then proceeded up the Missouri, where, at Chouteau's

Post near present-day Kansas City, he befriended Sacagawea's son Jean Baptiste Charbonneau, now eighteen. Paul Wilhelm went on to Fort Atkinson, but on his way downriver he picked up Jean Baptiste at the post and took him back to St. Louis. The duke apparently received permission from Clark to take Pomp to Europe as his manservant. On November 3, they embarked on a steamboat to New Orleans, and then sailed on the Rhode Island brig *Smyrna* to the East Coast and on to Europe.

Incredibly, the *métis* son of Sacagawea, who had been born with the assistance of two ground rattlesnake rattles and had journeyed with Lewis and Clark to the Pacific, then spent the next six years traveling through Europe and North Africa with Paul Wilhelm. He evidently learned German—supplementing his native French, English, and Hidatsa—and fathered a child with Anastasia Fries, a German soldier's daughter, before returning to the West in 1829.[44]

There were other changes in Clark's family. His brothers-in-law Dennis Fitzhugh and William Croghan both died in 1822 during an epidemic in Louisville. His sister Ann Clark Gwathmey died a year later. His son Julius was still living in Fincastle with Julia's widowed mother, Margaret Hancock. Margaret reported regularly on the boy's progress—"[He] runs every whare talks much better & is a fine sensable Child"—though she always qualified her assessment: "He don't talk as plain as mite be."[45]

On a leap year day, February 29, 1824, Harriet gave birth to her first child with Clark, a healthy boy. Initially undecided about a name—for a time the baby would be called Thomas Jefferson Clark, or "T.J."—the Clarks resorted to a familiar nickname: they called him "Pomp."

In the summer of 1824, Clark left St. Louis for a trip to the eastern seaboard with his sons Lewis and William and his stepson William Radford. The business at hand was to accompany the Indian agents Lawrence Taliaferro and his brother-in-law George Hancock Kennerly in escorting a delegation of Sauk, Fox, and Iowa Indians to a treaty-signing in Washington. Settlers were once again moving illegally onto Indian lands. Clark's objective was not to remove the settlers, however, but to persuade the tribes to give up all of their claims within the new state of Missouri.

Among the Sauks was a war chief of unusual force and ability whom Clark was assiduously cultivating. Keokuk, "the Watchful Fox," was head of the cooperative band of Sauks who lived west of the Mississippi. He was therefore a tribal rival of Black Hawk, head of the far more militant Sauk band on the Rock River known as the "British Band" because of its close ties to Canadian traders. The more Clark could build up the prestige of Keokuk, the lower would fall that of Black Hawk.

Impressed, as always, by the magnitude of the eastern cities, each tribe signed a treaty giving away its lands in Missouri for $500 in cash and a matching annuity. Kennerly and Taliaferro loaded up the chiefs with presents and took them home by way of New York and the partially constructed Erie Canal. Clark then took the boys on to what promised to be the highlight of the trip: the arrival in New York City of the Marquis de Lafayette, the French hero of the American Revolution, who had been invited for the forthcoming fiftieth anniversary of the nation's independence.

William Clark's first glimpse of New York would have been of a long, low smear of wooded land all but hidden behind a forest of ships' masts crowding the docks. One hundred and seventy thousand citizens shared the streets with some twenty thousand hogs scrabbling for garbage and vegetables dropped from horse carts. Clark and the boys stayed at the seventy-five-room City Hotel on the west side of lower Broadway between Thames and Cedar streets (one block from the site of the future World Trade Center).

Lafayette arrived on the sailing ship *Cadmus* amid the most tumultuous reception in the city's history. Lining the streets and docks was a cheering crowd of thousands. "The Nation's Guest" (as the newspapers called him) boarded a barouche drawn by four white stallions for the celebratory ride up Broadway to City Hall. That night the entire façade of the five-story City Hotel, the first building in the United States constructed as a hotel, was illuminated by lamplights spelling out Lafayette's name. Among the children in the crowd who witnessed Lafayette's arrival, in addition to Clark's sons, was the five-year-old Walt Whitman.

Lafayette resolved to visit each of the twenty-four states—and did. After calling on the eighty-eight-year-old John Adams in Massachusetts and spending a week at Monticello with Jefferson, then eighty-one, Lafayette methodically made his way across the country to New Orleans and the Mississippi.

At 9 a.m. on the morning of April 29, 1825, General Lafayette stepped off the steamboat *Natchez* to cries of joy from the crowd in the histori-cally French town of St. Louis. But the newly elected governor of Mis-souri, Frederick Bates, Meriwether Lewis's nemesis, was nowhere to be seen. It seemed that Bates had not received preapproval from the federal government for the expenses of greeting Lafayette. Nothing if not by-the-book, Bates decided to boycott the event and had sequestered himself at his farmhouse outside of town. He would die before the year was out.

Lafayette otherwise typically received an emotional welcome. Many Americans burst into tears upon first seeing the French hero. There was a tour to the nearby Indian mounds, a dinner with toasts, and a fancy-dress ball. Lafayette's secretary Auguste Levasseur marveled over the beautiful women and the hospitality that "made us completely forget that we were on the confines of a wilderness which the savages them-selves consider as insufficient for the supply of their simple wants."[46]

Clark would have had much to talk about with Lafayette. His brother Jonathan had been one of Lafayette's colonels at the Battle of Brandy-wine, and the French general knew well of George Rogers's triumphs in the Old Northwest. Naturally, Clark gave Lafayette and his entourage a tour of his Indian museum. The collection awed Levasseur, who described it in detail, especially the "articles worn by the Indian hunters, collars made of claws of prodigious size . . . These claws, Gen. Clark informed us, are from that most terrible of all the animals of the American conti-nent, the Grizzly Bear, of the Missouri, the ferocious instinct of which adds still more to the terror inspired by its enormous size and strength."[47]

Clark later sent a grizzly cub to Lafayette in Paris. The Frenchman acknowledged the gift in a graceful letter that wryly confirmed the bear's reputation:

> The grisley bear you had the goodness to send to me, has been the more admired on this side of the Atlantic as it was the first animal of the kind, living or dead, that had ever made an appearance in Europe. I was inclined to make a pet of him as he was thereby gentle, but it was thought wise to put him under the care of the Board of professors at the Jardin des Plantes, the first European museum of Natural Philosophy. There he was received with much gratitude to you the principal donator and to me . . . His large vile and ferocious temper have since been developed.[48]

After leaving St. Louis, Lafayette, who was opposed to slavery, made a point of visiting the free state of Illinois. He was traveling up the Ohio on the steamboat *Mechanic* when the boat rammed a snag after midnight, about 125 miles below Louisville; it sank in ten minutes. Lafayette lost his carriage and all his clothing. The Nation's Guest wound up huddling all night with a group of forlorn passengers on a wet riverbank waiting for a passing boat to pick them up so they could resume their journey.

The first superintendent of the new federal Bureau of Indian Affairs was to be Thomas L. McKenney, a former head of the Office of Indian Trade. Appointed by Calhoun, McKenney would become the federal government's principal administrator for Indian relations. His responsibilities would include monitoring the budgets, annuity distributions, and correspondence of the field superintendents, among them Clark's, and administering all funds dedicated to "the civilization of the Indians."[49] McKenney's full staff consisted of himself, two clerks, and a messenger.

By this time, virtually all of the top government officials with responsibility for Indian affairs had come to the view Jefferson had outlined in 1802: the tribes of the East "will either incorporate with us as citizens of the United States, or remove beyond the Mississippi."[50] As early as 1817, President Monroe had argued in his annual message to Congress, "The hunter state can exist only in the vast uncultivated desert. It yields to the more dense and compact form and great force of civilized population: and of right it ought to yield, for the earth was given to mankind to support the great number of which it is capable, and no tribe or people have a right to withhold from the wants of other more than is necessary for their own support and comfort." (A gratified John Jacob Astor congratulated Monroe for his early articulation of the rationale for Indian removal, assuring the President that "your message is the best publick document which has ever appeared in this country.")[51]

Advocates of removal claimed it was the only humane way to prevent the tribes' inevitable extermination. In a report to the President, Calhoun described the impact of white society on Indians: "They lose the lofty spirit and heroic courage of the savage state, without acquiring the virtues which belong to the civilized. Depressed in spirit, and debauched in morals, they dwindle away through a wretched existence, a nuisance to the surrounding country."[52] McKenney likewise concluded, "It is . . . very certain that, should they retain their present location, they will, in the course of a few years, be lost as a race."[53]

McKenney did not need to add that removal was the only alternative acceptable to whites. By framing the issue as a false dilemma—removal or extinction—he encouraged the false comfort of choosing the former. Clark could think of himself as a moderating influence in applying federal policy to the Indians—but only when the alternative was defined as extermination. The option never seriously considered was acculturation, allowing Indians with agriculture-based economies to live side by side with whites while retaining their tribal identities.

Clark's job became increasingly consumed by the politics of Indian removal. He complained to John O'Fallon, "I have more duties imposed on me without an increase of pay."[54] The government helped out by giving him the job of acting surveyor general for Missouri, Illinois, and Arkansas Territory—and a salary to go with it.

The first step in the removal process was the rapid acquisition of lands already occupied by those Indians who had moved west of the Mississippi. In March 1825, Clark persuaded the acculturated Delawares and Shawnees in southern Missouri to exchange their lands for territories farther west. The fact that these peaceful tribes had thoroughly embraced white agricultural practices, including slave ownership, gave them no reprieve. Acculturation was not impossible for Indians to achieve; it was impossible for whites to accept.

Writing to Calhoun in 1823, Clark urged that the government act quickly to purchase Missouri land from the Osage and Kansas tribes *before* they started farming, "as the difficulties of purchasing the lands from those tribes will increase and the removal of the emigrating Indians will be no easy task after they have once opened themselves farms."[55] It seemed that once the Indians started to behave like whites, it would be all the more difficult to remove them.

Accordingly, the Osage agent Alexander McNair—Clark's former political rival whom he had magnanimously hired after McNair left the governorship—brought forty-two chiefs and headmen of the Great and Little Osage bands to meet with Clark at his country house, Marais Castor, in May 1825. Although the Osages had been promised they could keep their lands forever and were the one tribe that had never gone to war against the United States, they were told that the Great Father needed their land. Clark made his point with a thinly concealed threat: "You know I have turned 3 Indian Armies from the direction of your towns and prevented other parties from sucking the blood of your people."[56]

Powerless to resist, the Osages signed a treaty on June 2, 1825, that surrendered almost all of their lands in Missouri, Arkansas, and present-day Kansas. They would retain a single strip of land 50 miles wide and 125 miles long in southern Kansas. The next day, June 3, Clark negotiated a similar treaty at Marais Castor with the Kansas tribe that extinguished their title to lands in Missouri's Jackson and Clay counties and in eastern Kansas.

In his letter accompanying the treaties sent to James Barbour, the new Secretary of War for recently elected President John Quincy Adams, Clark said that the treaties gave to the state of Missouri three or four million acres of "the richest and most beautiful land in this State, and will meet with a ready sale when it is brought into market." Moreover, the additional 100 million acres acquired west of Missouri were enough to house not only the Osages and Kansas but also the Creeks, who had recently signed a removal treaty—and there would still be enough land left over for "the gradual removal and collocation of the Indians" from the East. This western land was grassy and well watered, Clark observed, and "wonderfully adapted to an Indian population in the first stages of civilization." Finally, Clark pointed out that the annuities and other expenses mandated by the treaties could be covered by selling off as little as one-fifth of the acquired land.[57]

A future home was now prepared for the Eastern tribes. But how would they be finally dislodged? The opportunity grew out of the long-standing hostilities between the Santee Sioux (Dakotas) and the Chippewas (Ojibwas). During their trip to Washington the previous year, these tribes had asked the government to arbitrate their boundary disputes. It was decided to convene a grand council on the Upper Mississippi with the sole stated goal of promoting peace among the tribes by fixing boundaries between them. But fixing boundaries of the land, as everyone knew—including the Indians—was the necessary prelude to selling it.

To arbitrate the boundary disputes, Barbour appointed Clark as a peace commissioner, along with Lewis Cass, governor of the Michigan

Territory since 1813. They decided to hold the council at Prairie du Chien, the eight-mile-long meadow under the bluffs above the mouth of the Wisconsin River that had been the site of Clark's ill-fated gunboat campaign in 1814. Clark dispatched letters inviting the tribes to convene on July 29, it "being the full moon."[58]

Extensive preparations were made for the largest gathering of Indians and whites since the meeting at Portage des Sioux a decade earlier. The tribes expected to attend were the Dakota Sioux, Winnebagos, Menominees, Chippewas, Ottawas, Potawatomis, Sauks, Foxes, and Iowas. Clark prepared by advertising for 85,000 pounds of fresh beef, 900 barrels of flour, 300 bushels of feed corn, 40 bushels of salt, and 100 gallons of whiskey.[59] He had never forgotten the quartermaster skills he had first learned in Anthony Wayne's Legion.

The supply boats left on June 29, and Clark followed on July 6. His entourage included Thomas Biddle, the council's acting secretary and the younger brother of Nicholas Biddle. Clark also took along his thirteen-year-old son, William. Arriving at Prairie du Chien on July 30, Clark had a raised platform built so he and Cass could address the throng of Indians camped in the meadow.

Clark opened the council on August 6 with his familiar rhetorical device: "Friends and children . . . The Great Spirit has given us a clear day and we hope he has opened your ears and will prepare your heart for the good work before us." (On a subsequent rainy day, he altered his message only slightly: "You see we have met here under dark clouds. But we hope the Great Spirit will disperse it, as he will disperse all your evil thoughts & open your hearts to his wishes.") He went on to assure the suspicious tribes, "We want nothing, not the smallest piece of your land. Not a single article of your property."

Then the chiefs addressed the council. Keokuk once again impressed the commissioners and agents with his forceful orations. "Keokuk was, in all respects, a magnificent savage," McKenney said later. "Bold, enterprising, and impulsive, he was also politic, and possessed an intimate knowledge of human nature, and a tact which enabled him to bring the resources of his mind into prompt action." Ominously, though, Keokuk's fierce rival Black Hawk had come neither to the council nor to the previous year's trip to Washington. When the chiefs said they were powerless to control their headstrong young warriors, Governor Cass urged the elders to "take the tomahawks from them and throw them in the fire."[60]

The fixing of the tribal boundaries was an arduous process. The tribes were uncomfortable with the idea of imposing limits on their hunters and preferred to think of their borders as flexible. The permeable frontier had already been the reality on the continent for two centuries. Clark himself had acknowledged the usefulness of buffer zones when, in the previous treaties with the Osages and Kansas, he deliberately set up thirty-mile-wide zones between Indian and white land, "experience having convinced me of the necessity of preventing a white and Indian population from remaining in immediate contact with each other."[61]

The treaty was finally signed in mid-August by the representatives of the tribes and the government. Instead of the usual whiskey-fueled celebration, however, only a limited amount of liquor was handed out to the Indians. Cass was a zealous temperance man and apparently had his way. When the tribes complained about the parsimonious allotment, Clark brought out the remaining whiskey, carefully filled a row of kettles, and, to the horror of the Indians (and not a few whites), knocked each kettle over, spilling it all on the ground.

By the end of August, Clark had returned to St. Louis, and a tenuous peace prevailed on the Upper Mississippi. He had not been well, suffering once again from an ailment that had incapacitated him for twenty days of the two months he spent at Prairie. Many of the Indians themselves fell sick, apparently from dysentery, though a rumor that the whites had poisoned them at Prairie du Chien was circulated among the tribes for years.

But the superintendent's health was a secondary issue; he was bursting with curiosity to hear from his son Lewis. Shortly before leaving office, Secretary of War Calhoun had given Lewis an appointment to the United States Military Academy at West Point. For Clark and his family of generals, the most notable of all honors would be to study under West Point's renowned Colonel Sylvanus Thayer. Lewis was barely out the door—with $20 from his proud father jingling in his pocket—when Clark began his frequent inquiries: "Do my son, write the particulars, and keep nothing from me let it be what it may, either good or bad, and recollect that no person now living can be as much your friend and devoted to your true interest as your father."[62]

Clark peppered his son with news and advice. He urged him to treat everyone "with politeness which is the certain result of respect & attention." He cautioned him to "keep in mind my son that dissipation of any description grows and becomes a habit which is not easy to overcome, and should be avoided by all who wish future prosperity." Knowing what a soldier's life could be like, Clark added, "it may be well to keep in mind the importance of avoiding temptations." Lewis must have protested the warning, since a few weeks later his father hastened to assure him, "I have no fears of your becoming dissipated."[63]

Anxious over his first exams—understandably, since his father had reminded him that "the eyes of all your noumerous friends in this quarter and Virginia are upon you"—Lewis asked permission to resign before suffering the humiliation of failing. Clark grudgingly gave it and added that he had written to the American Fur Company's Ramsay Crooks in New York "to furnish you with such funds as you may require & need, by the permission of Colonel Thayer."[64] Fortunately for both father and son, Lewis took the exams and passed.

Typically, Clark ended his letters with a heartfelt message: "May the Guardian Angels of heaven defend you from harm and guide you in the paths of rectitude is the prayer of your affc't father."[65]

Clark continued to correspond with Thomas Jefferson. On Christmas Day of 1825, answering Jefferson's request to contribute Indian artifacts to the University of Virginia, Clark included pithy assessments of the development of his five sons: Lewis ("capacity & application"), William ("boald sprightly with good capacity deficient in application"), George ("application and mind equal to any boy of his age"), John Julius ("sprightly but unfortunately deformed"), and the President's namesake, Thomas Jefferson ("very promising").

Clark then turned to the subject of Indians. "In my present situation of Superintendent of Indian Affairs," he said, "it would afford me pleasure to be enabled to meliorate the condition of those unfortunate people placed under my charge, knowing as I do their [w]retchedness and their rapid decline—It is to be lamented that the deplorable situation of the Indians do not receive more of the humain feeling of the nation."[66] It was a strong view to express to a former President known for his willingness to "crush" those Indians with the temerity to oppose the advance of white civilization.

Clark's choice of words was interesting. He wanted to be "enabled" to help the Indians under his charge. He did not feel that he could do so independently. As ever, he remained the loyal military man—able to accept that he would never be made a captain, able to accept that he was not "enabled" to improve the treatment of Indians for whom he was responsible.

Unlike many of his contemporaries, Clark never labeled all native peoples simply "merciless savages." He differentiated between tribes—especially between cooperative tribes and uncooperative tribes. He clearly wanted the government to play a larger role in attending to "those unfortunate people" who listened to their Great Father. What was less clear was how to ameliorate their condition. Would it be by protecting their lands from the incursions of white settlers and trappers? Or would it be by removing them from their lands to a place far from the corrupting influence of whites? While the government gave lip service to the former, it aggressively pursued the latter.

The fact is that for most of his life, Clark embodied the contradictions and hypocrisies of the federal government's Indian policy. As a militiaman and soldier in the Ohio Valley, he had joined "punitive" raids against Indians who had been provoked to violence by illegal white settlers. During the expedition, he was able to establish necessarily amicable relationships with those tribes who were powerful enough to wipe out his entire party at will. With the relentless growth of the market economy in the decade after the War of 1812, even peaceful Indians became an obstacle if they were on land desired by whites. Clark's conviction that the Indians deserved "the humain feeling of the nation" had more to do with their treatment during their removal than with protecting their right to remain on the lands they owned. They should be protected, Clark thought, but they should also be removed.

Jefferson never answered Clark's letter. Six months later, the third President died, on July 4, 1826, the fiftieth anniversary of Independence Day and within hours of the death of John Adams, the nation's second President. At the American Philosophical Society, the eulogy to its founder was delivered by Nicholas Biddle.

In early 1826, Clark made his first courtesy call in Washington on the new Administration of John Quincy Adams. His superiors had reason to be well pleased with their Superintendent of Indian Affairs in St. Louis. In 1825, Clark had supervised the signing of seventeen treaties with the sovereign Indian nations, extinguishing their claims to more than 100 million acres of land. In so doing, he had started the mechanism that would lead to the removal of all of the original inhabitants of eastern North America. Clark received several letters of praise from McKenney and Barbour. He found them "most gratifying." The fifty-five-year-old superintendent allowed himself a rare moment of self-congratulation: "To discharge the Public trust confided to me, has occupied my feeble exertions for more than Thirty Years—and I believe it may be said that no one of its members have been more willing to extend a supporting arm, or have felt less regret in hazarding either person or property in its defense, than I have to the Government under which I have lived."[67]

Clark traveled in a Dearborn carriage to Washington, accompanied by the newlywed General Henry Atkinson and his wife, Mary Ann Bullitt, of Louisville. Soon after his arrival, he dined with Secretary of War Barbour, who evidently asked Clark to put into writing his thoughts about Indian relations. On March 1, 1826, Clark responded with a letter that not only expanded on the views he had privately expressed to Jefferson but was, for him, uniquely passionate.

"The events of the last two or three wars, from Genl. Wayne's campaign in '94 to the end of the operations against the southern tribes in 1818, have entirely changed our position with regard to the Indians," Clark began. "Before these events they were a formidable and terrible enemy; since then their power has been broken, their warlike spirit subdued, and themselves sunk into objects of pity and commiseration. While strong and hostile it was our policy and duty to weaken them; now that they are weak and harmless, and most of their lands fallen into our hands, justice and humanity require us to cherish and befriend them."[68]

Clark's view—that once the Indians were no longer a military threat and were no longer obstacles to American economic interests, then justice and humaneness could govern their treatment—marked him as moderate when it came to Indian affairs; most Americans wanted the Eastern tribes to be removed at once, or exterminated.

But how would the American government "cherish and befriend" the tribes? By teaching them "to live in houses, to raise grain and stock, to plant orchards." In other words, teach them to become Jefferson's yeoman farmers. It hardly seemed to matter that many Indians were already doing precisely that. Thanks to trade with the whites, the material culture of many Indians was indistinguishable from that of Euro-Americans.

Like his countrymen, Clark had devised a mythology of the Indians that required him to believe that the tribes had provoked all the bloodshed and were incapable of living like whites, or even alongside them. Instead, Clark proposed that "the tribes now within the limits of the States and Territories should be removed to a country beyond those limits, where they could rest in peace, and enjoy in reality the perpetuity of the lands on which their buildings and improvement should be made." Where would the Indians live in peace and tranquillity? "The country west of Missouri and Arkansas is the one intended to receive them."

Clark went on to list specific recommendations, ranging from employing agents "who are acquainted with the Indian character," assisting Indian families during their removal, buying agricultural equipment instead of dry goods, establishing common schools for Indian children, and exchanging permanent annuities for property ownership. Clark was realistic enough about Indian poverty to know that "It is vain to talk to people in this condition about learning and religion; they want a regular supply of food, and until that Is obtained the operations of the mind must like the Instinct of mere animals, be confined to warding off hunger and cold."

What Clark did not have room for in his plan was what many tribes—notably the Cherokees in Georgia and the Delawares and Shawnees in Missouri —had already achieved. They had successfully combined their native agricultural traditions with the white man's tools while *not* choosing to be assimilated. When Indians were starving, it was usually because they had given up their ancestral farmlands and become dependent on a precarious fur-trade economy with Euro-Americans.

Most of Clark's ideas fell on sympathetic ears in the Administration. Both Barbour and John Quincy Adams were committed to Indian removal, if not to the compassionate method Clark was urging. On March 10, Clark had dinner at the White House with President Adams. It would have been an interesting meeting between the two men, both from families of the nation's founders.

One of their topics would have been the familiar problem of alcohol in Indian country. Although virtually all government officials gave lip service to the laws prohibiting the importation of liquor, whiskey was everywhere—routinely brought in by traders, trappers, and even peace commissioners. Alcoholism was becoming a plague in Indian country. "I have ever been of the opinion that a more pernicious article could not be introduced among them," Clark wrote Elbert Herring, "as it is well known that not an Indian could be found among a thousand, who would not (after a first drink) sell his horse, his gun, or his last blanket for another drink—or even commit a murder to gratify his passion for spirits."[69] Clark's view that virtually all Indians were rendered helpless by alcohol was widely shared, despite evidence that white men were just as susceptible to the demon rum. But selectively pointing out alcohol's evil influence over Indians provided yet another justification for removing the Eastern tribes far from the reach of whiskey-toting traders. What was unusual about Clark's letter to Barbour was his willingness to oppose a policy that the government permitted and traders enthusiastically embraced.

In 1820, the newly reorganized Missouri Fur Company sent eight hundred gallons of whiskey to one of its posts. Agents felt helpless to stop it. "The facility with which whiskey can be introduced among the Indians, renders them very savage [and] ungovernerable," complained the agent Richard Graham. "A stop if possible should be put to it, but the law is so lame . . . that an agent can do nothing."[70]

In May 1822, a ban on the importing of "ardent spirits" had been imposed in Indian country, and the army given the task of interdicting smuggled goods. But loopholes permitted wines to escape the definition of "ardent spirits," and fur traders' boatmen were allowed to bring in personal supplies of whiskey that vastly exceeded what they could drink. Clark's Illinois agent Thomas Forsyth complained that "almost every settler's house is a whiskey shop . . . and when spoken to on the subject, the whiskey seller will say, prove it."[71]

Like many Kentuckians, the Clarks bought and sold whiskey routinely. William bought two hundred gallons when he returned to St. Louis in 1820, and John O'Fallon bought fifty-five barrels in Louisville in 1821 and another fifty-two barrels in 1822. The O'Fallon brothers set up a distillery on their farm in the mid-1820s, where they made rye and corn whiskey. Even if they retailed their alcohol locally, it is likely that much of it wound up in Indian hands.

The Chouteaus and John Jacob Astor's American Fur Company were adamantly opposed to any restrictions on the whiskey trade. When

Clark's agents seized alcohol being shipped up the Missouri by the American Fur Company, Astor protested so vehemently that McKenney at once wrote to Clark, ordering him to return to the company any furs that had been detained. Clark complied. Confronted with a conflict between the Indians' interests and direct orders from his superiors, he often argued for the former but obeyed the latter. The improvisational leadership style that served Clark so well during the expedition was absent when he was behind a desk.

Near the end of 1826, Clark encountered two tribes he could not control. The government ordered him to leave his jurisdiction and go down the Mississippi to persuade the Chickasaws and Choctaws to cede several million acres of their land and move west of the state of Missouri. In mid-October, Clark and John O'Fallon went first to Chickasaw Bluffs. Clark knew the Chickasaws well; they had fought with him at Fallen Timbers. But his entreaties failed; they refused to move, refused to visit the territory the government had prepared for them, and said that they would never cede their lands. Clark proceeded next to the Choctaw towns and received the same answer. They said they would never move. Clark reported to Barbour that his negotiations had failed. It would take another eight years for the government to move the Chickasaws and Choctaws to Kansas.

Clark would have been pleased to return to St. Louis for the Christmas holiday in 1826. A few months earlier, Harriet had given birth to their second son and Clark's sixth. They called him Edmund, after William's late brother. Edmund took after the Kennerly side of the family, with black hair and blue eyes; "a quite merry little fellow," William said.[72] Clark had barely gotten to know Edmund when the child fell sick during a heat wave the following summer. Clark rarely wrote personal entries in the Indian Office logbook. But on August 12, 1827, he entered one in a bold black script, pressing hard on his pen: "Edmond Clark (my Infant Son) died at 8½ A.M. (10 mo. 3 days old)."[73]

John Julius had returned to St. Louis, though Clark worried that his "deformity is becoming worse and more oppressive to him. I fear he will not live many years."[74] Of more immediate concern was the health of ten-year-old George Rogers Hancock Clark. In a bizarre hunting accident, a carelessly handled shotgun had discharged, shattering bones in his jaw and the roof of his mouth. George was carried home covered with blood. "It like to have killed your mama," Clark wrote to Lewis. "She & Mary [Radford, her daughter] dressed his wound. She will let no other person do it."[75] Henry, the mixed-race slave with whom George had been hunting, was so frightened of punishment that he ran away for twenty-four hours. George eventually recovered, though as an adult he wore a beard that concealed his scars.

William Preston Clark had been chronically unhappy at boarding schools in the East. Clark finally concluded that he had shown "so much discontent in the situations in which I have placed him I am fearful he will not learn & had as well be here at something."[76] After bringing William Preston home to work in the Kennerlys' dry-goods store, Clark made a revealing if forgiving assessment. William, he said, lacked "contentment of situation."[77]

Contentment of situation was not something the father lacked. The ability to accept difficulties and still soldier on was Clark's greatest strength. In another letter to Lewis, still struggling with his studies at West Point, he exhorted, "Try my dear boy to get thro, persevere and show what you can do . . . On you my son our greatest hopes rest, only persevere my dear boy and you will come out an ornament to the country which gave you burth. Nearly anything can be effected by perseverence."[78] Later, Clark pithily summarized the stoical outlook he lived by. "View the world as it is," he told his son. "Do not anticipate too much. The pleasant feelings of one day may never be realized in another, yet I hope many will be exceeded by you."[79]

By the 1820s, Clark had largely given up his ambitions to make his fortune in the dry-goods business. But he still believed deeply in land. Among his holdings were seventy-four thousand acres in western Kentucky that the state of Virginia had originally granted to his brother George Rogers in 1794 in belated recognition of his contributions during the Revolution. George Rogers had then turned the tract over to William in payment for his efforts to settle his debts in the late 1790s.

At the time of the grant, the land had little market value, since Virginia did not even own it. It was within the hunting grounds of the Chickasaw tribe. But a treaty negotiated by Andrew Jackson in 1818 extinguished the Chickasaw titles to Clark's grant. In April 1827, Clark put one hundred acres up for auction in a new town he called "Pa-Du-Cah" on the Ohio at the mouth of the Tennessee River.

Sounding like a real-estate agent hawking Florida land a century later, Clark touted its healthy location, steamboat access, rich soil, and "inexhaustible supplies of Oak and Pine timber." In short, "Few, if any points on the western waters, present so many advantages to the merchant, mechanic and capitalist."[80] Clark explained that he had named the town in honor of a lost tribe "once the largest nation of Indians known in this country, and now almost forgotten."[81]

Why would Clark name his new community after a vanished tribe? Though a statue of a "Chief Paduke" stands in present-day Paducah, Kentucky, the mysterious "Padoucas" were in truth most likely Apaches, whom the early French had once called the *padu-kesh* (enemy people).[82] Clark may have felt more at ease commemorating a conveniently vanished tribe than honoring more recent inhabitants, such as the Chickasaws, who were uncomfortably still present.

In the summer of 1827, the fragile peace on the Upper Mississippi began to unravel. The cause was the white settlers' lust for a glittering metal— not gold, but lead. It had been mined for centuries by Indian women around present-day Dubuque for ornaments and sparkling paint, and more intensely for bullets after the French introduced firearms in North America. After the 1825 Treaty of Prairie du Chien, adventurers rushed illegally onto Indian-owned lands to begin extracting the ore. The number of miners grew from about two hundred in 1825 to about four thousand in 1827. The following year, Clark reported that five steamboats were serving some six thousand whites illegally working the lead mines around the Fever River.

Conflicts were inevitable. The agent Joseph Street complained to Illinois governor Ninian Edwards that the "low, gross, blackguards" among the whites were flouting the rights of the Winnebagos to mine the land. But Edwards was a land speculator himself who wanted peace to preserve stable land prices, not Indian rights. When he heard that a party led by the Winnebago chief Red Bird had murdered two white boatmen and an infant to avenge liberties the men had taken with an Indian woman, Edwards threatened to call out the militia.

After several more threatening incidents, Clark met in St. Louis with Atkinson and Cass to discuss what to do about the Winnebago "attacks on our citizens."[83] Atkinson wound up taking a detachment of 580 U.S. infantrymen to the Upper Mississippi to squelch the so-called uprising. Though it was the first Indian campaign in the Old Northwest since the War of 1812, there were virtually no casualties. The Winnebago War amounted to little more than a show of force by Atkinson's regulars and a posse of mounted militia commanded by General Henry Dodge. Red Bird surrendered himself and died in custody. Cass negotiated a "temporary arrangement" with the Winnebagos in August 1828 that allowed whites to cross their lands and called for a treaty to be held for the purposes of a cession the next year.[84] But Ninian Edwards and his successor as governor, John Reynolds, continued to call for the expulsion of all Indians from Illinois.

Many Indians continued to remove themselves voluntarily. Almost all of them came through St. Louis to meet with Clark in his Council Room. These entries were made in Clark's logbook during the month of September 1826:

> *Sept. 10:* "Shawonee Chief and 7 men arrived others Depart"
> *Sept. 11:* "Potawatomy Chief Sanachwan & 7 men arrive"
> *Sept. 15:* "13 Kickapoos & 2 Shawenes arrive"
> *Sept. 16:* "4 Shawones & 3 Delewares arrive"
> *Sept. 19:* "8 Delawares arrive from Illinois"
> *Sept. 20:* "80 Osages arrive with agent for council"
> *Sept. 21:* "5 Peorias & 5 Piankashaws arrive"
> *Sept. 25:* "35 Delawars arrive with Chief Anderson"
> *Sept. 26:* "6 Indians arrive from the Eastward"
> *Sept. 27:* "Delawars arrive had a talk in Council house"
> *Sept. 28:* "Indian Council Commences"
> *Sept. 29:* "3 Potawatomies & 4 Kickapoos arrive"
> *Sept. 30:* "20 Shawnees arr."[85]

Before turning emigrating Indians over to one of his agents for relocation to their new homes, Clark provided lodging and provisions for them. In October 1826 he noted, "I have 33 Indians a visit and Purchased beef, pork, bacon, turkey, Whiskey, flour, lard, butter cakes apples potatoes vegetables appbl wine."[86] At one point, Clark paid his wife, Harriet, $20.50 for "making shirts for Indians."[87]

At the end of 1827, Clark advised McKenney that he was struggling to keep up with the flood of Indians pouring across the Mississippi. They were foraging for food and drawing complaints from local citizens. "I have taken upon myself to give some partial assistance to those Bands," he said. "The Tribes on this side of the Mississippi are wretched and moving from place to place . . . The distresses of the Indians of this Superintendency are so great and extensive, and complaints so frequent, it is, and has been impossible for me to report them. I therefore have taken upon myself a great deal, in acting as I thought best."[88]

Social life in St. Louis, lively since its French beginnings, was becoming robustly American, thanks to the army. In June 1826, Clark and Atkinson had ridden several miles south of St. Louis to find a site for a new arsenal to replace the aging cantonment at Bellefontaine. The ground was cleared on July 4, 1826, the day of Jefferson's death, and so the new fort was named Jefferson Barracks. The ready supply of officers guaranteed dancing partners for the Clark women. "My family have become so identified with the military that several parties given by the Sixth, First, and Third Regiments this Christmas and New Year's past [we were] the only family invited from this city," Clark boasted.[89] But that may have been due less to his prestige than to the presence of his pretty niece Henrietta Preston, who is "much admired, courted &c &c."[90]

The parties continued through the spring of 1828. At its dinner on St. Patrick's Day, the Missouri Hibernian Relief Society toasted General Clark with "Auld Lang Syne." Clark retreated to Marais Castor twice a week, tending to his orchard of apple, cherry, and peach trees. "This town improves astonishingly in Building & Population and will unquestionably grow to be a large City," Clark told his son Lewis. "Steam Boats are almost daily arriving and departing to & from the upper Mississippi, Missouri Illinois River & the Ohio."[91]

He continued to feel the "emence press of business in my department."[92] The Southern tribes—Chickasaws, Choctaws, and Creeks—had finally agreed to inspect the lands waiting for them beyond Missouri. But before resettling them, Clark said, it would be necessary "that some assistance should be given to remove them there: and, when there, to assist them in preparing the earth for cultivation, and provisions, until they could raise a support, &c. Without this aid, the Indians will be more wretched than they were before they moved."[93]

By the fall, Clark's thoughts had again turned toward Washington. No ordinary election year, 1828 was the year of the first presidential election ever held by popular vote. Determined to avenge the "corrupt bargain" by which Henry Clay had delivered the White House to John Quincy Adams in 1824, the sixty-two-year-old Andrew Jackson had won the first great landslide in American politics. In Missouri, Old Hickory won an astonishing 70 percent of the popular vote.

During the campaign, Adams had appointed Secretary of War Barbour as Ambassador to Great Britain. His replacement in the department was Peter Porter, a New Englander and one of the congressional War Hawks in 1812. Arriving on the job and finding no coherent Indian policy, Porter asked Clark and Cass to come to Washington to reorganize the Indian Office.

On October 29, Clark took the stage east with a larger-than-usual entourage. His party included his wife, Harriet; their four-year-old son, Pompy; her fourteen-year-old son, William Radford; his nieces Henrietta Preston and Eliza Anderson; and his great-niece Sarah Pearce (daughter of Jonathan's daughter Nancy). Attending to the group were two African-American slaves, Berry and Allen.

They took a steamboat from Louisville to Cincinnati, a city of some 1,500 brick buildings fronted with limestone sidewalks. At Wheeling, they boarded a stage to cross the Appalachians, despite the snow on the newly built National Road (today's U.S. 40). Clark was retracing in reverse the journey he and his family had taken to Kentucky in 1784–'85— but now he was traveling on a comfortable gravel road.

In Washington, Clark and his family boarded at Mrs. Handy's rooming house, next door to the President's House, "where I pay less than at the Tavern." He rented a piano for Harriet and observed "great bustle at this place as the members of Congress are coming in to the City & taking quarters."[94] While he and Cass set to work on their report, Harriet and the rest of the family went on to Philadelphia and New York with hopes of visiting Lewis at West Point.

Prevented by ice floes on the Hudson from visiting Lewis, Harriet and the family returned to the capital. The entire family then moved over to Washington's premier hotel, Gadsby's Indian Tavern, on the corner of Pennsylvania Avenue and Sixth Street. President-elect Jackson also stayed at Gadsby's before his inauguration in March. On February 18, William and Harriet attended a Mardi Gras celebration with President-elect Jackson, his nephew Andrew Jackson Donelson, and Donelson's wife, Emily.

In early February, Clark and Cass turned in their "bill for the general regulation of the intercourse with the Indians" to the lame-duck Adams Administration. It was a document of one hundred pages and fifty-six separate proposals that codified existing procedures and added new ones in every area of Indian administration. It was engaged not with policy but with practice. Whether it would be adopted would depend on the wishes of the new Jackson Administration.

The new President delivered his inaugural address under a glowering sky, which suddenly brightened to cheers from the crowd. Jackson proclaimed that his Administration would give Indians "humane and considerate attention" with a policy that was "consistent with the habits of our Government and the feelings of our people."[95]

What he meant was that the Eastern and Southern tribes would be moved beyond the Mississippi River.

Old Hickory's inebriated supporters then poured into the President's House, spilling punch and tracking their muddy boots on the carpets.

CHAPTER TEN

RESISTANCE AND REMOVAL

1829–1838

After Jackson's inauguration, Clark took his family and two servants back to St. Louis on a carriage over the National Road to Wheeling and then on the steamboat *Cleopatra* down the Ohio. But by the time Harriet threw open her house for a party for the officers at Jefferson Barracks that lasted until 3 a.m., Clark knew that his and Lewis Cass's ambitious plan for reforming the Indian Department had gone nowhere. Andrew Jackson was not interested in administrative fixes; the new President had far more sweeping changes in mind.

A more complicated man than the merciless Indian-hater portrayed by his enemies, Jackson could be sentimental about the natives. Earlier in his life, he adopted an Indian infant found on a battlefield and raised him as his son. For years, Jackson had felt that the policy of laboriously extinguishing Indian land titles, as if the tribes were sovereign nations, made no sense. Moreover, allowing the tribes to continue to live in the East under their own governance would lead inevitably to their destruction.

In his first annual message to Congress, presented in December 1829, Jackson cited the calamities that had already befallen tribes like the Mohegans, the Narragansetts, and the Delawares. They were virtually extinct. The same destiny would await the remaining tribes if the nation did not act "to preserve their much-injured race." The Indians had a choice: they could remain in the East and individually blend in with the white man's world, at the price of losing their own culture, or they could remove themselves to the West, where "they can be Indians, not cultural white men," and perpetuate their race while learning the "arts of civilization." Remaining in the East while retaining their "wandering ways," however, was not an option.[1]

The introduction of the Indian Removal Bill of 1830 ignited an opposition, largely along regional lines, that bitterly accused Jackson of dumping the Indians into Stephen Long's "Great American Desert." Church groups and humanitarians in the Northeast joined forces with Jackson's political rivals in an intensely fought battle. In the spring of 1830, New Jersey Senator Theodore Frelinghuysen took the floor of the chamber for a six-hour oration spread over three days. "We have crowded the tribes upon a few miserable acres of our Southern frontier: it is all that is left to them of their once-boundless frontier," he bellowed. "And still, like the horse-leech, our insatiable cupidity cries, give! Give! Give!"[2] Tennessee Congressman Davy Crockett thundered that "if he should be the only member of the House who voted against the bill, and the only man in the United States who disapproved it, he would still vote against it." The former Attorney General William Wirt—the same William Wirt who had turned down Clark's offer to edit his journals twenty years earlier—set about to organize a legal challenge.

Jackson prevailed. The Indian Removal Bill passed the House 102 votes to 97, and on May 28, 1830, Jackson signed it into law. It authorized the President to exchange public land in the West, beyond the states of Missouri and Arkansas, for Indian land in the East. It also appropriated $500,000—not nearly enough, as it turned out—to carry out its provisions.

William Clark's job suddenly became more complicated. The new law meant that the federal government was now committed to moving all of the Indians east of the Mississippi into the lands he supervised. If he was opposed to this policy, he never said so, privately or publicly. Like many Americans, he had most likely convinced himself that removal was the only way to save the Indians. The first problem Clark faced in executing the plan was that other people were already living on those lands; those tribes would not welcome intruders of any race. The superintendent at St. Louis nevertheless needed to acquire titles to these Indian lands in Missouri and beyond to make room for the flood tide of Eastern Indians coming across the Mississippi. He would need to relocate some tribes for the second time in his superintendency and somehow keep peace between the tribes and the settlers—and between the tribes themselves. And he would need to do it in a largely unsurveyed land area that extended for millions of square miles across half a continent.

Indians were not the only people pressuring Clark's office. Many white Americans stood to profit from the migration of Indians. They included not only farmers and plantation owners ready to move onto tribal homelands in the East but also merchants and other suppliers of equipment, food, and clothing purchased by the government for emigrating Indians. Prominent among these merchants was John O'Fallon, who was amassing a fortune in St. Louis, and the Kennerly brothers, who were less successful in their dry-goods and sutlering businesses.

No one profited more or caused more disruption than the whiskey traders. Alcohol was at one end of most transactions in the fur trade—not surprisingly, since the average adult American in 1830 consumed an estimated seven gallons of wine, beer, and spirits every year. Each of the traders' boatmen was allowed to take along a gallon of whiskey per month for personal use, but Clark routinely authorized traders to carry far more "ardent spirits" into Indian country than even the thirstiest boatmen could drink. One trader, William Sublette, was allowed to bring 450 gallons up the Missouri in 1832, even though he did not employ a single boatman. To a trader, it meant certain profit: a gallon of whiskey that cost $1 in St. Louis was worth $30 in Indian country.[3]

Even Clark's agents were beginning to protest the superintendent's willingness to accommodate his friends at the American Fur Company. To the agents, Clark's vacillations created too many opportunities for abuse. Their complaints about Clark's inaction were usually stated indirectly, as Lawrence Taliaferro's were after his post at St. Peter's was burned in 1830 by a "drunken Indian." Author of repeated warnings about whiskey abuses, Taliaferro told Clark that "it is a well established fact that almost every outrage which has been committed by the Indian tribes within the last twelve years can be safely traced to whiskey as the direct or primary cause."[4] A year later, the subagent Jonathan Bean erupted bitterly, "Liquor flows as freely here as the Missouri, if we might judge from the number of drunken Indians. Yet no one gives them a drop, or at lest no proof can be had. For God's sake, for the sake of humanity exert yourself to have this article stopped in this country."[5]

Pressures were building on the tribes from all sides. In early 1830, the Sauks and Foxes found themselves at war on two fronts. West of the Mississippi, the Dakota Sioux were fighting to drive them off the lands the American government had awarded them. East of the Mississippi, settlers and miners were eagerly moving onto the farms and mineral lands that the tribe had supposedly ceded in Harrison's Treaty of 1804, a concession reaffirmed at the 1816 treaty. The departing Illinois governor, Ninian Edwards, complained that the tribe was slow to remove itself as agreed. Further, unless the federal government acted, his militia would take matters into its own hands, and "those Indians will be removed, and that very promptly."[6] When the Sauks and Foxes returned to Saukenuk after their winter hunt in 1829, they found squatters there who had taken over the village and released cattle into their cornfields.

Thomas Forsyth, the competent agent to the tribe, observed to Clark, "It appears hard to me that the Indian property should be stolen, their huts torn down and burned down, and their persons insulted by Strangers." He went on to hope that "our Government will render some justice to those Indians, and not encourage those intruders."[7]

Instead, the government did the opposite: it put up the Indians' homelands in Illinois for public sale. When the Sauks and Foxes returned from their winter hunt in 1830, they found not squatters but whites with legal land titles plowing up the graves of their ancestors.

The government had long wanted to acquire the Indians' mineral-rich lands on the Mississippi near present-day Dubuque, Iowa. White miners had already crossed the Mississippi from Galena and illegally occupied the Indian villages there. The Sauks and Foxes refused to sell the land, however, and instead requested a council to survey the boundaries. The American Fur Company, anxious to end the disputes crippling its trade in the region, agreed that a council was a good idea. But fair arbitration was not their hope, nor their expectation. John Jacob Astor's son William urged Pierre Chouteau to keep the pressure on Clark to arrange the council, confident it would end in their favor: "As our Mr. Crooks says, 'give him no peace day and night.'"[8]

The council would be convened at Prairie du Chien. Clark dispatched his son William Preston Clark and Jonathan Bean up the Missouri to gather the Nakota Sioux and Omahas. He feared, however, that the Sauks and Foxes would not agree to come. "[They] have more national character than any tribes we have within this Superintendency," he warned McKenney, "and a firm and decisive course is necessary with them."[9]

On June 24, 1830, Clark departed for Prairie du Chien on the steamboat *Planet* with his co-commissioner at the council, Colonel Willoughby Morgan, and a military detachment commanded by Stephen Watts Kearny, the handsome young major from Jefferson Barracks. Harriet Clark came along, as did the six-year-old Pomp and Harriet's daughter, Mary Preston Radford.

Clark's entourage also included a special guest, a thirty-three-year-old lawyer–turned–portrait painter, George Catlin. Entranced by an Indian delegation that had passed through Philadelphia, Catlin had resolved to record this vanishing race for history. He had traveled to St. Louis and befriended "the venerable Governor Clark, whose whitened locks are still shaken in roars of laughter, and good jest among the numerous citizens, who all love him, and continually rally around him in his hospitable mansion."[10]

Clark opened the council on July 7. Among the principal chiefs in the throng was a familiar face: Big Elk, the Omaha whose eulogy to Black Buffalo had saved the council at Portage des Sioux in 1815. Much had since changed, including Big Elk's relative influence and that of his tribe. Competing with rival hunting bands of Sauks and Foxes for dwindling herds of bison, the Omahas were hungry and desperate. Big Elk told Clark that in traveling to the council, he had seen only a dozen bison "in passing thro' these peoples lands . . . which is perhaps all they have on them."[11]

After a week of talks, Keokuk and 112 other chiefs and headmen from the various tribes signed the treaty. They agreed to cede to the United States a forty-mile-wide swath of land in today's Iowa, intended to become a buffer zone separating the Dakota Sioux on the north from the Sauks and Foxes on the south. Clark told the Indians that he would not settle white people on this land—though with an eye to its long-term prospects for either race, he advised the Secretary of War that it was "fine farming and grazing country." (It later would become a new home for the emigrating Winnebagos.)

For Western nations like the Omahas, this was their first land cession. The delay did not improve their bargaining position. In exchange for little more than a meager annuity of $2,500 "for ten successive years" and the services of a blacksmith, the Omahas gave up rights to millions of acres of their traditional hunting grounds in western Iowa. Big Elk complained to Clark that annuities lasting only "ten winters" would not be enough. "In that time I may be dead," he said, "and what am I to leave to my Children?"[12]

On a cold January night earlier that year, as ice floes slid down the Mississippi, a mellow William Clark sat up late writing to his eldest child, Lewis. His son would graduate after all from West Point, and William felt warmed by paternal pride and comforts of the hearth. "Geo. [Rogers Hancock Clark] and John [Radford] is sitting by me in my office this night getting their lessons," he wrote. "Julias & Pompy in Bead, your ma[,] Mary [Radford] . . . and some gentlemen in the parlour. All well."[13]

All well, indeed. William was proud of Lewis. Despite threatening to resign before almost every examination, Lewis would graduate in the middle of his West Point class and was named color-bearer, which, as his father observed, was a substantial honor. In his letters to his son Clark wrote, "It is to me pleasure to be felt, the enjoyment of my children who is all to me at this stage of life."[14]

His domestic life with Harriet was also a joy. She had virtually adopted his children as her own, as he had hers. Her attractive daughter, Mary Radford, turned so many heads that she "has been a good deal envied by some of the contending young ladies of the city," Clark boasted. In fact, "to show her disregard to the contending parties she gave a great party, at which she had all concerned and nearly 200 other persons, all very social and merry."[15]

One of the turned heads was his son's. That previous April, Lewis had asked his father's advice about a subject of "a delicate but honourable nature"—namely, he was falling in love with Mary. His feelings were in some measure reciprocated. But Mary not only lived under the Clark roof, she was both his stepsister and his second cousin once removed. Clark pondered the problem long enough to makes notes to himself ("My dear son . . . I know of no legal impropriety in such a connection") before writing out an answer advising Lewis "not to discover your feelings & preference for a year or two longer by that time you will complete your education."[16]

Over the following year, however, it was Mary's feelings that changed. She became engaged to marry Major Stephen Watts Kearny, the dashing officer who had commanded the military mission to Prairie du Chien in July 1830. On Thursday morning, September 2, 1830, St. Louis's French and American elites gathered at the Clark home with officers from Jefferson Barracks to await what would be the town's most glamorous wedding in years.

The guests waited . . . and waited. James Kennerly appeared and announced that the ceremony had been delayed until 11 a.m. Still no bride. What could have happened? Learning belatedly of Mary's wedding, Meriwether Lewis Clark had rushed home in a last-minute effort to dissuade her. He was upstairs with her; she was in tears, unable to make up her mind. General Atkinson was said to be "so indignant at the idea of one of his officers & his favorite being treated so" that he stormed out, with Kearny in his wake.[17]

For two days, tense messages and notes were exchanged between the would-be bride and the disappointed groom. Finally, on a sweltering hot Sunday, September 5, Stephen Watts Kearny and Mary Preston Radford quietly married at the Clark farm, Marais Castor, with only two witnesses present. Mary would eventually bear eleven children with Kearny. Meriwether Lewis Clark and Kearny later became fast friends, and Kearny died at his old rival's house in 1848. Mary outlived her husband by fifty years. Her newspaper obituary, published in 1899, almost seventy years after the wedding, still remembered "the fame of her wondrous beauty."[18]

The changes shadowing the world of Big Elk and refashioning the one Clark's children would inherit were evident on the Mississippi. In the year 1832 alone, five hundred steamboats would dock at the St. Louis levee, all within sight of Clark's Indian Office. The boats themselves were notoriously uncomfortable and unreliable, throbbing and shaking from the clamor of their high-pressure boilers and showering travelers with sparks and soot. Accommodations were dreadful, often exposed to the elements. Overnight passengers would be awakened by cascades of rainwater pouring on them from the leaky decks. The overheated boilers were subject to catastrophic explosions. Clark's clerk noted in his 1828 daybook that the dilapidated steamboat *Car of Commerce* blew up on the

Lower Mississippi, killing twenty-four. In 1830, Clark sent his son William to New Orleans to pick up two family slaves, Henry and Clayburne, who had been hired out as steamboat stewards. On his return trip, William booked passage on the *Helen McGregor*. Outside Memphis, the steamboat's boiler exploded, killing or maiming 30 or 40 of its 410 passengers. Uninjured, William gave first aid to the victims.

Steamboats carried other dangers. In June 1830, Clark's clerk excitedly noted the arrival of the *Atlantic*, carrying "the excentric and no less strange <u>Woman</u>, Mrs. Ann Royall!"[19] Anne Newport Royall was a travel writer, an early crusading journalist, and one of the most controversial figures of her time. Publishing books and newspapers in Washington, she took on the Protestant churches, the anti-Freemason movement, Sunday mail service, restrictive immigration policy, and corporal punishment of sailors in the navy. John Quincy Adams described her as "a virago errant in enchanted armor."[20] The indignant Presbyterians had her charged and convicted as a common scold.

Royall had met William and Harriet Clark in passing during Andrew Jackson's inauguration in 1829. Understanding that Clark was "as generous as he was hospitable," she decided to visit him in St. Louis during one of her cross-country trips. Even before she disembarked at St. Louis, she cast a cold eye at soldiers bathing nude along the riverbank at Jefferson Barracks—and was further appalled to see that one of the wives aboard the vessel was delighted by the sight. Royall pronounced the entire fort to be a colossal waste of money: "There are no Indians within many hundred miles of this place."[21]

Upon disembarking, Royall encountered "a host of enemies," beginning with Augustin Kennerly ("a simpleton from his birth"), who assured her that Governor Clark was unavailable. When not a single tavern or hotel agreed to give her a room—no doubt feeling pressure from the local clergy—Royall wound up receiving a parade of curious visitors aboard the *Atlantic*. Augustin Kennerly lamented in the Indian Office daybook that "her turbulence & wanton vehemence, excited curiosity, while it keeps from her, the real friendship of all."[22]

Before departing, Royall was determined, despite the rebuffs, "to take a peep at the Indian Agency." Along the way, she encountered several young men who "gave me an insight of the infamous frauds of the agency in cheating the innocent Indians, and their overbearing conduct toward the subagents." They further informed her that "Clark could never be seen; he was surrounded by a parcel of harpies who denied admittance, stating 'that he was sick, or in bed, or in the country.'"[23]

That was all the challenge Royall needed. She made straight for Clark's Council House, a place she found to be "filled with trifles to allure the poor Indians out of their annuities—another part of the house, under the appearance of hospitality to the Indians, the more readily to fleece them, is allotted to those unsuspecting visitors. This was a large room on the first floor, and was then full of Indians. I pushed on briskly through them, and found Clark in a remote room, cooped up like an old rooster."[24]

The man who had stared down the Lakota Sioux in 1804 had met his match. "I am sick madam," Clark protested. "I cannot see company today, I am sick." Clark had been meeting with the Sauks to persuade them to attend the 1830 council at Prairie du Chien. But his complaint, reputation, and federal office drew from Royall the scornful opinion that the superintendent "is only the shadow of a man, scarcely sane, reduced to a skeleton, feeble, superannuated, and fit for no business in the world."[25] After "venting a little of her Spleenatic," as Kennerly put it, Mrs. Royall soon departed for Illinois.[26] "I had stormed the castle," she concluded, "and put the citizens to flight."[27]

The removal of Indians from the eastern United States began in earnest at a place in Mississippi with the deceptively lighthearted name of Dancing Rabbit Creek. On September 27, 1830, the Choctaws ceded 10,423,130 acres to the federal government—all of their land east of the Mississippi. The Treaty of Dancing Rabbit Creek was the first removal negotiated with what were known as the Five Civilized Tribes—the Cherokee, Chickasaw, Choctaw, Creek, and Seminole peoples. The removals started with these tribes because of their large numbers—the first stage alone of the Choctaw removal would uproot five thousand people—and because gold had been discovered on Cherokee land in 1829.

The geography of dispossession was far different in the Old Northwest. Dozens of smaller tribes lived along the waters of the Ohio, Great Lakes, and Upper Mississippi. Each involved a separate nation, a separate treaty, a separate removal. Each would need a separate home west of the Mississippi. Beginning in February 1831, removal treaties were negotiated in quick succession with the Menominees, Senecas, Shawnees, Ottawas, and Wyandots.

Indian families were moving across the Mississippi in increasingly large numbers. The federal government did little to care for them or protect them from unscrupulous whites, despite the efforts of the agents in the field. The agent Joseph Street reported to Clark that when he paid out an annuity of $3,000 to 349 Indians at Prairie du Chien in September 1830, a single trader had collected $2,300 of it by nightfall. The agent in southern Illinois, Pierre Menard, wrote to Clark that white men were stealing the horses belonging to the defenseless Senecas and Shawnees traveling through his district. "Although there is no obligation to clothe them," he went on to say, "it is impossible to refuse clothing to many women and children, suffering in cold weather."[28]

Wild game was vanishing across the Old Northwest, and in the harsh winter of 1830–'31 the choice for many Indians was to remove or to starve. Street advised Clark that "about 2/3rds of the Indians heretofore residing on the Wisconsin . . . have gone up the Mississippi saying they could not find game to live on since the white people had come on the Wisconsin."[29]

The Shawnee and Delaware agent in Missouri reported that whites were taking land and selling whiskey to his charges. "Great many of the Indians are in a suffering condition owing chiefly to the unusual hardness of the winter," he wrote to Clark. "I believe it to be my duty to have some provisions waggoned to them, particularly, to the Delawares." Their chief Anderson informed the agent that "the white people moved in among Them and took possession of their farms commenced seeding their fields and selling whiskey to his People so that he was compelled to move."[30]

Sometimes the Indians did not get far in their journey west. One group of Senecas tried to travel from Ohio to St. Louis, but the weather was "excessively cold," Clark wrote. "The Indians being frost bitten, sick, and some dying: and the whole party being much discouraged." The Senecas had not been given the blankets and rifles promised to them, so Clark provided these along with clothing, axes, hoes, plows, farming tools, and several horses.[31]

The situation was no better in the increasingly crowded wilderness west of the Mississippi. From the Osage villages on the Verdigris River, Clark's subagent Nathaniel Pryor reported that "the Osages appear to be a very unhappy people, and I think it is altogether attributable to the emigration of so many Red People to the West. The Game is entirely destroyed and they see that they must now cultivate the soil for a subsistence. They are extremely poor and they feel their inability to do any thing for themselves without the assistance of the Govt who, they are anxious would enable them to commence farming by furnishing them with the necessary means, and would like to have among them persons to instruct their young to spin and weave."[32]

The agent Paul Chouteau requested that the location of the principal Osage agency be moved. Why? "The Agency at present is surrounded by Indian villages, some within half a mile, consequently the crying of the Indians for lost relations the morning and evening (which is a religious ceremony amongst them) makes it very unpleasant to myself and my family."[33]

The agent John Dougherty at Fort Leavenworth reported that a group of Otoes "set out for their village today. They wintered, together with about half of the Oto tribe, a short distance below the Pawnee Republican village. Their account of the difficulties they encountered and the privations which they endured, during the continuance of the long protracted cold weather, is truly distressing . . . They lost a great number of their horses, and suffered themselves, extremely much, of hunger and cold; without the consolation of a profitable hunt."[34]

The Indian agents were overwhelmed by the scale of the tragedy unfolding around them. Clark pleaded for budgetary relief from Washington but instead was told to cut his expenses. He had always suffered physically when under stress, and, as Anne Royall had discerned, he frequently fell ill and complained of "dizziness."

Disease was once again sweeping through the tribes on the Missouri River. From Fort Leavenworth, Dougherty reported the effects of smallpox on the Pawnees: "Judging from what I saw during the four days I spent with them, and the information I received from the Chiefs . . . I am fully persuaded that one half the whole number of souls of each village have and will be carried off by this cruel and frightful distemper. They told me that not one under 33 years of age escaped the monstrous disease." It left a horrifying landscape behind. "They were dying so fast, and taken down at once in such large numbers, that they had ceased to bury their dead, [their bodies] were to be seen in every direction."[35]

Smallpox had last visited the Pawnees thirty-three years earlier; the survivors of that grim experience had developed immunity, while a new generation was now succumbing.

This vast tragedy was only a dim concern back in Washington. In 1831, Clark was asked by the War Department to submit a report, not on the epidemics but on the state of the fur trade. It, after all, had been one of the drivers of the Voyage of Discovery itself—"for the purposes of commerce," Jefferson had instructed. But even to Clark, with his long associations in the trade, the problems in the business of trapping and processing furs were beginning to pale beside the human disasters he was witnessing.

Clark tried to write the report as expected. The Santa Fe trade routes, he said, needed to be protected from the aggressive tribes of the Southwest. He proposed organizing a force of a thousand men to act as a mounted constabulary on the southwestern frontier, protecting traders from tribes and tribes from one another. The Rocky Mountain trade was "declining" because of "a very perceptible decrease of the furred animals," which he characteristically blamed on the British traders and hunters.[36]

But Clark saved his real passion for a topic that was seemingly tangential: "the necessity of an entire prohibition of [spirituous liquors] in the Indian country." He finally acknowledged that "the privilege of taking whiskey for the use of the Boatmen has been abused." As a result, he urged "the total & entire prohibition of this article in the Indian country under any pretence, or for any purpose whatever."

Reform was coming to Indian country, but the problems were multiplying even faster. The Jacksonians firmly believed that the last best hope for the removed Indians would be for them to eventually learn the "arts of civilization." But the tribes were unwilling to be assimilated. Efforts to send Indian children away to boarding school, for example, failed. The agent Cummins reported to Clark from his Delaware and Shawnee agency, "I have not been able to find one that was willing to send his Child so far from home even if the schooling would come gratis."[37] Dougherty told Clark he had no better luck with the tribes around Fort Leavenworth: "They were fully sensible of your kindness towards them in offering to instruct their children . . . but they . . . were unwilling to send off to so great a distance a single child alone without some one who could converse in its own language to accompany it—because the child would soon forget its own tongue and become estranged even from its Father and mother, be ashamed of their poverty, and abandon them in old age."[38]

A series of events in the second half of 1831 began as farce and ended in tragedy. In August, Clark's army friend Major Thomas Biddle, the brother of Nicholas, fought a duel with Spencer Pettis, a Jackson supporter who had recently been elected to the U.S. Congress. Enraged over Pettis's criticism of his brother's Bank of the United States, Biddle burst into Pettis's hotel room and cudgeled the sleeping congressman in his bed. At the resulting duel, Biddle demanded that their distance be set at a murderous five feet apart, to compensate for his nearsightedness. Biddle and Pettis fired simultaneously; both fell, mortally wounded. When Charles Dickens learned of this ludicrous combat during his 1842 visit, he pronounced both men "no great loss to the community."[39]

Another death struck the Clark family closer to home. On September 5, a distraught Clark wrote to Lewis that thirteen-year-old John Julius had succumbed to his long-standing disability. "We are all in grief at present. Dear little Julius died this morning, perfectly in his senses to the last. He wrote part of a letter to you. He had not the strength to finish it, pore little fellow." Almost visibly taking a breath and squaring his shoulders, Clark urged Lewis, "Bear up against all misfortunes, my son, and let your course be correct, and fortune may smile on you."[40]

Two months later Harriet Clark wrote Lewis, "Your Papa is still perplexed as ever in his office"; she hoped a new grandchild would lift his spirits.[41] Mary and Stephen Kearny were expecting their first baby by Christmas. But Mary's daughter was born just a week after her mother wrote to Lewis and died a few hours later.

Harriet herself was growing weaker. On Christmas Day of 1831, she died at home at the age of forty-three. The cause was not clear, but river travelers carried many infectious diseases to St. Louis. Harriet was buried in her black silk dress, without flowers.

In the space of three months, Clark had lost his son, his step-grandchild, and his wife. At the age of sixty-one, he was for the second time a widowed father raising a family whose youngest member was under eight years old. For once, his usual resolve deserted him. "My afflictions are as much as I can bear at present," he told Lewis in a rare emotional letter. "My spirits are low and my course indecisive."[42] Although he would soon be back at work, Clark seemed more aware of his own mortality. "I have had my shear of difficulties," he wrote, "& know not when they will end."[43]

In the same week that Harriet died, the French nobleman Alexis de Tocqueville and his companion Gustave de Beaumont were traveling down the Mississippi on a steamboat to New Orleans. They had nearly drowned a few days earlier when their boat hit a rock on the Ohio. They arrived at Chickasaw Bluffs on Christmas Day, just as the first group of Choctaw emigrants removed by the Treaty of Dancing Rabbit Creek were being ferried across the Mississippi. The sight prompted Tocqueville to a memorable description:

> The Indians came forward toward the shore with a despondent air; they first made the horses go, several of which, little accustomed to the forms of civilized life, took fright and threw themselves into the Mississippi, from which they could be pulled out only with difficulty. Then came the men, who, following their usual custom, carried nothing except their weapons; then the women, carrying their children attached to their backs or wrapped up in the blankets that covered them; they were, moreover, overburdened with loads that contained all their riches. Finally, the old people were led on. There was among them a woman of a hundred and ten years of age. I have never seen a more frightening figure. She was naked, with the exception of a blanket that allowed one to see, in a thousand places, the most emaciated body that one can imagine. She was escorted by two or three generations of grandchildren. To leave her country at that age to go seek her fate in a strange land, what misery! . . . There was, in the whole of this spectacle, an air of ruin and destruction, something that savored of a farewell that was final and with no return; no one could witness this without being sick at heart.

The sight led Tocqueville to an observation about the contradictions implicit in American attitudes toward Indians:

In the midst of this American society, so well policed, so sententious, so charitable, a cold selfishness and complete insensibility prevails when it is a question of the natives of the country . . . This world here belongs to us, they tell themselves every day: the Indian race is destined for final destruction which one cannot prevent and which it is not desirable to delay. Heaven has not made them to become civilized; it is necessary that they die. Besides I do not want to get mixed up in it. I will not do anything against them: I will limit myself to providing everything that will hasten their ruin. In time I will have their lands and will be innocent of their death.[44]

This was the dilemma Clark confronted—but was never able to solve.

Neither peace nor war prevailed on the Upper Mississippi. All eyes were on Black Hawk, the aging Sauk war leader. In the spring of 1831, Black Hawk had once again led his band back across the Mississippi, to the east bank, returning to his tribal home of Saukenuk. The fiery new Illinois governor, John Reynolds, at once wrote to Clark and threatened to call out the militia to remove the Indians, "dead or alive," in order to protect the citizens of his state.[45] Clark replied that he was doing all he could to remove the tribes. The stalemate continued until General Edmund P. Gaines appeared at Fort Armstrong on Rock River with an armed steamboat and ten companies of regular infantry. Black Hawk retreated westward across the Mississippi. He then grudgingly signed the so-called Corn Treaty, receiving food in return for his promise to remain west of the Mississippi and submit to Keokuk's authority.

Within a month, Clark's agent at Rock River, Felix St. Vrain, reported that white squatters were desecrating the same graves at Saukenuk that Black Hawk was so reluctant to abandon. "[I] found to my astonishment, that about fifteen or twenty graves had been uncovered and one entire corpse taken out from the grave, and put into the fire, and burned." Such atrocities reflected a broader lawlessness in the borderlands. "Some of these inhabitants make it their business to shoot at the Indians as they peaceably pass in the river, and if they happen to land their canoes are either destroyed or taken from them."[46]

St. Vrain continued to struggle against squatters illegally purchasing lead ore from Indians—"the Indian will have no other benefit from it than whiskey"—but his efforts were frustrated by the Indians' own tribal conflicts.[47] On July 31, 1831, the agent Joseph Street informed Clark that a group of Sauks and Foxes had fallen on a band of Menominees on the banks of the Mississippi and murdered twenty-five of them, "most of whom were drunk, and the women had hidden their guns and knives, to prevent their hurting each other."[48]

Over the summer, Secretary of War John Eaton had been forced to resign as a result of the controversy surrounding his marriage to his mistress, Peggy O'Neale. His replacement, Lewis Cass, immediately began to press Congress to adopt the Indian Office reforms he and Clark had proposed two years earlier. In briefing Cass on the long and troubled relationship between the United States and the Sauks and Foxes, Clark returned to two familiar themes: first, that Black Hawk's band "had been in the British interest during the late war, and were among our most distrustful Enemies on the frontiers"; second, that nothing could influence them other than a powerful display of military force.[49]

The resulting tragedy now seems to have been inevitable. Over the winter, the Sauks and Foxes refused to surrender the murderers of the Menominees to the American authorities. Keokuk put his finger on the ambiguous state of the tribes—part sovereign states, part wards of the state—when he asked, "Why do you not let us be as the Great Spirit made us and let us settle our own difficulties?" In March, Cass ordered General Henry Atkinson to take six companies of infantry from Jefferson Barracks, proceed to Rock River, and demand the murderers of the Menominees.

Meanwhile, Black Hawk had been encouraged by the Sauk chief Napope and the Winnebago Prophet, White Cloud, to believe that other Northern tribes and even the British would support his return to his ancestral lands. In the first week of April 1832, Black Hawk once again led his band of five hundred warriors and one thousand women and children to the east bank of the Mississippi.

By the time Atkinson arrived at Fort Armstrong with his troops aboard the steamboats *Chieftain* and *Enterprise*, Black Hawk was moving slowly up the Rock River in the direction of the Winnebago villages. It clearly was not a war party, and there had been no violence. His intent, it seemed, was to gain the support of the other tribes in resettling on his ancestral lands. A peaceful solution was still possible.

Instead of calming the situation, Atkinson wrote to Reynolds, telling the already belligerent Illinois governor that the borderlands of his state were under assault from Black Hawk. Alarmed, Reynolds promptly issued a call for 1,700 mounted militiamen. The militia was organized in a few weeks. Among the first volunteers was a gawky store clerk from New Salem, Abraham Lincoln. The twenty-three-year-old Lincoln was later reenlisted into service by Lieutenant Robert Anderson, whose father, Richard Anderson, had married Clark's sister Eliza.

From St. Louis, William Clark wrote Atkinson and Cass a series of increasingly bellicose letters, urging that the Sauks be "punished severely" and receive a "severe chastisement . . . which would serve as a warning to others."[50] Atkinson was a competent but cautious commander. The Indians called him the White Beaver, more out of deference to his snowy beard than to his energy. His principal aide was Lieutenant Meriwether Lewis Clark, on his first assignment out of West Point.

Atkinson began methodically pursuing the Indians up the Rock River. But his supply lines were stretching thin, and his troops were stumbling almost helplessly through swamps and thickets. He then made the grievous mistake of allowing the undisciplined mounted militia to ride out ahead of the U.S. regulars. On May 14, Major Isaiah Stillman and a group of 275 mounted militiamen were camped along Old Man's Creek (now Stillman's Run) when three Indians rode into their camp under a white flag.

The Indians tried to tell the whites that Black Hawk was ready to talk to the White Beaver about peace. But the disorganized militiamen had no interpreter with them. When other Indians were spotted in the area, shots rang out. One of the peace emissaries was killed in the camp; the others fled back to tell the main Sauk party about the whites' treachery. Black Hawk's warriors then attacked the approaching volunteers and routed them, killing eleven soldiers and leaving their grotesquely mutilated bodies to be found later by their unnerved comrades.

With the chance for peace gone, the fog of war settled over the Illinois Valley. A party of Winnebagos came upon the agent Felix St. Vrain and three other men carrying dispatches from Atkinson. They killed all four. A group of Potawatomis attacked an isolated community, killed fifteen settlers, including women and children, and carried off two young women, Sylvia and Rachel Hall, as prisoners. The Hall girls were later released and passed through St. Louis, where they spent a week with Clark. At his house, they recorded, they "were made as comfortable as his family and friends could make us."[51]

Clark could not contain his anger at Black Hawk's "blood thirsty savages." The image of the natives as savage murderers, dating to the frontier stories he'd heard from George Rogers as a child, boiled to the surface whenever Indians resisted his vision of their future. "A war of Extermination should be waged against them," he angrily wrote to Cass. "The honor & respectability of the Government requires it;—the pease & quiet of the frontier—the lives and safety of its inhabitants demand it." Clark was so furious that he once again authorized a measure he had previously disavowed: he would send the Dakota Sioux and Menominees "to execute vengeance against Black Hawk's band."[52]

Although Black Hawk was encumbered, moving what amounted to an entire village through the wilderness, he continued to elude Atkinson's troops. Lieutenant Jefferson Davis, serving with Abraham Lincoln in the same campaign, called it a "brilliant exhibition of military tactics . . . a feat of the most consummate management and bravery."[53] Frustrated by Atkinson's lack of success, Andrew Jackson ordered General Winfield Scott to proceed from New York with a thousand regular troops to join in the hunt for Black Hawk.

Clark remained at his farm near St. Louis, writing encouraging letters to Lewis: "Your fair is rought, recollect that your father has met with bad far and you are more stout with he was. Take care of yourself and do not unnecessarily expose yourself either to climate or the enemy." The soldier in Clark was never far below the surface. "I wish you had one or two Howitzers to route those fellows from their strong hole," he lamented.[54]

Unable to gain the support he expected from the Winnebagos and Potawatomis, Black Hawk began a desperate flight to the Mississippi. His people were starving, eating bark and digging roots. Atkinson's forces, meanwhile, had grown larger. Scott's reinforcements had been crippled by a cholera epidemic, but 2,000-man militia brigades had signed up, as had 350 mounted militia recruited by Colonel Henry Dodge in Illinois's mining district.

On July 21, Dodge and General James Henry came across the main body of Black Hawk's British Band as it was crossing the Wisconsin River. They attacked, killing about fifty Indians in what became known as the Battle of Wisconsin Heights. The chief Napope tried to arrange a truce to allow the Indians to cross to the Mississippi peacefully, but once again the whites did not have an interpreter.

As a result, for the next ten days Black Hawk's followers fled across present-day Wisconsin, with Atkinson's mounted troops close behind. On August 1, some 500 survivors from the original 1,500 Indians reached the Mississippi, just below the mouth of the Bad Axe River. They began building boats and rafts, only to see the steamboat *Warrior* chuffing up-river with U.S. troops aboard. Ignoring the Indians' white flag, the soldiers opened fire with an artillery piece and rifle volleys, killing 24 Indians before running out of fuel and dropping back down the river to load on more wood.

The next morning, Atkinson's land force attacked the band, which was pinned between it and the Mississippi. The Indians put up little resistance, as most were attempting to find shelter or help the women and children scramble across the river's mudflats and small islands. Then the *Warrior* reappeared, leveling a devastating fire at the Indians helplessly floundering and splashing through willows and water. The carnage was terrible; men, women, and children were shot indiscriminately, their bodies left to float downriver.

Somewhere between 150 and 300 Indians were killed at Bad Axe, which was less a battle than a massacre. The few exhausted Indians who made it across the Mississippi were hunted and killed by the Sioux. Black Hawk was captured by the Winnebagos and delivered to Colonel Zachary Taylor and the agent Joseph Street at Prairie du Chien. Taylor then sent Black Hawk and five of his co-leaders on the steamboat *Winnebago* to confinement at Jefferson Barracks. Their escort was Lieutenant Jefferson Davis.

Clark was delighted and relieved to hear the "glorious news," though he was not pleased to hear from Lewis that he wished to cut off the head of an Indian and then scalp it in order to evade orders against mutilating prisoners. He reprimanded Lewis, then reported back to Cass on the successful action at Bad Axe. By mid-August, three of his four boys had reassembled with him in St. Louis. "We all paraded at church today," he told his son George.[55]

It had been an unnecessary war, brought on by a stubborn Indian warrior, a belligerent Illinois governor, and incompetent militia officers. Already devastated by the war, the Sauks were forced to cede six million acres of land in a fifty-mile-wide strip along the Mississippi in present-day Iowa. Clark traveled to Fort Armstrong to advise General Scott and Governor Reynolds on the treaty terms. "It is expressly understood," the treaty said, "that no band or party of the Sac or Fox tribes shall reside, plant, fish, or hunt on any portion of the ceded country." They could no longer enter the land of their forefathers.

Afterward, one of Clark's former agents, Thomas Forsyth, blamed the superintendent for the war. Forsyth had been dismissed as subagent to the Sauks and Foxes in the early months of the Jackson Administration. He bitterly criticized Clark for failing to protect him from the Administration's newly introduced spoils system and for not attending to the legitimate complaints of Black Hawk's band. "It is very well known . . . that if I had remained at Rocky Island as Indian agent no trouble would ever have taken place between the white people and the Indians," he said, "and no other person is to blame but Gen'l William Clark."[56] Forsyth bitterly labeled Clark "a perfect ignoramus. But he is superintendent and can do no wrong."[57]

The superintendent had his hands full minding the shop in St. Louis, where an influential new player had arrived. John Jacob Astor's powerful American Fur Company had bought out its major rivals for the Missouri River fur trade: Pratte & Company and the Columbia Fur Company. The energetic Pierre Chouteau, Jr. ("Caddy"), who as a teenager had met Lewis and Clark in 1803, and the Scotsman Kenneth McKenzie were aggressively managing Astor's interests in the West.

In 1831, Chouteau personally escorted the company's new marvel, the triple-decker steamboat *Yellow Stone*, from Louisville to St. Louis. Chouteau hoped that the *Yellow Stone* could ascend the Missouri as far as Fort Union, the headquarters of the company's Upper Missouri Outfit at the mouth of the Yellowstone River. In its first voyage, it made it to Fort Tecumseh, opposite today's Pierre, South Dakota. But in its trip in the spring of 1832, the *Yellow Stone* made it all the way to Fort Union, carrying a load of trade goods and a group of passengers that included the painter George Catlin and two Nez Perce men, Rabbit Skin Leggings and No Horns on His Head.

The two Indians were the survivors of a group of three Nez Perces and a Salish man who had made a remarkable trip in the previous year, traveling with a trading party from west of the Continental Divide to St. Louis. They had been welcomed by Clark, surely curious to meet the first Indians from west of the Rockies he had seen since 1806. When two of the four Indians fell mortally ill in Clark's Indian Council House, two priests visited and administered last sacraments. The Indians later died and were buried in the Catholic cemetery.

During the visit, Clark had introduced the Indians to a man named William Walker, telling Walker that the warriors had come to St. Louis to learn the white man's religion. When Walker and others publicized the story of the "Nez Perce Christians," as they became known, it created an outpouring of evangelical fervor. Missionaries rushed into Indian country, including Dr. Marcus Whitman, whose wife, Narcissa, became the first white woman to cross the Continental Divide. Catlin painted the portraits of both Rabbit Skin Leggings and No Horns on His Head during their return trip.

Despite his concern about abuses, Clark continued to issue permits for extraordinary amounts of whiskey to be carried by boatmen up the Missouri. The legal loophole permitted only one gill (a half cup) per crewman per day, but Clark had allowed 12 gallons for each man going upriver in 1831 and a total of 1,500 gallons on the *Yellow Stone*'s first trip in 1832.

On July 9, 1832, however, Congress finally enacted a complete prohibition against carrying liquor into Indian country "under any pretence." Since news of the prohibition did not reach St. Louis until late August, Clark routinely issued a permit on July 9 for Chouteau to carry another 1,073 gallons for ninety-four men on the *Yellow Stone*'s second trip of the year.

By the time the *Yellow Stone* arrived at Cantonment Leavenworth in August, the military had learned of the new law. The officer of the day, a Lieutenant Jonathan Freeman, promptly confiscated twenty-eight barrels of whiskey found in the hold of the steamboat. The incident precipitated an uproar at the American Fur Company and an angry, pistol-waving confrontation farther upriver between the company trader Jean Cabanné and a competitor named Narcisse LeClerc.

Freeman sought legal advice from a judge in St. Charles, Missouri, who turned out to be Clark's friend George Shannon from the Lewis and Clark expedition. Shannon advised him to turn the entire mess over to the Superintendent of Indian Affairs at St. Louis. Acting on Clark's recommendation, Lewis Cass ended the brouhaha by ordering the whiskey returned to Chouteau and suspending Cabanné's trading license.

In 1832, America's most famous writer, Washington Irving, returned to his native country after spending seventeen years in Europe. Eager to replenish his materials, Irving embarked on a series of trips around the country. On Wednesday, September 12, he was on a packet boat churning up the Mississippi at 9 p.m. when, as he wrote in his journal: "Crash!—a steamboat, the *Yellow Stone*, coming down the stream at the rate of 15 miles an hour runs on us & staves in the upper works of our side . . . general alarm—some think the boat sinking—Kentucky lady threw herself into her husband's arms."[58]

Irving's boat had been rammed by Chouteau's *Yellow Stone*, running full throttle at night. But the smaller craft survived the accident and was repaired, and by the next morning Irving was enjoying the fragrant prairie flowers as a carriage drove him to visit William Clark at Marais Castor. The general was out hunting, so Irving waited, jotting random notes on the "Orchard bending & breaking with loads of fruit—negros—with tables under trees preparing meal—fire <sitting room> in open air—little negros, whooping & laughing—Civil Negro major domo who asks to take horses out . . . Sitting room, rifle & game bag &c in corners—Indian calumet over fire place . . . lovely day—golden sunshine—transparent atmosphere . . . the house looks out over rich level plain or prairie—green near at hand blue line at the horizon universal chirp & spinning of insects."[59]

Irving continued to admire the peach trees, grapevines, and beehives, when, amid a clamor of hoofbeats and "hallowing laughing," Clark suddenly hove up on horseback, with a gun on his shoulder and a dog at his heels. With him was his son Thomas Jefferson ("Jeff") on a calico pony. "Gov Clark fine healthy robust man, tall about 56—perhaps more [Clark was in fact sixty-two]," Irving wrote in his notebook. "His hair, originally light, now gray falling on his shoulders—Frank—intelligent."[60]

This was not the sickly man Anne Royall said she found cowering in his office. This was the vital William Clark that Catlin met, whose "whitened locks are still shaken in roars of laughter, and good jest."

Irving interviewed Clark over a bountiful dinner of fried chicken, bison and other game, roast beef, roast potatoes, tomatoes, and cakes. Clark at first talked to Irving guardedly about the Indian character—"Indians never quarrel & fight when sober—only when in liquor—& then lay it all to whiskey"—but soon observed that "Cherokees & Kickapoos used to say will fight, fight, fight, until we are all dead & then our bones will fight together—but they are now neighbours and friends thro necessity."[61] It was as succinct an encapsulation of Clark's opinion—and experience— of Indians as ever recorded.

When the conversation turned to slavery, Clark became more diplomatic. He told the New Englander that he had set three of his slaves free. One of them was probably Kitt, a man Clark gained title to in 1800 in settling a debt with George Rogers Clark. It is not clear whether Kitt was genuinely manumitted or "freed" in order to be hired into indentured servitude in the free state of Indiana.

Another freed slave, Clark said, was York, whom he had given a "large wagon & team of 6 horses to ply between Nash-/ville & Richmond." But even when presenting himself as a liberator of slaves, Clark could not help justifying the peculiar institution. All three of the slaves he had freed, he reported, had seen the error of their decision. They had "repented & wanted to come back."

As for York, Clark could not conceal his contempt. York, he said, had failed in his business. "He could not get up early enough . . . his horses were ill kept . . . fared ill." According to Clark, York had finally said, "Damn this freedom. I have never had a happy day since I got it." He had decided to return "to his old master" but had died in Tennessee.[62]

What is one to make of this implausible story? Was it the tortured logic of a slave owner convinced that servitude was what African-Americans really wanted? Or did Irving bend the story to put the national hero in a sympathetic light? The deep anger in Clark's voice was palpable, years after he had last seen York, when he sarcastically referred to his slave as "the hero of the expedition & adviser of the Indians."

Clark was most likely conflating a real event in his memory with another version he preferred to tell Irving. Twenty years earlier, Clark had sent York to Louisville in slavery. Later, he learned from his nephew that York "appeared wretched under the fear that he has incurred your displeasure" and "sorely repant of whatever miscounduct of his that might have lead to such a breach."[63] Either willingly or inadvertently, Clark had merged the report of York's regret for his misconduct with his imagined repentance for asking to be freed. It was not a coincidence that the same word, "repent," appears in both versions.

Simply by requesting his freedom and the right to live with his wife, York had so challenged Clark's personal code that the Virginian could frame it only as a mistake. Rather than manumitting York, Clark had probably allowed York to hire himself out, or sold him for a dollar, if only to be rid of him. There is no record of the Clark family freeing any slaves other than in legal charades. But, as with Indians, Clark needed to invent a narrative that was palatable.

Clark's views about slavery never changed, despite the impression he tried to give Irving. Just a few months before Irving arrived in St. Louis, Clark had purchased four "slaves for life" from Pierre Menard. The price: one dollar apiece. The slaves were in fact being moved from the free state of Illinois to the slave state of Missouri, where they would become part of the estate of Menard's daughter Alzière, who had married George Hancock Kennerly.

One of the family slaves Clark took to Jackson's inauguration was a man named Allen. In Washington, Allen apparently misbehaved in some fashion. In his account book, Clark recorded that he had to pay out $11.50 for "Allen folly." Then he matter-of-factly added that he gave another 50 cents "to a man to whip Allen."[64]

The morning after his interview with Clark, Irving rode out to Jefferson Barracks to see the imprisoned Black Hawk. He found not a frightening warrior but an old man in chains, "emaciated and enfeebled by the sufferings he has experienced," fanning himself with the tail feathers of a black hawk. Irving confessed, "I find it extremely difficult, even when so near the seat of action, to get at the right story of these feuds between the white and red men, and my sympathies go strongly with the latter."[65] It was a comment that could just as likely have applied to his conversation with Clark about his slaves.

During the Black Hawk War, white attitudes had become even more hardened against Indian tribes still east of the Mississippi. The schedule set in place by the Indian Removal Act of 1830 accelerated. In July, President Jackson nominated Clark as a co-commissioner charged with providing for the extinguishment of Indian titles remaining in the states of Illinois and Missouri. In October 1832, a month after Irving's visit, the tribes began arriving at Marais Castor for a series of treaty councils that would determine their future.

The first to appear were the Kickapoos. They were a sober and industrious people who were acculturated but not assimilated. The leader of the Vermillion Band, near the Illinois-Indiana border, was Kenekuk, the Kickapoo Prophet, a man with "a keen black eye, and a face beaming with intelligence."[66] Clark's agent Richard Graham observed, "This man has acquired an influence over his people through supposed revelations from God, which he urges on them with an eloquence, mildness, and firmness of manner."[67] Kenekuk's followers did not use whiskey or decorate themselves with war paint. Clark had told his superiors that Kenekuk's band were "the most orderly and sober Indians within the State of Illinois," and for years he had resisted demands for their removal.[68] But Kenekuk's people had taken in refugees from Black Hawk's destroyed force. This provided the state of Illinois a pretext for forcing Clark to act: the Kickapoos would be removed to present-day Kansas.

Two days later, Clark and his commissioners concluded a treaty with the Shawnees and Delawares from the Cape Girardeau region in Missouri. They had lived quietly in southern Missouri since the days of Spanish rule, and their land was considered ill suited for white settlement. But, as one sympathetic resident put it, their land "appears to have excited the jealousy and cupidity of idle and wandering persons in the county of Stoddard."[69] The governor of Missouri, John Miller, agreed that the white settlers clamoring for their removal had "unworthy motives" and—almost uniquely—threatened to call out the militia to protect the Indians.[70]

But no one could stave off the inevitable. The removal treaty called for the Shawnees and Delawares to give up all their land in Missouri for a combination of cash awards, livestock, and lifetime annuities of $100 to three of their chiefs. Before the month was out, Clark signed similar land-cession treaties at Marais Castor with the Kaskaskias and Peorias, the Piankashaws and Weas, and the Potawatomis. Clark told his son George that within the past two months at his farm, "I have concluded Treaties with about 400 Indians."[71]

Meanwhile, Indians and whites alike were suffering from the cholera epidemic sweeping up the Mississippi. More than six thousand people died in New Orleans in twelve days, and about another three hundred perished in St. Louis.

One of the disease's victims was Russel Farnham, an early Astorian and fur trader. In an era of many celebrated explorers and adventurers, Farnham stands out. A New Englander, he had joined Wilson Hunt Price's overland party that traveled to the Pacific Northwest and founded Astoria at the mouth of the Columbia in 1811. But when the post failed during the War of 1812, Farnham was given the task of delivering its proceeds to John Jacob Astor in New York. In order to avoid capture by the British, Farnham crossed the Bering Sea on Astor's brig, the *Pedlar*, and was dropped on the Kamchatka Peninsula. He then made his way, largely on foot, across Russia to St. Petersburg and then to Copenhagen. From there, he sailed to the West Indies and on to New York. Farnham was the first man to walk around the world, west to east. The only surviving portrait of the ruddy-faced, curly-haired Farnham states on its label: "Walked from Oregon to St. Petersburgh, 1813–1814."

Two hours after he showed the first symptoms of cholera in St. Louis, Farnham was dead.

As the *Yellow Stone* prepared to go up the Missouri in the spring of 1833, its passenger roster once again included a painter, the twenty-four-year-old Swiss artist Karl Bodmer. Bodmer was traveling with his patron, Maximilian, Prince of Wied Neuwied, an experienced naturalist and field ethnologist. Before issuing passports allowing for their travel into Indian country, Clark had given Maximilian and Bodmer a tour of his Indian museum and arranged for the now-mandatory trip to Jefferson Barracks to see Black Hawk. Echoing Catlin's impression, the Prince found Black Hawk to be "a little old man, perhaps seventy years of age, with gray hair, and a light yellow complexion; a slightly curved nose, and Chinese features to which the shaven head, with the usual tuft behind, not a little contributed."[72] The Sauk warrior had devolved into just another Indian curiosity.

The *Yellow Stone* eased away from the St. Louis levee amid the celebratory sounds of cheers, rifle shots, and crashing cannons. Maximilian and Bodmer traveled up the Missouri, observing the landmarks Lewis and Clark had made famous—the grave of the Omaha chief Blackbird, Floyd's Bluff, the Big Bend of the Missouri. On June 2 at Fort Pierre, the *Yellow Stone* loaded seven thousand bison robes for shipment back to St. Louis. The harvesting of furs on the Missouri had reached prodigious levels. Maximilian estimated that the traders were bringing down twenty-five thousand beaver skins and forty thousand to fifty thousand bison robes annually.

It could not last. Already, Maximilian recorded, the trade in muskrat pelts at Rock River on the Mississippi had collapsed from 130,000 pelts in 1825 to scarcely any at all. The steamboat traffic had continued to destroy the riparian habitat on the rivers; the *Yellow Stone* burned ten cords of wood each day. By 1841, all the available timber on the banks of the Missouri had been removed.

Above Fort Union, Maximilian and Bodmer transferred to another Chouteau steamboat, the *Assiniboin*, and finally to a keelboat to reach Fort McKenzie at the mouth of the Marias, the scene of Lewis and Clark's fork-in-the-river dilemma in 1805. Here Bodmer painted his memorable watercolors of the White Cliffs of the Missouri and the Blackfeet warriors. Here also Kenneth McKenzie, head trader at Fort Union, unloaded his ultimate weapon in the struggle to defeat the alcohol prohibition: his own distillery.

Since the law explicitly forbade *importing* alcohol, not *making* it, McKenzie had brazenly walked through the loophole. Fueled with Mandan corn, McKenzie's still was producing grain alcohol by the fall. Even after McKenzie's moonshine scheme was exposed by a rival trader, his boss, Pierre Chouteau, vehemently denied to Clark that any violations had been committed, conceding only that the company had conducted "experiments" to determine if "a wild Pear and Berries might be converted into wine."[73]

On February 9, 1834, Salmon P. Chase, a young lawyer in Cincinnati, stopped by a friend's house for dinner. Chase would later become a Secretary of the Treasury and Chief Justice of the Supreme Court during the Civil War; it would fall to him to swear in the new President, Andrew Johnson, after Abraham Lincoln's assassination. But on this Sunday night in 1834, Chase was a recently engaged twenty-six-year-old with wide eyes.

At the dinner table he was introduced to a traveler from the West. Chase was so struck by this man, a "Genl. Clarke," that later that night he put down a full description in his notebook:

> This gentleman resides far up the Missouri, between the State of that name & the Rocky Mountains. He was attired in a brown hunting shirt, which opened a little upon the breast. It was furnished with a small cape which was copiously fringed. A quantity of fringe also lined the back of the sleeve from the shoulder to the wrist. The skirts were also fringed. The whole was confined to the body by a crimson sash which was tied at one side and the ends hung down to the thigh. The whole dress was extremely picturesque and the whole appearance of the old veteran highly interesting. He was asked if there was a post office in his neighbourhood, & answered with perfect naiveté, that there was one about a hundred miles off to which he sent twice a month. He described several peculiar plants & flowers, & proved as interesting in conversation as he was in appearance.[74]

Chase was confused about the location of St. Louis, but his overall impression of the man was accurate. Much of Clark's appeal came from the combination of his physical vitality and his obvious intelligence, making him "as interesting in conversation as he was in appearance." In his dinner attire he combined the rugged hunting frock—the men of the expedition had similar ones—with the authority symbol of an officer's scarlet sash. George Washington had worn one that was eight feet long.

In 1834, Clark was at the height of his governmental powers, but there were some troubling personal concerns. He had always worried about money, and of late he had encountered serious difficulties. Many of them appeared to be at the hands of the Kennerly brothers, whose factoring business was beset with problems. A year earlier, William Preston Clark had cautioned his brother George, "You must not expect a fortune from our father's estate. He is using every exertion to give his children an education & will have but little to divide among them."[75]

When Chase met Clark, the superintendent was on his way to Washington to settle expense claims of $30,000 that the government had disallowed. "Uncle William I fear is much in debt," John O'Fallon wrote.

"Uncle is proud and much touch[y] on the subject of his pecuniary affairs any allusion to which wound his feeling most sensibly."[76] Without telling Clark, O'Fallon had quietly appealed for help from Cass and from Quartermaster General Thomas Jesup, the husband of his cousin Ann Croghan.

Clark stayed in Washington through the spring of 1834 to watch over a sweeping reorganization of the Indian Department. It was based almost entirely on the recommendations that he and Cass had made five years earlier. Indian territory would be defined as all lands west of the Mississippi not in a state or existing territory (clarifying Clark's jurisdiction and eventually reducing it as more states and territories were created). Accounting procedures were set up to help avoid the financial embarrassments that Clark and other agents had encountered. The War Department was given an explicit instruction to suppress wars between Indian tribes. However, a bill to create a new territory west of Arkansas and Missouri to be governed by Indians themselves—in effect, a de facto Indian state—failed.

In the closing days of 1834, Clark's health suddenly worsened. He may have had a slight stroke. James Kennerly noted in his diary that "Genl Clark is threatened with Palsy in right side tho is better today."[77] His usually faithful writing of letters and keeping of journals suddenly stopped. His large extended family began to wonder if the sixty-four-year-old general should still live in his large house. Two months later John O'Fallon worried, "The old gentleman is still quite feeble and his state of health is much impaired, so much so, that he cannot live more than a year or so unless his mind becomes more tranquilized and relieved."[78]

O'Fallon knew that the best way to relieve his uncle's mind would be to relieve his debts. He made arrangements to sell off the tract of 919 acres that Clark owned on the Indiana side of the Ohio, opposite Louisville, near the site of his and Lewis's departure for the Pacific in 1803. The sale was made by June, and O'Fallon reported "a most striking change in Uncle's spirits. As matters are now arranged, he will be able to spend two-thirds of his time at Lewis's and his plantation, by which I doubt not, that his latter days may be numbered the happiest of his life."[79]

In the summer of 1835, the aging Black Hawk appeared in St. Louis to complain to Clark about white incursions on Sauk lands west of the

Mississippi. It would have been an interesting reunion of the two old warriors. After the war, the army had escorted Black Hawk from Jefferson Barracks to Washington, where a testy Andrew Jackson reminded the Indian that "our young men are as numerous as the leaves in the woods."[80] Black Hawk was briefly imprisoned in Virginia, but after Clark and Cass appealed for his release, he was taken on a tumultuous journey through Baltimore, Philadelphia, and New York, where enthusiastic crowds gathered to gawk at the exotic warrior. He then returned on the Erie Canal to rejoin Keokuk's band near present-day Des Moines, Iowa.

Clark's assistant George Maguire was now handling more and more of the Indian Office business—issuing annuities, hiring blacksmiths, and placing advertisements for supplies for emigrating tribes. In his personal affairs, Clark relied on his domestic slaves as well as the O'Fallon and Kennerly brothers (and their families)—and a new friend, Edward Polkowski, a twenty-three-year-old Polish émigré who acted as a combination valet and companion.

Clark would soon negotiate his last treaty. In the summer of 1836, he had pointed out to Cass that both whites and Indians were occupying the rich lands around the Black Snake Hills, in what is now the northwestern corner of Missouri. Would the Sauks and Foxes, who had moved there after the Treaty of Prairie du Chien in 1830, agree to cede these lands?

In September 1836, Clark made his final trip up the Missouri to arrange this treaty. It was the farthest west he had proceeded since 1806. This time he traveled by steamboat, not on a keelboat dragged by cordelles against the powerful current. At Fort Leavenworth, he negotiated a treaty with the Iowas and the Sauks and Foxes by which they ceded two million acres to the United States in exchange for new land in Kansas and incidentals that included "one hundred cows and calves and five bulls, and one hundred stock hogs."[81]

This treaty, and a subsequent one with the Otoes, Missouris, Omahas, and Nakota and Dakota Sioux, constituted the Platte Purchase. The land acquired was so fertile that the agent Joshua Pilcher told friends that he hoped to invest in it. White settlers rushed onto the newly acquired land, displacing the Indians prematurely. The Iowas and Sauks and Foxes wound up starving on the west bank of the Missouri.

The apparatus for the last removals was completed. In the span of his public life, Clark had been a primary architect of a form of what is now called ethnic cleansing. He personally signed thirty-seven separate treaties with Indian nations, more than anyone in American history. He helped the United States extinguish Indian titles to 419 million acres of land. A total of 81,282 Indians was moved from the eastern United States to the lands west of the Mississippi; thousands more were moved out of Missouri, farther west.

His ostensible goal was not the elimination of a people, but rather the acquisition of their land. But the foreseeable consequences were just as devastating. During the years Clark lived in St. Louis, the prosperous frontier town became the leading refugee camp on the continent.

The case for removal rested upon several widely accepted assumptions. First, Indians, presumed to be culturally inferior, stood in the way of progress and were the all-too-willing foot soldiers for America's international competitors. Therefore, acquisition of their "unused" hunting grounds freed up valuable territory needed for American expansion and American security.

Second, even Americans sympathetic to the tribes thought that the removals offered the Indians their only hope of surviving as a people. Clark had particular reason to believe that the removals could eliminate the deadly conflicts between whites and Indians that had been an annual feature of his life since childhood. Relocated in the West, safe from the pernicious influence of unscrupulous traders, Indians could buy the time needed to master the white man's farming skills.

These convictions required what now seems to be a wholesale suspension of disbelief. Clark and his peers ignored the contradictory evidence that Eastern Indians were hugely successful agriculturists whose cultivated gardens and fields were equal to those of whites. Both William and George Rogers Clark had participated in military campaigns whose primary objective was to *destroy* the agricultural economy of the Indians.

Supporters of removal saw no conflict between the ruthless confiscation of Indian lands and the self-serving assertions of benevolence toward the tribes. In order to save the Indians, it would be necessary to remove them. They believed that the continuing resistance mounted by the tribes to American expansion could be best explained by the sinister machinations of the British.

Over time, Clark's attitude toward the Indians evolved, showing the same vacillations and contradictions displayed by his countrymen. In his youth, when Indians were equal to or even more powerful than whites,

Clark developed a valuable expertise in negotiating amicably with these potentially formidable foes. But after the War of 1812, when the Indians had lost their ability to play the British and Americans off against one another, the nation's attitude hardened toward the Indians, as did Clark's. His increasingly uncompromising behavior in treaty councils reflected his personal conviction that only the threat of overwhelming force could influence the tribes to see that their best interests lay in melting away before the advance of American civilization.

Within this rapacious climate Clark was, if anything, a moderating influence. Other leaders were far more ruthless. Beginning in 1804, William Henry Harrison bullied, bribed, and divided the tribes in order to force on them treaties extinguishing their title to millions of acres of land. As Secretary of War from 1831 to 1836, Lewis Cass did more than anyone with the possible exception of Andrew Jackson to carry out the Indian removals. Cass believed that the Eastern Indians were products of an irretrievably inferior culture and that their removal was morally justified since their ancestors had killed off the ancient Mississippian Mound Builders. Almost no one west of the Appalachians advocated, as Clark did, that emigrating Indians be treated with "the humain feeling of the nation."

Even though his earlier generosity to the tribes and his opposition to white squatters had cost him the Missouri governorship, Clark continued to display conspicuous compassion toward the Indians. He delayed removing peaceful tribes like the Kickapoos—an act that outraged the governor of Illinois—and stretched his budgets to feed and clothe impoverished Indians crossing the Mississippi to move west. Americans who visited Clark in St. Louis routinely commented on his kindliness toward the Indians. It was almost as if the republic's citizens shared with the Indians a deep-seated need to believe in this kindly "Red-Headed Chief." If the powerful superintendent of Indians in St. Louis was so trusted and beloved by his charges, was that not convincing proof of the benevolence of the government's policies?

The cruelties of Clark's time and the strengths of his character did not contradict one another; they lived within him. He was a man whose complexity encompassed both.

The relations between other races were also beginning to break down. The approximately eight thousand residents of St. Louis included several thousand black slaves and a much smaller number of free blacks. Threatening events such as Nat Turner's Rebellion in Virginia in 1831 had put St. Louis's slave owners on edge. On October 31, 1835, an ad hoc meeting of citizens was held at the courthouse for the purpose of organizing "Committees of Vigilance" to block the entry and activities of free blacks in St. Louis.

Clark did not attend the meeting, but it is likely that he supported it. Among those who agreed to serve on the committees were most of the town's leading citizens — Pierre Chouteau, Jr., Thomas Hart Benton, William Ashley, Dr. Bernard Farrar, and two of his sons, Meriwether Lewis Clark and William Preston Clark.[82] (Clark himself was either unwilling or, more likely, unable to attend.)

The citizens passed a series of resolutions designed "to guard our families and property against the ill consequences, which have resulted from allowing free persons of color to reside among us." The proposed restrictions would forbid the entry of free blacks into the state, prohibit any blacks from preaching in church, prohibit large groups of blacks from gathering "for any reason whatsoever," force emancipated blacks to leave the city and county, and require steamboat captains to turn over a list of any free blacks arriving on their vessels.

The citizens were particularly incensed by the presence in St. Louis of Elijah Lovejoy, a Presbyterian pastor whose newspaper, the *St. Louis Observer*, had become the region's leading abolitionist voice. Facing down regular death threats, Lovejoy continued to publish until a mob wrecked his press in July 1836. He then moved across the river to Alton, Illinois, where mobs destroyed two more of his presses. Finally, on November 7, 1837, as he was standing guard over his fourth printing press, thugs stormed his office, killed him with a shotgun blast, and threw the printing press into the Mississippi.

Against this backdrop, the events that led to the famous *Dred Scott* decision were beginning to unfold. Clark had almost certainly encountered Scott, who worked as a domestic servant at the boardinghouse run by his owner, a Virginian named Peter Blow. After Blow died in 1832, Scott was sold to John Emerson, an army surgeon at Jefferson Barracks. Emerson took him to Fort Armstrong and then Fort Snelling in Minnesota. There Scott married a woman named Harriet, who was owned by Lawrence Taliaferro, Clark's Indian agent for the Upper Mississippi.

Both Scotts were later returned to St. Louis by their then owner, John F. A. Sanford, Clark's former subagent at the Mandan villages. Scott's appeal for freedom, based on his residence in free states for seven years, bore the name *Scott v. Sanford.* Its rejection by the Supreme Court in 1857 contributed directly to the Civil War.

Clark continued to feel ill in January 1837. Anything that upset him emotionally appeared to cause his health to collapse. His grip on his responsibilities was clearly weakening. Pilcher would say later that his "infirmities and goodness of heart [had] induced an implicit reliance upon every thing recommended by his subordinates."[83] To help out, the War Department dispatched Captain Ethan Allen Hitchcock to St. Louis as disbursing officer in the Indian Office—in effect, putting him in charge of Clark's budget. The grandson of the Green Mountain Boy Ethan Allen, Hitchcock was a former commandant of cadets at West Point with a deserved reputation for integrity and compassion.

Hitchcock was at once impressed with the superintendent's "humanity & kindness, which never fails." Not long after arriving, he told his superiors in Washington how Clark had come across a group of fourteen destitute Indians who had been hired by a local museum owner to dance for the public. Clark was so offended by the spectacle that he personally "offered to furnish them means, even out of his private purse to enable them to go home, instead of doing which they are about dancing their way to Washington."[84]

Clark drew up his last will and testament on April 14, 1837.

Three days later, the steamboat *St. Peters* left St. Louis for its annual spring trip to drop off supplies at the American Fur Company's posts along the Upper Missouri River.

For years, the federal government had been concerned about the periodic outbreaks of smallpox among the Western tribes. On their journey upriver in 1804, Lewis and Clark had seen Oto and Arikara villages abandoned after earlier epidemics. Protecting the Indians' health was more than a humanitarian issue; smallpox also threatened traders and agents.

In 1832, Congress appropriated $12,000 to fund an inoculation program for "the several tribes." That summer two physicians, David Davis and Meriwether Martin, traveled on the *Yellow Stone* upriver from Leavenworth. Using the milder form of *Variola major* called cowpox, they successfully vaccinated the tribes, overcoming their initial resistance. By the fall they had vaccinated about three thousand people at a cost of $1,800—but they had not reached the Mandans or most of the Arikaras. Could they continue next spring?

The reply was no. "It is not the present intention of the Government to prosecute this business," said Commissioner of Indian Affairs Elbert Herring.[85] He suggested that the surplus funds be diverted to "aid to emigrating tribes."

Matters stood there until the 1837 voyage of the *St. Peters*. Clark first heard from Edwin James at Council Bluff that three Otoes had died of smallpox while hunting in the Potawatomis' country.

Then a chilling letter arrived from the subagent William Fulkerson at the Mandan villages: "It is with regret I have to communicate to you that the small pox had broke out in this country and is sweeping all before it—unless it be checked in its mad career I would not be surprised if it wiped the Mandans and Rickaree [Arikara] Tribes of Indians clean from the face of the earth. I also understand that its broken out among the Assinaboines and Black feet Indians where it is also causing great havoc and distress."[86]

The *St. Peters* had carried smallpox upriver to the Mandans and Arikaras, the tribes left unprotected five years earlier. As the disease flamed through the Missouri Valley, the agents frantically speculated as to its origins. A blanket stolen from an infected crewman on the *St. Peters* by an Arikara? An infected Blackfeet man who left the steamboat to return to his tribe?

Returning to St. Louis, Pilcher reported to Clark that the disease had in fact broken out on the *St. Peters* before it had passed Fort Leavenworth. A mulatto crewman was the first to show symptoms, but the captain had refused to have the man put ashore as a precaution. Pilcher sent messengers ahead to warn the Lakota Sioux to stay away from the river, "but I think it likely that [the disease] will be communicated to most of the tribes from the Platte to the Yellow Stone."[87] He would not be able to fulfill Clark's order to gather a delegation of chiefs to go to Washington, since "when they are afflicted with a disease so distructive and alarming to all Indians, it renders the execution of your orders still more embarrassing."[88] He would later report that the chiefs he had selected for the trip had in fact died.

The enormity of the scourge left Pilcher and the other agents struggling for words. "The country through which it has passed is literally depopulated and converted into <u>one great grave yard</u>," Pilcher said.

> The Mandans, consisting of 1600 souls, had been reduced by the 1st of October last to thirty-one persons. The Groventres or Minetaries a tribe about one thousand strong . . . one half perished and the disease was still raging . . . The Riccasas . . . one half of them had fallen, and the disease was raging with unabated fury, not more than one out of fifty recovering from it, and most of those that survived, subsequently committed suicide . . . some by shooting, others by stabbing, and some by throwing themselves from the high precipieces along the Missouri. The great band of Assineboine, say ten thousand strong, and the Crees numbering about three thousand have been almost annihilated.

By early 1838, "the disease had reached the Blackfeet of the Rocky Mountains."[89]

Only the nomadic Lakota Sioux had thus far escaped, protected by their far-ranging bison hunts from the epidemic that devastated more sedentary peoples living in earth lodges along the river bottoms. Pilcher proposed to go upriver to somehow find the Lakotas and inoculate them before it was too late. "It is a very delicate experiment among those wild Indians," Pilcher acknowledged to Clark, "because death from any other cause, while under the influence of vaccination, would be attributed to that and no other cause. Nevertheless, if furnished with the means, I will cheerfully risk an experiment which may preserve the lives of fifteen or twenty thousand Indians."[90]

Clark authorized Pilcher to hire a doctor, Joseph R. De Prefontaine, to join him on a search for the Lakota Sioux. In April 1837, the two men boarded Atkinson's old wheel boat, *Antelope*, retrofitted for steam, and left on their mission. At every stop along the river above Council Bluff, De Prefontaine inoculated throngs of desperate Indians, who had lost any fears of the procedure. De Prefontaine was so inundated by "the mass of men, women and children that crowded around me" that Pilcher ordered him to stop keeping records of their names and gender and simply vaccinate as many as he could.[91] When the supply of government vaccine ran out, the doctor got out his personal supply and used it up as well. The scope of the tragedy they were witnessing, Pilcher said, "no human power can estimate."[92] Although De Prefontaine fell sick while trying to locate the Lakotas near the South Platte, he ultimately vaccinated about three thousand persons.

In the spring of 1837, Clark made what would be his last trip to the East Coast. Traveling with Lewis and his wife, Abby, son William, and his Polish friend "Kosky," he went to Philadelphia and West Point and then on to New York City as an honored guest (along with the future commodore Matthew Perry) at the July 4 dinner of the Corporation of the City of New York. Back in Washington, he called on Joel Poinsett, the Secretary of War in the new Martin Van Buren Administration. He would very likely have discussed with Poinsett the Second Seminole War and the plans to remove the Cherokees from their home in Georgia. He then proceeded on to Warm Springs, Virginia, "with a view of my taking the warm baith," before returning to St. Louis in the fall.[93]

Clark arrived just as the Missouri militia was evicting the last of the Osages from the state. Acting on rumors of "depredations" in the southwestern part of Missouri, Governor Liburn Boggs, a Jacksonian who had defeated Ashley in the last election, had called up five hundred mounted riflemen to remove the Osages and some equally unfortunate Delawares and Shawnees. By December 2, there were no more Osages in Missouri.

Ethan Allen Hitchcock would later report that Clark had ruefully told him during this time that his 1808 Osage treaty "was the hardest treaty on the Indians he ever made and that if he was to be damned hereafter it would be for making that treaty."[94]

Early in 1838, Meriwether Lewis Clark and Abby moved from their two-room cottage behind the old Indian Agency Council Room into the new house they had built at Fifth and Olive Street. Soon Clark moved in with them; the general was suffering from vertigo and occasional falls. His son Jeff was sent to live with James Kennerly's family at Jefferson Barracks.

The Indian Agency Council Room had been converted into offices and the upstairs rooms opened up for rent. The first boarders in Lewis and Abby's cottage were a thirty-one-year-old West Point graduate, Robert E. Lee, his wife, Mary Custis Lee, and two of their three children. Captain Lee had been sent to St. Louis by the Army Corps of Engineers to solve river-channel problems interfering with navigation. (Abraham Lincoln would have encountered the same migrating sandbars when he passed through St. Louis on a flatboat seven years earlier.) Lee was just a year ahead of Meriwether Lewis Clark at West Point. It is certain that the Clarks would have dined with the attractive young couple from Virginia.

On July 5, 1838, James Kennerly noted in his diary that he had gone to Lewis's house to see his uncle and found the general "quite unwell."[95]

Kennerly's reports did not get better:

August 27: "Quite unwell"
August 29: "Quite sick"
August 30: "Not expected to live"

On Thursday, September 1, Ethan Allen Hitchcock wrote to Indian Commissioner Carey A. Harris, "General Clark is very near [death]. Day before yesterday he was supposed at one time to have died but he revived so as yesterday to ~~apparently~~ distinguish his friends; ~~but~~ today he does not know his own family & his demise appears to be hourly expected."[96]

William Clark died at nine o'clock that evening. At sixty-eight, he was the last of the ten Clark siblings. He had outlived his friend Meriwether Lewis by twenty-nine years.

The military funeral the following Monday was the largest St. Louis had ever seen. The procession wended from Meriwether Lewis Clark's brick house to John O'Fallon's farm four miles away. First came the St. Louis Greys militia, with their banners tightly furled with black ribbons, marching to muffled drums. The carriage with the coffin was drawn by four white horses. Next came Clark's fellow Masons, then a servant leading the General's horse, in full caparison, followed by a train of carriages and men on horseback that extended a full mile.

When the cortège reached the burial site at O'Fallon's farm, just south of the confluence of the Mississippi and the Missouri, Clark was laid to rest. Rifle volleys echoed over the rivers.

On the Upper Missouri, far out of touch with St. Louis, Joshua Pilcher continued to send in his reports. He would not learn of Clark's death until he returned downstream to Council Bluff two months later. In October, he wrote to Clark to give him the good news that he had visited tribes throughout the agency and at last was "happy to find that the <u>small pox</u> has long since disappeared."[97]

During Clark's final illness, the United States Army had begun to move the Cherokee Nation west of the Mississippi. Seventeen thousand Cherokees were herded into camps in Georgia and Tennessee and then forcibly marched a thousand miles to Indian territory in present-day Oklahoma. At least four thousand men, women, and children died along what became known as the Trail of Tears.

In 1832, the state of Ohio and the rest of the new republic prepared to celebrate the one-hundredth anniversary of the birth of George Washington. A few months before that, two brothers named McDowell had been digging on the banks of the Wabash River, near the town of Fort Recovery, Ohio, built on the site of St. Clair's Defeat in 1791. The youths were startled to come upon a small cannon buried in the mud. The cannon was one of six lost by Arthur St. Clair's artillerymen in 1791. It had lain undisturbed for forty-one years. The finders hauled the cannon to Greenville, Ohio, where it was rubbed and polished to a surprising brightness.

Then, on George Washington's one-hundredth birthday, many of the hundred citizens of Greenville gathered to watch it primed with gunpowder.

The first shot, a four-pound ball, was fired at a large burr oak tree about 150 yards away. It missed. The next two shots also missed. But a fourth was fired, which struck the oak about twelve feet from the ground. Eyewitnesses said that the shot split the tree exactly in half, opening a fissure running fifteen feet up the trunk from the point of impact and down to its roots. The boys and men tried to pry the ball free to continue the shooting. But they finally gave up. The ball was buried too deeply in the wood to be retrieved.

NOTES

ABBREVIATIONS USED IN NOTES

ASP/IA
American State Papers, Class II, Indian Affairs, 2 vols. (Washington, D.C.: Gales and Seaton, 1832–1861)

Draper
Collected by Lyman Copeland Draper. Archives Division, State Historical Society of Wisconsin, Madison. Includes the papers of Jonathan Clark and William Clark.

FHS
Filson Historical Society, Louisville, Ky.

GRC
George Rogers Clark

GRC Papers (Draper)
George Rogers Clark Papers. In the Lyman Copeland Draper Manuscripts, Archives Division, State Historical Society of Wisconsin, Madison.

KSHS
Kansas State Historical Society, Topeka

MHS
Missouri Historical Society, St. Louis

ML
Meriwether Lewis

MLC
Meriwether Lewis Clark

MLC Papers
Meriwether Lewis Clark Papers. In the Clark Family Papers, Missouri Historical Society, St. Louis.

TJ
Thomas Jefferson

WC
William Clark

WC Papers (Draper)
William Clark Papers. In the Lyman Copeland Draper Manuscripts, Archives Division, State Historical Society of Wisconsin, Madison.

WC Papers (KSHS)
William Clark Papers. 34 vols. Kansas State Historical Society, Topeka.

WC Papers (MHS)
William Clark Papers. In the Clark Family Papers, Missouri Historical Society, St. Louis.

WHMC
Western Historical Manuscripts Collection, Ellis Library, University of Missouri, Columbia. Includes William Clark journal for 1798 and notebook for 1798–1801.

PROLOGUE: A DARK AND BLOODY GROUND

1. Capt. Buntin to Arthur St. Clair, *Annals of the West*, ed. James H. Perkins (Pittsburgh: James R. Albach, 1858), 598.

2. Winthrop Sargent, 1 February 1792, "Winthrop Sargent's Diary," *Ohio Archaeological and Historical Quarterly* 33, no. 3 (1924): 272.

3. Diary of Maj. Ebenezer Denny, 7 November 1791, in *The St. Clair Papers: The Life and Public Services of Arthur St. Clair*, ed. William H. Smith (Cincinnati: Robert Clarke, 1882), 2:262.

4. St. Clair to Knox, 19 July 1791, 8 August 1791, *St. Clair Papers*, in Wiley Sword, *President Washington's Indian War* (Norman: University of Oklahoma Press, 1985), 152.

5. William David Butler, *The Butler Family in America* (St. Louis, 1909), in Sword, *President Washington's Indian War*, 161.

6. Denny Diary, 30 October 1791, *St. Clair Papers*, 2:257.

7. Clarence M. Burton, ed., *Michigan Pioneer and Historical Collections*, 2d ed., 40 vols., 24:331, Lansing, 1877–1929, in Sword, *President Washington's Indian War*, 169.

8. Denny Diary, in *St. Clair Papers*, 2:257; Sargent, 31 October 1791, "Sargent's Diary," 251.

9. St. Clair to Knox, 21 October 1791, Henry Knox Papers (microfilm), University of Michigan Graduate Library, Ann Arbor, in Sword, *President Washington's Indian War*, 168.

10. Burton, *Michigan Pioneer*, 24:332, in Sword, *President Washington's Indian War*, 168–69.

11. Denny Diary, 4 November 1791, in *St. Clair Papers*, 2:258.

12. Testimony of Capt. Slough, in *St. Clair Papers*, 2:634–35.

13. Sargent, "Sargent's Diary," 258.

14. Ibid., 259.

15. Account of Benjamin Van Cleve, in Perkins, *Annals of the West*, 584.

16. Denny Diary, in *St. Clair Papers*, 260.

17. Sargent, "Sargent's Diary," 265.

18. Account of Maj. Jacob Fowler, *Historical Collections of Ohio* (Columbus, Ohio: Henry Howe, 1891), 2:489.

19. Sargent, "Sargent's Diary," 268–69.

20. Gen. St. Clair to Secretary of War, 9 November 1791, *St. Clair Papers*, 2:262–67.

21. Account of Jackson to Johonnet, 12 July 1826, *People's Press and Exposition* (Xenia, Ohio), in *The Archaeology of Fort Recovery, Ohio*, Occasional Monographs of the Upper Miami Valley Archaeological Research Museum, no. 6 (Arcanum, Ohio, 1996), 53.

22. Account of Benjamin Van Cleve, in Perkins, 584–85.

23. Emilius O. Randall and Daniel J. Ryan, *History of Ohio* (New York: Century History Company, 1912), 541.

1. AMERICA'S FIRST WEST: 1722–1772

1. Thomas Jefferson, *Autobiography*, in Donald Jackson, *Thomas Jefferson and the Stony Mountains: Exploring the West from Monticello* (Norman: University of Oklahoma Press, 1993), 21.

2. Daniel K. Richter, *Facing East from Indian Country: A Native History of Early America* (Cambridge: Harvard University Press, 2001), 174, quoting Kathryn E. Holland Braund, *Deerskins and Duffels* (Lincoln: University of Nebraska Press, 1993), 30.

3. John Mack Faragher, *Daniel Boone: The Life and Legend of an American Pioneer* (New York: Holt, 1992), 43–44.

4. Ibid., 22.

5. Bakeless Papers, New York Public Library. Notes for unpublished book called *How They Lived*.

6. *The Journal of Nicholas Cresswell, 1774–1777* (London: Jonathan Cape, 1925), 49.

7. John Mack Faragher and Robert V. Hine, *The American West: A New Interpretive History* (New Haven: Yale University Press, 2000), 71–99.

8. Jane T. Merritt, "Metaphor, Meaning, and Misunderstanding: Language and Power on the Pennsylvania Frontier," in *Contact Points: American Frontiers from the Mohawk Valley to the Mississippi, 1750–1830*, ed. Andrew R. L. Cayton and Fredrika J. Teute (Chapel Hill: University of North Carolina Press, 1998), 60–87.

9. Elizabeth A. Perkins, "Distinctions and Partitions amongst Us: Identity and Interaction in the Revolutionary Ohio Valley," in *Contact Points*, 232–33.

10. Alden T. Vaughan, "From White Man to Redskin: Changing Anglo-American Perceptions of the American Indians," *American Historical Review* 87, no. 4 (1982): 925.

11. Sir Walter Raleigh, *The Discoveries of the Large, Rich, and Bewtiful Empire of Guiana* (London, 1596), ibid., 922.

12. William Wood, *New Englands Prospect* (London, 1634), 62–63, in Karen Ordahl Kupperman, *Indians and English: Facing Off in Early America* (Ithaca: Cornell University Press, 2000), 58.

13. Vaughan, "White Man to Redskin," 948.

14. Quoted in "British Administrative Policy," in *The New Encyclopedia of the American West*, ed. Howard Lamar (New Haven: Yale University Press, 1998).

15. John Edwin Bakeless, *Background to Glory: The Life of George Rogers Clark* (Lincoln: University of Nebraska Press, 1992), 21–22.

16. Stephen Aron, *How the West Was Lost: The Transformation of Kentucky from Daniel Boone to Henry Clay* (Baltimore: Johns Hopkins University Press, 1996), 6.

2. GENERAL GEORGE ROGERS CLARK: 1772–1789

1. Journal of David Jones, Draper 1-L-9, in John Edwin Bakeless, *Background to Glory: The Life of George Rogers Clark* (Lincoln: University of Nebraska Press, 1992), 22.

2. Francis Baily, *Journal of a Tour in Unsettled Parts of North America in 1796 & 1797*, ed. Jack D. L. Holmes (Carbondale and Edwardsville: Southern Illinois University, 1969), 82.

3. Draper 1-J-52–53, 1-L-8, in Bakeless, *Background to Glory*, 22.

4. John A. Jakle, *Images of the Ohio Valley: A Historical Geography of Travel, 1740 to 1860* (New York: Oxford University Press, 1977), 104.

5. GRC to Samuel Brown, 17 June 1798, papers of TJ, 30:512–15.

6. Quoted in Thomas Jefferson, *Notes on the State of Virginia* (New York: Penguin Books, 1999), 67–68.

7. Jefferson, *Notes on Virginia*, 67. Despite Clark's correction that it was Greathouse, not Cresap, who killed Logan's family, Jefferson never made the correction.

8. See Elizabeth A. Perkins, *Border Life: Experience and Memory in the Revolutionary Ohio Valley* (Chapel Hill: University of North Carolina Press, 1998), 58.

9. *The Journal of Nicholas Cresswell, 1774–1777* (London: Jonathan Cape, 1925), 70–72.

10. William Fleming, "Journal" (1780), in John Mack Faragher, *Daniel Boone: The Life and Legend of an American Pioneer* (New York: Holt, 1992), 166.

11. Draper 1-L-23, in Bakeless, *Background to Glory*, 31.

12. Dragging Canoe paraphrased in John Haywood, *The Civil and Political History of the State of Tennessee* (1803), in Faragher, *Daniel Boone*, 112.

13. GRC to Jonathan Clark, 26 February 1776, FHS.

14. *Journal of Cresswell*, 78.

15. A Kentuckian quoted in Andrew R. L. Cayton, *Frontier Indiana* (Bloomington: Indiana University Press, 1996), 82.

16. GRC, *George Rogers Clark Papers, 1771–1781*, ed. James Alton James, 2 vols. (Springfield, 1912), *Collections of the Illinois State Historical Library, Virginia Series*, vol. 3, 210.

17. John Dabney Shane interview with Jacob Stevens, Draper 12-CC-48, in Perkins, *Border Life*, 136.

18. Speech of Cornstalk, 7 November 1776, Morgan Letterbook (1776), quoted in Colin G. Calloway, *The American Revolution in Indian Country: Crisis and Diversity in Native American Communities* (Cambridge and New York: Cambridge University Press, 1995), 166.

19. Ibid.

20. R. Douglas Hurt, *The Ohio Frontier: Crucible of the Old Northwest, 1720–1830* (Bloomington: Indiana University Press, 1969), 66.

21. Gen. Edward Hand to Jasper Yeates, 24 December 1777, in Reuben Gold Thwaites and Louise P. Kellogg, eds., *Frontier Defense on the Upper Ohio*, 188, quoted in Stephen Aron, *How the West Was Lost: The Transformation of Kentucky from Daniel Boone to Henry Clay* (Baltimore: John Hopkins University Press, 1996), 41. See also Calloway, *American Revolution in Indian Country*, 168.

22. TJ to GRC, 3 January 1778, in *The Papers of Thomas Jefferson*, ed. Julian P. Boyd et al., 30 vols. to date (Princeton: Princeton University Press, 1950–), 2:132–33.

23. George Rogers Clark, *The Conquest of the Illinois*, ed. Milo M. Quaife (Chicago: R. R. Donnelley and Sons, 1920), 34.

24. Clothing description from "How It Was," unpublished manuscript, John Edwin Bakeless Papers, Series 2 (Writings), boxes 21–22, Manuscripts and Archives Division, New York Public Library (hereafter Bakeless Papers).

25. Clark, *Conquest of the Illinois*, 41–42.

26. Ibid., 39.

27. Ibid., 69–70.

28. Ibid., 71–75.

29. Ibid., 113.

30. GRC to Patrick Henry, 3 February 1779, *George Rogers Clark Papers*, 98, quoted in *Papers of Thomas Jefferson*, 2:246.

31. Clark, *Conquest of the Illinois*, 116–17.

32. Ibid., 119.

33. Clark, *Conquest of the Illinois*, 132.

34. George Rogers Clark, *Col. George Rogers Clark's Sketch of His Campaign in the Illinois in 1778–9* (1869, rpt. New York: Arno Press, 1971), 105–6.

35. Ibid., 106.

36. Ibid., 73.

37. "Governor Hamilton's Report," in George Rogers Clark, *The Capture of Old Vincennes, The Original Narratives of George Rogers Clark and of His Opponent Gov. Henry Hamilton*, ed. Milo M. Quaife (Indianapolis: Bobbs-Merrill, 1927), 196.

38. GRC to Patrick Henry, 29 April 1779, *Papers of Thomas Jefferson*, 2:256.

39. June 15, 1779, *George Rogers Clark Papers*, 336.

40. James Alton James, *The Life of George Rogers Clark* (Chicago: University of Chicago Press, 1928), 204.

41. James, *George Rogers Clark Papers*, 144, 167, 189, quoted in Calloway, *American Revolution in Indian Country*, 48.

42. "Governor Hamilton's Report," Clark, *Capture of Old Vincennes*, 200.

43. TJ to GRC, 1 January 1780, *Papers of Thomas Jefferson*, 3:259. The editors of *The Papers of Thomas Jefferson* note that in his draft of this letter, Jefferson had first written, then deleted: "I think the most important object which can be proposed with such a force is the extermination of those hostile tribes of Indians who live between the Ohio and Illinois who have harassed us with eternal hostilities, and whom experience has shewn to be incapable of reconciliation. The Shawanese, Mingos, Munsies and Wiandots can never be relied on as friends, and therefore the object of the war should be their total extinction, or their removal beyond the lakes of the Illinois river and peace."

44. Henry Wilson account in Hurt, *Ohio Frontier*, 57–58.

45. Ibid., 85.

46. Ibid., 67.

47. John Shane interview with William Clinkenbeard, c. 1840s, Draper 11-CC-66, in Perkins, *Border Life*, 89.

48. GRC to TJ, 22 August 1780, *Papers of Thomas Jefferson*, 3:561.

49. Josiah Herndon to Jonathan Clark, 23 October 1779, Draper 1-L.

50. TJ to Virginia Delegates in Congress, 18 January 1781, *Papers of Thomas Jefferson*, 4:398–400.

51. John Floyd to TJ, 16 April 1781, ibid., 5:467.

52. Lowell H. Harrison, *George Rogers Clark and the War in the West* (Lexington: University Press of Kentucky, 1976), 81.

53. *Calendar of Virginia State Papers*, 3:337, ibid., 90.

54. Daniel K. Richter, *Facing East from Indian Country: A Native History of Early America* (Cambridge, Mass.: Harvard University Press, 2001), 222–23, quoting C. Hale Sipe, *The Indian Wars of Pennsylvania, of the French and Indian War, Pontiac's War, Lord Dunmore's War, The Revolutionary War and the Indian Uprising from 1789 to 1795* (Harrisburg, Pa.: Telegraph Press, 1929), 650.

55. Emily Foster, ed., *The Ohio Frontier: An Anthology of Early Writings* (Lexington: University Press of Kentucky, 1996), 66–67.

56. Daniel Drake, *Pioneer Life in Kentucky, 1785–1800*, ed. Emmet F. Horine (New York: Henry Schuman, 1948), 26–27, in Daniel Blake Smith, "This Idea in Heaven," in *The Buzzel about Kentuck: Settling the Promised Land*, ed. Craig Thompson Friend (Lexington: University Press of Kentucky, 1999), 92.

57. J.D.F. Smith, *A Tour of the United States of America*, 2 vols. (London, 1784), 1:345–46, in Alden T. Vaughan, "From White Man to Redskin: Changing Anglo-American Perceptions of the American Indians," *American Historical Review* 87, no. 4 (1982): 942.

58. W. H. Bogart, *Daniel Boone, and the Hunters of Kentucky* (1875); Boston: Lee and Shepard, Publishers, 125.

59. "Journal of Daniel Boone," *Ohio Archaeological and Historical Publications* 13 (1904): 276, in Calloway, *American Revolution in Indian Country*, 54.

60. TJ to GRC, 26 November 1782, *Papers of Thomas Jefferson*, 6:204–5.

61. Benjamin Harrison to GRC, 2 July 1783, *George Rogers Clark Papers*, 246.

62. Quoted in Frederick Palmer, *Clark of the Ohio: A Life of George Rogers Clark* (New York: Dodd, Mead and Company, 1929), 52.

63. 3 November 1783, Jonathan Clark Diary, FHS.

64. TJ to GRC, 4 December 1783, *Letters of the Lewis and Clark Expedition, with Related Documents, 1783–1854*, ed. Donald Jackson (Urbana and Chicago: University of Illinois Press, 1978), 2:654–55.

3 · LIEUTENANT BILLY CLARK: 1789–1795

1. GRC to TJ, 8 February 1784, *Letters of the Lewis and Clark Expedition, with Related Documents, 1783–1854*, ed. Donald Jackson (Urbana and Chicago: University of Illinios Press, 1978), 2:655–56.

2. GRC to Gov. Harrison, 18 February 1782, Clark MSS, Virginia State Library, in *George Rogers Clark Papers*, ed. James Alton James, 2 vols. (Springfield: Illinois State Historical Library, 1912), 260.

3. Indian delegation in St. Louis, *Spain in the Mississippi Valley*, vol. 3, pt. 2:117, in Colin G. Calloway, *The American Revolution in Indian Country: Crisis and Diversity in Native American Communities* (Cambridge and New York: Cambridge University Press, 1995), 281.

4. "John D. Shane's Interview with Benjamin Allen," *Filson Club History Quarterly* 5 (1931): 65, in Daniel Blake Smith, "This Idea in Heaven," in *The Buzzel about Kentuck: Settling the Promised Land*, ed. Craig Thompson Friend (Lexington: University Press of Kentucky, 1999), 88.

5. John D. Shane interview with Col. John Graves [c. 1845], Draper 12-CC-54, Elizabeth A. Perkins, *Border Life: Experience and Memory in the Revolutionary Ohio Valley* (Chapel Hill: University of North Carolina Press, 1998), 60.

6. Nicholas Meriwether to William Meriwether, 7 August 1784, FHS.

7. Diary of Dr. John Croghan, Draper 10-J-230, in Ludie J. Kinkead, "How the Parents of George Rogers Clark Came to Kentucky in 1784–85," *Filson Club Quarterly* 3 (October 1928): 3.

8. Francis Baily, *Journal of a Tour in Unsettled Parts of North America in 1796 & 1797*, ed. Jack D. L. Holmes (Carbondale and Edwardsville: Southern Illinois University, 1969), 120.

9. William Croghan to GRC, 19 November 1785, Draper 1-L.

10. Temple Bodley, *George Rogers Clark: His Life and Public Services* (Boston and New York: Houghton Mifflin, 1926), 273.

11. John Clark to Jonathan Clark, 29 March 1786, Draper 2-L.

12. John May to Patrick Henry, 14 July 1786, Palmer, *Virginia State Papers*, 4:157, 166, in Wiley Sword, *President Washington's Indian War: The Struggle for the Old Northwest, 1790–1795* (Norman: University of Oklahoma Press, 1985), 33.

13. Ibid.

14. WC, Journal of Hardin's Campaign, 5 August 1789–5 March 1790, WC Papers (MHS).

15. Knox to Harmar, ASP/IA, 1:97.

16. Quoted in William B. Skelton, *An American Profession of Arms: The Army Officer Corps, 1784–1815* (Lawrence: University Press of Kansas, 1992), 306.

17. Knox to Harmar, Draper 2-W-324, 330, quoted in Sword, *President Washington's Indian War*, 95, 121.

18. Colonial Office Records, Public Archives of Canada, Q Series, in Sword, *President Washington's Indian War*, 99.

19. TJ to Harry Innes, 7 March 1791, *The Papers of Thomas Jefferson*, ed. Julian P. Boyd et al., 30 vols. to date (Princeton: Princeton University Press, 1950–), 19:521.

20. Innes to TJ, 30 May 1791, ibid., 20:480–81.

21. WC, Journal of Scott's Expedition, in WC Papers (MHS).

22. "Expeditions of Generals Scott and Wilkinson in May and August, 1791," in Samuel L. Metcalfe, comp., *A Collection of Some of the Most Interesting Narratives of Indian Warfare in the West . . .* (Lexington, Ky.: Printed by W. G. Hunt, 1821), 112.

23. 3 June 1791, WC, Journal of Scott's Expedition (MHS).

24. Metcalfe, 117.

25. Harry M. Ward, *Charles Scott and the "Spirit of '76"* (Charlottesville: University Press of Virginia, 1988), 114.

26. GRC Papers (Draper), 2-L-28, quoted in Jay H. Buckley, "William Clark: Superintendent of Indian Affairs at St. Louis, 1813–1838" (Ph.D. diss., University of Nebraska, Lincoln, 2001).

27. 26 July 1791, WC, Journal of Wilkinson's Expedition, in WC Papers (Draper), series J, Draper MSS.

28. Gen. Wilkinson to Gov. St. Clair, Metcalfe, *Narratives*, 127.

29. 12 August 1791, Journal, WC Papers (Draper), series J.

30. Wilkinson to Gov. St. Clair, Metcalfe, *Narratives*, 127.

31. Ibid., 123.

32. 10 August 1791, Journal, WC Papers (Draper), series J.

33. Opinion of the General Officers, undated, in Ward, *Charles Scott*, 120.

34. Washington to Gov. Henry Lee, 30 June 1792, in Glenn Tucker, *Mad Anthony Wayne and the New Nation: The Story of Washington's Front-Line General* (Harrisburg, Pa.: Stackpole Books, 1973), 226.

35. William Clark's Journal and Memo Book, 1792, WC Papers (MHS).

36. Knox to Wayne, 20 July 1792, in *Anthony Wayne, a Name in Arms: Soldier, Diplomat, Defender of Expansion Westward of a Nation; The Wayne-Knox-Pickering-McHenry Correspondence*, ed. Richard C. Knopf (Pittsburgh: University of Pittsburgh Press, 1960), 42.

37. WC to Jonathan Clark, 2 September 1792, in *Dear Brother: Letters of William Clark to Jonathan Clark*, ed. James J. Holmberg (New Haven: Yale University Press, 2002), 19.

38. 24 November 1792, Journal and Memorandum Book of William Clark, 1792–94, MHS.

39. 29 November 1792, ibid.

40. 10–12 December 1792, ibid.

41. 15–17 December 1792, ibid.

42. Ibid.

43. 3 February 1793, WC Journal, 1792–94, MHS.

44. Abraham P. Nasatir, ed., *Before Lewis and Clark: Documents Illustrating the History of the Missouri, 1785–1804*, 2 vols. (Lincoln: University of Nebraska Press, 1990), 1:135–42.

45. 31 March 1793, WC Journal, 1792–94, MHS.

46. 2 June 1792, ibid.

47. 3 June 1792, ibid.

48. 15 April–15 May 1792, ibid.

49. Wayne to Knox, 9 May 1793, in *Anthony Wayne, a Name in Arms*, 234–35.

50. Wayne to Knox, 29 April 1793, ibid., 231–33.

51. Wayne to Knox, 9 May 1793, ibid., 234–35.

52. Baily, *Journal*, 142–43.

53. Talk of the Chickasaw Chiefs at Silver Bluffs, Clements Library, McHenry Papers, in Calloway, *American Revolution in Indian Country*, 241.

54. Wayne to Knox, 20 June 1793, in *Anthony Wayne, a Name in Arms*, 246–47.

55. Alexander MacKenzie, *Alexander Mackenzie's Voyage to the Pacific Ocean in 1793, with Historical Introduction and footnotes by Milo Milton Quaife* (New York: Citadel Press, 1967), 311.

56. Wayne to Knox, 8 August 1793, ibid., 263.

57. Wayne to Knox, 17 September 1793, ibid., 272–75.

58. Wayne to O'Fallon, 16 September 1793, Draper 54-J-23.

59. WC to Jonathan Clark, 25 May 1794, Draper 2-L.

60. 4 January 1794, WC Journal, 1792–94, MHS.

61. 19 February 1794, ibid.

62. Ibid.

63. 28 February 1794, 3 March 1794, WC Journal, 1792–94, MHS.

64. 16 April 1794, ibid.

65. 1–30 April 1794, ibid.

66. Wayne, Public Order of the Commander-in-Chief, 17 May 1794, in *Kentucky Gazette*, 31 May 1794, cited in Buckley, "William Clark."

67. WC to Jonathan Clark, 25 May 1794, Jonathan Clark Papers, Draper 2-L.

68. 30–31 July 1794, "William Clark's Journal of General Wayne's Campaign," *Mississippi Valley Historical Review* 1, no. 3 (1914): 420–21.

69. 3 August 1794, ibid., 422.

70. 4 August 1794, ibid., 423.

71. 7 August 1794, ibid., 423.

72. Wayne to Knox, 14 August 1794, ASP/IA, 1:490.

73. 9 August 1794, "Clark's Journal of Wayne's Campaign," 424.

74. WC to Jonathan Clark, 18 August 1794, Draper 2-L.

75. 12 August 1794, "Clark's Journal of Wayne's Campaign," 425.

76. 20 August 1794, ibid., 430.

77. Quoted in Glenn Tucker, *Tecumseh: Vision of Glory* (New York: Russell & Russell, 1973), 69–71, 300.

78. 21 August 1794, "Clark's Journal of Wayne's Campaign," 430.

79. 18 August 1794, ibid., 427.

80. WC to Jonathan Clark, 18 August 1794, Draper 2-L.

81. C. B. Brown, ed., *A View of the Soil and Climate of the United States by C. F. Volney* (1804; rpt., New York, 1968), 382, quoted in Calloway, *American Revolution in Indian Country*, 289.

82. Wilkinson to Brown, 28 August 1794, Wilkinson Papers, Chicago Historical Society, quoted in Sword, *President Washington's Indian War*, 282.

83. Wayne to Knox, 29 January 1795, *Anthony Wayne, a Name in Arms*, 383.

84. 25 August 1794, "Clark's Journal of Wayne's Campaign," 433.

85. 8 October 1794, ibid., 441.

86. 22 October 1794, ibid., 444.

87. 24 September 1794, ibid., 439.

88. WC to Edmund Clark, 23 November 1794, Jonathan Clark Papers, Draper 2-L.

89. WC to Jonathan Clark, 25 November 1794, ibid.

90. Ibid.

91. WC to Fanny Clark O'Fallon, 1 June 1795, *Dear Brother*, 273.

92. Frazer E. Wilson, *Around the Council Fire: Proceedings at Fort Greene Ville in 1795, Culminating in the Signing of the Treaty of Greene Ville* (Mt. Vernon, Ind.: Windmill Publications, 1990), 29.

93. Wayne to Pickering, 8 March 1795, *Anthony Wayne, a Name in Arms*, 386–91.

94. Burton, *Michigan Pioneer*, 34:736, quoted in Sword, *President Washington's Indian War*, 318.

95. Wayne to Knox, 12 February 1795, *Anthony Wayne, a Name in Arms*, 384–85.

96. Wilson, *Around the Council Fire*, 31.

97. Richard C. Knopf, ed., *A Surgeon's Mate at Fort Defiance* (Columbus, Ohio, 1957), quoted in Andrew R. L. Cayton, "Power and Civility in the Treaty of Greenville," in *Contact Points: American Frontiers from the Mohawk Valley to the Mississippi, 1750–1830*, ed. Andrew R. L. Cayton and Fredrika J. Teute (Chapel Hill: University of North Carolina Press, 1998), 257.

98. *The Correspondence of Lt. Gov. John Graves Simcoe*, ed. E. A. Cruikshank and A. F. Hunter (Toronto, 1923–31), 2:334, in Sword, *President Washington's Indian War*, 278.

99. Quoted in Harvey Lewis Carter, *The Life and Times of Little Turtle: First Sagamore of the Wabash* (Urbana: University of Illinois Press, 1987), 149.

100. Wilson, *Around the Council Fire*, 48.

101. Ibid., 65.

102. Ibid., 70.

103. See Richter, *Facing East from Indian Country*, 135–37, for an analysis of these rituals.

104. Samuel Gardner Drake, *Book of Indians of North America* (Boston, 1834), 56–57, in Sword, *President Washington's Indian War*, 335.

4. SOLDIER AND CITIZEN: 1795–1803

1. James O'Fallon to Fanny O'Fallon, 23 November 1793, Draper 2-M-47.

2. John Clark to Jonathan Clark, 9 February 1795, Draper 2-L-39.

3. WC to Fanny, 9 May 1795, *Dear Brother: Letters of William Clark to Jonathan Clark*, ed. James J. Holmberg (New Haven: Yale University Press, 2002), 269.

4. Ibid.

5. Wayne to Pickering, 3 September 1795, in *Anthony Wayne, a Name in Arms: Soldier, Diplomat, Defender of Expansion Westward of a Nation; The Wayne-Knox-Pickering-McHenry Correspondence*, ed. Richard C. Knopf (Pittsburgh: University of Pittsburgh Press, 1960), 454.

6. Ibid.

7. WC, 29 September 1795, ed. Samuel W. Thomas, "William Clark's 1795 and 1797 Journals and Their Significance," *Bulletin of the Missouri Historical Society* 25, no. 4, pt. 1 (July 1969): 280.

8. Transcript of a contemporary copy of a report to Major General Wayne on descent of Ohio with dispatches to New Madrid, 4 November 1795, WC Papers (MHS).

9. American Historical Association, *Annual Report for 1896*, 1092.

10. Clark's Report to Wayne, MHS.

11. Ibid.

12. Clark Report, Voorhis Collection, MHS.

13. TJ to André Michaux, 30 April 1793, *Letters of the Lewis and Clark Expedition, with Related Documents, 1783–1854*, ed. Donald Jackson (Urbana and Chicago: University of Illinois Press, 1978), 2:669–72.

14. Ibid.
15. American Historical Association, *Annual Report for 1896*, 995–96, quoted in Lawrence Kinnaird, ed., *Annual Report of the American Historical Association for 1945*, vol. 4, "Spain in the Mississippi Valley," pt. 3, "Problems of Frontier Defense," xxiii.
16. "André Michaux's Travels into Kentucky, 1793–96," in *Early Western Travels, 1748–1846*, ed. Reuben Gold Thwaites, vol. 3 (Cleveland: Arthur H. Clark, 1904), 65–66, 89–90.
17. Clark's Report to Wayne, pen-and-ink sketch plan of Fort St. Ferdinand at Chickasaw Bluffs, MHS.
18. Pickering to Wayne, 7 November 1795, *Anthony Wayne, a Name in Arms*, 467.
19. Wayne to Pickering, 12 November 1795, ibid., 471.
20. General Orders, Fort Greenville, 16 November 1795, National Archives, Record Group 94, 106–08, Records of the Adjutant General's Office, 1780–1917, Courts-Martial Orders 1792–1799, quoted in E. G. Chuinard, "The Court-Martial of Ensign Meriwether Lewis," *We Proceeded On* 8, no. 4 (November 1982): 12–15.
21. William B. Skelton, *An American Profession of Arms: The Army Officer Corps, 1784–1815* (Lawrence: University Press of Kansas, 1992), 55.
22. Chuinard, "Court-Martial of Ensign Lewis," 15.
23. GRC to WC, June 1796, GRC Papers, MHS.
24. GRC to Jonathan Clark, 11 May 1792, W. H. English, *Conquest of the Country Northwest of the River Ohio, 1778–83*, in *George Rogers Clark Papers*, ed. James Alton James, 2 vols. (Springfield: Illinois State Historical Library, 1912), 417–18.
25. WC to Edmund, 18 August 1797, Draper 2-L-45.
26. GRC to WC, 1 September 1797, WC Papers (MHS).
27. WC, 9 September 1797, "William Clark's 1795 and 1797 Journals," 291.
28. WC, 10 September 1797, ibid., 292.
29. Ibid.
30. WC, 12–18 September 1797, ibid., 292.
31. WC to Edmund Clark, 14 December 1797, Draper 2-L.
32. Quoted in David J. Weber, *The Spanish Frontier in North America* (New Haven: Yale University Press, 1992), 290.
33. WC Notebook, 1798–1801, WHMC. Unless otherwise indicated, all of Clark's subsequent journal entries in this chapter are from his 1798–1801 notebook in the Western Historical Manuscripts Collection.
34. Charles Dickens, *American Notes and Pictures from Italy* (London: Oxford University Press, 1957), 171.
35. WC 1798 Journal, undated entry. This courier was not Meriwether Lewis, then an army paymaster in Charlottesville. It was most likely another Virginian, Captain Thomas Lewis.
36. John Bradbury, "Travels in the Interior of America: In the Years 1809, 1810, and 1811," in *Early Western Travels*, vol. 5 (1904), 211.
37. Clark to Biddle, 15 August 1811, *Letters of the Expedition*, 2:571.
38. Francis Baily, *Journal of a Tour in Unsettled Parts of North America in 1796 & 1797*, ed. Jack D. L. Holmes (Carbondale and Edwardsville: Southern Illinois University, 1969), 25.
39. Ibid., 272.
40. 6 June 1799, Draper 2-L-50.
41. Quoted in *George Rogers Clark Papers*, 445.
42. William to Jonathan, 30 July 1799, Draper 2-L-51.
43. John Clark's Will, 26 July 1799, typescript in WC Papers (MHS).

44. After his regular army duty, Clark was commissioned on May 28, 1800, as a captain of a troop of cavalry in the Jefferson County militia, First Regiment, Kentucky Militia.

45. Stephen Ambrose, *Undaunted Courage: Meriwether Lewis, Thomas Jefferson, and the Opening of the American West* (New York: Simon and Schuster, 1996), 63, citing TJ to Martha Jefferson Randolph, *The Family Letters of Thomas Jefferson*, ed. Edwin Morris Betts and James Adam Bear, Jr. (1966; rpt., Charlottesville: University Press of Virginia, 1986), 202.

46. *Jefferson's Memorandum Books: Accounts, with Legal Records and Miscellany, 1767–1826*, ed. James Adam Bear, Jr., and Lucia C. Stanton (Princeton: Princeton University Press, 1997), 2:1062 n. 33.

47. ML to WC, 27 June 1801, WC Papers (MHS).

48. WC to Jonathan Clark, 13 August 1801, *Dear Brother*, 30–31.

49. WC to Biddle, 15 August 1811, *Letters of the Expedition*, 2:571.

50. George Dangerfield, *Chancellor Robert R. Livingston of New York, 1746–1813* (New York, 1960), 309–11, in Jon Kukla, *A Wilderness So Immense: The Louisana Purchase and the Destiny of America* (New York: Knopf, 2003), 238.

51. WC to Jonathan Clark, 4 February 1802, *Dear Brother*, 40–41.

52. TJ to Robert R. Livingston, 18 April 1802, *State Papers and Correspondence Bearing upon the Purchase of the Territory of Louisiana* (Washington, D.C.: U.S. Congress, 1903), 15–16, in Kukla, *A Wilderness So Immense*, 232.

53. GRC to TJ, 12 December 1802, *Letters of the Expedition*, 7–8.

54. Jefferson's Message to Congress, 18 January 1803, ibid., 1:10–13.

55. Livingston to James Madison, 11 April 1803, *Papers of James Madison: Secretary of State Series*, ed. Robert J. Brugger, Mary A. Hackett, David B. Mattern, et al. (Charlottesville, 1986–), 4:500–02, in Kukla, *A Wilderness So Immense*, 269.

56. Hurst to WC, 25 June 1803, WC Papers (MHS).

57. *Dear Brother*, 99 n. 16.

58. Josiah Espy, 1805, quoted in Frederick Palmer, *Clark of the Ohio: A Life of George Rogers Clark* (New York: Dodd, Mead and Company, 1929), 461.

59. ML to WC, 19 June 1803, *Letters of the Expedition*, 1:57–60.

60. WC to ML, 18 July 1803, ibid., 1.

5. "Ocian in view! O! the joy!": 1803–1806

1. WC to ML, 24 July 1803, *Letters of the Lewis and Clark Expedition, with Related Documents, 1783–1854*, ed. Donald Jackson (Urbana and Chicago: University of Illinois Press, 1978), 1:112–13.

2. ML to WC, 3 August 1803, ibid., 1:115–17.

3. ML to TJ, 22 July 1803, ibid., 1:111–12.

4. ML to WC, 28 September 1803, ibid., 1:112–13.

5. *A Journey through the West: Thomas Rodney's 1803 Journal from Delaware to the Mississippi Territory*, ed. Dwight L. Smith and Ray Swick (Athens: Ohio University Press, 1997), 50.

6. Ibid., 53.

7. WC to ML, 21 August 1803, *Letters of the Expedition*, 1:117.

8. WC to ML, 11 September 1803, ibid., 1:123.

9. ML, 10 September 1803, *Journals of the Lewis and Clark Expedition*, ed. Gary E. Moulton, 13 vols. (Lincoln: University of Nebraska Press, 1983–2001), 2:76. Journal citations hereafter are identified by date, volume, and page number.

10. 16 September 1803, 2:83.

11. Francis Baily, *Journal of a Tour in Unsettled Parts of North America in 1796 & 1797*, ed. Jack D. L. Holmes (Carbondale and Edwardsville: Southern Illinois University, 1969), 120.

12. Ibid., 121.

13. *Thomas Rodney's 1803 Journal*, 124–25.

14. Personal Diary of Jonathan Clark, 1 June 1770–20 November 1811, FHS.

15. Charles Dickens, *American Notes and Pictures from Italy* (London: Oxford University Press, 1957), 171.

16. 22 November 1803, 2:101.

17. 23 November 1803, 2:108.

18. 28 November 1803, 2:117.

19. 22 December 1803, 2:140.

20. 26 March 1804, 2:181.

21. 9 January 1804, 2:154.

22. 4 January 1804, 2:150.

23. Detachment Order, 3 March 1804, 2:178.

24. *Black Hawk: An Autobiography*, ed. Donald Jackson (1955; rpt., Urbana: University of Illinois Press, 1990), 51.

25. Stoddard to Dearborn, 3 June 1804, *Glimpses of the Past* 2 (1933–35), MHS, 111, quoted in ibid., 52 n. 21.

26. 30 March 1804, 2:183.

27. 28 April 1804, 2:206.

28. Henry Dearborn to ML, 26 March 1804, *Letters of the Expedition*, 172.

29. ML to WC, 6 May 1804, ibid., 179.

30. 14 May 1804, 2:215.

31. "Autobiography of Peachy R. Gilmer," excerpted in Richard Beale Davis, *Francis Walker Gilmer: Life and Learning in Jefferson's Virginia* (Richmond, Va.: Dietz Press, 1939), 361.

32. 14 July 1804, 2:377.

33. 7 August 1804, 3:455–56.

34. James Bruff to James Wilkinson, 5 November 1804, *Letters of the Expedition*, 1:215.

35. 13 October 1804, 3:170. For a definitive account of the expedition's military culture, see Robert J. Moore, Jr., and Michael Haynes, *Lewis & Clark: Tailor Made, Trail Worn: Army Life, Clothing & Weapons of the Corps of Discovery* (Helena, Mont.: Farcountry Press, 2003).

36. 3 February 1805, 3:285.

37. 13 February 1805, 3:293.

38. 27 October 1805, 5:345.

39. 14 August 1805, 5:93.

40. Lewis to Clark, 6 May 1804, *Letters of the Expedition*, 1:179–80.

41. L. R. Masson, ed., *Les Bourgeois de la Compagnie du Nord-Ouest . . .* , 2 vols. (1889–90; rpt., New York: Antiquarian Press, 1960), 1:336.

42. 12 August 1805, 5:75–76.

43. 20 August 1804, 2:495.

44. 24 July 1805, 4:423.

45. 12 August 1806, 8:158.

46. 14 August 1806, 9:350.
47. TJ to ML, 16 November 1803, *Letters of the Expedition*, 1:137.
48. 23 March 1804, 2:180.
49. TJ to ML, 22 January 1804, *Letters of the Expedition*, 1:166.
50. 25 September 1804, 3:113.
51. Ibid.
52. 25 September 1804, 9:68.
53. Lincoln to TJ, 17 April 1803, *Letters of the Expedition*, 1:34–36.
54. 12 October 1804, 3:163. Clark similarly called the Teton Sioux "generally ill-looking & not well made" (26 September 1804, 3:117).
55. 16 October 1804, 3:178.
56. "Estimate of the Eastern Indians," 3:386–447. A magpie and a prairie dog also survived the trip to Monticello.
57. Ibid., 3:418.
58. 20 January 1805, 3:277.
59. 1 April 1805, 3:327.
60. 28 July 1805, 5:9.
61. 30 April 1805, 4:89.
62. Clark apparently attributed her illness to venereal disease acquired from Charbonneau.
63. Members of the Lemhi Shoshone tribe say that Pomp is a Shoshone name meaning "firstborn" or "lots of hair" (Stephenie Ambrose Tubbs and Clay Straus Jenkinson, *The Lewis and Clark Companion: An Encyclopedic Guide to the Voyage of Discovery* [New York: Henry Holt, 2003]).
64. 24 November 1805, 6:84. Her "Potas" were roots of wapato, *Sagittaria latifolia*.
65. 30 November 1805, 6:97.
66. 25 December 1805, 6:137.
67. 5 May 1806, 7:209.
68. 12 May 1806, 7:247.
69. 5 May 1806, 7:212.
70. 22 November 1804, 3:239.
71. 26 September 1804, 3:116.
72. 27 September 1804, 3:121.
73. 12 October 1804, 3:164.
74. 19 August 1805, 5:121.
75. 24 December 1805, 6:136.
76. "Nicholas Biddle Notes," *Letters of the Expedition*, 2:503.
77. Peter Ronan, *History of the Flathead Indians* (1890; rpt., Minneapolis: Ross & Haines, 1965), 44.
78. A thorough discussion of the expedition's sexual encounters with the natives is in James P. Ronda's definitive study, *Lewis and Clark among the Indians* (Lincoln: University of Nebraska Press, 1984).
79. Jay H. Buckley, "William Clark: Superintendent of Indian Affairs at St. Louis, 1813–1838" (Ph.D. diss., University of Nebraska, Lincoln, 2001), 76.
80. 10 October 1805, 5:258. The possibility that Clark also fathered children with his African-American slaves cannot be ruled out. The Eva Emery Dye Papers at the Oregon Historical Society contain a letter from Peter H. Clark, a prominent nineteenth-century educator, in which he claims to be a grandson of the explorer.

81. 28 June 1804, 2:327; 2 July 1804, 2:341; 3 August 1804, 2:440.

82. "Missouri River Miscellany," 3:479–80.

83. 4 July 1804, 2:346–47.

84. 5 January 1805, 3:268.

85. 13 October 1804, 3:169.

86. For an excellent discussion of this and other Indian mapmaking, see Carolyn Gilman, *Lewis and Clark—Across the Divide* (Washington, D.C.: Smithsonian Books, 2003), 135–64.

87. Jerry Garrett, "Lewis and Clark Expedition Place Names" (unpublished paper, 2003), courtesy of the writer.

88. 29 April 1805, 4:87. This stream in Roosevelt County, Montana, is known today as Big Muddy Creek.

89. For this information and supporting documentation, the author is grateful to Nettie Oliver, genealogical specialist at the Filson Historical Society.

90. 29 May 1805, 4:215–16.

91. Gary Moulton, editor of the University of Nebraska Press edition of the *Journals of the Lewis and Clark Expedition*, believes that Lewis changed the "Big Horn" to "Judieths" River during the expedition and that his use of her childhood name rather than her frequently used name of "Julia" in adulthood suggests that the change was made at the earlier date (personal communication to the author, 28 February 2003). Clark continued to name geographical features after women, most memorably commemorating his sister Frances with "Fanny's Bottom," now Crims Island in Columbia County, Oregon. Lewis contributed "Marias River," in Montana, named for his cousin Maria Wood.

92. 1 January 1805, 3:267.

93. 10 October 1804, 3:156–57.

94. 9 October 1804, 3:155.

95. Robert B. Betts, *In Search of York: The Slave Who Went to the Pacific with Lewis and Clark*, rev. ed. (Boulder: Colorado Associated University Press, 2000), 36, 39.

96. Biddle Notes, *Letters of the Expedition*, 2:503.

97. 7 November 1805, 6:58.

98. 14 February 1806, 6:309.

99. For the definitive treatment of Clark's mapmaking contributions, see John Logan Allen, *Passage through the Garden: Lewis and Clark and the Image of the American Northwest* (Urbana: University of Illinois Press, 1975).

100. For more on the mythical Multnomah, see ibid.

101. Clark and his men were not the first Europeans to see Pompy's Tower. Ten months earlier, François-Antoine Larocque, a French Canadian trader who had previously visited the captains at Fort Mandan, ascended the Yellowstone with two companions and described the formation the natives called "Erpian Macolié." See "Narrative of François-Antoine Larocque," in *Early Fur Trade on the Northern Plains: Canadian Traders among the Mandan and Hidatsa Indians, 1738–1818*, ed. W. Raymond Wood and Thomas D. Thiessen (Norman: University of Oklahoma Press, 1985), 194.

102. Speech for the Yellowstone Indians, undated, 8:213–15.

103. 23 July 1806, 8:212.

104. Colter would go on to spend another four years in the Mountain West and was the first white man to bring back a description of the area that became Yellowstone National Park.

105. Clark to Charbonneau, 20 August 1806, *Letters of the Expedition*, 1:315–16.

106. 20 August 1806, 8:310.
107. Biddle Notes, *Letters of the Expedition*, 2:527.

6. THIS WILD COUNTRY: 1806–1809

1. *The Journals of Zebulon Montgomery Pike, with Letters and Related Documents*, ed. Donald Jackson, 2 vols. (Norman: University of Oklahoma Press, 1966), 1:277.
2. 20 September 1806, *Journals of the Lewis and Clark Expedition*, ed. Gary E. Moulton, 13 vols. (Lincoln: University of Nebraska Press, 1983–2001), 8:367. Journal citations hereafter are identified by date, volume, and page number.
3. 22 September 1806, 8:370.
4. 23 September 1806, 8:370–71.
5. J. Rankin to Amos Stoddard, 4 August 1804, in Lloyd A. Hunter, "Slavery in St. Louis, 1804–1860," *Bulletin of the Missouri Historical Society* 30 (July 1974), 256.
6. TJ to William Henry Harrison, 27 February 1803, in *The Writings of Thomas Jefferson*, ed. Andrew A. Lipscomb and Albert E. Bergh, vol. 10 (Washington, D.C.: Thomas Jefferson Memorial Association, 1905), 269–70, quoted in *Major Problems in the Early Republic, 1787–1848: Documents and Essays*, ed. Sean Wilentz (Lexington, Mass.: D. C. Heath, 1992), 130–31.
7. Gov. Wilkinson to the Secretary of War, 8 September 1805, *The Territorial Papers of the United States*, ed. Clarence Edwin Carter (Washington, D.C.: GPO, 1934–75), 14:196–200.
8. "Diary of William Joseph Clark," 20 May 1805, *The Register of the Kentucky State Historical Society*, vol. 25, no. 73, 193–206.
9. TJ to the Indian Delegation, 4 January 1806, *Letters of the Lewis and Clark Expedition, with Related Documents, 1783–1854*, ed. Donald Jackson (Urbana and Chicago: University of Illinois Press, 1978), 1:280–83.
10. WC to ML, 18 July 1803, ibid., 1:110–11.
11. WC to Dearborn, 10 October 1806, ibid., 1:347. Clark had been promoted to first lieutenant the previous March.
12. 5 November 1806, Personal Diary of Jonathan Clark, FHS.
13. Josiah Espy, "A Tour in Ohio, Kentucky, and Indiana Territory, in 1805," in *Ohio Valley Historical Series: Miscellanies*, quoted in James Alton James, *The Life of George Rogers Clark* (Chicago: University of Chicago Press, 1928), 459.
14. Samuel Gwathmey, interview by Lyman Draper, 1846, Draper 10-J-212.
15. Ibid., 10-J-213.
16. *Political Correspondence and Public Papers of Aaron Burr*, ed. Mary-Jo Kline, 2 vols. (Princeton: Princeton University Press, 1983), 2:995–1007.
17. Citizens of Fincastle to Lewis and Clark, 8 January 1807, *Letters of the Expedition*, 1:358.
18. Clark to the Citizens of Fincastle, after 8 January 1807, ibid., 1:359.
19. WC to Edmund Clark, 5 March 1807, ibid., 2:694–95.
20. WC to Jonathan Clark, 22 January 1807, *Dear Brother: Letters of William Clark to Jonathan Clark*, ed. James J. Holmberg (New Haven: Yale University Press, 2002), 119–22.
21. WC to Edmund Clark, 5 March 1807, *Letters of the Expedition*, 2:694–95.
22. WC to Jonathan Clark, 22 January 1807, *Dear Brother*, 119–22.
23. Reuben Lewis to Mary G. Marks, 29 November 1807, Meriwether Lewis Collection, MHS.

24. WC to ML, after 15 March 1807, *Letters of the Expedition*, 2:387–88.

25. WC to the Secretary of War, 18 May 1807, *Territorial Papers*, 14:124.

26. 3 September 1804, Elliott Coues, ed., *History of the Lewis and Clark Expedition*, 3 vols. (New York: Dover), 1:133.

27. Wilkinson to Pike, 18 July 1806, quoted in Richard Edward Oglesby, *Manuel Lisa and the Opening of the Missouri Fur Trade* (Norman: University of Oklahoma Press, 1965), 37.

28. WC to the Secretary of War, 1 June 1807, *Territorial Papers*, 14:126–27.

29. Extracts of letters addressed to the War Department, ASP/IA, 1:798.

30. WC to the Secretary of War, 17 July 1807, *Territorial Papers*, 14:136–37.

31. WC to the Secretary of War, 1 June 1807, ibid., 14:126–27.

32. WC to Jonathan Clark, 9 September 1807, *Dear Brother*, 126.

33. WC to TJ, 20 September 1807, *Jefferson Papers*, Series 1, General Correspondence, 1751–1827, Library of Congress.

34. Nathaniel Pryor to WC, 16 October 1807, *Letters of the Expedition*, 2:432–37.

35. WC to Jonathan Clark, 10 December 1808, *Dear Brother*, 184.

36. The three crates wound up in Havana after the vessel carrying them was forced ashore during the embargo of American shipping by the British. Jefferson was still trying to locate them fifteen months later and apparently never succeeded.

37. ML to WC, 29 May 1808, WC Papers (MHS).

38. Thomas Riddick to Frederick Bates, 2 July 1808, *The Life and Papers of Frederick Bates*, ed. Thomas Maitland Marshall, 2 vols. (St. Louis: Missouri Historical Society, 1926), 2:5–7.

39. WC to Jonathan Clark, 2 July 1808, *Dear Brother*, 139–41.

40. 21 July 1808, ibid., 143–44.

41. Ibid.

42. 17 August 1808, MHS.

43. ML to Dearborn, 1 July 1808, *Territorial Papers*, 14:196–203.

44. TJ to ML, 21 August 1808, ibid., 14:219–21.

45. Ibid.

46. TJ to Secretary of the Navy Robert Smith, 12 July 1804, *Letters of the Expedition*, 1:199n.

47. Quoted in Frederick J. Fausz, "'They Have Become a Nation of Quakers': The Removal of the Osage Indians from Missouri," *Gateway Heritage* 21, no. 1 (Summer 2000): 28–39.

48. WC to Dearborn, 18 August 1808, *Territorial Papers*, 14:207–10.

49. TJ to ML, 24 August 1808, ibid., 14:219–21.

50. William Clark, *Westward with Dragoons: The Journal of William Clark on His Expedition to Establish Fort Osage, August 25 to September 22, 1808*, ed. Kate L. Gregg (Fulton, Mo.: Ovid Bell Press, 1937), 21.

51. Ibid., 36.

52. Ibid., 38.

53. Ibid., 39.

54. WC to Dearborn, 23 September 1808, *Territorial Papers*, 14:224–28.

55. ML to TJ, 15 December 1808, McCarter and English Indian Claims Cases, box 18, Princeton Collections of Western Americana, Princeton University Library.

56. Ibid.

57. WC to Jonathan Clark, 5 October 1808, *Dear Brother*, 153–56.

58. WC to Jonathan Clark, 9 November 1808, ibid., 160–62.
59. WC to Jonathan Clark, 10 December 1808, ibid., 181–84.
60. WC to John Hite Clark, 15–16 December 1808, ibid., 278–79.
61. WC to Jonathan Clark, 9 November 1808, ibid., 160–62.
62. WC to Jonathan Clark, 17 December 1808, ibid., 186–88.
63. WC to Jonathan Clark, 2 January 1809, ibid., 189–91.
64. WC to Jonathan Clark, 21 January 1809, ibid., 193–94.
65. WC to Jonathan Clark, 2 January 1809, ibid., 189–91.
66. Ibid.
67. WC to Jonathan Clark, 21 January 1809, ibid., 193–94.
68. WC to MLC, 12 October 1831, MLC Papers.
69. WC to Edmund Clark, 15 April 1809, *Dear Brother*, 283–84.
70. *Missouri Gazette*, 23 November 1808.
71. WC to Dearborn, 5 April 1809, *Territorial Papers*, 14:260.
72. Ibid.
73. WC to Dearborn, 30 April 1809, ibid., 14:271.
74. Quoted in Donald Jackson, "A Footnote to the Lewis and Clark Expedition," *Manuscripts* 24 (Winter 1972): 3–21.
75. Frederick Bates to Richard Bates, 17 December 1807, *Life and Papers of Bates*, 2:237.
76. Frederick Bates to Richard Bates, 15 April 1809, ibid., 1:64.
77. Frederick Bates to Richard Bates, 9 November 1809, ibid., 2:108–112.
78. Frederick Bates to Richard Bates, 14 July 1808, ibid., 1:67–73.
79. ML to Pierre Chouteau, 8 June 1809, *Territorial Papers*, 14:348–52.
80. Eustis to ML, 15 July 1809, ibid., 14:285–86.
81. ML to Eustis, 18 August 1809, ibid., 14:290–93.
82. William C. Carr to Charles Carr, 24 August 1809, William C. Carr Papers, MHS.
83. Ibid.
84. Eustis to WC, 7 August 1809, *Territorial Papers*, 14:289–90.
85. WC to Jonathan Clark, 26 August 1809, *Dear Brother*, 209–11.
86. WC to Eustis, 20 February 1810, ASP/IA, 1:765.
87. TJ to WC, 10 September 1809, WC Papers (MHS).
88. WC to Jonathan Clark, 28 May 1809, *Dear Brother*, 200–02.
89. WC to Jonathan Clark, 26 August 1809, ibid., 209–11.
90. WC, September 1809, William Clark 1809 Memorandum Book, WHMC.
91. Julia Hancock Clark, 8 October 1809, ibid., 60.
92. WC, 8 October 1809, ibid.
93. Gwathmey interview, 1846, Draper 10-J-214.
94. WC to Jonathan Clark, 28 October 1809, *Dear Brother*, 216–18.

7. LIFE WITHOUT LEWIS: 1809–1813

1. Neely to TJ, 18 October 1809, *The Territorial Papers of the United States*, ed. Clarence Edwin Carter, 28 vols. (Washington, D.C.: GPO, 1934–75), 14:332–34.
2. Ibid.
3. WC to Jonathan Clark, 26 November 1809, *Dear Brother: Letters of William Clark to Jonathan Clark*, ed. James J. Holmberg (New Haven: Yale University Press, 2002), 228–30.
4. WC to Jonathan Clark, 28 October 1809, ibid., 216–18.

5. WC to Jonathan Clark, 30 October 1809 and 8 November 1809, ibid., 224–26.

6. WC to Jonathan Clark, 26 November 1809, ibid., 228–30.

7. WC to Jonathan Clark, 8 November 1809, ibid., 225–26.

8. Ibid.

9. C. and A. Conrad and Co. to TJ, 13 November 1809, *Letters of the Lewis and Clark Expedition, with Related Documents, 1783–1854*, ed. Donald Jackson (Urbana and Chicago: University of Illinois Press, 1978), 2:468–69.

10. 6 December 1809, WC 1809 Memorandum Book, ibid., 2:724.

11. 7 December 1809, ibid., 2:725.

12. Undated entry, WC 1809 Memorandum Book, WHMC, 70.

13. Ibid., 43.

14. 17 December 1809, WC 1809 Memorandum Book, *Letters of the Expedition*, 2:725.

15. WC to Jonathan Clark, 12 January 1810, *Dear Brother*, 233–34.

16. Memorandum of Lewis's Personal Effects, [23 November 1809], *Letters of the Expedition*, 2:470–72.

17. Clark's Memorandum on the Journals, [c. January 1810], ibid., 2:486.

18. WC to William D. Meriwether, 26 January 1810, ibid., 2:490–91.

19. Charles Willson Peale to Rembrandt Peale, 3 February 1810, ibid., 2:493–94.

20. WC to Nicholas Biddle, 20 February 1810, ibid., 2:494.

21. Biddle to WC, 3 March 1810, ibid., 495.

22. Biddle to WC, 7 July 1810, ibid., 550.

23. WC to Jonathan Clark, 3 July 1810, *Dear Brother*, 244–45.

24. Washington Irving, *Astoria* (Portland, Oreg.: Binfords & Mort, 1967), 110.

25. WC to Jonathan Clark, 16 July 1810, *Dear Brother*, 248–49.

26. WC to Jonathan Clark, 14 December 1810, ibid., 251–52.

27. WC to Eustis, 28 September 1810, *Territorial Papers*, 14:415–16.

28. George Rogers Clark Floyd to his wife, 14 August 1810, quoted in John Sugden, *Tecumseh: A Life* (New York: Henry Holt, 1997), 198.

29. Capt. Johnston, 7 August 1810, ASP/IA, 1:799.

30. Sugden, *Tecumseh*, 198.

31. *Louisiana Gazette*, 28 November 1810.

32. WC to John Hite Clark, 27 October 1810, *Dear Brother*, 289–90.

33. WC to Edmund Clark, 16 July 1810, ibid., 248–49.

34. WC to Eustis, 28 September 1810, *Territorial Papers*, 14:415–16.

35. WC to John Hite Clark, 27 October 1810, *Dear Brother*, 289–90.

36. WC to Jonathan Clark, 31 January 1811, ibid., 254–55.

37. WC to Biddle, 7 December 1810, *Letters of the Expedition*, 2:562–64.

38. WC to Biddle, 7 and 20 December 1810, ibid., 2:562–65.

39. The original of Clark's 1810 map is in the Beinecke Rare Books and Manuscript Library at Yale University. This discussion is indebted to the work of many historical geographers, most notably John Logan Allen's groundbreaking *Passage through the Garden*.

40. Bradbury to William Roscow, 24 July 1810, in *Letters of the Expedition*, 458–59 n. 1.

41. John Bradbury, *Travels in the Interior of America: In the Years 1809, 1810, and 1811*, vol. 5 of *Early Western Travels*, ed. Reuben Gold Thwaites (Cleveland: Arthur H. Clark, 1904), 5:58–59.

42. H. M. Brackenridge, *Journal of a Voyage up the River Missouri: Performed in 1811*, vol. 6 of *Early Western Travels*, ed. Reuben Gold Thwaites (Cleveland: Arthur H. Clark, 1904), 6:30.

43. Ibid., 6:31–32.

44. George Hancock to WC, 14 February 1811, WC Papers (MHS).

45. John O'Fallon to WC, 13 May 1811, ibid.

46. Boilvin to Eustis, 11 February 1811, *Territorial Papers*, 14:438–41.

47. Secretary of War to Boilvin, 14 March 1811, ibid., 14:443–44.

48. *Letter Book of George C. Sibley, 1808–11*, quoted in Kate L. Gregg, "The War of 1812 on the Missouri Frontier," *Missouri Historical Review* 33 (October 1938): 6.

49. Sibley to WC, 22 July 1811, George C. Sibley Papers, MHS.

50. WC to Madison, 10 April 1811, *Territorial Papers*, 14:445–46.

51. Eustis to WC, 31 May 1811, ibid., 14:451.

52. WC to Eustis, 3 July 1811, ASP/IA, 1:800.

53. *Louisiana Gazette*, 4 July 1811.

54. Harrison to Eustis, 17 September 1811, ASP/IA, 1:801.

55. WC to Eustis, 23 November 1811, ibid., 1:802.

56. Henry Duncan to WC, 5 April 1811, WC Papers (MHS).

57. *Louisiana Gazette*, 26 August 1811.

58. WC to Shannon, 20 April 1811 and 18 August 1811, WC Papers (MHS).

59. WC to Jonathan Clark, 30 August 1811, *Dear Brother*, 262–63.

60. Biddle to WC, 28 June 1811 and 8 July 1811, *Letters of the Expedition*, 2:568–69.

61. WC to Biddle, 15 August 1811, ibid., 2:571–72.

62. WC to Jonathan Clark, 14 September 1811, *Dear Brother*, 264–65.

63. John O'Fallon to Lyman Draper, 1847, draft of original letter, WC Papers (MHS).

64. "Appraisement Bill of the Slaves and Personal Estate of Jonathan Clark," 1811, Jonathan Clark Papers, FHS.

65. An excellent source on this event is James Lal Penick, Jr., *The New Madrid Earthquakes*, rev. ed. (Columbia: University of Missouri Press, 1981).

66. Bradbury, *Travels in the Interior of America*, 204.

67. *Lorenzo Dow's Journal* (Joshua Martin, 1849), 344–46, reprinted in *The Virtual Times*, "The New Madrid Earthquake," http://www.hsv.com/genlintr/newmadrd.

68. Account of George Heinrich Crist submitted by Floyd Creasey to *The Virtual Times*, "The New Madrid Earthquake," http://www.hsv.com/genlintr/newmadrd.

69. WC to John Armstrong, 23 June 1812, John Armstrong Papers, Indiana Historical Society, Indianapolis.

70. WC to Eustis, 13 February 1812, *Territorial Papers*, 14:518–20.

71. Zebulon Pike, 3 December 1805, "Journal of the Mississippi River Expedition," in *The Journals of Zebulon Montgomery Pike, with Letters and Related Documents*, ed. Donald Jackson, 2 vols. (Norman: University of Oklahoma Press, 1966), 1:64–65.

72. Capt. Horatio Stark to Col. Daniel Bissell, 6 January 1810, *Territorial Papers*, 14:506.

73. WC to Eustis, 13 February 1812, ibid., 14:518–20.

74. Harrison to Eustis, 24 January 1812, ibid., 8:161.

75. Edwards to Eustis, 3 March 1812, ibid., 16:193.

76. John Johnston to Gov. Howard, 9 March 1812, ibid., 14:534.

77. Rhea to War Department, 14 March 1812, ASP/IA, 1:806.

78. *Louisiana Gazette*, 21 March 1812, cited in John Louis Loos, "A Biography of William Clark, 1770–1813," 2 vols. (Ph.D. diss., Washington University, 1953), 1006.

79. 25 April 1812, ibid., 1017.

80. Secretary of War to Territorial Governors, 19 June 1812, *Territorial Papers*, 14:552 n. 21.

81. Quoted in Louise P. Kellogg, "The Capture of Mackinac in 1812," State Historical Society of Wisconsin, *Proceedings* (1912), 141.
82. Wilt Letter-Book, cited in Gregg, "War of 1812" (October 1938): 18.
83. *National Intelligencer*, 6 August 1812.
84. WC to Ninian Edwards, 16 August 1812, *The Edwards Papers*, ed. E. B. Washburne (Chicago: Chicago Historical Society, 1884), 80–81.
85. Biddle to WC, 4 July 1812, *Letters of the Expedition*, 2:577–78.
86. WC to Biddle, 6 August 1812, ibid., 2:578.
87. Howard to Eustis, 20 September 1812, *Territorial Papers*, 14:593–94.
88. Ibid.
89. WC to Eustis, 24 October 1812, ibid., 14:602–03.
90. *Black Hawk: An Autobiography*, ed. Donald Jackson (1955; Urbana: University of Illinois Press, 1990), 66.
91. Dickson to Jacob Franks, 2 October 1812, "Dickson and Grignon Papers, 1812–1815," ed. Reuben Gold Thwaites, *Collections of the State Historical Society of Wisconsin* 11 (1888): 271–72.
92. John O'Fallon to Fanny Fitzhugh, 11 February 1813, Fitzhugh Family Collection, MHS.
93. Joseph Charless to John Armstrong, 7 February 1813, *Territorial Papers*, 14:629–31.
94. Frederick Bates to Benjamin Howard, 27 February 1813, ibid., 14:637–39.
95. Pierre Chouteau to John Armstrong, 5 March 1813, ibid., 14:639–40.
96. Benjamin Howard to Pierre Chouteau, April [1813], ibid., 14:674–75.
97. Edward Hempstead to Madison, 4 March 1813, ibid., 14:636–37.

8. Territorial Governor: 1813–1820

1. Sibley to WC, 9 July 1813, Sibley Papers, MHS.
2. WC to Armstrong, 12 September 1813, *The Territorial Papers of the United States*, ed. Clarence Edwin Carter, 28 vols. (Washington, D.C.: GPO, 1934–75), 14:697–98.
3. Howard to WC, 24 September 1813, quoted in Kate L. Gregg, "The War of 1812 on the Missouri Frontier," *Missouri Historical Review* 33 (January 1939): 197.
4. WC to Armstrong, 12 September 1813, *The Territorial Papers of the United States*, ed. Clarence Edwin Carter, 28 vols. (Washington, D.C.: GPO, 1934–75), 14:697–98.
5. WC to Sibley, 15 December 1813, Sibley Papers, MHS.
6. WC to Col. George Hancock, 27 October 1813, FHS.
7. Biddle to WC, 23 March 1814, *Letters of the Lewis and Clark Expedition, with Related Documents, 1783–1854*, ed. Donald Jackson (Urbana and Chicago: University of Illinois Press, 1978), 2:598–99.
8. Dickson to Lt. John Lawe, 31 August 1813, "Dickson and Grignon Papers, 1812–1815," ed. Reuben Gold Thwaites, *Collections of the State Historical Society of Wisconsin* 11 (1888): 273.
9. Dickson to Lawe, 5 December 1813 and 4 February 1814, ibid., 291.
10. *Missouri Gazette*, 8 May 1813.
11. Julia Clark to George Hancock, 27 February 1814, WC Papers (MHS).
12. WC to Armstrong, 6 January 1814, *Territorial Papers*, 14:727–28.
13. WC to Armstrong, 18 December 1813, ibid., 14:723–24.
14. WC to George Sibley, 17 March 1814, Sibley Papers, MHS.
15. WC to Armstrong, 6 January 1814, *Territorial Papers*, 14:727–28.

16. *Missouri Gazette*, 28 May 1814.

17. WC to GRC, 27 December 1813, Draper 55-J.

18. WC to Armstrong, 2 February 1814, *Territorial Papers*, 14:738–40.

19. WC to Armstrong, 28 March 1814, ibid., 14:746–47.

20. WC to Secretary of War, 4 May 1814, ibid., 14:762–63.

21. *Niles' Weekly Register*, 20 August 1814.

22. Lt. Col. McKay to Lt. Col. Robert McDouall, 1 August 1814, "Papers from the Canadian Archives — 1767–1814," *Collections of the State Historical Society of Wisconsin* 12 (1892): 116.

23. Lt. Col. Robert McDouall to Gen. Drummond, 16 July 1814, "Capture of Fort M'Kay, Prairie du Chien, in 1814," *Collections of the State Historical Society of Wisconsin* 11 (1888): 260–63.

24. WC to Armstrong, 28 June 1814, *Territorial Papers*, 14:775–76.

25. *Niles' Weekly Register*, 20 August 1814.

26. *Missouri Gazette*, 18 July 1814.

27. *Niles' Weekly Register*, 20 August 1814.

28. James Neal Primm, *Lion of the Valley: St. Louis, Missouri, 1764–1980*, 3d ed. (St. Louis: Missouri Historical Society Press, 1998), 102–03.

29. *Missouri Gazette*, 22 October 1814.

30. Wilt to Joseph Herzog, 6 August 1814, Christian Wilt Papers, MHS, in Gregg, "War of 1812," *Missouri Historical Review* 33 (April 1939): 334.

31. George Sibley to Samuel H. Sibley, 12 August 1814, Sibley Papers, MHS.

32. Ibid.

33. WC to Armstrong, 20 August 1814, *Territorial Papers*, 14:786–87.

34. Ibid.

35. WC to Nicholas Biddle, 16 September 1814, *Letters of the Expedition*, 2:599–600.

36. Ibid.

37. WC to Edmund Clark, 25 December 1814, Clark Family Papers, FHS.

38. 1 October 1814, *The Life and Papers of Frederick Bates*, ed. Thomas Maitland Marshall, 2 vols. (St. Louis: Missouri Historical Society, 1926), 2:283–91.

39. Monroe to the Indian Commissioners, 11 March 1815, *Territorial Papers*, 15:14–15.

40. Ibid.

41. Capt. Andrew Bulger to Lt. John Lawe, April 1815, "Dickson and Grignon Papers," 313.

42. WC to Monroe, 17 April 1815, *Territorial Papers*, 15:25–26.

43. William Russell to Secretary of War, 29 May 1815, ibid., 15:57.

44. *Missouri Gazette*, 10 June 1815, dateline.

45. Timothy Flint, *Recollections of the Last Ten Years in the Valley of the Mississippi*, ed. George R. Brooks (Carbondale and Edwardsville: Southern Illinois University Press, 1968), 89–91.

46. "The Road West in 1818: The Diary of Henry Vest Bingham," ed. Marie George Windell, *Missouri Historical Review* 40, no. 2 (January 1946): 186.

47. William Campbell Preston to Susan S. Preston, 9 August 1816, Smithfield Preston Foundation Papers, Special Collections Department, University Libraries, Virginia Polytechnic Institute, Blacksburg.

48. H. M. Brackenridge, *Journal of a Voyage up the River Missouri: Performed in 1811*, vol. 6 of *Early Western Travels*, ed. Reuben Gold Thwaites (Cleveland: Arthur H. Clark, 1904), 28–29.

49. *Missouri Gazette*, 17 June 1815.
50. Commissioners to Secretary of War, 22 May 1815, MHS, Indian Collection.
51. Undated clip from *Missouri Gazette*, June/July 1815.
52. *Missouri Gazette*, 10 June 1815.
53. Clark, Edwards, and Chouteau to Daniel Bissell, 11 July 1815, General Daniel Bissell Papers, Mercantile Library, University of Missouri, St. Louis, quoted in *Missouri Gazette*, 15 July 1815.
54. *Missouri Gazette*, 15 July 1815.
55. Ibid.
56. *Niles' Weekly Register*, 14 October 1815.
57. Flint, *Recollections*, 112.
58. *Missouri Gazette*, 5 August 1815.
59. Ibid.
60. Ibid.
61. *Missouri Gazette*, 29 July 1815.
62. WC to John O'Fallon, 25 April 1818, John O'Fallon Papers, MHS. The wounded officer was William G. Shade of the Fort Crawford garrison at Prairie du Chien.
63. *Missouri Gazette*, 22 July 1815.
64. William Clark, Ninian Edwards, and Auguste Chouteau to William H. Crawford, Secretary of War, 18 October 1815, in *Treaties with Twenty-one Tribes*, McCarter and English Indian Claims Cases, box 17, Princeton Collections of Western Americana, Princeton University Library.
65. Ibid.
66. Ibid.
67. Edwards to Crawford, 24 September 1816, *Territorial Papers*, 17:398–99.
68. Charles J. Latrobe, *The Rambler in North America* (1835), cited in "A Glimpse of St. Louis in 1816," *Glimpses of the Past* (1830): 98–99.
69. William Lovely to WC, 1 October 1813, *Territorial Papers*, 15:51.
70. For a particularly insightful discussion of the impact of the market economy on the factory system, see Andrew C. Isenberg, "The Market Revolution in the Borderlands: George Champlin Sibley in Missouri and New Mexico, 1808–1826," *Journal of the New Republic* 26 (Fall 2001): 445–65.
71. Proclamation by William Clark, 4 December 1815, *Territorial Papers*, 15:191–92.
72. John Heath to Frederick Bates, 14 January 1816, *Life and Papers of Bates*, 2:297.
73. Crawford to WC, 5 February 1816, *Territorial Papers*, 15:113–14.
74. WC to Biddle, 31 March 1816, *Letters of the Expedition*, 2:609–10.
75. *The Reminiscences of William C. Preston*, ed. Minnie Clare Yarborough (Chapel Hill: University of North Carolina Press, 1933), 16–19.
76. Ibid., 20.
77. Treaty with the Sacs of Rock River, 13 May 1816, ASP/IA, 2:94.
78. Biddle to WC, 29 May 1816, *Letters of the Expedition*, 2:613–15.
79. *Missouri Gazette*, 12 October 1816.
80. WC to Biddle, 17 October 1816, *Letters of the Expedition*, 2:626.
81. WC to TJ, 10 October 1816, ibid., 2:623–25.
82. John O'Fallon to Dennis Fitzhugh, 11 August 1817, Fitzhugh Family Papers, MHS.
83. *Missouri Gazette*, 9 August 1817.
84. *Missouri Gazette*, 27 September 1817.
85. WC to Crawford, 1 October 1815, ASP/IA, 2:77–78.

86. Commissioners to Crawford, 7 December 1816, Arthur G. Mitten Collection, Indiana Historical Society.

87. Ibid.

88. WC to Acting Secretary of War George Graham, 15 May 1817, *Territorial Papers*, 15:260–61.

89. Benjamin O'Fallon to WC, 10 May 1817, *Territorial Papers*, 15:262.

90. Benjamin O'Fallon to WC, 29 November 1817, Western Americana Collection, Beinecke Rare Book and Manuscript Library, Yale University.

91. Benjamin O'Fallon to WC, 20 May 1818, *Territorial Papers*, 15:407–13.

92. William Russell to Charles Lucas, 22 February 1817, John B. C. Lucas Papers, MHS.

93. Notes of J.B.C. Lucas, 28 February 1818, Lucas Papers, MHS.

94. Jean Baptiste Charles Lucas to John Quincy Adams, ca. September 1826, *Letters of Hon. J.B.C. Lucas from 1815 to 1836*, ed. John B. C. Lucas (St. Louis, 1905), 79.

95. WC to Crawford, 28 September 1816, *Territorial Papers*, 15:177–78.

96. John O'Fallon to Fanny Fitzhugh, 18 February 1818, Fitzhugh Family Collection, MHS.

97. Political Notes of J.B.C. Lucas, 17 March 1818, Lucas Papers, MHS.

98. WC to George Sibley, 12 May 1818, Sibley Papers, MHS.

99. WC to Calhoun, 9 July 1818, ASP/IA, 2:176.

100. WC to John O'Fallon, 5 October 1818, O'Fallon Papers, MHS.

101. "Road West in 1818: Diary of Bingham," 184–85.

102. Calhoun to WC, 8 May 1818, *Territorial Papers*, 15:391.

103. WC to Calhoun, October 1818, ibid., 15:454–55.

104. James Haley White, "Early Days in St. Louis," *Glimpses of the Past* 6 (January–March 1939): 5–13.

105. Accounts of Superintendent of Indian Affairs, 22 January 1820, ASP/IA, 2:291.

106. *Forty Years of Pioneer Life: Memoir of John Mason Peck, D.D.*, ed. Rufus Babcock (Carbondale: Southern Illinois University Press, 1965), 90.

107. Floyd Calvin Shoemaker, *Missouri's Struggle for Statehood, 1804–1821* (1916; rpt., New York: Russell and Russell, 1969), 85.

108. Thomas Forsyth to WC, 4 November 1818, Forsyth Papers, MHS.

109. Charless to Lucas, 24 January 1818, Lucas Papers, MHS.

110. Charless to Lucas, 18 April 1819, Lucas Papers, MHS.

111. WC to John O'Fallon, 10 October 1819, O'Fallon Papers, MHS.

112. WC to "Mr. Editor," January 1820, WC Papers (MHS).

113. *St. Louis Enquirer*, 19 July 1820.

114. *Missouri Gazette*, 19 July 1820.

115. *St. Louis Enquirer*, 15 July 1820.

116. *Missouri Intelligencer*, 19 August 1820.

117. 27 July 1820, Small Journal of Trip to Washington, Memoranda and Expenses, 1817–20, WC Papers (MHS).

118. John O'Fallon to Gen. T. A. Smith, 27 July 1820, quoted in Shoemaker, *Missouri's Struggle for Statehood*, 264.

119. John O'Fallon to Dennis Fitzhugh, 18 August 1820, Fitzhugh Family Papers, MHS.

120. *Missouri Gazette*, 23 August 1820.

121. Thomas Hart Benton, *Thirty Years' View; or, A History of the Working of the American Government for Thirty Years, from 1820 to 1850*, 2 vols. (New York: D. Appleton and Co., 1854–56), 1:28.

122. Memo and Account Book: 1820–1825, WC Papers (MHS).

9. "The Red-headed Chief": 1820–1829

1. John Calhoun to Thomas Smith, 16 March 1818, in *The Missouri Expedition, 1818–1820: The Journal of Surgeon John Gale, with Related Documents*, ed. Roger L. Nichols (Norman: University of Oklahoma Press, 1969), 89–90.

2. Secretary of War to Benjamin O'Fallon, 8 March 1819, *The Territorial Papers of the United States*, ed. Clarence Edwin Carter, 28 vols. (Washington, D.C.: GPO, 1934–75), 15:520–21.

3. 3 August 1804, *Journals of the Lewis and Clark Expedition*, ed. Gary E. Moulton, 13 vols. (Lincoln: University of Nebraska Press, 1983–2001), 2:441.

4. Benjamin O'Fallon to WC, 9 July 1819, WC Papers (MHS).

5. Calhoun to WC, 21 October 1820, *Territorial Papers*, 15:659.

6. Mary Margaret Clark to WC, 13 July 1821, WC Papers (MHS).

7. Dennis Fitzhugh to John O'Fallon, 10 June 1821, O'Fallon Papers, MHS.

8. Marshall D. Hier, "Frontier Scandal, *Stokes v. Stokes* Revisited," http://www.bamsl.org/barjour/winter01/Hier.htm.

9. John Scott to Secretary of State John Quincy Adams, 27 February 1821, *Territorial Papers*, 15:705.

10. Calhoun to WC, 2 April 1821, ibid., 15:712–15.

11. Calhoun to WC, 4 June 1821, ibid., 15:731–33.

12. S. T. Fitzhugh to John O'Fallon, 16 October 1821, John O'Fallon Papers, MHS.

13. WC Memo and Account Book, 1820–1825, WC Papers (MHS).

14. John O'Fallon to Dennis Fitzhugh, 2 November 1821, Fitzhugh Family Papers, MHS.

15. John O'Fallon to Dennis Fitzhugh, 22 December 1821, ibid.

16. WC Memo and Account Book, 1820–1825, WC Papers (MHS).

17. Sibley to Thomas L. McKenney, 1 October 1820, in Jay H. Buckley, "William Clark: Superintendent of Indian Affairs at St. Louis, 1813–1838" (Ph.D. diss., University of Nebraska, Lincoln, 2001), 139.

18. Calhoun to Monroe, 2 February 1822, ASP/IA, 2:200–201.

19. *St. Louis Enquirer*, reprinted in *Missouri Intelligencer*, 17 September 1822, in Dale L. Morgan, ed., *The West of William H. Ashley: The International Struggle for the Fur Trade of the Missouri, the Rocky Mountains, and the Columbia . . .* (Denver: Old West Publishing Company, 1964), 19.

20. See William R. Nester, *The Arikara War: The First Plains Indian War, 1823* (Missoula, Mont.: Mountain Press, 2001).

21. The author is grateful to J. Frederick Fausz of the University of Missouri, St. Louis, for his background paper "Partners in Pelts," which contains an excellent discussion of fur trade and manufacturing.

22. O'Fallon to Calhoun, 9 April 1822, Morgan, ed., *Ashley*, 6.

23. WC to Calhoun, 9 August 1822, ibid., 18.

24. *St. Louis Enquirer*, 9 April 1822, ibid., 6–7.

25. Jedediah Smith, Journal, 1822, ibid., 12.

26. WC to Calhoun, 16 January 1823, ibid., 20.

27. James C. Elyman's Notebook, 10 March 1823, ibid., 23.

28. O'Fallon to Ashley's Deserters, 19 June 1823, ibid., 34.

29. O'Fallon to WC, 24 June 1823, ibid., 36–37.

30. O'Fallon to Ashley, 20 June 1823, ibid., 35–36.

31. O'Fallon to WC, 3 July 1823, ibid., 44–45.

32. WC to Calhoun, 4 July 1823, ibid., 45–46.
33. Leavenworth's Final Report, 20 October 1823, ibid., 55.
34. *Missouri Republican*, 15 October 1823, ibid., 58.
35. *Detroit Gazette*, 17 October 1823, in Nester, *Arikara War*, 188–89.
36. Leavenworth to Gen. Henry Atkinson, 22 November 1823, Morgan, ed., *Ashley*, 64–67.
37. WC to Calhoun, 18 September 1823, ibid., 61.
38. WC to Calhoun, 29 March 1824, ibid., 75.
39. Leavenworth to Atkinson, 22 November 1823, ibid., 64–67.
40. Quoted in *Wheel Boats on the Missouri: The Journals and Documents of the Atkinson-O'Fallon Expedition, 1824–26*, ed. Richard E. Jensen and James S. Hutchins (Helena: Montana Historical Society Press, 2001), 194.
41. Benjamin O'Fallon to WC, Morgan, ed., *Ashley*, 82–83.
42. George Kennerly to James Kennerly, 1 August 1825, James Kennerly Papers, MHS.
43. *Missouri Republican*, 22 January 1823.
44. Albert Furtwangler, "Sacagawea's Son: New Evidence from Germany," *Oregon Historical Quarterly* 102, no. 4 (2001): 518–23. The child, a boy named Anton Fries, died in infancy.
45. Margaret Strother Hancock to WC, 18 December 1821 and 16 June 1822, WC Papers (MHS).
46. Auguste Levasseur, *Lafayette in America in 1824 and 1825; or, Journal of a Voyage to the United States*, 2 vols. in 1, trans. John D. Godman (Philadelphia: Carey and Lea, 1829), 2:128.
47. Ibid., 124.
48. Lafayette to WC, 1 February 1830, WC Papers (MHS).
49. James D. Horan, *The McKenney-Hall Portrait Gallery of American Indians* (New York: Crown, 1972), 58.
50. TJ to William Henry Harrison, 27 February 1803, *The Writings of Thomas Jefferson*, vol. 10, ed. Andrew A. Lipscomb and Albert E. Bergh (Washington, D.C.: Thomas Jefferson Memorial Association, 1905), 369–70.
51. Astor to Monroe, 6 December 1817, quoted in Buckley, "William Clark," 135.
52. Calhoun to Monroe, 8 February 1822, ASP/IA, 2:200–01.
53. McKenney to Barbour, December 1825, ibid., 2:652.
54. WC to O'Fallon, 8 August 1824, John O'Fallon Papers, MHS.
55. WC to Calhoun, 8 December 1823, WC Papers (MHS), in Robert Ralph Russell, "The Public Career of William Clark, 1813–1838" (M.A. thesis, Washington University, 1945).
56. WC to Osage Nation, undated, WC Papers, KSHS, 2:87–89.
57. WC to Secretary of War Barbour, 11 June 1825, ASP/IA, 2:591–92.
58. WC to Iowa Nation, 12 April 1825, WC Papers, KSHS, 2:87–89.
59. *Missouri Republican*, 11 April 1825.
60. Quoted in Charles A. Abele, "The Grand Council and Treaty at Prairie du Chien, 1825" (Ph.D. diss., Loyola University, Chicago, 1969).
61. WC to Barbour, 11 June 1825, ASP/IA, 2:591–92.
62. WC to MLC, 3 July 1825, MLC Papers.
63. WC to MLC, 4 April 1825 and 24 September 1825, ibid.
64. WC to MLC, 30 November 1825, ibid.
65. WC to MLC, 12 April 1827, ibid.
66. WC to TJ, 25 December 1825, Thomas Jefferson Papers, Series 1, General Correspondence: 1751–1827, Library of Congress.

67. WC to Thomas L. McKenney, 4 January 1826, quoted in Russell, "Public Career of William Clark."

68. WC to Barbour, 1 March 1826, WC Papers (MHS).

69. WC to Elbert Herring, 3 December 1831, quoted in William E. Unrau, *White Man's Wicked Water: The Alcohol Trade and Prohibition in Indian Country, 1802–1892* (Lawrence: University Press of Kansas, 1996), 36.

70. Quoted in Joseph P. Herring, *Kenekuk, the Kickapoo Prophet* (Lawrence: University Press of Kansas, 1988), 41.

71. Forsyth to WC, 9 April 1824, quoted in Unrau, *White Man's Wicked Water*, 11.

72. WC to MLC, 27 April 1827, MLC Papers.

73. "William Clark's Diary, May, 1826–February, 1831," ed. Louise Barry, *Kansas Historical Quarterly* 16, no. 1 (February 1948): 32.

74. WC to MLC, 10 September 1826, MLC Papers.

75. WC to MLC, 25 February 1827, ibid.

76. WC to MLC, 12 April 1827, ibid.

77. WC to MLC, 18 May 1828, ibid.

78. WC to MLC, 10 December 1827, ibid.

79. WC to MLC, 27 October 1829, ibid.

80. Broadside for lots in the town of Paducah, 1827, WC Papers (MHS).

81. WC to MLC, 27 April 1827, MLC Papers.

82. John P. Dyson, "The Naming of Paducah," *Register of the Kentucky Historical Society* 92, no. 2 (1994): 149–74.

83. *Missouri Republican*, 12 July 1827.

84. *Indian Treaties: 1778–1883*, comp. and ed. Charles J. Kappler (1904; rpt., Mattituck, N.Y.: Amereon House, 1972), 292–94.

85. Entries for September 1826, "Clark's Diary," 14–15.

86. WC, 8 October 1826, in Account Book, 25 May 1825 to 14 June 1828, Everett D. Graff Collection of Western Americana, Newberry Library, Chicago.

87. 19 May 1827, ibid.

88. WC to Col. McKenney, 10 December 1827, Buckley, "William Clark," 201.

89. WC to MLC, 7 January 1828, MLC Papers.

90. WC to MLC, 8 February 1828, ibid.

91. WC to MLC, 18 May 1828, ibid.

92. WC to MLC, 18 October 1828, ibid.

93. WC to McKenney, 10 December 1827, Buckley, "William Clark," 201.

94. WC to George Rogers Hancock Clark, 30 November 1828, George Rogers Hancock Clark Papers, MHS.

95. Robert V. Remini, *Andrew Jackson and His Indian Wars* (New York: Viking, 2001), 226.

10. RESISTANCE AND REMOVAL: 1829–1838

1. Quoted in Robert V. Remini, *Andrew Jackson and His Indian Wars* (New York: Viking, 2001), 232.

2. Ibid., 234.

3. See William E. Unrau, *White Man's Wicked Water: The Alcohol Trade and Prohibition in Indian Country, 1802–1892* (Lawrence: University Press of Kansas, 1996).

4. Lawrence Taliaferro to WC, 17 August 1830, KSHS, 6:5.

5. Jonathan Bean to John Dougherty, 21 June 1831, excerpted in Dougherty to WC, 10 November 1831, KSHS, 6:374.

6. Edwards to WC, 25 May 1828, quoted in William T. Hagan, *The Sac and Fox Indians* (Norman: University of Oklahoma Press, 1958), 107.

7. Forsyth to WC, 4 June 1829, ibid., 111.

8. Quoted in David Lavender, *The Fist in the Wilderness* (Garden City, N.Y.: Doubleday, 1964), 400.

9. WC to McKenney, 19 June 1830, quoted in Robert Ralph Russell, "The Public Career of William Clark, 1813–1838" (M.A. thesis, Washington University, 1945).

10. George Catlin, *Letters and Notes on the Manners, Customs, and Conditions of the North American Indians*, 2 vols. (1841; rpt., New York: Dover, 1973), 2:30.

11. "Extracts from Minutes of a Council Held at Prairie du Chien, 7 July 1830," McCarter and English Indian Claims Cases, box 2, Princeton Collections of Western Americana, Princeton University Library.

12. Ibid.

13. WC to MLC, 28 January 1830, WC Papers (MHS).

14. WC to MLC, 27 October 1829, ibid.

15. WC to MLC, 28 January 1830, ibid.

16. WC to MLC, 26 April 1829, ibid.

17. Mary Kennerly Taylor to Eva (Emery) Dye, no. 43, Dye Collection (microfilm), Oregon Historical Society, Portland.

18. *St. Louis Globe-Democrat*, 2 July 1899.

19. Entry for 12 June 1830, "William Clark's Diary, May 1826–February 1831," ed. Louise Barry, *Kansas Historical Quarterly* 16, no. 1.

20. Bessie Rowland James, *Anne Royall's U.S.A.* (New Brunswick, N.J.: Rutgers University Press, 1972), viii.

21. Anne Royall, *Mrs. Royall's Southern Tour; or, Second Series of the Black Book*, 3 vols. (Washington, D.C., 1830–31), 3:142.

22. Entry for 12 June 1830, "William Clark's Diary," 395.

23. *Mrs. Royall's Southern Tour*, 3:153.

24. Ibid., 154.

25. Ibid.

26. Entry for 16 June 1830, "William Clark's Diary," 395.

27. *Mrs. Royall's Southern Tour*, 3:155.

28. Menard to WC, 8 October 1830, WC Papers, KSHS, 6:16.

29. Street to WC, 14 October 1830, ibid., 6:32–34.

30. Cummins to WC, 2 April 1831, ibid., 6:166–67.

31. WC to Herring, 20 December 1831, ibid., 4:319–22.

32. Pryor to WC, 22 January 1831, ibid., 6:104.

33. Paul Chouteau to WC, 20 January 1831, ibid., 6:100–01.

34. John Dougherty to WC, 15 March 1831, ibid., 6:122.

35. Dougherty to WC, 29 October 1831, ibid., 6:351.

36. "William Clark's 1830 Report on the Fur Trade," *Oregon Historical Quarterly* 48, no. 1 (1947): 25–33.

37. Cummins to WC, 13 January 1831, WC Papers, KSHS, 6:97.

38. Dougherty to WC, 30 October 1831, ibid., 6:353.

39. Charles Dickens, *American Notes and Pictures from Italy* (London: Oxford University Press, 1957), 184.

40. WC to MLC, 5 September 1831, MLC Papers.

41. Harriet Clark to MLC, 6 November 1831, ibid.

42. WC to MLC, 29 December 1831, ibid.

43. WC to MLC, 28 January 1832, ibid.

44. Tocqueville to his mother, 25 December 1831, as quoted in Louis P. Masur, *1831: Year of Eclipse* (New York: Hill and Wang, 2001), 135.

45. Reynolds to WC, 26 May 1831, WC Papers, KSHS, 6:194–95.

46. Felix St. Vrain to WC, 23 July 1831, ibid., 6:237–38.

47. St. Vrain to WC, 29 July 1831, ibid., 6:243.

48. Street to WC, 1 August 1831, ibid., 6:245–47.

49. WC to Cass, 12 August 1831, ibid., 6:245–54.

50. WC to Atkinson, 16 April 1832, WC Papers (MHS); WC to Cass, 20 April 1832, WC Papers, KSHS, 4:356–57.

51. Statements of J. W. Hall and his sisters Rachel Munson and Sylvia Horn in Frank E. Stevens, *The Black Hawk War: Including a Review of Black Hawk's Life* (Chicago: Frank E. Stevens, 1903), 155–56.

52. WC to Cass, 8 June 1832, WC Papers, KSHS, 4:376–78.

53. Quoted in Roger L. Nichols, *General Henry Atkinson: A Western Military Career* (Norman: University of Oklahoma Press, 1965), 171.

54. WC to MLC, 19 June 1832, MLC Papers.

55. WC to George Rogers Hancock Clark, 19 August 1832, George Rogers Hancock Clark Papers, MHS.

56. Thomas Forsyth, "Report on Black Hawk War," Draper 9-T-54–59, cited in *Black Hawk: An Autobiography*, ed. Donald Jackson (1955; rpt., Urbana: University of Illinois Press, 1990), 109n.

57. Quoted in *The Indian Tribes of the Upper Mississippi Valley and Region of the Great Lakes as Described by Nicholas Perrot*, ed. Emma Helen Blair, 2 vols. in 1 (1911; rpt., Lincoln: University of Nebraska Press, 1996), 2:189n.

58. Washington Irving, *Journals and Notebooks*, vol. 5, *1832–1859*, ed. Sue Fields Ross (Boston: Twayne Publishers, 1986), 57.

59. Ibid., 61.

60. Ibid.

61. Ibid., 70.

62. Ibid., 63.

63. John O'Fallon to WC, 13 May 1811, WC Papers (MHS).

64. WC, Account and Memo Book, 30 October 1828 to 21 March 1829, WC Papers (MHS).

65. *The Western Journals of Washington Irving*, ed. John Francis McDermott (Norman: University of Oklahoma Press, 1944), 15–16.

66. John Treat Irving, quoted in Joseph P. Herring, *Kenekuk, the Kickapoo Prophet* (Lawrence: University Press of Kansas, 1988), 39.

67. Richard Graham, ibid., 43.

68. WC, ibid., 54.

69. Godfrey Lesieur to Gov. John Miller, 6 October 1831, WC Papers, KSHS, 6:311–12.

70. Gov. Miller to WC, 25 October 1831, WC Papers, KSHS, 6:307.

71. WC to George Rogers Hancock Clark, 29 October 1832 and 11 November 1832, George Rogers Hancock Clark Papers, MHS.

72. Prince Maximilian, quoted in *Western Journals*, 83n.

73. Chouteau to WC, 22 November 1833, in Barton H. Barbour, *Fort Union and the Upper Missouri Fur Trade* (Norman: University of Oklahoma Press, 2001), 167.

74. *The Salmon P. Chase Papers*, vol. 1, *Journals, 1829–1872*, ed. John Niven et al. (Kent, Ohio: Kent State University Press, 1993), 1:79–80.

75. William P. Clark to George Rogers Hancock Clark, 27 February 1833, George Rogers Hancock Clark Papers, MHS.

76. John O'Fallon to Charles Thruston, 8 March 1834, John O'Fallon Papers, FHS.

77. James Kennerly Diary, 1826–1838, 1 January 1835, James Kennerly Papers, MHS.

78. John O'Fallon to Charles Thruston, 7 March 1835, John O'Fallon Papers, FHS.

79. O'Fallon to Thruston, 4 June 1835, ibid.

80. *Niles' Weekly Register* 8 (1833), 256, cited in *Black Hawk: An Autobiography*, 9.

81. *Indian Treaties: 1778–1883*, comp. and ed. Charles J. Kappler (1904; rpt., Mattituck, N.Y.: Amereon House, 1972), 469.

82. *Missouri Argus*, 6 November 1835.

83. Pilcher to Crawford, 6 July 1839, quoted in John Sunder, *Joshua Pilcher: Fur Trader and Indian Agent* (Norman: University of Oklahoma Press, 1968), 141.

84. Ethan Allen Hitchcock to Commissioner C. A. Harris, 11 January 1838, Ethan Allen Hitchcock Papers, Beinecke Library, Yale University.

85. Quoted in Donald Jackson, *Voyages of the Steamboat Yellow Stone* (New York: Ticknor and Fields, 1985), 67.

86. William Fulkerson to WC, 20 September 1837, WC Papers, KSHS, 34:86.

87. Pilcher to WC, 10 June 1837, ibid., 34:86–87.

88. Pilcher to WC, 1 July 1837, ibid., 34:88.

89. Pilcher to WC, 27 February 1838, ibid., 34:94–95.

90. Ibid.

91. Joseph R. De Prefontaine to Pilcher, 9 July 1838, WC Papers, KSHS, 34:135.

92. Pilcher to WC, September 1838, ibid., 34:132–35.

93. WC to George Rogers Hancock Clark, 25 August 1837, George Rogers Hancock Clark Papers, MHS.

94. *A Traveler in Indian Territory: The Journal of Ethan Allen Hitchcock*, ed. Grant Foreman (Cedar Rapids, Iowa: Torch Press, 1930), 56.

95. James Kennerly Diary, MHS.

96. Ethan Allen Hitchcock to C. A. Harris, 1 September 1838, Hitchcock Papers.

97. Pilcher to WC, 27 October 1838, WC Papers, KSHS, 34:139–40.

BIBLIOGRAPHY

MANUSCRIPT SOURCES

Armstrong, John. Papers. Manuscript Collections Department, William Henry Smith Memorial Library, Indiana Historical Society, Indianapolis.

Bakeless, John Edwin. Papers, 1913–77. Manuscripts and Archives Division, New York Public Library.

Bissell, Daniel. Papers. St. Louis Mercantile Library, University of Missouri, St. Louis.

Carr, William C. Papers. Missouri Historical Society, St. Louis.

Clark, George Rogers. Papers. In the Lyman Copeland Draper Manuscripts. Archives Division, State Historical Society of Wisconsin, Madison.

Clark, Jonathan. Papers. Filson Historical Society, Louisville, Ky.

Clark, Meriwether Lewis. Papers. Missouri Historical Society, St. Louis.

Clark, William. Account Book, 25 May 1825 to 14 June 1828. Everett D. Graff Collection of Western Americana, Newberry Library, Chicago.

———. Memorandum Book, 1809. Western Historical Manuscript Collection, State Historical Society of Missouri, Columbia.

———. U.S. Office of Indian Affairs, Central Superintendency, St. Louis, Missouri, 1807–55. Also known as William Clark Papers, 34 vols., Kansas State Historical Society, Topeka.

Clark Family Collection. Missouri Historical Society Archives, St. Louis. Includes papers of William Clark, George Rogers Clark, Meriwether Lewis Clark, George Rogers Hancock Clark, and other family members.

Draper Manuscripts. Collected by Lyman Copeland Draper. Archives Division, State Historical Society of Wisconsin, Madison. Includes papers of Jonathan Clark and William Clark.

Dye, Eva Emery. Papers, 1879–1942. Oregon Historical Society, Portland.

Filson Historical Society Collections. Louisville, Ky.

Fitzhugh Family Collection. Missouri Historical Society, St. Louis.

Forsyth, Thomas. Papers. Missouri Historical Society, St. Louis.

Hitchcock, Ethan Allen. Papers, 1798–1870. Beinecke Library, Yale University, New Haven, Conn.

Jefferson, Thomas. Papers, Series 1, General Correspondence: 1751–1827. Library of Congress, Washington, D.C.

Kennerly, James. Papers. Missouri Historical Society, St. Louis.

Lewis, Meriwether. Papers. Missouri Historical Society, St. Louis.

Lucas, John B. C. Papers. Missouri Historical Society, St. Louis.

McCarter and English Indian Claims Cases. Princeton Collections of Western Americana, Princeton University Library.

O'Fallon, John. Papers. Missouri Historical Society, St. Louis.

Sibley, George C. Papers. Missouri Historical Society, St. Louis.

Smithfield Preston Foundation Papers. Special Collections Department, University Libraries, Virginia Polytechnic Institute, Blacksburg, Va.

PUBLISHED PRIMARY SOURCES

American State Papers: Documents, Legislative and Executive, of the Congress of the United States. 38 vols. Washington, D.C.: Gales and Seaton, 1832–61.

Bates, Frederick. *The Life and Papers of Frederick Bates.* Edited by Thomas Maitland Marshall. 2 vols. St. Louis: Missouri Historical Society, 1926.

Before Lewis and Clark: Documents Illustrating the History of the Missouri, 1785–1804. Edited by Abraham P. Nasatir. 2 vols. 1952. Reprint, Lincoln: University of Nebraska Press, 1990.

Benton, Thomas Hart. *Thirty Years' View; or, A History of the Working of the American Government for Thirty Years, from 1820 to 1850.* 2 vols. New York: D. Appleton and Co., 1854–56.

Bingham, Henry Vest. "The Road West in 1818: The Diary of Henry Vest Bingham." Edited by Marie George Windell. *Missouri Historical Review* 40, no. 2 (January 1946): 174–204.

Black Hawk: An Autobiography. Edited by Donald Jackson. 1955. Reprint, Urbana: University of Illinois Press, 1990.

Burr, Aaron. *Political Correspondence and Public Papers of Aaron Burr.* Edited by Mary-Jo Kline. 2 vols. Princeton: Princeton University Press, 1983.

"Capture of Fort M'Kay, Prairie du Chien, in 1814." *Collections of the State Historical Society of Wisconsin* 11 (1888): 254–70.

Catlin, George. *Letters and Notes on the Manners, Customs, and Conditions of the North American Indians.* 2 vols. 1841. Reprint, New York: Dover, 1973.

Chase, Salmon P. *The Salmon P. Chase Papers.* Vol. 1, *Journals, 1829–1872.* Edited by John Niven et al. Kent, Ohio: Kent State University Press, 1993.

Clark, George Rogers. *The Capture of Old Vincennes: The Original Narratives of George Rogers Clark and of His Opponent Gov. Henry Hamilton.* Edited by Milo M. Quaife. Indianapolis: Bobbs-Merrill, 1927.

———. *Col. George Rogers Clark's Sketch of His Campaign in the Illinois in 1778–9.* 1869. Reprint, New York: Arno Press, 1971.

———. *The Conquest of the Illinois.* Edited by Milo M. Quaife. Chicago: R. R. Donnelley and Sons, 1920.

———. *George Rogers Clark Papers.* Edited by James Alton James. 2 vols. Springfield: Illinois State Historical Library, 1912.

Clark, William. *Dear Brother: Letters of William Clark to Jonathan Clark.* Edited by James J. Holmberg. New Haven: Yale University Press, 2002.

———. *Westward with Dragoons: The Journal of William Clark on His Expedition to Establish Fort Osage, August 25 to September 22, 1808.* Edited by Kate L. Gregg. Fulton, Mo.: Ovid Bell Press, 1937.

————. "William Clark's Diary, May, 1826–February, 1831." Edited by Louise Barry. Parts 1–4. *Kansas Historical Quarterly* 16, no. 1 (February 1948): 1–39; no. 2 (May 1948): 136–74; no. 3 (August 1948): 275–305; no. 4 (November 1948): 384–410.

————. "William Clark's 1830 Report on the Fur Trade." *Oregon Historical Quarterly* 48, no. 1 (1947): 25–33.

————. "William Clark's Journal of General Wayne's Campaign." Edited by R. C. McGrane. *Mississippi Valley Historical Review* 1, no. 3 (1914): 419–44.

Cresswell, Nicholas. *The Journal of Nicholas Cresswell, 1774–1777.* London: Jonathan Cape, 1925.

Denny, Ebenezer. *Military Journal of Major Ebenezer Denny, an Officer in the Revolutionary and Indian Wars, with an Introductory Memoir.* Philadelphia: Historical Society of Pennsylvania, 1859.

DeRegnaucourt, Tony. *General Anthony Wayne and the Ohio Indian Wars: A Collection of Unpublished Letters and Artifacts.* Arcanum, Ohio: Upper Miami Valley Archaeological Research Museum, 1995.

Dickens, Charles. *American Notes and Pictures from Italy.* London: Oxford University Press, 1957.

"Dickson and Grignon Papers, 1812–1815." *Collections of the State Historical Society of Wisconsin* 11 (1888): 271–315.

Early Fur Trade on the Northern Plains: Canadian Traders among the Mandan and Hidatsa Indians, 1738–1818. Edited by W. Raymond Wood and Thomas D. Thiessen. Norman: University of Oklahoma Press, 1985.

Flint, Timothy. *Recollections of the Last Ten Years in the Valley of the Mississippi.* Edited by George R. Brooks. Carbondale and Edwardsville: Southern Illinois University Press, 1968.

Gale, John. *The Missouri Expedition, 1818–1820: The Journal of Surgeon John Gale, with Related Documents.* Edited by Roger L. Nichols. Norman: University of Oklahoma Press, 1969.

Hitchcock, Ethan Allen. *A Traveler in Indian Territory: The Journal of Ethan Allen Hitchcock.* Edited by Grant Foreman. Cedar Rapids, Iowa.: Torch Press, 1930.

Indian Treaties: 1778–1883. Compiled and edited by Charles J. Kappler. 1904. Reprint, Mattituck, N.Y.: Amereon House, 1972.

The Indian Tribes of the Upper Mississippi Valley and Region of the Great Lakes as Described by Nicholas Perrot. Edited by Emma Helen Blair. 2 vols. in 1. 1911. Reprint, Lincoln: University of Nebraska Press, 1996.

Irving, Washington. *Journals and Notebooks.* Vol. 5, *1832–1859.* Edited by Sue Fields Ross. Boston: Twayne Publishers, 1986.

————. *The Western Journals of Washington Irving.* Edited by John Francis McDermott. Norman: University of Oklahoma Press, 1944.

Jefferson, Thomas. *Jefferson's Memorandum Books: Accounts, with Legal Records and Miscellany, 1767–1826.* Edited by James Adam Bear, Jr., and Lucia C. Stanton. 2 vols. Princeton: Princeton University Press, 1997.

————. *The Papers of Thomas Jefferson.* Edited by Julian P. Boyd et al. 30 vols. to date. Princeton: Princeton University Press, 1950–.

————. *The Writings of Thomas Jefferson.* Edited by Andrew A. Lipscomb and Albert E. Bergh. 20 vols. Washington, D.C.: Thomas Jefferson Memorial Association, 1905.

The Journals of the Lewis and Clark Expedition. Edited by Gary E. Moulton. 13 vols. Lincoln: University of Nebraska Press, 1983–2001.

Kinnaird, Lawrence, ed. *Spain in the Mississippi Valley, 1765–1794.* 3 vols. Washington, D.C.: GPO, 1946–49.

Letters of the Lewis and Clark Expedition, with Related Documents, 1783–1854. Edited by Donald Jackson. 2d ed., with additional documents and notes. 2 vols. Urbana: University of Illinois Press, 1978.

Levasseur, Auguste. *Lafayette in America in 1824 and 1825; or, Journal of a Voyage to the United States.* 2 vols. in 1. Translated by John D. Godman. Philadelphia: Carey and Lea, 1829.

The Lewis and Clark Journals: An American Epic of Discovery. The Abridgment of the Definitive Nebraska Edition. Edited by Gary E. Moulton. Lincoln: University of Nebraska Press, 2003.

Lucas, John Baptiste Charles. *Letters of Hon. J.B.C. Lucas from 1815 to 1836.* Compiled by John B. C. Lucas. St. Louis: n.p., 1905.

Mackenzie, Alexander. *Alexander Mackenzie's Voyage to the Pacific Ocean in 1793.* With historical introduction and footnotes by Milo Milton Quaife. New York: Citadel Press, 1967.

Major Problems in the Early Republic, 1787–1848: Documents and Essays. Edited by Sean Wilentz. Lexington, Mass.: D. C. Heath, 1992.

Masson, L. R., ed. *Les Bourgeois de la Compagnie du Nord-Ouest . . .* 2 vols. 1889–90. Reprint, New York: Antiquarian Press, 1960.

Metcalfe, Samuel L., comp. *A Collection of Some of the Most Interesting Narratives of Indian Warfare in the West . . .* Lexington, Ky.: Printed by W. G. Hunt, 1821.

Morgan, Dale L., ed. *The West of William H. Ashley: The International Struggle for the Fur Trade of the Missouri, the Rocky Mountains, and the Columbia . . .* Denver: Old West Publishing Company, 1964.

The Ohio Frontier: An Anthology of Early Writings. Edited by Emily Foster. Lexington: University Press of Kentucky, 1996.

"Papers from the Canadian Archives—1767–1814." *Collections of the State Historical Society of Wisconsin* 12 (1892): 23–132.

Peck, John Mason. *Forty Years of Pioneer Life: Memoir of John Mason Peck, D.D.* Edited by Rufus Babcock. 1864. Reprint, Carbondale: Southern Illinois University Press, 1965.

Pike, Zebulon Montgomery. *The Journals of Zebulon Montgomery Pike, with Letters and Related Documents.* Edited by Donald Jackson. 2 vols. Norman: University of Oklahoma Press, 1966.

Preston, William Campbell. *The Reminiscences of William C. Preston.* Edited by Minnie Clare Yarborough. Chapel Hill: University of North Carolina Press, 1933.

Rodney, Thomas. *A Journey through the West: Thomas Rodney's 1803 Journal from Delaware to the Mississippi Territory.* Edited by Dwight L. Smith and Ray Swick. Athens: Ohio University Press, 1997.

Royall, Anne. *Mrs. Royall's Southern Tour; or, Second Series of the Black Book.* 3 vols. Washington, D.C., 1830–31.

St. Clair, Arthur. *A Narrative of the Manner in Which the Campaign against the Indians, in the Year One Thousand Seven Hundred and Ninety-one, Was Conducted, under the Command of Major General St. Clair . . .* Philadelphia: Printed by Jane Aitken, 1812.

———. *The St. Clair Papers: The Life and Public Service of Arthur St. Clair.* Edited by William Henry Smith. Cincinnati: Robert Clarke & Co., 1882.

Sargent, Winthrop. "Winthrop Sargent's Diary." Edited by Charles Sprague Sargent. *Ohio Archaeological and Historical Quarterly* 33, no. 3 (1924): 237–82.

The Territorial Papers of the United States. Edited by Clarence Edwin Carter. 28 vols. Washington, D.C.: GPO, 1934–75.

Thwaites, Reuben Gold, ed. *Early Western Travels, 1748–1846.* 32 vols. Cleveland: Arthur H. Clark, 1904–07.

Wayne, Anthony. *Anthony Wayne, a Name in Arms: Soldier, Diplomat, Defender of Expansion Westward of a Nation; The Wayne-Knox-Pickering-McHenry Correspondence.* Edited by Richard C. Knopf. Pittsburgh: University of Pittsburgh Press, 1960.

Wheel Boats on the Missouri: The Journals and Documents of the Atkinson-O'Fallon Expedition, 1824–26. Edited by Richard E. Jensen and James S. Hutchins. Helena: Montana Historical Society Press, 2001.

White, James Haley. "Early Days in St. Louis." *Glimpses of the Past* 6 (January–March 1939): 5–13.

SECONDARY SOURCES

Abele, Charles A. "The Grand Council and Treaty at Prairie du Chien, 1825." Ph.D. diss., Loyola University, Chicago, 1969.

Allen, John Logan. *Lewis and Clark and the Image of the American Northwest.* 1975. Reprint, New York: Dover, 1991. Originally published as *Passage through the Garden: Lewis and Clark and the Image of the American Northwest.*

Ambrose, Stephen. *Undaunted Courage: Meriwether Lewis, Thomas Jefferson, and the Opening of the American West.* New York: Simon and Schuster, 1996.

Aron, Stephen. *How the West Was Lost: The Transformation of Kentucky from Daniel Boone to Henry Clay.* Baltimore: Johns Hopkins University Press, 1996.

Bakeless, John Edwin. *Background to Glory: The Life of George Rogers Clark.* 1957. Reprint, Lincoln: University of Nebraska Press, 1992.

Barbour, Barton H. *Fort Union and the Upper Missouri Fur Trade.* Norman: University of Oklahoma Press, 2001.

Berkhoffer, Robert F. *The White Man's Indian: Images of the American Indian from Columbus to the Present.* New York: Knopf, 1978.

Berlin, Ira. *Many Thousands Gone: The First Two Centuries of Slavery in North America.* Cambridge: Harvard University Press, 1998.

Betts, Robert B. *In Search of York: The Slave Who Went to the Pacific with Lewis and Clark.* Rev. ed. Boulder: Colorado Associated University Press, 2000.

Bodley, Temple. *George Rogers Clark: His Life and Public Services.* Boston and New York: Houghton Mifflin, 1926.

Bogart, W. H. *Daniel Boone, and the Hunters of Kentucky.* 1854. Boston: Lee and Shepard, Publishers, 1875.

Boughter, Judith A. *Betraying the Omaha Nation, 1790–1916.* Norman: University of Oklahoma Press, 1998.

Buckley, Jay H. "William Clark: Superintendent of Indian Affairs at St. Louis, 1813–1838." Ph.D. diss., University of Nebraska, Lincoln, 2001.

Calloway, Colin G. *The American Revolution in Indian Country: Crisis and Diversity in Native American Communities.* Cambridge and New York: Cambridge University Press, 1995.

Carter, Harvey Lewis. *The Life and Times of Little Turtle: First Sagamore of the Wabash.* Urbana: University of Illinois Press, 1987.

Cayton, Andrew R. L. *Frontier Indiana.* Bloomington: Indiana University Press, 1996.

Cayton, Andrew R. L., and Fredrika J. Teute, eds. *Contact Points: American Frontiers from the Mohawk Valley to the Mississippi, 1750–1830.* Chapel Hill: University of North Carolina Press, 1998.

Chuinard, E. G. "The Court-Martial of Ensign Meriwether Lewis." We Proceeded On 8, no. 4 (November 1982): 12–15.

Clokey, Richard M. William H. Ashley: Enterprise and Politics in the Trans-Mississippi West. Norman: University of Oklahoma Press, 1980.

Crotty, Gene. The Visits of Lewis & Clark to Fincastle, Virginia. Roanoke: History Museum and Historical Society of Western Virginia, 2003.

Cruikshank, Ernest Alexander. "Robert Dickson, the Indian Trader." Collections of the State Historical Society of Wisconsin 12 (1892): 133–53.

DeRegnaucourt, Tony. The Archaeology of Fort Recovery, Ohio: St. Clair's Defeat (November 4, 1791) and Wayne's Victory (June 30 and July 1, 1794). Occasional Monographs of the Upper Miami Valley Archaeological Research Museum, no. 6. Arcanum, Ohio: Upper Miami Valley Archaeological Research Museum, 1996.

Dillon, Richard. Meriwether Lewis: A Biography. New York: Coward-McCann, 1965.

Douglas, Walter B. Manuel Lisa. Annotated and edited by Abraham P. Nasatir. New York: Argosy-Antiquarian, 1964.

Dowd, Gregory Evan. A Spirited Resistance: The North American Indian Struggle for Unity, 1745–1815. Baltimore: Johns Hopkins University Press, 1992.

Dyson, John P. "The Naming of Paducah." Register of the Kentucky Historical Society 92, no. 2 (1994): 149–74.

Edmunds, R. David. The Shawnee Prophet. Lincoln: University of Nebraska Press, 1983.

Faragher, John Mack. Daniel Boone: The Life and Legend of an American Pioneer. New York: Holt, 1992.

Fausz, J. Frederick. "Partners in Pelts." Public lecture.

———. "'They Have Become a Nation of Quakers': The Removal of the Osage Indians from Missouri." Gateway Heritage 21, no. 1 (Summer 2000): 28–39.

Fischer, David Hackett, and James C. Kelly. Bound Away: Virginia and the Westward Movement. Charlottesville: University Press of Virginia, 2000.

Foley, William E. The Genesis of Missouri: From Wilderness Outpost to Statehood. Columbia: University of Missouri Press, 1989.

Foley, William E., and C. David Rice. The First Chouteaus: River Barons of Early St. Louis. Urbana: University of Illinois Press, 1983.

Friend, Craig Thompson, ed. The Buzzel about Kentuck: Settling the Promised Land. Lexington: University Press of Kentucky, 1999.

Furtwangler, Albert. "Sacagawea's Son: New Evidence from Germany." Oregon Historical Quarterly 102, no. 4 (2001): 518–23.

Garrett, Jerry. "Lewis and Clark Expedition Place Names." Unpublished paper, 2003.

Gilman, Carolyn. Lewis and Clark—Across the Divide. Washington, D.C.: Smithsonian Books, 2003.

Gregg, Kate L. "The War of 1812 on the Missouri Frontier." Missouri Historical Review 33 (October 1938): 3–22; (January 1939): 184–202; (April 1939): 326–48.

Hagan, William T. The Sac and Fox Indians. Norman: University of Oklahoma Press, 1958.

Harrison, Lowell H. George Rogers Clark and the War in the West. Lexington: University Press of Kentucky, 1976.

Hartley, Robert E. Lewis and Clark in the Illinois Country. Westminster, Co.: Xlibris and Sniktau Publications, 2002.

Hay, Thomas Robson, and M. R. Werner. The Admirable Trumpeter: A Biography of General James Wilkinson. Garden City, N.Y.: Doubleday, Doran & Company, 1941.

Herring, Joseph P. *Kenekuk, the Kickapoo Prophet.* Lawrence: University Press of Kansas, 1988.

Horan, James D. *The McKenney-Hall Portrait Gallery of American Indians.* New York: Crown, 1972.

Howe, Henry L. *Historical Collections of Ohio.* Vol. 2. Columbus: Henry Howe & Son, 1891.

Hunter, Lloyd A. "Slavery in St. Louis, 1804–1860." *Bulletin of the Missouri Historical Society* 30 (July 1974): 233–65.

Hurt, R. Douglas. *The Ohio Frontier: Crucible of the Old Northwest, 1720–1830.* Bloomington: Indiana University Press, 1996.

Isenberg, Andrew C. *The Destruction of the Bison: An Environmental History, 1750–1920.* Cambridge and New York: Cambridge University Press, 2000.

———. "The Market Revolution in the Borderlands: George Champlin Sibley in Missouri and New Mexico, 1808–1826." *Journal of the New Republic* 26 (Fall 2001): 445–65.

Jackson, Donald. *Among the Sleeping Giants: Occasional Pieces on Lewis and Clark.* Urbana: University of Illinois Press, 1987.

———. "A Footnote to the Lewis and Clark Expedition." *Manuscripts* 24 (Winter 1972): 3–21.

———. *Thomas Jefferson and the Stony Mountains: Exploring the West from Monticello.* 1981. Reprint, Norman: University of Oklahoma Press, 1993.

———. *Voyages of the Steamboat Yellow Stone.* New York: Ticknor and Fields, 1985.

Jakle, John A. *Images of the Ohio Valley: A Historical Georgraphy of Travel, 1740 to 1860.* New York: Oxford University Press, 1977.

James, Bessie Rowland. *Anne Royall's U.S.A.* New Brunswick: Rutgers University Press, 1972.

James, James Alton. *The Life of George Rogers Clark.* Chicago: University of Chicago Press, 1928.

Jenkinson, Clay Straus. *The Character of Meriwether Lewis: "Completely Metamorphosed" in the American West.* Reno, Nev.: Marmath Press, 2000.

Kellogg, Louise P. "The Capture of Mackinac in 1812." State Historical Society of Wisconsin, *Proceedings* (1912), 124–45.

Kinkead, Ludie J. "How the Parents of George Rogers Clark Came to Kentucky in 1784–85." *Filson Club Quarterly* 3 (October 1928): 1–4.

Kukla, Jon. *A Wilderness So Immense: The Louisiana Purchase and the Destiny of America.* New York: Knopf, 2003.

Kupperman, Karen Ordahl. *Indians and English: Facing Off in Early America.* Ithaca: Cornell University Press, 2000.

Lamar, Howard, ed. *The New Encyclopedia of the American West.* New Haven: Yale University Press, 1998.

Lavender, David. *The First in the Wilderness.* Garden City, N.Y.: Doubleday, 1964.

Lilley, James D. "George Catlin and Washington Irving Meet Black Hawk: Landscapes of Colonial Violence in the Emerging U.S. Nation." Paper presented at Princeton University, 27 December 2001.

Limerick, Patricia Nelson. *The Legacy of Conquest: The Unbroken Past of the American West.* New York: W. W. Norton, 1987.

Linklater, Andro. *Measuring America: How an Untamed Wilderness Shaped the United States and Fulfilled the Promise of Democracy.* New York: Walker & Company, 2002.

Loos, John Louis. "A Biography of William Clark, 1770–1813." 2 vols. Ph.D. diss., Washington University, 1953.

Masur, Louis P. *1831: Year of Eclipse*. New York: Hill and Wang, 2001.

Moore, Robert J., Jr., and Michael Haynes. *Lewis & Clark: Tailor Made, Trail Worn: Army Life, Clothing & Weapons of the Corps of Discovery*. Helena, Mont.: Farcountry Press, 2003.

Nester, William R. *The Arikara War: The First Plains Indian War, 1823*. Missoula, Mont.: Mountain Press, 2001.

Nichols, Roger L. *Black Hawk and the Warrior's Path*. Wheeling, Ill.: Harlan Davidson, 1992.

———. *General Henry Atkinson: A Western Military Career*. Norman: University of Oklahoma Press, 1965.

Oglesby, Richard Edward. *Manuel Lisa and the Opening of the Missouri Fur Trade*. Norman: University of Oklahoma Press, 1965.

Owens, Robert M. "Jeffersonian Benevolence on the Ground: The Indian Land Cession Treaties of William Henry Harrison." *Journal of the Early Republic* 22, no. 3 (Fall 2002): 405–35.

Palmer, Frederick. *Clark of the Ohio: A Life of George Rogers Clark*. New York: Dodd, Mead and Company, 1929.

Penick, James Lal, Jr. *The New Madrid Earthquakes*. Rev. ed. Columbia: University of Missouri Press, 1981.

Perkins, Elizabeth A. *Border Life: Experience and Memory in the Revolutionary Ohio Valley*. Chapel Hill: University of North Carolina Press, 1998.

Perkins, James H. *Annals of the West*. Pittsburgh: W. S. Haven, 1858.

Primm, James Neal. *Lion of the Valley: St. Louis, Missouri, 1764–1980*. 3d ed. St. Louis: Missouri Historical Society Press, 1998.

Prucha, Francis Paul. *American Indian Treaties: The History of a Political Anomaly*. Berkeley: University of California Press, 1994.

Randall, Emilius O., and Daniel J. Ryan. *History of Ohio*. New York: Century History Company, 1912.

Remini, Robert V. *Andrew Jackson and His Indian Wars*. New York: Viking, 2001.

Richter, Daniel K. *Facing East from Indian Country: A Native History of Early America*. Cambridge: Harvard University Press, 2001.

Ronan, Peter. *History of the Flathead Indians*. 1890. Reprint, Minneapolis: Ross & Haines, 1965.

Ronda, James P. *Jefferson's West: A Journey with Lewis and Clark*. Monticello: Thomas Jefferson Foundation, 2000.

———. *Lewis and Clark among the Indians*. Lincoln: University of Nebraska Press, 1984.

———, ed. *Voyages of Discovery: Essays on the Lewis and Clark Expedition*. Helena: Montana Historical Society Press, 1998.

Russell, Robert Ralph. "The Public Career of William Clark, 1813–1838." M.A. thesis, Washington University, 1945.

Shoemaker, Floyd Calvin. *Missouri's Struggle for Statehood, 1804–1821*. 1916. Reprint, New York: Russell and Russell, 1969.

Skelton, William B. *An American Profession of Arms: The Army Officer Corps, 1784–1815*. Lawrence: University Press of Kansas, 1992.

Steffen, Jerome O. *William Clark: Jeffersonian Man on the Frontier*. Norman: University of Oklahoma Press, 1977.

Stevens, Frank E. *The Black Hawk War: Including a Review of Black Hawk's Life*. Chicago: Frank E. Stevens, 1903.

Sugden, John. *Blue Jacket: Warrior of the Shawnees*. Lincoln: University of Nebraska Press, 2000.

———. *Tecumseh: A Life*. New York: Henry Holt, 1997.

Sunder, John. *Joshua Pilcher: Fur Trader and Indian Agent*. Norman: University of Oklahoma Press, 1968.

Sword, Wiley. *President Washington's Indian War: The Struggle for the Old Northwest, 1790–1795*. Norman: University of Oklahoma Press, 1985.

Thomas, Samuel W. "William Clark's 1795 and 1797 Journals and Their Significance." *Bulletin of the Missouri Historical Society* 25, no. 4 (July 1969): 277–95.

Tubbs, Stephenie Ambrose, and Clay Straus Jenkinson. *The Lewis and Clark Companion: An Encyclopedic Guide to the Voyage of Discovery*. New York: Henry Holt, 2003.

Tucker, Glenn. *Mad Anthony Wayne and the New Nation: The Story of Washington's Front-Line General*. Harrisburg, Pa.: Stackpole Books, 1973.

Unrau, William E. *White Man's Wicked Water: The Alcohol Trade and Prohibition in Indian Country, 1802–1892*. Lawrence: University Press of Kansas, 1996.

Vaughan, Alden T. "From White Man to Redskin: Changing Anglo-American Perceptions of the American Indians." *American Historical Review* 87, no. 4 (1982): 917–53.

Wallace, Anthony F. C. *Jefferson and the Indians: The Tragic Fate of the First Americans*. Cambridge: Belknap Press of Harvard University Press, 1999.

Ward, Harry M. *Charles Scott and the "Spirit of '76."* Charlottesville: University Press of Virginia, 1988.

Weber, David J. *The Spanish Frontier in North America*. New Haven: Yale University Press, 1992.

White, Richard. *The Middle Ground: Indians, Empires, and Republics in the Great Lakes Region, 1650–1815*. Cambridge: Cambridge University Press, 1991.

Wides, Harry Emerson. *Anthony Wayne, Trouble Shooter of the American Revolution*. New York: Harcourt, Brace, 1941.

Wilson, Frazer E. *Around the Council Fire: Proceedings at Fort Greene Ville in 1795, Culminating in the Signing of the Treaty of Greene Ville . . .* Mt. Vernon, Ind.: Windmill Publications, 1990.

Wishart, David J. *The Fur Trade of the American West, 1807–1840*. Lincoln: University of Nebraska Press, 1979.

Wood, W. Raymond. *Prologue to Lewis & Clark: The Mackay and Evans Expedition*. Norman: University of Oklahoma Press, 2003.

WEB SITES

Fallen Timbers Battlefield Archaeological Project. Heidelberg College, Tiffin, Ohio. http://www.heidelberg.edu/offices/chma/fallen-timbers

Hier, Marshall D. "Frontier Scandal, *Stokes v. Stokes* Revisited." http://www.bamsl.org/barjour/winter01/Hier.htm

ACKNOWLEDGMENTS

This book is about journeys—the many arduous ones taken by William Clark during his lifetime but also the wonderful ones I have taken in his footsteps two centuries later. My own journey on this trail began at Clark Elementary School in St. Louis, named for William, who co-founded the first school board in the city. It led down Union Boulevard to the Missouri Historical Society, a major repository of Clark papers, where I played as a boy under a statue of Thomas Jefferson. Since then, later journeys have taken my wife, Sarah, and me from the attic of Fotheringay, the Hancock family manor in Virginia that is still in private hands, to the wild and scenic White Cliffs stretch of the Missouri River. Along the way I have met many of the delightful people attracted by the romance of the Lewis and Clark story. Less romantically, perhaps, I have spent equally rewarding hours with archivists, librarians, interpretative-center guides, and passionate scholars—most especially Native Americans—dedicated to telling the complete story of Clark's life, with its often unsettling contradictions.

The mainspring of this enterprise from the start has been Thomas LeBien, publisher and editor at Hill and Wang, who welcomed the idea of a full biography of William Clark and nurtured it to fruition with intellectual enthusiasm, expert editing, and discerning judgment. He has been the best editor a writer could hope for. His colleagues at Farrar, Straus and Giroux—notably Kristy McGowan, Susan Goldfarb, Lynn Buckley, and Sarita Varma—have been equally gracious and professional.

The primary sources for this book—the letters and documents produced by William Clark over his lifetime—reside in archival collections
around the country. Prominent among them is the Missouri Historical
Society, whose president, Dr. Robert R. Archibald, also serves as president of the National Council of the Lewis and Clark Bicentennial. His
colleagues Carolyn Gilman, Karen M. Goering, and Duane Snedekker
have all been immensely helpful. At other archival collections, I am
especially indebted to the generous help of James J. Holmberg and
Nettie Oliver at the Filson Historical Society, Charles T. Cullen and
Robert Karrow at the Newberry Library in Chicago, Justin Dragosanti-
Brantingham at the Kansas State Historical Society, John Neal Hoover
and Charles Brown at the St. Louis Mercantile Library, Robert Cox at
the American Philosophical Society, Harry Miller at the State Historical
Society of Wisconsin, and George Miles at the Beinecke Rare Book and
Manuscript Library at Yale University.

In a category by itself is the amazing Princeton University Library,
whose open stacks make it the best library in the world for a working
writer. Its superb holdings in the Princeton Collections of Western Americana were built over many years by its justly celebrated curator, Alfred
L. Bush. The Princeton Library is also home to the Papers of Thomas
Jefferson, the extraordinary project whose thirty-first volume covers the
death of George Washington and the events preceding the tumultuous
presidential election of 1800. I have benefited from the advice of its general editor, Barbara Oberg, and its former assistant editor Shane Black-
man, as well as from Jeff Looney, editor of the forthcoming Jefferson
Papers Retirement Series at Monticello.

In assembling these materials, I have been ably assisted by a formidable group of researchers. Katherine Douglass, former editor of the Missouri Historical Society's *Gateway Heritage* magazine, worked heroically
to unearth the riches in Clark collections, not only in St. Louis but also
at the Filson Historical Society in Louisville and at the Western Historical Manuscript Collection in Columbia, Missouri. Zoë Davidson ana-
lyzed the voluminous McCarter and English Indian Claims Cases
Collection at Princeton University. Loralee Nolletti read and deciphered
the microfilms of Clark's important Indian superintendency records at
the Kansas State Historical Society. Amanda Martin assisted on several
research projects, and Donna Aceto tracked down all the visual materi-

als. Special thanks go to Gretchen M. Oberfranc, editor of the *Princeton University Library Chronicle*, who checked my sources and documentation to ensure that due citations were appropriately given.

I am deeply grateful that parts or all of the completed manuscript were read in a neonatal state by several of the most outstanding scholars and editors I know. They were Andrew C. Isenberg of the Department of History at Princeton University; Robert J. Moore, Jr., historian at the Jefferson National Expansion Memorial in St. Louis; Gary E. Moulton, editor of the definitive University of Nebraska edition of *The Journals of the Lewis and Clark Expedition*; Dustin Griffin of the Department of English at New York University, and Gale Griffin; Jim Merritt, editor of *We Proceeded On*, the lively quarterly journal of the Lewis and Clark Trail Heritage Foundation; Amy Mossett, a Mandan/Hidatsa tribal historian; and Stephenie Ambrose Tubbs, co-author of *The Lewis and Clark Companion*. They all pulled me back from more precipices than I care to remember.

Every journey begins with its first tentative steps, and mine were helped by early conversations with two smart friends, A. Scott Berg and Robert Fagles, both students of heroes and journeys, who encouraged me to believe that this was a trip worth taking. My literary agent, Robin Straus, a friend for twenty-five years, has given wise counsel from the beginning. I thank many other valued friends and supporters encountered along the way, including Peyton (Bud) Clark, Gene Crotty, Anne M. Daniel, Connie Escher, Jerry Garrett, Robert Gatten, Will Howarth, Stephanie Kearny, Mary-Jo Kline, Stu Knapp, Dr. William R. Leahy Jr., James D. Lilley, Emily McCulley, David Nicandri, Chet Orloff, Eugene Peters, Jane Sarles, Mark Wethli, Sean Wilentz, and many members of the Lewis and Clark Trail Heritage Foundation.

My most steadfast companion on this journey, and in life, is my wife, Sarah, who, with our children, Rebecca, Landon, and Cassie, joined me on the physical landscape from Monticello to the Pacific and, in a deeper sense, in traveling the complex interior landscape of the American character during the early republic. To paraphrase both Clark and Lewis, there is no person on earth with whom I would rather share its fatigues, its dangers, and its honors.

INDEX

Active (schooner), 101

Adams, John, 86, 101, 105, 277, 285

Adams, John Quincy, 242, 245, 281, 285, 287, 294, 303

African-Americans, *see* blacks

Aird, James, 147, 151, 204

Albany, Treaty of, 13

Alien and Sedition Acts (1798), 104, 106

Allen (slave), 260, 294

Allen, Ethan, 329

Allen, Paul, 208, 216, 239

American Fur Company, 188, 243, 263, 264, 284, 288–89, 298, 299, 315–17, 329

American Philosophical Society, 91, 111, 160, 183, 186, 200, 285

American Revolution, *see* Revolutionary War

Amherst, Lord Jeffrey, 21–22

Anderson, Ann Clark, 162–64, 170

Anderson, Eliza (Clark's niece), 294

Anderson, Eliza Clark, 16, 50, 87, 153, 163, 312

Anderson, Richard Clough, 57, 153, 163, 178, 312

Anderson, Lieutenant Robert, 312

Antelope (steamboat), 331

Anthony (slave), 255, 260

Apaches, 281

Arbuckle, Captain Matthew, 33

Argus of Western America, 178

Arikaras, 97, 132, 137, 142, 152, 160, 174–75, 268–72, 274, 329, 330

Arkansas River, 166, 176, 193, 215, 258

Arketarnashar (Eagle Feather), 152, 161

Armstrong, John, 67–68, 97, 107, 113, 185, 211, 217, 219, 221, 223

Army, U.S., 56, 60, 101, 121, 147, 265, 293, 334; Clark's promotion denied by, 155; Corps of Engineers of, 124, 333; High Plains forts built by, 256–58; Missouri Legion of, 269–70; Ohio Valley Indian campaign of, 8–12, 57–59, 63–82; at Three Flags Ceremony, 122–23; *see also* Legion of the United States

Arnold, Benedict, 42

Arrowsmith, Aaron, 139

Ashe, Thomas, 160

Ashley, William H., 224, 260, 263, 266–71, 274–75, 328, 332

Assiniboin (steamboat), 322

Assiniboins, 330, 331

Astor, John Jacob, 188, 226, 243, 263, 264, 279, 288–89, 298, 299, 315, 321

Astor, William, 299

Astoria expedition, 193–94, 226, 321

Atkinson, General Henry, 257, 258, 273, 274, 286, 292, 311–14, 331

Atkinson, Mary Ann Bullitt, 286, 302

Atlantic (steamboat), 303

Audubon, John James, 178, 201

Bad Axe, Battle of, 314
Baily, Francis, 25, 70, 104, 118
Bakewell, Thomas W., 201
Bank of St. Louis, 254, 262
Bank of the United States, 308
Barbour, James, 281, 286–89, 294
Barton, Benjamin Smith, 185–87
Barton, David, 240, 267
Bates, Frederick, 173–75, 188–89, 204, 211, 278
Bates, Richard, 174
Bazadone, Laurent, 94, 95, 110, 112
Bean, Jonathan, 299
Beaumont, Gustave de, 309
Beaver (keelboat), 273–74
Becknell, William, 263
Beckwourth, Jim, 248
Ben (slave), 106, 171, 260
Benoit, François Marie, 129
Benton, Thomas Hart, 240–42, 255, 264, 267, 273, 328
Berkeley, William, 84
Berry (slave), 255, 260, 294
Biddle, Charles, 185
Biddle, Jane Craig, 200
Biddle, Nicholas, 143, 185–87, 192–93, 199–200, 208, 216, 223, 236–37, 240, 282, 285, 308
Biddle, Thomas, 282, 308
Big Bone Lick fossil beds, 48, 159–60, 163
Big Elk (Ongpatonga), 229–31, 300–302
Big Soldier, 168, 207
Bingham, George Caleb, 227
Bingham, Henry Vest, 227, 247
Bird family, 14
Bissell, General Daniel, 232
Blackbird, 231, 321
Black Buffalo (Un-tongar-Sarbar), 131–32, 228–30, 300
Black Cat (Posecopsahe), 133
Blackfeet, 144, 193, 205, 270, 272, 273, 322, 330, 331
Blackfish, 32
Black Hawk (Makataimeshekiakiak), 123, 209–10, 221, 222, 225, 228, 277, 282, 310–15, 319–21, 324–25
Black Hills, 143; map of, 193
Black Moccasin (Omp-se-ha-ra), 133

blacks: enslaved, *see* slaves; free, 149, 175, 188, 269, 328
Blondeau, Maurice, 206, 211
Blow, Peter, 328
Blue Jacket, 5, 8, 9, 27, 58–59, 75, 78, 82–84, 190
Blue Licks, Battle of, 44, 54
Bodmer, Karl, 321–22
Boggs, Liburn, 332
Boilvin, Nicholas, 196
Bonaparte, Napoleon, 109, 110, 112, 224
Boone, Daniel, 16, 23, 26, 27, 29, 32, 44, 45, 50, 54, 131, 160, 167, 193, 205, 224, 256
Boone, Israel, 44
Boone, James, 26
Boone, Nathan, 167, 205, 256
Boone, Rebecca, 16
Bowman, Major Joseph, 35
Brackenridge, Henry Marie, 194, 227
Bradbury, John, 101, 193–94, 201–2
Braddock, General Edward, 16
Bradford, Samuel, 208
Bradford & Inskeep, 216, 239
Bradshaw, Lieutenant, 82
Brandywine, Battle of, 47, 59, 64, 278
Brant, Joseph, 20, 43, 82
Brant, Molly, 20
Bratton, William, 117
Breckenridge, Letitia, 164
Bridger, Jim, 217, 248, 268
British, 5, 8, 19–23, 52, 59, 83, 85, 86, 105, 110, 152, 158, 159, 171, 173, 190–91, 195–96, 198, 205, 228, 231, 232, 256, 257, 321, 326; French conflicts with, 15–16, 21, 148; in fur trade, 19, 97, 129, 131, 147, 150, 157, 165, 166, 172, 199, 203, 204, 244, 263–64, 270, 272–74; intermarriage of Indians and, 20; in Pontiac's War, 22; during Revolutionary War, 30, 32, 33–47, 55, 64, 96, 121; Royal Navy, 102–3; and Scott's Wabash expedition, 60, 62; Spain and, 98; and U.S. Army's Ohio Valley campaign, 70, 71, 74, 77–79, 82; in War of 1812, 206–7, 209–11, 214–25, 229, 234, 235, 311, 327
Brock, General Isaac, 210
Brown, Captain James, 60

Brulé bands, *see* Lakotas
Buckongahelas, 8
Buffalo Medicine (Tar-ton-gar-wa-ker), 131
Buffon, Georges Louis Leclerc de, 28, 160
Builderback, Charles, 43
Bulger, Andrew, 225
Bullock, William Fontaine, 141
Bunker Hill, Battle of, 199, 210
Bureau of Indian Affairs, 273, 279
Burr, Aaron, 147, 148, 154, 185
Butler, Major General Richard, 7, 9–11

Cabanné, Jean, 317
Cadmus (ship), 277
Cahokia, Treaty of, 35–36
Calhoun (steamboat), 260
Calhoun, John C., 242, 247–48, 251, 256, 257, 259, 261, 264, 265, 267, 268, 272, 279–80, 283
Cambridge University, 186
Campbell, Colonel John, 62, 163, 172, 196, 204
Campbell, Lieutenant John, 192, 221
Campbell, Major William, 78, 79
Canada, 150, 166, 201, 244, 256; militia of, 75
Car of Commerce (steamboat), 302–3
Carr, William C., 176, 232
Cass, Lewis, 281–83, 292, 294–96, 311, 312, 317, 324, 325, 327
Catawbas, 13
Catherine the Great, Empress of Russia, 90
Catlin, George, 300, 316, 318
Cession, Treaty of, 112
Chabot, Madame, 100
Chapline, Captain Abraham, 57
Charbonneau, Jean Baptiste "Pomp" ("Pompy"), 134, 135, 144–46, 186, 194, 249, 254, 260, 276
Charbonneau, Lisette, 249
Charbonneau, Toussaint, 128–29, 134, 135, 137, 144–45, 194, 249, 260, 270, 274
Charless, Joseph, 163, 210–11, 226, 232, 240, 251, 253
Charlotte, Treaty of, 27–28
Chase, Salmon P., 322–23

Chenoweth massacre, 56
Cherokees, 22–23, 29–30, 32, 39, 45, 70, 71, 189, 215, 233, 235, 243–44, 246–48, 287, 304, 318, 332, 334
Cheyennes, 274
Chickawsaws, 43, 70–73, 76, 88–90, 92, 166, 180, 289, 290–91, 293, 304
Chieftain (steamboat), 311
Chinooks, 136
Chippewas, *see* Ojibwas
Chloe (slave), 177, 188, 260
Choctaws, 92, 289, 293, 304
cholera, 313, 321
Chouteau, Auguste, 131, 157, 167, 224, 237, 247–48
Chouteau, Auguste Pierre, 158, 172, 223
Chouteau, Paul, 306
Chouteau, Pierre, 124, 152–54, 156–58, 167–69, 172, 174, 175, 181, 211–12, 223, 299, 322
Chouteau, Pierre, Jr., 315–17, 328
Chouteau family, 96, 122, 139, 149, 288
Christy, Major, 209
Civil War, 322, 329
Clamorgan, Jacques, 97
Clark, Abby (daughter-in-law), 332–33
Clark, Ann (sister), *see* Gwathmey, Ann Clark
Clark, Ann Rogers (mother), 13–17, 47, 50, 60, 106, 107
Clark, Benjamin (uncle), 16
Clark, Edmund (brother), 16, 47, 55, 81, 94, 95, 105, 112, 153, 169, 170, 191, 223, 245, 289
Clark, Edmund (son), 289
Clark, Eleanor (niece), 47
Clark, Eliza (sister), *see* Anderson, Eliza Clark
Clark, Frances "Fanny" (sister), *see* Fitzhugh, Fanny Clark O'Fallon Thruston
Clark, George Rogers (brother), 25–30, 47, 52, 55, 56, 65, 86, 92, 113, 119, 124, 133, 153–54, 181, 230, 271, 313, 326; alcoholism of, 59, 94, 106; birth of, 15, 16; death of, 244–45; debts of, 87, 94–95, 97, 107–8, 110, 112, 169, 176, 218, 290, 318; education of, 17; exploration by, 24–25, 48–50, 97; failing health of, 178, 239;

Clark, George Rogers (*cont.*)
  fossils collected by, 48, 160; fort named
  for, 215; French and, 91, 106, 278; as Indian commissioner, 53; land grant to, 46,
  84, 209; and O'Fallon's schemes, 60, 88;
  pension for, 184; during Revolutionary
  War, 30, 31, 33–45, 57, 66, 79, 81, 90,
  96, 111, 121, 177, 197, 199; Wilkinson's
  campaign to discredit, 54, 64, 73, 147
Clark, George Rogers Hancock (son), 239,
  251, 255, 259, 284, 289–90, 301, 314,
  320, 323
Clark, Harriet Kennerly Radford (second
  wife), 107–8, 155, 260, 262–63, 276,
  289–90, 293, 294–95, 300, 301, 303,
  308–9
Clark, John (ancestor), 14
Clark, John (father), 13–17, 23, 25, 30, 39,
  41, 47, 50–53, 60, 87, 91, 95, 106, 107, 113
Clark, John, Jr. (brother), 16, 18, 47, 55
Clark, John Hite (nephew), 170, 191
Clark, John Julius (son), 247, 251, 255,
  259, 276, 284, 289, 301, 308
Clark, Jonathan (brother), 25, 30, 42, 53,
  62, 94, 112, 141, 162, 178; birth of, 15,
  16; children of, 65–66, 170, 294; death
  of, 200; education of, 17–18; move to
  Kentucky of, 108–10; during Revolutionary War, 47, 55, 278; William's letters to,
  79, 81, 106, 108, 153, 156, 160, 164, 165,
  169–71, 176, 179, 182, 184, 199
Clark, Jonathan (grandfather), 15, 119
Clark, Julia Hancock (first wife), 142, 155,
  172, 176, 177, 182–84, 186, 188, 207,
  216, 263, 276; birth of children of, 171,
  200, 217, 239, 247; childhood of, 107–8;
  death of, 254, 255, 262; illness of, 223,
  239, 246, 247, 250–52; Kennerly cousins
  of, 219, 259–60; marriage of, 156, 159,
  161–64, 181
Clark, Lucy (sister), *see* Croghan, Lucy
  Clark
Clark, Mary (part-Indian granddaughter),
  138
Clark, Mary Margaret (daughter), 217,
  251, 255, 259, 261–62
Clark, Meriwether Lewis (son), 276, 277,
  301–2, 308, 309, 332–33; in Atkinson's

campaign against Black Hawk, 312, 314;
  birth of, 171; childhood of, 176, 186, 207,
  216, 231, 248, 255, 259; education of,
  251; at West Point, 283–84, 290, 294, 301
Clark, Richard (brother), 16, 39, 47, 52, 55
Clark, Sarah "Sally" (sister-in-law), 47, 65–
  66, 119
Clark, Thomas Jefferson (son; later Jefferson Kearny Clark), 276, 284, 294, 300,
  301, 314, 317, 332
Clark, William: adolescence of, 47, 50, 52;
  birth of, 16; birth of children of, 171,
  200, 217, 239, 247, 276, 289; business
  ventures of, 169–70, 172, 191, 199, 267,
  290; childhood of, 17, 18; commissioned
  lieutenant in U.S. Army, 64–69; death of,
  333–34; debts of, 323–24; declining
  health of, 324, 329, 332–33; and earthquakes of 1811, 201–2; education of, 57;
  family life of, 194, 255, 259–60, 276,
  289–90, 301; first visit to St. Louis of, 95–
  97; fossil collecting for Jefferson by, 159–
  61, 177; and George Rogers's financial
  problems, 87, 94–95, 97, 107–8, 110,
  112, 169, 176, 218, 290, 318; as governor
  of Missouri Territory, 212–14, 235–37,
  240–52; at Greenville, 84, 86–88; and
  Harriet's death, 308–9; Indian Museum
  of, 237, 275, 278, 321; Irving's visit to,
  317–20; and Julia's death, 254, 255, 262;
  in Kentucky militia, 12, 55–57, 59–63;
  and Lafayette's visit, 277–78; land speculation by, 209, 237, 290–91; in Legion of
  the United States Indian campaign, 70–
  82; and Lewis's death, 176–82; marriage
  of Harriet and, 262–63; marriage of Julia
  and, 156, 159, 161–64, 181; military mission to Spanish of, 89–92, 201; Missouri
  gubernatorial campaign of, 252–55, 275;
  Mulberry Hill plantation managed by,
  97, 106, 108; New Orleans journey of,
  97–105, 109; and parents' deaths, 106,
  107; during preparations for expedition
  with Lewis, 113–15, 117–25; and publication of expedition journals, 182–87,
  192–93, 199–200, 208, 209, 216, 239; return to civilian life of, 93; during Revolutionary War, 39, 41; Sacagawea's son as

ward of, 194, 249, 276; as slave owner, 106–7, 164–65, 170–71, 195, 232, 260, 318–19, 328–29; as Superintendent of Indian Affairs, 259, 261, 264–65, 267–70, 272, 273, 276–77, 279–81, 284–89, 292–95, 297–308, 310–17, 323–28, 330–31; as territorial Indian agent, 155–59, 161, 165, 167–69, 171–74, 188–92, 196–99, 203–6, 212; treaties with Indians negotiated by, 67–69, 226–34, 237–39, 281–83, 285–86, 320, 325–26, 332; on Voyage of Discovery, 125–53, 256–58, 322; during War of 1812, 207–10, 212, 214–25; in Washington, 105, 108, 155–56, 212, 242–44, 251, 285, 286, 294–95, 324, 332; will of, 329

Clark, William M. (cousin), 57

Clark, William Preston (son), 276, 277, 282, 284, 299, 303, 314, 323, 328, 332; birth of, 200; childhood of, 207, 216, 248, 255, 259; education of, 251, 290

Clarke, Peter (half-Indian son), 138

Clatsops, 136, 137

Clay, Henry, 206, 249, 252, 294

Clayburne (slave), 303

Clemson, Captain Eli, 167

Cleopatra (steamboat), 296

Clermont, 207

Clyman, James, 268

Cole, Captain William, 189

Coles, Isaac, 184

Collins, John, 123, 125, 126

Colter, John, 116, 123–24, 144, 158, 193

Columbia (ship), 65

Columbia River Fur Company, 315

Columbus, Christopher, 19

Comanches, 166

Commodore Perry (gunboat), 228

Concord, Battle of, 30

Congress, U.S., 103–4, 106, 184, 208, 240, 257, 264–65, 279, 296, 308, 311; army expanded by, 57, 64; Clark's promotion to colonel rejected by, 155, 200; inquiry into St. Clair's Defeat by, 9, 63; liquor sales to Indians prohibited by, 316; militias authorized by, 57; smallpox inoculation program funded by, 329; and statehood for Missouri, 249; Voyage of Discovery funded by, 111, 113; War of 1812 declared by, 206

Conner, John, 115, 117

Connolly, Dr. John, 26

Conrad, John, 186, 208

Constellation (frigate), 103, 103

Constitution, U.S., 64, 206

Continental Army, 4, 5, 49, 54, 55, 59, 60, 62, 64, 72, 93

Continental Congress, 5, 39, 44, 49, 53

Cook, Captain James, 139

Cornstalk, 27, 32–33

"Corn Treaty," 310

Cornwallis, Charles, 1st Marquess Cornwallis, 43

Corps of Discovery, *see* Voyage of Discovery; *names of specific members*

cotton plantations, 109, 234

Crawford, Captain John, 65

Crawford, Redford, 172, 204

Crawford, Colonel William, 43–44, 122

Creeks, 66, 71, 92, 218, 281, 293, 304

Crees, 331

Creoles, 105, 131, 149, 174, 208, 240, 245, 246

Cresap, Colonel Michael, 26, 28

Cresswell, Nicholas, 29, 31

Crist, George Heinrich, 202

Crockett, Davy, 297

Croghan, Colonel George, 159, 198, 222

Croghan, Lucy Clark (Clark's sister), 16, 50, 59, 94–95, 119, 153, 178, 259

Croghan, William, 43, 52, 59, 95, 99, 119, 159, 178, 276

Crooks, Ramsay, 264, 284, 299

Crows, 144, 274

Croyable (schooner), 104

Cruzatte, Pierre, 130, 145

Cumberland Gap, 26, 29, 30, 50, 107, 154, 182

Cummins, John, 273, 307

Cupid (slave), 18–19, 106

Cus-ka-lah (Clatsop Indian), 137

Dafney (slave), 106

Dancing Rabbit Creek, Treaty of, 304, 309

Davis, David, 330

Davis, Jefferson, 313, 314

Daytime Smoke (Halahtookit), 138

Dearborn, Henry, 111, 123, 148, 152, 155, 157, 159, 165, 166, 168, 173

Decatur, Stephen, 104

Declaration of Independence, 19, 32, 116–17

Delaware (schooner), 104

Delawares, 5, 16, 20, 21, 27, 30, 71, 78, 95, 115, 157, 307; agrarian, 280, 287; alcohol sold to, 305; Christian, slaughter of, 43; in delegation to Washington, 206; Osages and, 189; removal of, 292, 296, 332; Spanish and, 46; treaties with, 53, 83, 122, 229, 233, 248, 320; victories against U.S. Army of, 8, 58, 66; in War of 1812, 222

Dennie, Joseph, 186

Denny, Major Ebenezer, 7–8, 10, 54

De Prefontaine, Dr. Joseph R., 331–32

Detroit, 8, 15, 45; during Revolutionary War, 33, 34, 36, 39, 42

Detroit Gazette, 271

Devil's Race-Ground, 99

Dickens, Charles, 99, 120, 308

Dickson, Joseph, 144, 158

Dickson, Robert, 147, 151, 203–4, 207, 209–11, 216–20, 224, 225, 244, 263

Dodge, General Henry, 292

Donelson, Andrew Jackson, 295

Donelson, Emily, 295

Dougherty, John, 306–8

Dougherty, Major, 70

Dow, Lorenzo, 202

Dragging Canoe, 30, 43

Drouillard, George, 121, 157, 176, 189, 193

dueling, 147, 185, 172, 191–92, 196, 204, 232, 242, 308

Duncan, Henry, 199

Dunmore, Lord, *see* Murray, John, 4th Earl of Dunmore; *see also* Lord Dunmore's War

Eagle Feather, *see* Arketarnashar

earthquakes, 201–2

Easter (slave), 106, 163, 171

Easton, Rufus, 208, 240–41

Eaton, John, 311

Eaton, Peggy O'Neale, 311

Ebenene (Ebony) (slave), 260

Edinburgh, University of, 6, 17

Edwards, Ninian, 205, 208, 209, 224, 233–34, 291, 292, 299

Elinipsico, 33

Eliott, Lieutenant, 92–93

Ellicott, Andrew, 139

Elliott, Matthew, 8, 78

Elliott massacre, 51

Emerson, John, 328

Enlightenment, 29, 98, 133

Enterprise (steamboat), 311

Espy, Josiah, 153–54

Eustis, William, 175–77, 182, 184, 189, 191, 196, 197–99, 203, 206–7, 210

Evans, John Thomas, 97

Fallen Timbers, Battle of, 78, 80, 82, 86, 190, 198, 289

Farnham, Russel, 321

Farrar, Ann "Nancy" Clark Thruston, 260

Farrar, Bernard Gaines, 191–92, 232, 260, 328

Fearson, Henry Bradshaw, 249

Federal (barge), 69

Federalists, 101, 104, 148, 156, 185, 206

Field, Joseph, 117, 162

Field, Reubin, 117, 122, 162

Fink, Mike, 249, 268

Finney, Treaty of, 53, 54

Fire Prairie, Treaty of, 167–69

Fitzhugh, Dennis, 153, 181, 191, 254, 260, 262, 276

Fitzhugh, Fanny Clark O'Fallon Thruston, 16, 18, 50, 59–60, 81–82, 87, 107, 141, 210, 250, 260

Fitzpatrick, Thomas, 268

Five Civilized Tribes, 304

Flaget, Bishop Benedict, 171

Flint, Timothy, 226–27, 230

Floyd, Charles, 117, 124, 127, 129–30, 141, 142

Floyd, John, 42

Fontaine, Colonel Aaron, 141
Fontaine, Martha "Marthey," 141
Forsyth, Thomas, 227, 250, 288, 299, 315
Fort Wayne, Treaty of, 198
Fowler, Major Jacob, 10
Foxes, see Sauks and Foxes
France (slave), 106
Franklin, Benjamin, 23
Frazer (Frazier), Robert, 123
Freeman, Lieutenant Jonathan, 316–17
Frelinghuysen, Theodore, 297
French, 5, 20, 25, 60, 101, 104–6, 120, 121, 148, 152, 166, 291; fur trade of, 15, 96, 149, 150, 158; and Louisiana Purchase, 109–12, 122–23; navy of, 103; during Revolutionary War, 34, 35, 37, 40; in Seven Years War, 16, 21
French Revolution, 73
Fries, Anastasia, 276
Fulkerson, William, 330
Fulton, Robert, 201
fur trade, 19, 22, 122, 145, 177, 223, 231, 260, 263–75, 287; British, 97, 129, 131, 147, 150, 157, 165, 166, 172, 199, 203, 204, 244, 247, 263–64, 270, 272–74; decline in, 307, 322; French, 15, 96, 149, 150, 158; in St. Louis, 133, 139, 188, 191; see also American Fur Company; Missouri Fur Company

Gaines, General Edmund P., 310
Gallatin, Albert, 139
Gass, Patrick, 127
Gayoso de Lemos, Manuel, 89–90, 101, 102
Genêt, Edmond Charles, 91
George III, King of England, 22
Georgia, removal of Indians from, 334
Germantown, Battle of, 47, 59, 64
Geyer, Henry, 232
Ghent, Treaty of, 224–25
Gibson, George, 117
Giddings, Salmon, 262
Gilmer, Peachy, 126
Girty, Simon, 8, 44, 78, 122
Godoy, Manuel, 98

Goforth, William, 160
Gomo, 190
Goodrich, Silas, 136
Governor Clark (gunboat), 221, 225, 228
Graham, Captain Duncan, 228
Graham, James, 191–92
Graham, Richard, 288, 320
Gratiot, Charles, 96, 131
Gray, Captain Robert, 65
"Great American Desert," 258
Great Comet of 1811, 202
Greathouse brothers, 26, 28
Great Plains, see "Great American Desert"
Greene, Nathanael, 72
Greenville, Treaty of, 82–86, 122, 131, 144, 168, 198, 229
Grey Eyes, 268, 270
Griffin, John, 155
Griffin, Mary Hancock, 155, 217
Gwathmey, Ann Clark, 16, 25, 26, 47, 153, 276
Gwathmey, George, 198
Gwathmey, Owen, 25, 47, 223

Halahtookit, see Daytime Smoke
Hall, Hugh, 126
Hall, Rachel, 313
Hall, Sylvia, 313
Hamilton, Alexander, 147, 185
Hamilton, Henry, 36–40, 79, 121
Hamtramck, Major John, 56, 67, 78
Hancock, Caroline, see Preston, Caroline Hancock
Hancock, Colonel George, 107, 156, 161, 182, 195, 216, 254, 262
Hancock, Forrest, 144, 158
Hancock, Judith "Julia," see Clark, Julia Hancock
Hancock, Margaret, 217, 276
Hand, General Edward, 33
Hardin, Colonel John, 55, 56, 60, 66, 67
Harding, Chester, 275
Harmar, General Josiah, 5, 8, 58, 67–68, 72, 80
Harris, Carey A., 333
Harrison, Benjamin, 46

Harrison, William Henry, 77, 150–51, 156, 173, 190, 197–99, 205, 215, 217, 239, 299, 327

Harry (slave), 106

Harvard University, 4, 210

Hassler, Ferdinand Rudolph, 185

Hay, John, 121, 122

Hay, Major Jehu, 38, 121

"headrights" system, 14

Heath, John, 236

Helen McGregor (steamboat), 303

Hempstead, Edward, 208, 240

Henderson, Richard, 29–31

Henry (slave), 303

Henry, Andrew, 172, 267, 268, 20

Henry, General James, 313–14

Henry, Patrick, 31, 33, 36, 37, 39, 46, 53

Hero (brig), 102–3

Herring, Elbert, 288, 330

Hidatsas, 123, 187, 274

Hitchcock, Captain Ethan Allen, 329, 332, 333

Hood's Ferry, Battle of, 42

Hooke, Lieutenant Moses, 115, 116

Hortis, Francis, 159

House of Representatives, U.S., 108, 240, 297; *see also* Congress, U.S.

Howard, General Benjamin, 188, 204, 205, 207, 209, 211–15, 222, 223

Hull, William, 208

Hunt, George, 204

Hunt, Wilson Price, 193, 194, 321

Hurst, Henry, 112

Huston, Lieutenant, 82

Ibos, 17

Illinois, 83, 121, 177–78, 233–34, 291–92, 299, 305, 319; Black Hawk War in, 310–15; removal of Indians from, 320, 327; Revolutionary War campaign in, 33–39, 44, 46, 47, 52, 57, 81, 154

Indian Removal Act (1830), 297, 320

Indians, 5, 14, 19–21, 25, 49–52, 103, 105, 156, 159, 163, 170, 174, 182, 194, 195, 253–55, 258, 284–87, 324; alcohol traded to, 287–89, 298, 305, 311, 315–17, 322; Calhoun's policy toward,

242, 256, 259, 261, 264–65; delegations to Washington of, 124, 151–55, 206–7, 276–77; and earthquakes of 1811, 203; enslavement of, 17; French alliance with, 16, 21; fur trade with, 15, 19, 22, 97, 150, 157–58, 172, 223, 231, 267, 271, 272, 298, 299; hunting practices of, 3–4, 20; intermarriage between white men and, 20; Jackson's policy toward, 295–97; Jefferson's policy toward, 150, 151, 165–66, 176, 190, 243, 279; and Louisiana Purchase, 123; removal of, 279–80, 292–93, 296–98, 304–6, 326; during Revolutionary War, 30–46; in St. Louis, 96, 149; slaughter by militias of, 55–56, 61–62; smallpox among, 22, 306–7, 329–32; Tocqueville on, 309–10; treaties with, 52–53, 82–86, 167–69, 198, 226–34, 239, 274, 280–83, 285–86, 299–301, 327; U.S. Army's Ohio Valley campaign against, 8–12, 57–59, 63–82; and Voyage of Discovery, 125, 131–38, 140–43, 186, 192; and War of 1812, 206–7, 208–11, 213, 218, 222–25, 234, 235; *see also specific tribes*

Insurgente (ship), 103

Iowas, 165, 166, 196, 218, 223, 233, 276, 282, 325

Iroquois, 4, 22–23, 25, 26, 32, 52, 82

Irving, Washington, 166, 188, 317–20

Jackson, Andrew, 218, 224, 241, 290, 294, 295, 296–97, 303, 307, 308, 313, 315, 319, 320, 325, 327

James (slave), 106, 163

James, Edwin, 330

Jamestown colony, 21

Jarrot, Nicholas, 122

Jay's Treaty, 85

Jefferson, Peter, 14

Jefferson, Thomas, 14, 15, 46, 84, 90–91, 105, 108, 153, 154, 169, 173, 175, 186, 196, 203, 240, 284–86; biographical sketch of Lewis by, 216; death of, 285, 293; delegation of chiefs to, 152, 155; fossil collection of, 48, 159–61, 163, 177; George Rogers Clark and, 24, 49–50, 59,

97; Indian policy of, 150, 151, 165–66, 176, 190, 243, 279; Lafayette's visit to, 277; land speculation by, 23; and Lewis's death, 181; and Louisiana Purchase, 109–11; in Paris, 50, 90; during Revolutionary War, 28, 32–34, 39, 41, 42; slaves owned by, 17; and Voyage of Discovery, 110–11, 113, 115, 117, 118, 127, 130–33, 139, 143, 182–83, 200, 307; yeoman farmer ideal of, 197, 264

Jesseaume, René, 153
Jesup, Ann Croghan, 324
Jesup, Thomas, 324
Johnson, Andrew, 322
Johnson, Richard Mentor, 215–16
Johnson, William, 20, 22, 23
Johnston, John, 83, 205
Jones, Reverend David, 82
Jones, John Gabriel, 31
Jones, John Rice, 95
Juba (slave), 106, 173, 232
Judith ("Judieths") River, 141–42
Jumping Fish, 150

Kansas Indians, 165, 196, 233, 280, 281, 283
Kaskaskias, 83, 320
Kearny, Major Stephen Watts, 274, 300, 302, 308
Kearny, Mary Radford, 262, 290, 300–302, 308
Kekionga, 6
Kenekuk, 320
Kennerly, Alzière Menard, 319
Kennerly, Augustin, 260, 303, 304, 323, 325
Kennerly, Elizabeth, 260
Kennerly, George Hancock, 219–21, 228, 231–32, 246, 259–60, 274, 276–77, 319, 323, 325
Kennerly, Harriet, see Clark, Harriet Kennerly Radford
Kennerly, James, 219–21, 249, 259–60, 262, 274, 302, 323–25, 332–33
Kennerly, Mary Hancock, 262
Kenney, James, 20
Kenton, Simon, 54
Kentucky, 106, 114, 209, 210, 215, 246, 290–91; dueling in, 191; emigration to

St. Louis from, 149; militia of, 5, 7, 9–10, 31, 39–41, 55–58, 60, 62; during Revolutionary War, 30–33, 37, 39, 40, 42, 44, 45; settlement of, 5, 26, 29, 46, 50–52, 93–94, 107; slaves in, 95, 106–7, 108–9, 135; surveying of, 25, 27, 30, 47, 94
Keokuk, 228, 276, 282, 300, 310, 311, 325
Kickapoos, 60, 61, 74, 83, 131, 157, 173, 189, 228, 229, 233, 292, 318, 320, 327
King, Nicholas, 139
King, Rufus, 110
Kitt (slave), 106
Knox, Henry, 6, 8, 58, 64, 65, 68, 69, 71, 72, 79, 97

Labbadie, Sylvestre, 172
Labiche, François, 153
Lafayette, Marquis de, 277–79
Lalawethika, see Tenskwatawa
Land Ordinance of 1785, 57
Latrobe, Charles, 234–35
Leavenworth, Colonel Henry, 257–59, 269–74
Leavenworth, Treaty of, 325
LeClerc, Narcisse, 317
Lécuyer (trader), 97
Ledyard, John, 90
Lee, Colonel Henry "Light Horse Harry," 64
Lee, Mary Custis, 333
Lee, Robert E., 333
Legion of the United States, 69–84, 93, 108, 114, 115, 282
Levasseur, Auguste, 278
Lew (slave), 106
Lewis, Colonel Andrew, 27
Lewis, Isham, 203
Lewis, Lilburn, 203
Lewis, Meriwether, 84, 99, 113–25, 154–56, 183–85, 198–200, 208, 246, 274, 315, 333; court-martial of, 92–93; death of, 178–82, 187, 209; fossils collected for Jefferson by, 160; as governor of Louisiana Territory, 155, 163–66, 168–77, 184, 188, 213, 218, 278; as Jefferson's personal aide, 108, 109; on Voyage of Discovery, 125–53, 157, 158, 181, 322, 324, 329

Lewis, Reuben, 156, 172, 175, 182, 246
Lexington, Battle of, 30
Leyba, Fernando de, 40
Leyba, Teresa de, 40
Lincoln, Abraham, 312, 313, 322, 333
Lincoln, Levi, 132
Lisa, Manuel, 129, 157–58, 160, 172,
  174–76, 189, 194, 199, 205, 223, 224,
  227, 228, 256, 263
Little Big Horn, Battle of, 12
Little Otter, 72
Little Soldier, 270–71
Little Turtle, 5, 8, 9, 58, 60, 78, 79, 82–86,
  154, 229
Litty (slave), 255
Livingston, Robert, 109–11
Logan (Tah-gah-ju-te), 26–28, 31, 33
Logan, Benjamin, 53, 54
Loise, Paul, 167
Lolo Trail, 138
Long, Major Stephen H., 257, 258, 297
Lord Dunmore's War, 27, 32, 55
Lorimier, Agatha, 120
Lorimier, Louis, 45, 120
Louis XV, King of France, 151
Louisiana Gazette, 189, 192, 197, 199, 205,
  206
Louisiana Purchase, 109–12, 122–23, 148,
  150, 206, 210
Louisiana Territory, 147, 150, 173; Lewis as
  governor of, 155, 163–66, 168–77, 184,
  188, 213, 218, 278
Louisville, 51, 56; slaves in, 232, 260;
  steamboats from, 275; mercantile busi-
  ness in, 170
Lovejoy, Elijah, 328
Lovely, William, 235, 243, 246
Lowry, Lieutenant John, 72
Lucas, Ann, 242
Lucas, Charles, 237, 241–42
Lucas, John B. C., 240–42, 245–47, 251
Luttig, John C., 205

Mackay, James, 97, 113
Mackenzie, Alexander, 70–71, 110, 139
Madison, James, 17, 173, 175, 177, 178,
  180, 184, 188, 197, 212, 233, 236, 242

Maguire, George, 325
Main Poc (Withered Hand), 190
Maiouitinong, Le, 158
Makataimeshekiakiak, *see* Black Hawk
Mandans, 97, 123, 124, 132, 142, 153, 158,
  161, 171, 181, 257, 272–74, 321, 329–31
Mannahoacs, 13
maps, 120, 139–41, 192–93, 258
Marie Antoinette, Queen of France, 73
Marks, John, 108, 182
Marks, Lucy, 180, 182, 208
Marshall, Humphrey, 94
Marthey's River, 141
Martin, Meriwether, 330
Mason, George, 2, 33, 113
Mason, Stevens Thomson, 113
Massas, 85
Maximilian, Prince of Wied Neuwied,
  321–22
May, John, 53
McClellan, Robert, 82, 146, 159, 226, 232
McDonald, Angus, 271
McDowell brothers, 334
McGary, Hugh, 32, 54
McKay, William, 219–20
McKee, Alexander, 8, 44, 60, 71, 78
McKenney, Thomas L., 279, 280, 286,
  293, 300
McKenzie, Charles, 129
McKenzie, Kenneth, 315, 321
McNair, Alexander, 194, 211, 252–55, 280
McNair, Andrew, 232
Mechanic (steamboat), 279
Melgares, Facundo, 147
Menard, Pierre, 66, 172, 305, 319
Menominees, 190, 207, 211, 233, 282, 305,
  311, 313
Meriwether, William D., 183
Merry, Anthony, 152
Miami (galley), 44
Miamis, 4, 5, 9, 53, 62, 78, 82–84, 154,
  248; *see also* Weas
Michaux, André, 90–91, 97, 111, 113
Michilimackinac Company, 172, 204
Miller, John, 320
Mingos, 26, 28, 30–32
Minitarees, *see* Hidatsas
Mink (keelboat), 273–74

Mississippi River, 111, 117, 120, 121, 148, 154, 305; effect of New Madrid earthquake on, 202; forts on, 257, 259; freezing over of, 171, 204; gunboat expedition up, 214–15, 218–20; pro-British tribes on, 158, 172, 173, 195, 206, 214–17, 223–25, 244; return of expedition to, 148–49; during Revolutionary War, 33–35, 39, 40; Rock River Rapids, 221; Spanish on, 88–90, 99; steamboats on, 302–3, 309, 315–17, 322; trade on, 15, 54, 70, 81, 151, 243, 265; U.S. control of navigation on, 234; Voyage of Discovery on, 114, 125, 126, 131, 139

Mississippian culture, ancient, 96, 327

Missouri, 235, 260, 261, 287, 294, 297; Clark as territorial governor of, 212–14, 235–37, 240–52; congressional delegation of, 240–41, 267; militia of, 223; population growth in, 234; removal of Indians from, 320, 326, 332; slavery in, 252, 319; statehood for, 249–50, 252–56, 261, 327

Missouri Enabling Act (1820), 252

Missouri Company, 97

Missouri Compromise, 252

Missouri Fur Company, 205, 223, 263, 268–71, 288

Missouri Gazette, 163, 165, 171, 172, 214, 221, 226–28, 230, 232, 240–42, 251, 253

Missouri Intelligencer, 253

Missouri Legion, 269–70

Missouri River, 214, 222–23, 227, 228, 233, 236, 305; Big Bend of, 272; dugout canoes on, 229; exploration of, 67–68, 97, 110, 113, 114, 118, 121, 124–26, 130–34, 137, 139–48, 193–94; falls of, 185; Forks of, 205; fur trade on, 157, 159, 166, 172, 194, 199, 223, 243, 247, 263, 265–75, 298; Indian names for, 192; mapping of, 192–93; return of Sheheke to Mandan village on, 158, 161, 171–72; steamboats on, 257–58, 273, 321–22, 315, 329

Missouris, 152, 257, 325

Mitain (Indian wife of Manuel Lisa), 157

Mohawks, 20, 43, 151

Mohegans, 296

Molly (slave), 106

Moluntha, 54

Monacans, 13

Monmouth, Battle of, 47, 59

Monroe, James, 110, 224–25, 242, 247, 248, 251, 252, 264, 265, 273, 279

Moore, T., 116

Moravians, 43

Morgan, George, 32

Morgan, Colonel Willoughby, 300

Morrison, William, 172

Murray, John, 4th Earl of Dunmore, 23, 26–29

Muskrat (keelboat), 273–74

Nancy (slave), 106, 164, 260

Napoleonic Wars, 206

Napope, 311, 314

Narragansetts, 296

Natchez (steamboat), 278

Natchez Trace, 71, 180

National Intelligencer, 207, 263

Navahos, 263

Navy, U.S., 101, 103

Neelly, James, 180, 181

Nemacolin Trail, 50

New Jersey, College of, 78, 185

New Orleans, 15, 81, 100–101, 109, 111, 122; Battle of, 224; cholera epidemic in, 321; slaves in, 101; Spanish control of, 21, 40, 54, 88, 97–98, 105; steamboats from, 275

New Orleans (steamboat), 201, 202

Newman, John, 123, 125

New York: Corporation of the City of, 332; Lafayette in, 277

Nez Perces, 132, 136, 138, 143, 316

Niles Weekly Register, 220, 230

North West Company, 129, 188

Northwest Ordinance of 1787, 57

Northwest Passage, 88, 193

Northwest Territory, 4–6; see also Old Northwest

Notes on the State of Virginia (Jefferson), 28

Ochanee, 138

Office of Indian Trade, 191, 207, 279

O'Fallon, Benjamin, 87, 107, 194, 219, 232, 244–46, 258, 260, 267, 269, 270, 273, 274, 288, 325

O'Fallon, Fanny Clark, *see* Fitzhugh, Fanny Clark O'Fallon Thruston

O'Fallon, Harriet Stokes, 260

O'Fallon, James, 59–60, 62, 71, 87, 88

O'Fallon, John Julius, 206, 207, 219, 241, 246, 262, 267, 288, 289, 298, 324, 325, 333; in campaigns against Indians, 198, 210; childhood and youth of, 87, 107, 194; correspondence of, 195, 254, 262–63, 280, 323–24; marriage of, 260–61; on Yellowstone expedition, 257, 258

Ohio Company, 15

Ohio River, 27, 39, 41, 51, 99, 111, 115–16, 139, 148; exploration of, 24–25; Falls of, 34, 40, 44, 46, 47, 53, 63, 75, 98, 112, 117, 118, 142, 162, 178; Forks of, 15, 16, 26; fossil beds on, 159; freezing of, 95; Long Reach of, 25; military expeditions on, 74, 86, 120, 154; steamboats on, 201, 202, 245, 296, 309; trade on, 15, 70

Ojibwas (Chippewas), 40, 53, 83, 85, 233, 281, 282

Old Northwest, 150, 158, 190; removal of Indians from, 304

Old York (slave), 17, 47, 74, 106

Oldham, Colonel William, 10

Omahas, 152, 157, 165, 223, 229, 247, 299–301, 322, 325

Omp-se-ha-ra, *see* Black Moccasin

O'Neal massacre, 204

Oneidas, 26

Ongpatonga, *see* Big Elk

Ordway, John, 122–24, 127–28, 130, 132, 137, 144, 153

Oregon, 65, 131

Osages, 151, 156, 165–69, 175, 211–12, 214, 233, 236, 292, 305–6; conflicts between other tribes and, 196, 211, 215, 222, 247, 248; delegations to Washington of, 124, 152–55, 206, 207; depredations against settlers charged against, 217, 332; in fur trade, 131, 149, 166, 168, 264; Spanish and, 157, 165–66; treaties with, 167–69, 176, 194, 243–44, 246, 280–81, 283

Otoes, 152, 196, 257, 306, 325, 329, 330

Ottawas, 22, 53, 72, 83, 282, 305

Pacific Northwest, 65, 110

Paris, Treaty of, 21, 45, 46

Partisan, The (Torto-hongar),131–32, 228

Patterson, Robert, 117

Patterson, William Ewing, 117

Paulus Hook, Battle of, 47

Pawhuska (White Hair), 152, 157, 165–68

Pawnees, 147, 165, 247, 306–7

Peale, Charles Wilson, 185

Pearce, Nancy Clark, 294

Pearce, Sarah, 294

Peck, John Mason, 250

Pedlar (brig), 321

Pennsylvania, 26; colonial, 16, 22; Indians of, 4; militia of, 43, 58; during Revolutionary War, 39; University of, 185

Peorias, 292, 320

Perkins, Lieutenant Joseph, 220–21

Pernier, John, 180, 181

Perry, Commodore Matthew, 332

Perry, Oliver Hazard, 215

Petalla, 33

Peter (slave), 106

Pettis, Spencer, 308

Piaheto, *see* Arketarnashar (Eagle Feather)

Piankashaws, 83, 230, 233, 292, 320

Pickering, Anthony, 88, 89, 92

Pike (steamboat), 245

Pike, Zebulon, 77, 148, 193, 203–4

Pilcher, Joshua, 263, 269–71, 325, 329–32, 334

Pippo (slave), 106

Plains Indians, 270; *see also specific tribes*

Planet (steamboat), 300

Platte Purchase, 35

Pocahontas, 20

Poinsett, Joel, 332

Point Pleasant, Battle of, 27, 32, 189

Polkowski, Edward, 325, 332

Poncas, 97, 152, 274

Pontiac, 22

Portage des Sioux, 226; Treaty of, 227–33, 282

Porter, Peter, 294

Port Folio, 186, 208
Posecopsahe, *see* Black Cat
Potawatomis, 74, 83, 166, 189, 190, 196, 228, 230, 248, 275, 282, 292, 312–13, 320, 330
Potts, John, 122, 158, 193
Powhatans, 19
Prairie du Chien, 191, 195, 224, 225, 228, 245, 257, 299–300, 302, 304, 305; Treaty of, 282–83, 291, 325; during War of 1812, 209–11, 218–21
Pratte & Company, 315
Preston, Caroline Hancock, 107, 155, 250, 259, 262
Preston, Henrietta, 293, 294
Preston, Major William, 152, 155, 161, 200
Preston, William Campbell, 227, 237–39
Pricilla (slave), 106
Princeton, Battle of, 3, 59
Proclamation of 1763, 22, 29
Pryor, Nathaniel, 117, 124, 158, 161, 164, 175, 204, 268, 305–6

Quapaws, 166, 247–48
Quashquame, 150

Raccoon (keelboat), 273–74
Rachel (slave), 177, 188
Radford, Harriet Kennerly, *see* Clark, Harriet Kennerly Radford
Radford, John, 155, 262
Radford, Mary, *see* Kearny, Mary Radford
Radford, William, 262, 276, 277, 294
Raleigh, Walter, 21
Ramsay family, 225
Red Bird, 291, 292
Red Hawk, 33
Reed, Moses, 126
Republicans, 206
Revere, Paul, 4
Revolutionary War, 3, 5, 17, 30–47, 54, 55, 62, 64, 67, 96, 104, 108, 121, 235, 277
Reynolds, John, 292, 310, 312, 315
Robertson, Donald, 17
Robertson, Rachel Rogers, 17
Rocheblave, Phillippe François de Rastel, Chevalier de, 34, 35

Rocky Mountains, 114, 143, 157, 160, 258, 275, 307; map of, 193; smallpox in, 331
Rocky Mountains (keelboat), 268
Rodney, Caesar, 116
Rodney, Thomas, 116–17
Rogers, John, 14
Rogers, Captain John, 39
Rogers, Joseph, 41
Rogers, Rachel, 14
Rolfe, John, 20
Ronan, Peter, 138
Roosevelt, Lydia, 201
Roosevelt, Nicholas, 201
Rosalle (Rosalie) (slave), 260
Rose (slave), 17, 74, 106
Royall, Anne Newport, 303–4, 306, 318
Rush, Benjamin, 136
Russell, Captain Gilbert, 180
Russell, William, 240, 245

Sacagawea, 129, 134–37, 144, 145, 187, 194, 249, 260, 276
St. Clair, General Arthur, 5–12, 23, 58–60, 62–64, 66, 67, 72, 73, 75, 77, 78, 152, 210, 334
St. Dominique, 112, 150, 195
St. Louis, 68, 96–97, 162–64, 189, 225, 244, 248–49, 257, 308; cholera epidemic in, 321; Creole elite of, 149, 174, 208, 240, 245, 246; dueling in, 191–92, 232; effect of New Madrid earthquake on, 201; fur trade in, 133, 139, 157, 266, 267, 275, 315, 329; Indian Office in, 156, 165, 191, 265, 285–86, 292–93, 317, 326–27; Lafayette in, 277–78; mercantile businesses in, 169–70, 245, 298; politics in, 239–42, 251–55; during preparations for Voyage of Discovery, 121–26; public hangings in, 177; return of Voyage of Discovery to, 147, 149, 153; slaves in, 149–50, 195, 232, 260, 327–28; social life in, 293; Spanish control of, 35, 40, 96, 106; steamboats in, 275, 302–3, 315, 321; Three Flags Ceremony in, 122–23, 149; treaty-making in, 237–39; tribal delegations in, 248, 206; during War of 1812, 217, 224

St. Louis Enquirer, 248, 253, 265, 267

St. Louis Missouri Fur Company, 172, 175, 191, 194, 205; *see also* Missouri Fur Company

St. Louis Observer, 328

St. Mary's, Treaty of, 248

St. Peters (steamboat), 329, 330

St. Vrain, Felix, 310–12

Salishes, 132, 138, 142, 316

Sanford, John F. A., 32

San Ildefonso, Treaty of, 109

San Lorenzo, Treaty of, 98

Santa Fe Trail, 263

Santees, 203

Saones, 274

Sargent, Winthrop, 4, 8–12

Sauks and Foxes, 122, 165, 173, 206, 209, 218, 234, 243, 310–15, 321, 324–25; battles against, 221, 222, 225; British and, 40, 166, 190, 215, 217, 227–28; delegation to Washington of, 276–77; at Portage des Sioux, 228, 229, 231; at Prairie du Chien, 282, 299–300; Spanish and, 123; treaties with, 150, 156, 233, 237–39, 277, 300, 325

scalping, 10, 11, 54, 56, 62, 75, 226, 314

Schoolcraft, Henry Rowe, 249

Scippio (slave), 171, 251

Scott (slave), 177, 188

Scott, General Charles, 5, 59–64, 76, 79, 147, 246

Scott, Dred, 328–29

Scott, John, 240–41, 249, 251, 267

Scott, General Winfield, 313, 315

Selkirk, Lord Thomas, 263

Seminoles, 304, 332

Senate, U.S., 155, 206, 233, 255, 297; *see also* Congress, U.S.

Senecas, 44, 305

Seven Years War, 16, 21

Shannon, George, 116, 160, 187, 199, 207, 317

Shannon, John, 179

Shannon, Captain William, 94

Shawnees, 16, 20, 21, 23, 29, 57, 71, 77, 157, 158, 172, 292, 307, 332; agrarian, 197, 280, 287; burning of settlements of, 27, 54; in delegation to Washington, 206,

207; Iroquois cession of lands of, 22, 25–26, 52; mixed-race children of, 7, 120, 121; Osages and, 166, 189; during Revolutionary War, 30, 32–33, 39, 41, 44, 45; Spanish and, 46; treaties with, 27–28, 53, 54, 82–84, 229, 233, 248, 305, 320; victories against U.S. Army of, 5, 8, 58, 66, 70, 75–76; in War of 1812, 222

Shaylor, Major Joseph, 87, 93

Shields, John, 117, 122–24

Sheheke (Shehek-shote), 133, 140, 153, 155, 158, 161, 171, 172, 174, 181, 187, 268

Shoshones, 132, 134, 137, 143, 181, 187

Sibley, George, 196, 214, 215, 217, 222, 247, 264

Simmons, William, 184

Simpson, George, 273

Simpson, Robert, 241

Sink Hole, Battle of, 225–26

Siouan-speaking peoples, 13

Sioux, 40, 152, 158, 161, 166, 186, 196, 228–31, 272; Dakota (Santee), 203, 207, 223, 231, 281, 282, 299, 300, 313, 325; Hunkpapa, 270, 274; Lakota (Teton), 128, 131, 133–34, 137, 187, 229–31, 243, 270, 271, 274, 304, 330–32; Nakota, 204, 223, 299, 325; Oglala, 270, 274; Yankton, 231, 274

Slaughter, Colonel George, 57

Slaughter, Nelly, 57

slaves, 17–19, 25, 47, 50, 163, 170–71, 176, 177, 188, 234, 249–51, 255, 260, 262, 294; diminutives given to, 135; dividing families of, 164–65; freeing of, 318; hiring out of, 164, 250, 303; in Kentucky, 95, 107–9; and Missouri Compromise, 252; monetary value of, 200; murders of, 203; in St. Louis, 96, 149–50, 250, 327–28; sales of, 171, 232; uprisings of, 195; of Virginia planters, 17, 82, 108; whipping of, 164, 250

Slough, Jacob, 9

smallpox, 22, 73, 74, 306–7, 329–32

Smith, Ann, 260–61

Smith, Jedediah, 268, 269

Smith, Captain John, 21

Smith, General Samuel, 104–5

Smyrna (brig), 276

Soulard, Antoine, 139

Spanish, 35, 46, 60, 67, 86, 94, 102, 105, 152, 158, 194, 222, 235, 263; George Rogers Clark and, 40, 54, 96–97, 106, 201; Indians and, 70, 71, 88–92, 157, 165, 166, 320; land grants of, 148, 149, 173, 253; and Louisiana Purchase, 109, 110, 122–23, 206; Louisiana territory ceded by French to, 21; passport issued to William Clark by, 99, 101; Pinckney's Treaty with, 98; Wilkinson and, 88, 122, 147

Stanwix, Treaty of, 22, 25–26, 52

Star (ship), 101–4

Stark, Horatio, 211

steamboats, 245, 257–58, 260, 273, 275, 278–79, 291, 294, 296, 300–3, 309–11, 314–17, 321–22, 329–31

Stephens, Aaron, 269

Steuben, Baron Friedrich von, 42, 126

Stillman, Major Isaiah, 312

Stoddard, Captain Amos, 122–23, 150, 152

Stokes, Marianne, 260–61

Stokes, William, 260–61

Stony Point, Battle of, 64

Street, Joseph, 291, 305, 311, 314

Stuart, John, 19

Sublette, William, 298

Supreme Court, U.S., 322, 329

surveying, 24, 25, 27, 30, 46, 47, 49, 94, 139

Sweet Breeze, 9

Sycamore Shoals, Treaty of, 29

Tah-gah-ju-te, *see* Logan

Taliaferro, Lawrence, 276–77, 299, 328

Talleyrand-Périgord, Charles-Maurice de, 111

Tallmadge, James, 249

Tarleton, Colonel Banastre, 79

Tar-ton-gar-wa-ker, *see* Buffalo Medicine

Taylor, Colonel Zachary, 222, 314

Tecumseh, 8, 78, 158, 172, 189–89, 197, 198, 203, 204, 215–16

Temple, Benjamin, 178

Temple, Nelly Clark, 178

Tener (slave), 106

Tennessee, 29, 148, 241; removal of Indians from, 334

Tenskwatawa (Shawnee Prophet), 158, 172, 189, 190, 197–99, 205

Thames River, Battle of the, 215

Thayer, Colonel Sylvanus, 283, 284

Thompson, David, 139

Thruston, Charles Mynn, Sr., 95, 107

Thruston, Fanny Clark, *see* Fitzhugh, Fanny Clark O'Fallon Thruston

Tillier, Rudolphe, 173

Tippecanoe, Battle of, 198–99, 203, 204

tobacco, 15, 17, 97, 98

Tocqueville, Alexis de, 309–10

Todd, Colonel John, 44

Tompkins, Barrett, 68

Torto-hongar, *see* Partisan, The

Totowin, 203

Toussaint L'Ouverture, 112, 195

Trail of Tears, 334

Transylvania Colony, 23, 29

Trenton, Battle of, 3, 59

Trout, The, 158

Trudeau, Zenon, 96

Truteau, Jean Baptiste, 97

Tsiyu-Gûnsíni, *see* Dragging Canoe

Turner, Nat, 328

Tzi-kal-tza, 138

Ugulayacabe, 70

Underwood, Jemmy, 71

Un-tongar-Sarbar, *see* Black Buffalo

Vallé, François, II, 96

Valley Forge, 64, 72

Van Buren, Martin, 332

Van Cleve, Benjamin, 10, 11

Vancouver, George, 139

Venos (slave), 106, 164

Vigo, Francis, 66, 90

Virginia, 13–18, 20, 22, 23, 26, 47, 49; dueling in, 191; immigration to Kentucky from, 5, 26, 29, 50, 107, 108, 141; militia of, 16, 27, 33, 46, 84; slaves in, 82, 109, 135; during Revolutionary War, 30, 31, 33, 39–41, 94, 121; University of, 284

Voyage of Discovery, 113, 125–46, 182, 195, 228, 249, 256, 257, 307, 317; prep-

Voyage of Discovery (*cont.*) arations for, 114–25; publication of journals of, 182–87, 192–93, 199–200, 208, 209, 216, 239; return journey of, 147–53, 181

Waanowrabai, 231
Walker, William, 316
Walk-in-Rain, 166, 167
War Department, U.S., 68, 124, 165, 184, 189, 207, 233, 273, 307, 324, 329
Warfington, Richard, 124
War of 1812, 199, 206–7, 209–11, 214–25, 229, 234, 235, 253, 258–59, 263, 266, 285, 292, 311, 321, 327
Warrior (steamboat), 314
"Warrior's Path," 16
Washington, George, 16, 22, 43, 47, 72, 83, 101, 154, 323, 334; presidency of, 5, 58–59, 63–65, 84, 86, 88, 91, 92, 109, 162, 253; slaves owned by, 17; Wilkinson in cabal against, 54
Wayne, General Anthony, 11, 64–65, 68–73, 75–79, 81–86, 88–93, 108, 114, 147, 190, 198, 229, 274, 282, 286
Weas, 55, 58, 60, 74, 83, 320
Weiser, Peter, 158
Wells, Samuel, 10
Wells, William, 8–10, 77, 154, 208
"Welsh Indians of Prince Madoc," 97
Werner, William, 122
Western Engineer (steamboat), 258
West Point, U.S. Military Academy at, 283–84, 290, 294, 301, 312, 329, 332, 333
Wetmore, Alphonso, 249
Whiskey Rebellion, 84
White Cloud (Winnebago Prophet), 311
White Eyes, George, 78
Whitehouse, Joseph, 123, 127, 135
Whitman, Marcus, 316
Whitman, Narcissa, 316
Whitman, Walt, 277
Whitney, Eli, 109

Wilderness Road, 50, 107
Wilkinson, Ann Biddle, 3, 148
Wilkinson, Benjamin, 172
Wilkinson, General James, 3–5, 11, 61–64, 66–68, 76–77, 79–80, 88, 92, 151, 157, 159, 172; Burr and, 148, 154; campaign to discredit George Rogers Clark by, 54, 64, 73, 147
Willard, Alexander Hamilton, 126, 176, 204
Williamson, David, 43
Wilt, Christian, 207, 222
Winchester, James, 104
Winchester, General James, 210
Winnebago (steamboat), 314
Winnebagos, 40, 166, 189, 190, 198, 204, 207, 211, 219–21, 233, 282, 291–92, 300, 311–14
Wirt, William, 183, 185, 186, 297
Wisconsin Heights, Battle of, 314
Withered Hand, *see* Main Poc
Wood, William, 21
Wür ttemberg, Paul Wilhelm, Duke of, 275–76
Wyandots, 4, 30, 43, 53, 82, 83, 248, 305
Wythe, George, 33

XYZ Affair, 101

Yanktonais, 274
Yazoo Company, 60
"Yazoo Strip," 98
yellow fever, 73, 104–5, 108
Yellow Stone (steamboat), 315–17, 321–22, 330
Yellowstone expedition, 257–58
Yellow Stone Packet (keelboat), 268, 269
York, 17, 74, 106, 153, 154, 162, 163, 223, 232, 318–19; Clark's displeasure with, 170, 177, 195, 319; on Voyage of Discovery, 117, 134, 137, 142–43, 187
Yorktown, British surrender at, 43